Story Bible

for

Adults

John Berthe

2014

Table of Contents

Introduction	3
Genesis	4
Exodus	28
Summary of the Law Given to Moses	37
Numbers	44
Leviticus	52
Deuteronomy	52
Joshua	54
Judges	61
Ruth	74
The First Book of Samuel	76
The Second Book of Samuel	93
The Kings and Chronicles	110
Psalms	113
Job	115
Proverbs	118
Joel	149
Hosea	151
Amos	152
Jonah	153
Isaiah	156
Micah	157
Nahum	165
Zephaniah	166
Habakkuk	166
Jeremiah	167
Ezekiel	168
Obadiah	171
Esther	172
Daniel	175
Ezra	180
Haggai and Zachariah	183
Nehemiah	185
Malachi	190
The Gospels	191
The Acts of the Apostles	255
The Letter from James	263
The Letter to the Galatians	271
The Two Letters to the Thessalonians	276
The First Letter to the Corinthians	278
The Second Letter to the Corinthians	280
The Letter to the Romans	280
The Letter to the Ephesians	290
The Letter to the Colossians	291
The Letter to Philemon	291

- The Letter to the Philippians 292
- The First Letter to Timothy 292
- The Letter to Titus 293
- The Second Letter to Timothy 293
- The Letter to the Hebrews 294
- Peter's two letters 294
- Jude's Letter 295
- The First Letter of John 295
- The Second Letter of John 296
- The Third Letter of John 296

The Revelation of Jesus Christ to John 297

Introduction

The Uncensored Story Bible for Adults gives readers a chance to get an authentic feel for the entire Bible with a quicker read. The whole Bible devotes more of its words to narrative than to any other category of scripture (prophecy, or law, or poetry, or epistle). On a straight read through of the Bible there are long sections of law, prophecy and writings interlaced between narrative sections.

This work extracts the narrative from the other writings and presents it in continuous single strand. The story begins with Adam evicted from the garden and dangles to a stop with Paul stuck in the Roman legal system. Brief summaries of law, prophecy, or writings appear as they enter the story. This book does not contain commentary. There are scriptural addresses on every page so the original is easily referred to.

The story is condensed (including every character and event) with three principle methods.

First: Merging repeated narrative into a single strand, for instance, where Kings and Chronicles overlap repeatedly, a single strand emerges. The same is true in the Gospels. Where many events appear in all four books they are merged into a single strand that is shorter, and all inclusive.

Second: Lists, such as, genealogies, or tribal ledgers, priestly listing, or census, are referred to; not listed.

Third: Repeated stories are referred to; not retold. Often, in recorded public prayers or sermons, large sections of narrative are restated. Salomon's dedication of the temple, or Steven's message before he was martyred are two examples, of dozens that help condense the story by referring to, not repeating, previous content.

The net result is that the 350,000 narrative words in scripture are culled down to 130,000 in *The Uncensored Story Bible for Adults*. The entire Bible is 850,000 words. This book makes the complete uncensored story available to anyone who can read a beach novel.

The story doesn't come continuously in scripture, you simply can't read the Bible to get the single strand narrative like this. Understanding the sequence of characters and events in the Bible story, aids in every other aspect of Bible study.

Lots of folks have started to read the whole bible never to finish. *The Uncensored Bible Story for Adults* is an invitation for more people to read the Bible story and come to their own conclusions.

Genesis

Genesis Chapter 1 *Creation*

In the beginning God created the heavens and the earth. The earth was dark and disorganized. Then God created light. He separated light from darkness and the first day of creation ended. On the second day, God separated water from land. On the third day, He created every kind of plant. On the fourth day, He made the sun, moon and stars. On the fifth day, He created every living thing in the sea and every kind of bird. God started the sixth day creating all the land animals and ended the day by making man. He was very pleased with the results of his engineering. He said, "This is very good!" He blessed His creation, so it would flourish. The seventh day of that first week was a rest day.

Genesis Chapter 2 *Adam and Eve*

God made man from the earth and breathed His own image into him. He made Adam first, then Eve. Adam was thrilled when he saw Eve. God put man in charge of the earth and gave him just one rule: Adam and Eve were not to eat fruit from one particular tree in the middle of the Garden of Eden. God made man to enjoy a relationship with him. He liked spending time with Adam and Eve.

Genesis 3:1-8 *The fall*

One day Eve was walking by the forbidden tree and she noticed a crafty serpent in its branches. The serpent said to Eve, "Does God say you can't eat the fruit from this tree?" Eve answered, "You're correct serpent; we're not supposed to touch it or we'll die." Then the serpent hissed, "That's not true. You won't die from eating this fruit. God doesn't want you to eat it, because He knows if you do you'll be as aware as He is. You'll know the difference between right and wrong." Eve noticed that the fruit looked very good, so she took a piece and ate some. Then she shared the rest with Adam. When they finished eating, they felt embarrassed about being naked so they made clothes out of fig leaves. When God came to visit that afternoon, Adam and Eve hid from Him.

Genesis 3:9-24 *The penalty*

God knew what had happened. He cursed the serpent and told him a descendent of Eve would some day crush his head. He told Eve, "Your pain in childbirth will be increased, but you will always desire your husband and he will rule over you. Then he told Adam,

"Because you didn't obey my command about eating from this tree, the ground has become cursed. You'll have to work for every fruit it provides you. You'll sweat to get the food you need. And you will die, be buried, and become earth again. I made you from the earth and you'll return to it."

Genesis 4:1-15 *Cain and Able*

Adam and Eve began having children. They had two boys. One was named Cain and the other Abel. Cain worked as a farmer and Abel was a rancher. They both wanted to give God an offering. So Cain brought some of his crop, and Abel brought his best animals. God approved of Abel's offering, but wasn't impressed with Cain's. This upset Cain. God said, "Cain, try to do a little better next time. Don't dwell on this situation or you may do something you regret." Cain did something very regrettable. He murdered his brother Abel. On His next visit God asked, "Cain, where's Abel?" Cain shot back, "Hey I'm not his baby-sitter." Then God said, "Cain, I've got a bad feeling about this; I know you've killed your brother. You're going to be punished. You will be banished from this region. You'll be hated by everybody, but I won't let anybody kill you."

Genesis 4:25-5:32 *The Generations of Adam until Noah*

Adam and Eve produced more offspring. Their children also had children. People were living a long time. Adam lived 930 years. One of Adam's grandsons named Methuselah, lived 969 years. Another of Adam's grandchildren, named Enoch, had an excellent relationship with God. When he'd lived about 365 years, God invited him to come straight to heaven and Enoch accepted. After about a dozen generations, Noah was born.

Genesis 6 *Noah builds the ark*

Things were getting extremely bad on the earth. God looked at the Earth and said to Himself, "These folks don't think about
anything but evil!" He started to feel as though He'd made a mistake creating the earth in the first place and He was extremely upset about it. There was one man who respected God. His name was Noah. God told Noah and his three sons, Shem, Ham and Japheth, to build a large ship called an ark. The ark was 450 feet long, 75 feet wide and 45 feet high. It had three levels, with separate areas and rooms. It took 100 years for Noah and his sons to build the ark.

Genesis 7:1-9:19 *The flood and the rainbow*

When the ark was finally finished, with provisions collected and put inside, a male and a female of every kind of animal in the world came to the ark. When they were inside,

God closed the hatch Himself. Then the floodgates of heaven were opened and the fountains of the deep were released. These conditions did not let up for 40 days. The water covered even the highest mountain peaks by over 20 feet. The water remained that high for 150 more days. Then the water started slowly going down. Seven months and 17 days after the start of the flood, the ark finally hit dry ground. Noah, his family, and all the animals stayed in the ark for another few months. Finally God told Noah it was safe to come out of the ark. Then Noah built an altar to God. God said he'd never destroy the earth with a flood again. His promise was sealed with the first rainbow.

Genesis 9:20-29 *Noah and his sons*
Noah planted a vineyard. One day he was drinking wine he had produced. He became drunk and passed out in his tent. His youngest son Ham saw him lying naked on his bed and reported it to his brothers. His brothers carefully covered Noah with out viewing his nakedness or waking him up. When Noah came to his senses asking how he'd ended up covered in the tent, he was angry Ham hadn't covered him respectfully, saving him some embarrassment, like his brothers quickly did when they were told about his predicament. So he pronounced blessing on Shem and Japheth, and pronounced a curse on Ham.

Genesis 10-11 *The Tower of Babel*
Noah and his sons got busy having children. The earth became populated again. In those days everybody spoke the same language. The men on the earth began building a great city called Babel. In the center of the city they began a tower that would reach into the heavens. God knew with this much organization, men would soon get to the point where they could do anything...and it would probably be bad. So He mixed up their languages. The tower was abandoned and people separated into groups with the same language. The groups each went in different directions around the world.

Genesis 12:1-3 *God's promise to Abram*
A dozen generations after the flood there was a man named Abram and his wife, Sarai (who had not been able to bear children), lived in the land of Ur. God talked to Abram and said, "Abram, leave your family and your neighborhood. Go to the place I show you. I will make your offspring a great nation. Every family of earth will benefit because of you and your family!"

Genesis 12:4-10 *Abram arrives in Canaan*
So Abram left the area. He took Sarai, his nephew, Lot, and all the people and livestock he had accumulated. They traveled to the northern part of what is now called Israel.

Abram was 75 when the trip began. When he first arrived in Canaan, as Israel was called at the time, he stopped in a region that was called Moreh. God talked to him again and said, "This is the land I'm going to give to you and your descendants." So Abram built an altar to God there. At that time a significant drought developed in Canaan so Abram traveled south into Egypt where the Nile River provided water even during a drought.

Genesis 12:11-16 *Abram's deception*
Now Abram's wife Sarai was a very attractive lady. Abram was concerned that when the Egyptians saw her, they'd want to possess her and they would kill him because he was her husband. So Abram asked Sarai to tell the Egyptians that she was his sister so they would spare him and treat him well because of her. When they arrived in Egypt, Pharaoh's officials saw her. They told Pharaoh a lovely woman had come in from out of the area. So Sarai was taken to Pharaoh's house and Abram was rewarded for his beautiful "sister" with a gift of livestock and servants from Pharaoh.

Genesis 12:17-20 *Abram leaves Egypt enriched*
Then everybody in Pharaoh's house became ill. Pharaoh realized the sickness was invading his house because Sarai was more than Abram's sister. He called Abram in and berated him, "What are you trying to do by telling me she's your sister? You take her back so all my people can get well!" Pharaoh then instructed his men to escort Abram and all his possessions out of Egypt. Abram's wealth had greatly increased in Egypt.

Genesis 13:1-13 *Abram and Lot separate*
Abram traveled back to Canaan. Abram and his brother Lot had so much livestock that some trouble started between their servants. Then Abram met with Lot and said, "Lot, we're relatives, but we're getting too crowded. You decide where you want to go, and I'll go the other way." The drought was over and they were living in the hill country. Lot did some scouting and the valley looked inviting so Lot said, "Abram, I'm heading down to the valley with my people, good luck to you, wherever you decide to go." Lot settled in an urban area called Sodom and Gomorrah.

Genesis 13:14-18 *God expounds on His promise to Abram*
Abram went back up to North Canaan and visited the altar he had built. Then God came to him again and said, "Abram, I am going to make your descendants as numerous as the dust of the earth. No one can say how much dust there is on the earth, nor will any one be able to say how many descendants you have. I want you to

look around from east to west, north to south, this is all going to be your family's country."

Genesis 14 *Abram saves Lot*
Meanwhile Lot was falling into some bad luck down in Sodom and Gomorrah. A sinister tribe attacked the city. The king of Sodom and Gomorrah, along with Lot and his family, were taken captive. When Abram heard of it, he put together a group of his loyal servants and they rescued Lot, his family, and the king. The king offered Abram the loot the robbers had stolen, but Abram turned him down. He didn't want anyone believing he became wealthy as a mercenary. Abram met a priest named Melchizedek, who was from God, and he gave Melchizedek 10% of the loot. Abram also reimbursed himself the expenses for the rescue.

Genesis 15:1-6 *Abram questions and believe*
When Abram returned home he had a vision from God. God said He was Abram's shield and that He was going to bless him abundantly! Abram asked, "How can I be a great nation when Sarai can't have children?" God took him outside and they looked up at the stars. God said, "There are too many stars to count, your descendants will also be too many to count." Abram believed God. As far as God was concerned, Abram could do no wrong, because he believed.

Genesis 15:7-21 *The borders*
Then God told Abram how to conduct a ceremony to make their agreement binding. Abram set things up for the ceremony and then fell into a deep sleep. God talked to him in his sleep. God told him that his family would eventually be captives in a foreign country for 400 years, but God would deliver them from that bondage. He also told Abram that he would live a long and successful life. When Abram awoke, he finished the ceremony. God told Abram the borders of the country his people would inhabit. God also said He would help Abram's family defeat the nations living in the land.

Genesis 16 *Hagar and Ishmael*
After a few more years and no children, Sarai started to get a little nervous about her biological clock ticking away. She told Abram to have sexual relations with Hagar, her Egyptian maid. Abram did as Sarai instructed and Hagar became pregnant. When her condition was apparent, Hagar started getting uppity around Sarai, so Sarai complained to Abram. Abram told Sarai to do what she wanted with Hagar so Sarai threw Hagar out of the camp. Hagar ended up out in the desert alone, but she found a spring of water. An Angel from God came down and said, "Hagar...what's wrong?"

Hagar answered, "I'm out here, because my mistress kicked me out of camp." The angel said, "Go back to camp and be submissive to Sarai. You are going to have a boy and he will be quite a fellow. He and his people will be fighters. They'll live out to the east of his brother's people." She followed the angel's advice and went back to Sarai and gave birth to a son. Abram named him Ishmael. Abram was 86 years old when Ishmael was born.

Genesis 17 *New names and circumcision*
Thirteen years later, Sarai still had not become pregnant! God came to Abram again. "Abram I am the God you've trusted all these years. I am going to do all the things I've told you. You are going to be a great Nation! Your name isn't Abram any more; it is Abraham. As a mark for the world to know you and your family are my people, from now on all the males in your family will be circumcised." (This is where the foreskin of the man's penis is cut off). God continued, "Sarai will now be called Sarah, because she is going to have a child." Abraham fell down laughing and said, "Come on God, how are a lady 90 years old and a man 100 years old going to have a baby? Why don't you let Ishmael be my heir?" God replied, "Ishmael is going to be a great nation too, but My agreement with you is that Sarah will be the mother of the nation. She'll have a son in the next year." Soon after this exchange, Abraham circumcised himself and his household.

Genesis 18:1-15 *The birth of Isaac announced*
Later, Abraham was sitting at his tent door in the heat of the day when he saw three men standing nearby. Abraham ran to them and offered refreshment and comfort. When they accepted, he set his house buzzing to present a nice meal. After eating the men said, "Where is Sarah?" Abraham replied, "She's in the tent." Then the Lord said, "I'm coming back at this time next year. Sarah will have a baby by then." Sarah overheard this in the tent and she giggled to herself at how outlandish the whole thing sounded. Then God said to Abraham, "Why did your wife laugh? Does she think this is impossible for Me? When I'm back next year, we'll be looking at a cute little baby boy." Sarah denied that she giggled but God looked over and said, "You can't fool God, Sarah, I know what a giggle is!"

Genesis 18 *Abraham cuts a deal with the Angel of the Lord*
So the three men got up to leave and Abraham walked them out of camp. God thought to himself, "Hum, I'd guess I better let Abraham know what we're down here for, after all he is my main man right now." God said to Abraham, "Abraham, Sodom and Gomorrah are stinking up the valley with some horrible sin. I'm going down to check it out myself and deal with it." This was a bit disconcerting to Abraham because his

nephew, Lot, lived in Sodom and Gomorrah. So Abraham probed God about his intentions. He tried to couch it delicately so he started off like this. "God, You and I know You are a righteous God. If there were, say, 50 good people down there, You couldn't destroy the city then, could You? God said, "No." Abraham went a little further. "God, You're the Lord and You can do whatever You want, but I've got to think that if there were 45 good people in the city, You'd have to spare it as well." God agreed again and said, "Yes, if there were 45 good people, I'd be hard pressed to kill them along with the wicked so I wouldn't destroy the city." Abraham kept gradually reducing the number of righteous folks required to spare the city. Abraham ultimately got God to commit that He wouldn't destroy the city if there were even 10 good people. Abraham figured with Lot and his family, there should at least be 10 good people. Then the Lord went towards Sodom and Gomorrah and Abraham went back to his tent.

Genesis 19:1-11 *The Angels in the city*
The two Angels approached Sodom and Gomorrah in the early evening. Lot was at the gate of the city. Lot had to practically beg the Angels to stay at his house because they wanted to stay in the square. When they got to Lot's house, he made them dinner. Then all the men of the city came around Lot's house and made an indecent proposal to the Angels. They would not be satisfied till they got their hands on the Angels for sex. The men got angry with Lot when he would not comply. Lot even offered his virgin daughters as an alternative! When the evil men began to enter the house by force, the Angels pulled Lot inside and made the horny crowd outside blind so they couldn't even find the door.

Genesis 19:12-29 *The destruction of Sodom and Gomorrah*
The Angels told Lot to get his family out of the city because they were going to destroy it. Lot told his wife, his daughters and his daughters' boyfriends about what the Angels said. The boyfriends thought he was joking. The Angels wanted Lot and his family out Sodom and Gomorrah, so they escorted them to the edge of town. The boyfriends stayed behind. Lot got the Angels to agree not to destroy a small town nearby so he could go there. As they were fleeing, Lot's wife turned back and looked at the fire that was coming down on Sodom and Gomorrah. She turned into a pillar of salt. Abraham saw the smoke from Sodom and Gomorrah from where he had spoken to the Lord.

Genesis 19:30-38 *Lot and his daughters*
Lot didn't feel comfortable in the little town. So he and his daughters went into the wilderness where they lived in a cave in the mountains. Lot's daughters became concerned that they wouldn't have children. So each of them, on separate nights, got

their father blackout drunk and had sexual relations with him. They both became pregnant. Their sons ended up being fathers of two nations: Moab and Ammon.

Genesis 20:1-7 *Abraham's deception of Abimelech*
Abraham decided to head back down to south Israel again. He traveled to a territory that was ruled by a king named Abimelech. Sarah was still quite an attractive lady, and Abraham was still concerned he'd get killed because of her. So they said Sarah was his sister again. Abimelech was attracted to Sarah. When he heard she was Abraham's sister, he asked her to come into his home, but held off on having any relations with her. One night, as he was sleeping, God appeared to Aimelech in a dream and said, "You are a dead man because you have taken a married woman." Abimelech said, "Hold on; I haven't slept with her and besides, they said she was Abraham's sister!" God answered, "Yes you are right; I know your intentions were honorable and, frankly, I influenced your decision not to sleep with her. Return her to Abraham, and we'll forget the whole thing. Have Abraham pray for you because he is a prophet."

Genesis 20:9-18 *Abimelech's response*
So Abimelech did as God said. He called Abraham in and yelled at him, "What the heck are you thinking man! Don't you know because of your lie, I could have had my whole nation destroyed by God! Why would you do such a thing?" Abraham answered, "I didn't know if you would have any respect for God, and she is my half sister. As you know, she is a fine looking woman, so we made this deal that if we got in a spot where I might get killed because of her, we'd say she's my sister." Then Abimelech gave Abraham many new sheep and goats. He added 1000 pieces of silver as a vindication for poor Sarah. Abraham prayed for Abimelech and he was blessed with many children.

Genesis 21:1-7 *The birth of Isaac*
Finally Sarah became pregnant! When she had the baby, Abraham named him Isaac. He circumcised Isaac when he was eight days old according to the agreement God had made with him. Abraham was 100 years old. Sarah was pleased and radiant about the whole thing. It was a load off her back to finally give Abraham a child!

Genesis 21:8-21 *Sarah against Hagar*
There were bad feelings between Sarah and Hagar again. Sarah told Abraham she wanted Hagar and her son, Ishmael, sent away. This bothered Abraham because Ishmael was his son. God spoke to Abraham, "Don't be worried about your son Ishmael; I'm going to make him a great nation. Do what Sarah has asked you." So early the next morning, Abraham gave Hagar and her son water and bread. Then he sent them away. Soon the water ran out, so Hagar put Ishmael in the shade. She

went away and cried out to God, "Don't let me see the boy die!" God spoke from heaven, "Hagar, I've heard your cries. Don't worry; I'm going to make him a great nation! Get up and take the boy by the hand." When Hagar got up she saw a spring of water. She and Ishmael drank and refilled their water skin. In time Ishmael became a skilled archer. When he was a man, Hagar got him a wife from Egypt.

Genesis 21:22-34 *Water rights*
Back in Abraham's camp, King Abimelech came in with his commanders. He wanted to make a treaty with Abraham because of Abraham's wealth and power. Abraham felt fine about the treaty, but there had been a problem between some of Abraham's men and Abimelech's, over who owned the water in a certain well. Abraham's water rights became part of the treaty.

Genesis 22:1-6 *God requires a sacrifice*
After all this happened, God tested Abraham. God said, "Take your only son Isaac, whom you love, to the mountains of Moriah. I will show you where to sacrifice him as a burnt offering." The next day Abraham, Isaac, two of Abraham's hired hands, a donkey loaded with supplies, and wood for the burnt offering, started a journey to the mountains. After three days of travel, Abraham saw the place. He told the hired hands to stay with the donkey while he and Isaac went up to worship.

Genesis 22:7-19 *The sacrifice is provided*
On the way up Isaac asked, "Dad, we've got the wood for a burnt offering, but we don't have an animal, what's up?" Abraham replied, "God will provide the offering, son." When they arrived at the spot, Abraham prepared the fire, tied Isaac up, put him on the wood and was raising the knife to kill his own son when the Angel of the Lord called from heaven, "Abraham! Abraham!" Abraham answered, "Yes, I'm right over here!" The Angel said, "There's no question about your loyalty to God since you were ready to sacrifice your own son, your only son, whom you love, because I said so!" Just then Abraham looked up and saw a ram with his horns caught in a bush, so the sacrifice was provided. Then the Angel of the Lord said, "Abraham, because you were ready to give your only son, I will indeed make your family a great nation. They will exceed the number of the stars in the sky and the sand on the beach. The whole world will be blessed by your family because you have obeyed my voice!"

Genesis 23 *Sarah passes*
Sarah died when she was 127 years old. When it came time to bury her, Abraham didn't own any land for her grave. So he said to the folks living around him, "Let me

buy a piece of property to bury my wife." They all said, "Abraham, you've been around here so long and you're so rich, you're like a prince to us. Pick any field you want; it's yours, free of charge." So Abraham said, "I like a field Ephron owns. Let me buy it." Ephron was sitting right there and he said, "Abraham, the field is yours, please bury your wife there." Abraham replied, "No Ephron, I want to pay fair market value; have you had it appraised lately?" "Yes I have." returned Ephron, "It's worth 400 shekels of silver, but what's that between you and me, just bury your wife." Finally Abraham got his way, Ephron took the 400 shekels and the property was deeded over to Abraham. Sarah was buried there.

Genesis 24:1-9 *Abraham makes arrangements for Isaac's future*
Abraham kept getting older and richer. Abraham was concerned about a wife for Isaac. He didn't want him to marry one of the local girls. On the other hand, he didn't want him to go back to his family and never come back, but he did want him to marry one of the family girls. He called the general manager of his whole enterprise and had a meeting with him. He explained his concerns and asked the manager to go back to his family and find a suitable bride for Isaac. The manager was concerned that he might not be able to accomplish it. Abraham assured him that God, who had kept all His promises, would be with him. The manager had always been with Abraham, so he knew how great God was. He felt that with God's help, he could do it, so he promised Abraham he would try.

Genesis 24:10-27 *Rebekah*
The manager went to Abraham's family with 10 camels and many other fine gifts. When he got to the city of Nahor where Abraham's relatives lived, he stopped his camels near a well. He prayed to God and said, " God of my boss Abraham, please help me be successful today, and keep showing how faithful you are to Abraham by helping me. I'm standing here by a well. Some of the young girls are coming out for water. I'm going to ask one for a drink. If she's the one for Isaac, let her say: "Sure, I'll give you a drink, plus I'll get some water for your camels too." Before he was even finished praying a beautiful young girl, named Rebekah, came by with her water pot. He asked her for a drink and she said: "Sure, I'll give you a drink, plus I'll get some water for your camels too." Needless to say the manager was astonished. He gave her a batch of jewelry that would make a lady on Rodeo Drive blush and he asked, "By the way, I'm hoping to stay in town tonight. Who's your Dad? Maybe I could stay with your family?" She answered, "Bethuel's my Dad, and sure you can stay with us!" The manager was amazed again because he recognized Bethuel as a family name of Abraham's and he knew Abraham wanted Isaac's bride to be from his family. The manager bowed low and

exclaimed, "The God Abraham has blessed me because He has led me right here to his relatives!"

Genesis 24:28-60 *Laban releases Rebekah*
Then Rebekah ran home and told her older brother, Laban, about what had happened. He looked at the jewelry and ran outside to meet Uncle Abraham's general manager He said, "Don't stand out here, we've got the house all set up for you and a place for your camels" So Laban took the camels and Rebekah took the manager inside and got him taken care of. Dinner was set. Before they started to eat, the manager said, "I just can't eat till I get my business finished and tell you why I've come: I am the General Manager of your Uncle Abraham's estate. It's a big job because your Uncle Abraham is very rich. He's got livestock, gold and all kinds of investments. I manage a great number of hired hands and servants. Abraham is going to give his entire estate to his son Isaac. He wants Isaac to marry a girl in the family. So he sent me on this seemingly impossible task of coming here, finding you all, getting the right girl, and bringing her home." Then he told them about his prayer, how Rebekah did just as he prayed, and how he then realized she was a relative of Abraham's He continued, "So I'm starting to feel like being on a mission from God is a pretty great thing, but still I need to hear it from you. Will you make my trip successful by letting me take Rebekah back to marry Isaac? Bethuel and Laban looked at each other and said, "This sure seems like it's God's work to us. Why don't you stay with us for 10 days; then you can go." The manager (being a man of business) really wanted to get the deal done, so he said, "I'm too excited, I really want to get back." Then Bethuel and Laban asked Rebekah. She said she'd be happy to go right away.

Genesis 24:61-67 *Isaac and Rebekah*
When the manager, Rebekah, and their caravan got into the land, Isaac was out in the hills meditating. He saw Rebekah from way off and Rebekah saw him. There was an immediate chemistry between them. They got married right away. It helped Isaac get over the loss of his mother. Isaac was 40 years old when he married.

Genesis 25:1-11 *Abraham's final days*
Abraham married again to a girl named Keturah. She had many children. Abraham gave plenty of wealth to his new family while he was alive. When he finally died, Isaac and Ishmael buried him in the same cave at the end of the field Abraham had bought to bury Sarah in. Isaac stayed in Israel and inherited all of Abraham's wealth. Abraham's second family with Keturah moved east.

Genesis 25:12-18 *Ishmael's Family*

Ishmael and his 12 sons didn't have friendly relations with Isaac. They moved east.

Genesis 25:19-26 *Esau and Jacob*

Rebekah had some trouble getting pregnant for a while. Isaac prayed about it regularly and then Rebekah became pregnant with twins! She could tell it was twins because there seemed to be a constant struggle in her womb. She prayed about it. God told her, "You've got two nations in your womb. One will be stronger than the other. The older will serve the younger." When she gave birth, the first child was a hairy redheaded baby. The second child came literally on the heels of the first. He had a firm hold on the heel of the first as he came out! They named the first baby Esau, the second, Jacob. Isaac was 60 years old when the boys were born.

Genesis 25:27-34 *Esau sells his birthright to Jacob*

Esau was an outdoorsman. He was hairy, loved to hunt, and didn't stay around camp much. Jacob, on the other hand, was a smooth skinned, gentler person. He liked being in camp. Isaac preferred Esau because he enjoyed all the nice game he brought home. Rebekah was partial to Jabob. One day Jabob was cooking some red stew when Esau came in from a long period in the field. Esau was starved so He asked Jacob for some of the stew. Jabob said, "No problem brother, but first sell your rights as the first born to me." Esau replied gruffly, "Heck Jabob, if I don't eat soon I'll die, so what good is being born first to me? You can have my birthright! Give me some food!" It was pretty clear; Esau didn't have much use for the birthright.

Genesis 26:1-11 *Isaac deceives Abimelech*

There was another drought in Israel at this time. Isaac and his clan started to head south to Egypt again but God told Isaac he'd take care of him in Cannan. They did get as far south as King Abimelech's land. Isaac used the same story Abraham had used, saying his wife was his sister, and Rebekah ended up in Abimilech's household! One day Isaac was visiting her. They were out in the courtyard, and Isaac was hugging and kissing Rebekah in a way he would never kiss and hug a sister. Abimelech saw them. He yelled out to them, "Sister! My foot! Why did you tell me she was your sister? If one of us had relations with her, we would have been guilty!" Isaac gave him the old song and dance about being afraid of getting killed because of his beautiful wife. Abimelech forgave him and granted him safe residence in his country.

Genesis 26:12-22 *Water rights*

So Isaac stayed and established a prosperous farm. In fact, it was so prosperous that it made Abimelech nervous. He told Isaac to leave because he was getting too rich. Isaac left and started re-digging wells his father had dug. (The Philistines had filled them all up). Every well was a good one. Every time he hit water, all the local people would claim the well was theirs. Isaac had to dig four wells before he got one for his family.

Genesis 26:23-35 *Treaty with Abimelech and Esau's choices*
God appeared to Isaac. He assured him that all the promises He made to his father Abraham would be kept with Isaac and his family. Later Abimelech came down with his commanders. He asked for a treaty with Isaac. He could see how God was blessing Isaac. Isaac didn't have a problem with this, so they made a treaty and had a big feast together. Isaac's servants dug another good well and developed a town around it called Beersheba. In the meantime, Esau married a couple of local girls, which caused much grief for Isaac and Rebekah.

Genesis 27:1-17 *Rebekah's plan*
By this time, Isaac was getting old. His eyesight was failing. He called Esau in and said, "Esau, I'm not long for this world, I want you to get me some nice wild meat and cook it just the way I like it. After I've eaten it, I'll give you my blessing." So Esau headed out. Rebekah heard what Isaac said to Esau, and called Jacob into her tent. She said, "Jacob, your father has sent Esau out to get him some good food so he can give Esau his blessing. I want you to have that blessing, so here's the plan. I'm going to make some stew just the way your father likes it. You put on some of Esau's clothes, take the food into your father and get the blessing." Jacob reasoned, "Hold on Mom; what if he realizes what I'm doing and I end up getting a curse instead of a blessing?" "Don't worry son, I've got it all figured out, just go get the clothes so we can accomplish it before your brother comes back."

Genesis 27:18-29 *Jacob receives blessing intended for Esau*
When Jacob got back with the clothes a fantastic stew was ready. Rebekah had some goatskins, which she put on Jacob's hands and neck. "This way when your father wants to touch you, he'll surely think your Esau." Jacob took the stew into his Dad's tent. "Here's the stew you asked for." Isaac answered, "Wow, that was fast!" Jacob had to think quickly. "Uh ya, well ah, God really blessed me out there!" "That's fine Son; why don't you come over here so I can feel you. You sound like Jacob." Jacob went over and Isaac reached out to touch his hand. "Well, you sure feel like Esau, Come here and give me a hug." Jacob did as he was told. When Isaac grabbed his neck and smelled Esau's clothes, he said, "Ahhh, the smell of my son Esau is like the smell of a field that God has blessed. May God bless you in all that you do. May nations and people serve you,

and that would include your brother. Anyone who curses you is cursed and anyone who blesses you is blessed!"

Genesis 27:30-40 *Esau's blessing*
Just after Jacob left the tent with the blessing, Esau came in with his stew. "Get up Dad, and have some of this tasty stew I've made for you, so you can bless me." Isaac started to shake. "Why that little schemer Jacob has already been here, and I've given my blessing to him!" Esau cried out, "Darn that little wimp! Don't you have any blessing for me Dad?" Isaac moaned back, "Oh Esau, I've already made him your master; everything he does will be blessed. What's left for you?" "Just give it your best shot Dad." Isaac blessed Esau like this: "Esau, you won't always have the best place to live, and you're going to have to fight to get everything you do get. But eventually you'll get free from the yoke of serving your brother."

Genesis 27:41-28:9 *Jacob sent away*
After all this took place, Esau had a grudge against Jacob. He planned to kill him the day his father died. Rebekah heard about his plans and went in to see Isaac. "Isaac, Esau is going to kill Jacob as soon as you die. I couldn't handle losing both of you in one day. I want Jacob to go back to live with our relatives. He'll be away from Esau, and maybe he'll marry a family girl, unlike those two local girls Esau is tangled up with!" So Isaac called Jacob in, blessed him and sent him away. Esau heard about the whole thing. He knew his parents were upset about his local wives, so he married a daughter of Isaac's half brother Ishmael.

Genesis 28:10-22 *Stairway to heaven*
Jacob headed out of Israel. His first night on the road, he used a nice rock for a pillow. He had quite a dream that night. He saw a ladder going up to heaven. Angels were going up and down the ladder. God stood at the top and said to Jacob, "I'm the God of your Father and Grandfather. All the promises I made to them, I also will keep with you. You are the father of a great nation who will bless all the families on earth. I'll be with you every day and take care to see that you are blessed." Jacob woke up the next morning in awe. He exclaimed, "Wow! This is some place. It's like a stairway to heaven!" He took the rock he slept on and used it to start a pillar of rocks to commemorate the place. Then he made a vow and said, "If God will be with me on this journey and I get home safe, then the Lord will be my God, this stone pillar will be a monument to him, and I'll give God 10% of everything I make!"

Genesis 29:1-12 *Jacob meets Rachel*

Jacob kept traveling and finally got to the area where his relatives lived. He saw a well with three flocks of sheep. He walked up to the shepherds there, "Hi guys; any of you know Laban? He's my Uncle." They replied, "Sure we know him, as a matter of fact his daughter Rachel is heading this way to water her sheep." (Rachel was a shepherdess) When Rachel got there, Jacob kissed her and told her who he was. She ran and told her father while Jacob stayed and watered the flock.

Genesis 29:13-20 *Jacob's agreement with Laban*

When Laban saw Jacob he was quite happy. He could see family features in him. After Jacob had been there a month, Laban said, "Jacob, just because you're family, doesn't mean you need to work for free. How much do you want me to pay you?" Now Jacob had deep feelings for Rachel. She had an older sister named Leah. Frankly, Leah was not very attractive, but Rachel was a knock out! Jacob told Laban he would work for him seven years if he could have Rachel as his wife. Laban said, "Well, better I give her to you than anybody else...you got a deal!" Jacob loved Rachel and the seven years went by in a flash.

Genesis 29:21-30:13 *Laban's "deal" and Jacob's first sons*

At the wedding feast, Laban deceived Jacob. He put Leah in the wedding tent instead of Rachel. Jabob didn't realize till the next morning that he'd been tricked. Laban explained that it was their custom for the older girl to get married first. Then they cut a new deal; Jacob would get Rachel in a week, but he'd have to work another seven years. Leah and Rachel were both given maids by Laban. Leah's maid's name was Zilpah. Rachel's maid's name was Bilhah. Leah immediately started having children. She had four boys: Reuben, Simeon, Levi, and Judah. She hoped that having all these children would make Jacob love her, but he still loved Rachel even though Rachel wasn't having any children. Rachel told Jacob to have relations with her maid so she could at least get on the "baby derby" scoreboard. Bilhah got pregnant and had a boy they named Dan. Bilhah got pregnant again, and this son they named Naphtali. Leah wasn't going to sit on her lead. She told Jacob to have relations with her maid, so Zilpah got pregnant, and this son was named Gad. Zilpah got pregnant again, so they named this boy Asher.

Genesis 30:14-24 *Joseph*

One day one of Leah's son's, Reuben, went out and got some fruit. When Rachel saw the fruit, she asked Leah if she could have it. Leah said, "First you take the love of my husband; now you want my son's fruit." Rachel snapped back, "OK fine, you can be with Jacob tonight, but give me the fruit." So Leah slept with Jacob and got pregnant that night. She named this boy Issachar. Leah got pregnant again, and they named this boy Zebulun. Poor Leah still didn't have Jacob's love; he still continued to love only Rachel. Later Leah had another child...finally a girl! Her name was Dinah. At last Rachel got pregnant and she named her child Joseph.

Genesis 30:25-31:16 *The dealings of Jacob and Laban turn sour*
After Joseph was born, Jacob talked to Laban about returning to Israel. Laban knew he was being blessed because of Jacob. He started negotiations with Jacob to convince him to stay. They settled on a deal in which Jacob would take all the black and speckled cattle and Laban would keep all the regular cattle. As new stock was born, the speckled would go to Jacob and the regular ones to Laban. Soon Jacob put three days distance between his herd and Laban's animals. Jacob was still in charge of both herds. To increase his own wealth, Jacob used every cattle trick he knew. Most of the new cattle turned out speckled or black and they were good quality animals. Jacob was getting very rich, very fast. This caused friction between Jacob and Laban. Laban kept changing the rules on their agreement. Nevertheless, with God's help, Jacob kept getting richer and richer. God told Jacob it was time to return to Israel. He talked to his wives about it. They both said, "Jacob, our interest is with you and our family. Dad sold us to you for 14 years of your labor. Now he seems to be losing all that you've made him."

Genesis 31:17-55 *Jacob leaves Laban*
Without announcing their intentions to Laban, Jacob and the eastern franchise of "Patriarch's Ranch and Farm" started their trip back to Israel. On the sly, Rachel took some precious family idols from her Dad's tent. Laban found out about Jacob's departure three days later. He also realized his favorite statues were missing. He got some men together and pursued Jabob. The night before he caught up, God appeared to Laban in a dream and said, "Laban, you be careful tomorrow with Jacob; don't say either good or bad to him." When Laban caught up with Jacob, he did tone down his emotions. He scolded Jacob for leaving without telling him, he said he would liked to have had a party for him. Then he came to the issue of the stolen idols. Jacob, who did not know Rachel had stolen anything said, "Go ahead and search our whole camp, whoever has stolen those items will be executed!" So Laban searched every tent. Finally he got to Rachel's tent. She hid the statues under a camel saddle and sat on the saddle. Her father searched the tent and she said, "Sorry I can't get up Dad. I'm having my period, so I have to stay seated." So Laban never found the stolen statues. There was still tension between Laban and Jacob, but Laban didn't have power in the negotiation. They came to an agreement in which Jacob would be good to Laban's

daughters and neither Jacob or Laban would come after the other to do harm. Then Laban went home.

Genesis 32:1-12 *The impending reunion of Jacob and Esau*
Jabob now had to face a reunion with Esau, the brother he cheated and fled from. He was nervous about it. He sent runners to Esau with this message; "I'm coming to see you. In the 20 years I've been away I've done very well, I hope you're not mad anymore." It was signed: Your Servant, Jacob. The runners came back to Jacob and said, "We got the message to Esau, He's coming to meet you, and he's bringing 400 men with him!" Jacob split his group into two segments. He figured if Esau went after one, the other could escape. He prayed to God and said, "God, You told me to come over to the land of my relatives. You said You'd prosper me. I'm not worthy of Your blessing, yet I came with only my staff and now I have two large companies crossing the Jordan River back into the land! I need you to protect me from Esau. Remember, You promised to make me a great nation!"

Genesis 32:13-32 *Gifts for Esau and Jacob wrestles*
He made camp and put together some gifts for Esau, hoping it might loosen him up a bit. He separated 200 female goats and 20 male goats, 200 ewes and 20 rams, 30 milking camels and their colts, 40 cows and 10 bulls, and finally 20 female and 10 male donkeys! He set them up in individual herds and sent them one by one towards Esau with a space between each herd. He instructed his hands driving the herds like this, "When you see Esau and he asks you, 'Whose animals are these and where are you going with them,' reply, 'They are your brother Jacob's. He has sent them ahead as a gift for you and he is coming behind us!'" So nine separate herds went off before Jacob. Then he sent all his wives, children and all the rest he had, across the stream. He camped alone that night. A man came and wrestled with Jacob all night long. After wrestling all night, there was no clear winner. The man said, "Let me go." But Jacob answered, "Not until you bless me." The man answered, "What's your name?" "It's Jacob." The man continued, "Now your name is Israel because you have wrestled with God and with man, and you have prevailed!" Jacob felt like the man was God. The "man" injured Jacob's hip with a touch at the end of the wrestling match.

Genesis 33 *Jacob meets with Esau and settles in the land*
Jacob crossed over the next morning. When he got to his camp he could see Esau and his 400 men raising dust on the horizon. He arranged his family with the maids and their sons in front, then Leah and her children, then finally Rachel and Joseph in the rear. Jacob went out in front of the whole procession. When he met Esau, he bowed

down to the ground seven times. Esau ran up to him, and they hugged, kissed and cried together. Esau said, "Jacob, you have a big family!" After he met everyone Esau said, "Jacob, I appreciate all the cattle you sent ahead, but I have plenty, you don't need to give me anything." Jacob replied, "Esau, please keep them. I'm thankful you're not going to kill me." So Esau kept the gifts. Esau wanted Jacob to join with him and go back into the land. Jacob told him it wouldn't be practical because of all the young cattle he was driving and the children. So he sent Esau ahead. The next day Jacob and his group started heading a different direction, towards a place called Succoth. He built a house there. Nearby was a place called Shechem. Jacob bought some land there and built a nice altar to God, as he promised when he started the trip.

Genesis 34 *Dinah and her brothers*
Before long, the son of a local king was attracted to Jacob and Leah's daughter, Dinah. The young man's name was Shechem. His dad's name was Hamor the Hivite. There was a "date rape" incident between Shechem and Dinah. Word of it got back to Jacob. Shechem loved Dinah and asked his dad to get her for his wife. Dinah's brothers also heard about the rape incident. They were very angry about it. Hamor came to Jacob and his sons and said, "My son loves your daughter and sister. If you will let them get married, then you can marry our girls, and we'll just be one big happy family. I will also pay you whatever you ask as a dowry for Dinah. Jacob's sons decided to avenge Dinah, so they said, "Sure, that sounds great but there is one problem. We could never let our sister marry anyone who is uncircumcised. So if we're going to be "one happy family" all your people are going to have to be circumcised." Hamor went back to the city and explained the offer to his constituents. He said, "You know how rich these guys are.... heck, we'll double the amount of our wealth in one day!" So all the men of the city agreed, and they were all circumcised. Three days later these fellows weren't moving much because of the pain of their circumcisions. Then two of Jacob's sons, Simeon and Levi, went into the city with their swords, unannounced, and killed Hamor, Shechem and every male in the city. They took everything else: the animals, the jewels, all the women, and children. Jacob was upset at his sons. He said, "Great, now everybody around here is going to be after us!" Levi and Simeon answered, "Better that, than have our sister treated like a prostitute!"

Genesis 35:1-15 *"Jacob" becomes "Isreal"*
God told Jacob it would be a good idea to leave the area. His sons and all the people living with them had acquired some bad habits, from local customs. Many had idols and wore rings in their ears. Jabob told them to get rid of all it. So with a more patriarchal and conservative appearance, they left the area. Because the people in the towns they passed were frightened, there were no attacks on Jacob and his family.

The Story Bible for Adults

When they got to a place called Bethel, Jacob set up an altar for God. God came to him and said, "Jacob, you have a new name, it's Israel. You are going to be a great nation. Many nations will come from you. All the land I promised to your fathers, I'm going to give to you and your descendants."

Genesis 35:16-36:43 *The sons of Jacob (and Esau)*
They headed towards Bethlehem. Rachel was pregnant again and went into labor on the way. She died giving birth to Israel's last son, Benjamin. Now Israel had 11 sons from four women. Leah's sons were Reuben, Simeon, Levi, Judah and Issachar. Rachel was the mother of Joseph and Benjamin. Dan and Naphtali were Bilhah's sons. Zilpah, Leah's maid, had Gad and Asher. Isaac died when he was 180 years old. Esau and Jacob were never close again. They lived in different regions. Esau became a great company and grew into the nation of Edom.

Genesis 37:1-11 *Joseph's dreams*
Everyone knew that Joseph was Israel's favorite son. He displayed his love by giving Joseph a resplendent, multi-colored tunic. Israel's other sons didn't get along with Joseph, because Joseph delivered a bad report about them to their father. Things got worse between Joseph and his brothers when Joseph started having dreams. In one dream, he and his brothers were making piles of wheat in the field and Joseph's pile was the biggest. The brother's piles bowed down to Joseph's pile! In another dream, 11 stars and the sun and moon where bowing down to Joseph. Joseph told his dad about this one, and even Israel was offended.
"So you think even your mother and I are going to bow down to you?" But Israel did remember Joseph's dream.

Genesis 37:12-36 *Joseph sold*
One day Israel told Joseph to go to the fields and check on his brothers. They saw "the dreamer" coming from a distance and decided to kill him. Reuben the oldest said, "Let's just throw him in this deep pit, then we'll think of something." Reuben was planning to come back and save him later. The brothers roughed him up, tore off his fancy jacket and threw him in the pit with no food or water. Then they sat down to eat. A caravan of traders came by heading for Egypt. Judah suggested they sell Joseph to the caravan. Everyone agreed, because they wouldn't have to feel guilty about killing their own brother. The price for Joseph was 20 shekels of silver. To create their alibi, Joseph's fancy coat was covered with animal blood and torn to make it look as if a lion killed him. When poor Reuben returned, Joseph was sold and gone. Reuben had no choice

but to go along with the plan. Jacob suffered bitterly when he heard the story of Joseph's "death" and nearly died from grief.

Genesis 38 *Judah and Tamar*

While Joseph was in Egypt, Judah, Jacob and Leah's fourth son, and his wife had three sons. The oldest one, named Er, grew up and took a wife named Tamar. He was a bad fellow and died young. The custom, designed to keep family lines intact, was for the younger brother to have relations with his older brother's widow. The second son, named Onan, had relations with Tamar but he ejaculated on the ground, so there was no pregnancy. God was upset about this practice, so Onan died young too. Judah told Tamar he'd send his youngest son, Shelah, to her as soon as he was mature. But Judah didn't send him because he was afraid Shelah would die too. Later, Judah's wife passed away. Judah had to go through the town where Tamar lived on the way to shear some sheep. Tamar realized Judah wasn't going to send the youngest son to her. So she dressed like a prostitute along Judah's route of travel. When Judah saw her, he wanted to have sex with her. He wasn't carrying enough money so he left his identification seal with her to hold until he sent her a sheep for payment. Tamar became pregnant by Judah. When Judah sent the sheep to pay the "service", no one in the town knew of any prostitute. Judah figured he'd have to get a new identification seal and put the matter behind him. About three months later word got to Judah that his former daughter-in-law, Tamar, had become a prostitute and had gotten pregnant. He said, "Bring her to me, we'll burn her at the stake." When they came to take her she said, "The man who made me pregnant is the man who owns this identification seal!" Needless to say Tamar was spared and when she gave birth she bore twins. It was a breach birth. First a hand came out and the midwife tied a thread to it. The hand went back in and the other twin was born first. They named him Perez. The child with the thread on his hand was named Zerah.

Genesis 39:1-6 *Joseph and Potiphar*

Meanwhile in Egypt, Joseph was sold by the caravan to an Egyptian official named Potiphar. God blessed everything Joseph touched. Pretty soon he was in charge of Potiphar's entire estate. Potiphar was doing so well by Joseph that he stopped worrying about anything that had to do with business. With Joseph in charge, all he concerned himself with were things like: what to have for supper.

Genesis 39:7-23 *Joseph lands in prison*

Joseph was a very handsome man. Potiphar's wife wanted relations with Joseph. Joseph always turned her down. One day he was in the house while no one else was there and Potiphar's wife couldn't restrain herself any longer and she tried to rape

Joseph! She ripped his shirt as Joseph escaped and left the house. She told her husband that Joseph had tried to rape her. Joseph was thrown into Pharaoh's jail. In jail, Joseph gained alliance with the warden by helping him. Soon, once again, Joseph was running everything! But he was still a prisoner.

Genesis 40 *Joseph interprets dreams for fellow prisoners*
Later, two of Pharaoh's helpers were thrown into jail. One was a baker, the other served drinks to Pharaoh and his family. After these two fellows had been in jail for a few weeks they both had dreams. When Joseph saw them the next day they were distraught. He said, "What's the problem guys?" They explained the vivid dreams and neither of them knew what his dream meant. Joseph said, "No problem gentlemen, my God can help me interpret them for you!" Here's the cocktail server's dream: He saw a vine in front of him with three branches on it. It had succulent grapes, so he squeezed the grapes into Pharaoh's cup and served it to him. Joseph interpreted the dream like this: "The three branches are three days. In three days you're going to be out of here and back at your old job! If you could speak well of me to Pharaoh, I'd sure appreciate it!" When the baker saw how good the interpretation was for the server, he asked Joseph to interpret his dream; He had a basket on his head with three loaves of bread for Pharaoh. Birds were eating the bread out of the basket. Joseph's interpretation: "You've got three days before Pharaoh cuts your head off. He'll hang you from a tree and birds will come to eat your corpse." In three days it all happened just as Joseph predicted. The server went back to work and the baker was hung on a tree. The server didn't say anything to Pharaoh about Joseph.

Genesis 41:1-16 *Pharaoh needs a dream interpreter*
Two years later Pharaoh had a dream. In his dream he was standing by the Nile River. Seven healthy cows were coming out of the river. After them came seven skinny cows. The skinny cows ate the fat cows. He woke up, then fell back to sleep and had a second dream. In it he saw seven ears of grain come up on a single stalk. They were plump and good. Then seven ears of thin and scorched grain came up, they ate the plump ears. He woke up again and realized it was all a dream. Pharaoh was worried about his dreams, so he sent for his wise men and magicians. They had no idea what the dreams were about. The cocktail server finally remembered Joseph and told Pharaoh about Joseph's proven ability to interpret dreams. Joseph was immediately sent for, cleaned up, and brought before Pharaoh. Pharaoh said, "I hear you can interpret dreams." Joseph answered, "I can't, but God certainly can!"

Genesis 41:17-36 *Joseph interprets Pharaoh's dreams (and makes a recomendation)*

Pharaoh then told Joseph the dreams. Joseph answered, "Both the dreams are together because God is telling you what will certainly happen. There are to be seven good years for cattle and crops in Egypt. Then there will be seven bad years. You had two similar dreams because God is showing you how surely these things will come to pass. My advice is: put a wise person in charge of this situation. Take full advantage of the good years. Stockpile all you will need for the bad years. Then Egypt will come through beautifully!"

Genesis 41:37-57 *Joseph manages Egypt*

Pharaoh was very impressed and said, "Who could better supervise Egypt's food supply than you? God showed you the meaning of my dreams. Joseph, I'm putting you in charge. You are now second in command of Egypt. Nobody raises a foot around here unless you say so. Here's my special ring which I'm giving to you!" They took Joseph out and dressed him up like an important Egyptian, which he now certainly was, and paraded him around in a chariot. All the Egyptians bowed low to Joseph. (He was thirty years old.) Joseph took an Egyptian wife and moved into a wing of the palace. He traveled all over Egypt, managing the storage of food for the famine. The year before the famine came, Joseph had two sons by his Egyptian wife. He named his first Manasseh and the second Ephriam. There was so much extra food in Egypt it was impossible to inventory all of it! After seven good years the famine came and people started to cry to Pharaoh for food. Pharaoh simply handed the matter over to Joseph. Because the famine was world wide, Joseph was selling the whole world bread.

Genesis 42:1-28 *The brothers go to Egypt*

Which of course means, up in Cannan, Jacob and his sons were starting to feel the pinch. Jacob told his ten sons to go to Egypt and buy some grain. Joseph's full brother Benjamin stayed at home with Jacob. When the brothers arrived in Egypt, Joseph saw them. They didn't recognize him, it had been over ten years and he looked like the most important Egyptian around, because Joseph was the most important man in Egypt besides Pharaoh himself. When they approached him and bowed down, Joseph remembered his own dreams. He handled them roughly, speaking through an interpreter. "You guys look fishy to me. I believe you're spies. You've come to find our weak spots so you can attack Egypt!" They humbly replied, "Oh no! We are honest men, all sons of one father. There were twelve of us, but one died. The youngest stayed at home with our father." Joseph had his interpreter answer, "Fine, you bring me the young one at home and I'll know you're not spies." He put them in prison for three days to think about it. They were brought before Joseph again. Joseph announced, "Here's the deal: I'm keeping this one." He pointed to Simeon. "The rest of you take food and return to your father. If you come back without your youngest brother, you won't see my face. You will be immediately and permanently incarcerated!" The brothers didn't realize Joseph could understand what they said. Reuben said, "What did I tell you guys? The whole Joseph affair is blowing up in our face! We are guilty of his blood and now we're paying for it." At this Joseph quickly left and went back in his office to cry in private. Joseph had his people load sacks for his brothers. He told the Egyptians to put the money his brothers paid for the grain right inside the opening of each sack and to provide ample provisions for their trip back to Israel. On their first stop out of Egypt, one of the brothers took his sack down and found the money. "Dog gone it," they all cried. "Now that ruler is going to think we stole the grain!"

Genesis 42:29-43:15 *Troubled homecoming*
When they got home, they told Jacob what transpired in Egypt. Jacob was not pleased. They decided to hold tight and hope the drought would end. The famine didn't get any better. When Jacob's grain ran out again, the conversation between him and his sons got testy. "Why the heck did you have to even mention Benjamin?" wailed Jacob. "His brother Joseph is dead and now you want to take Benjamin! If anything happened to Benjamin....that would be it....I'd die that same day!" Judah answered, "Dad, that guy in Egypt was sharp. He got whatever information he wanted from us! Still, we need food! So send Benjamin with me. I will take responsibility. In the time we've been sitting here yakking about it, we could have been to Egypt and back already!" Jacob was livid, "I have no choice. Take the boy, get the food and get back here. If we don't do it we're all going to die anyway. Take the ruler a sampler of nice things from around here. Pack it with balm, honey, aromatic gum, myrrh, pistachio nuts and almonds. Take twice the money you need. Take the same amount that was left in the sacks and enough to buy the new load. May God protect you and give you success."

Genesis 43:16-45:28 *The brothers return to Egypt*
When Jacob's sons arrived in Egypt, the brothers were told to come to Joseph's house at noon. They were nervous because of the money left in the sacks on the last trip. They approached one of Joseph's servants. He said, "Don't worry about it, your God is with you." Then he brought in Simeon, the brother who had been left in Egypt. Now the brothers were seated in Joseph's dining room. They were arranged from the oldest to the youngest. They looked at each other in astonishment. Joseph did not eat with them. Food was delivered from his table. Benjamin's portion was the biggest. After lunch Joseph ordered the Egyptians to prepare sacks for his brothers. This time he had his own silver cup put in the top of Benjamin's bag.

The next morning the brothers headed off. They were followed. The Egyptians stopped them and demanded, "Why have you stolen our master's important cup? The brothers responded, "Hey, we didn't steal any cup, go ahead and search, if you find it, the one who has it will die." So the Egyptians searched each bag from the oldest to the youngest and found it in Benjamin's bag. They were escorted back to Egypt. "What have you done to me?" said Joseph when they were brought before him. Judah came forward and pleaded. "Sir, we can't leave the boy here. He is the youngest of us and his father loves him so. He loves him even more because a wild animal killed his brother. If he loses this son he will die on the spot. Please take me instead of the boy!"

Joseph couldn't fool them any longer. He sent all the Egyptians out of the room and cried, "It's me, Joseph! I am your brother; you sold me to the caravan. Your intentions were bad, but God actually had a very important plan for me. This is how God will see our family through this terrible drought. There are going to be five more years of drought. You all will need to come here to Egypt. We have plenty here. I'm in charge of everything. Our family can be reunited. Go back and get Dad and all you possess. Bring them to Egypt. I've got a nice place picked out for you on the delta. It's fertile there even during the drought and you won't bother the Egyptians out there."

The brothers were sent back to Jacob with a very nice caravan. It was designed to bring Joseph's father down to Egypt in comfort and style. When Jacob heard the whole story he could hardly believe it. Jacob had a night vision. God said, "Jacob, I am the God of your father, don't be afraid to go to Egypt, I will make you a great nation there and Joseph will shut your eyes."

Genesis 46:1-47:12 *Jacob arrives in Egypt*
When Jacob got to Goshen, Joseph harnessed his chariot and went up to meet his father, he cried on his shoulder for a long time. Jacob's immediate family, his sons, their wives and grandchildren totaled 66 people when they got into Egypt. This didn't include servants and ranch hands and all the cattle. Egyptians were prejudiced against shepherds and folks who lived in tents like Joseph's family. Pharaoh met a few of Joseph's bothers and Jacob. Because of his love and trust in Joseph, Pharaoh agreed to have them live in the delta region called Goshen. He asked them to run his livestock as well. In turn, Jacob gave Pharaoh a blessing.

Genesis 47:13-26 *Joseph makes Pharaoh the richest man in history*
The famine continued. Joseph was busy selling grain to all the people in Egypt and all the surrounding areas. After the third year of the famine, the people's money was in Pharaoh's account. The next year the people needed food again. They had no money so

they brought in all their livestock. It was added to Pharaoh's riches. The next year the people had nothing left to give but their land, so all the land in Egypt and the surrounding areas became the property of Pharaoh. From that time on a fifth of the crops went to Pharaoh because he owned the land. Pharaoh's wealth and power increased exponentially under Joseph's management. Pharaoh became the most powerful man on earth because of Joseph.

Genesis 47:27-49:33
Jacob lived 17 years in Egypt. When it was time for him to die, Joseph came to him with his sons. Jacob made Joseph promise that he would take his body out of Egypt and bury it in the family plot, in Canaan. Jacob blessed all of his sons. Joseph's son's, Manasseh and Ephraim, were included. Jacob's longest blessing was to Judah. He said the king of all Israel would come from Judah's family.

Genesis 50 *Joseph forgives his brothers*
When Jacob died, his sons and Joseph took a nice trip to the family plot in Canaan. Pharaoh instituted official mourning in Egypt for Jacob. After Jacob was buried, his sons thought Joseph would finally get his revenge, and they talked to him about it. Joseph assured them they were forgiven. "God is bigger than your bad intentions. Everything has turned out just as God intended."

Exodus

Exodus 1 *Joseph forgotten in Egypt*
Jacob's family flourished on the Nile river delta. After a few hundred years Joseph's accomplishments had been long forgotten and the increasing Hebrew population presented a threat to Pharaoh. He was afraid they would rebel, so he made them slaves. The Hebrews were forced to run a brick-making operation. The hard work didn't slow the Hebrew population explosion, so Pharaoh made them work harder. The harder the Hebrews worked, the more babies they had. So Pharaoh told the Hebrew midwives to kill all male babies as they were being born, but the midwives feared God more than Pharaoh. They told him that Hebrew women gave birth so quickly, it was impossible to arrive in time. Finally Pharaoh ordered all male Hebrew babies killed.

Exodus 2:1-10 *Moses*
During this time a married couple from the family of Levi had a baby boy. The mother couldn't stand to see him killed so she hid him for three months and nursed him. When

hiding him was impossible, she made a little boat out of reeds and tar. She set the child in it and released it into the river. One of the child's sisters watched from a distance to see what would happen. At that moment the Pharaoh's daughter was coming down to the river to bathe. She found the baby and loved it. The baby's sister approached and said, "I know a Hebrew woman who can nurse that baby!" Pharaoh's daughter answered, "Good, you take the child to her. I'll pay her to nurse the baby. When he's old enough he'll come live with me and will be my son." Pharaoh's daughter named the baby Moses.

Exodus 2:11-25 *Moses flees Egypt and lands in Midian*
When Moses became a young man the suffering of his own people distressed him. One day he was walking near the brick factory when he saw an Egyptian beating a Hebrew. He killed the Egyptian and buried him in the sand. The next day he saw two Hebrews fighting and said, "Why are you brothers fighting?" They answered, "Who made you boss? Are you going to kill us the way you killed the Egyptian yesterday?" At this Moses knew he had been found out. He fled Pharaoh and Egypt and went far away to a place called Midian. The priest of Midian had seven daughters. One day they were out watering their sheep when some thugs tried to run them off. Moses protected them and helped water their sheep. When the daughters told their father, he invited Moses to dinner. Moses married one of the daughters named Zipporah. In time, Moses and Zipporah had a son. Moses lived many years in Midian. In Egypt things were getting worse for the Hebrews.

Exodus 3 *God calls Moses to deliver Israel from Egypt*
One day Moses was pasturing the flock when he saw an incredible sight. A bush was on fire, but it didn't burn up. God spoke to Moses from the burning bush. "Moses, I am the God of your ancestors, Abraham, Isaac and Jacob. I've seen how the Egyptians are treating My people. I want you to go back to Egypt and lead My people to the land I promised Abraham, Isaac and Jacob." Moses objected, "I don't think I'm qualified!" God answered, "Don't worry Moses, I'll be with you! Moses replied, "When I go down to Egypt, who do I say has sent me?" "I AM WHO I AM; say "I AM" sent you. That's my name forever. When you get to Egypt, meet with the Elders of Israel and tell them that God is ready to deliver them. Then go to Pharaoh and say: Our God wants us to go out in the wilderness for three days to offer sacrifices and worship. Pharaoh will not let you go. The miracles I perform in Egypt will force him to let you go. By the time I get done with Pharaoh he will send you away with riches and be happy to see you go!"

Exodus 4:1-17 *Signs*
Then Moses asked God what he should do if the Hebrews didn't believe he had been sent from God. God said, "Throw your walking stick on the ground." When Moses did, the stick turned into a snake. Moses was afraid of it. God said, "Grab it by the tail." When Moses did, it turned back into a stick. God then told Moses to put his hand in his pocket and pull it out. When he did, his hand came out leprous and white as snow. When he put it back in and pulled it out, it was healthy and normal as before. God added, "If they don't believe you after this, take some water from the Nile River and pour it on the ground. It will become blood." Moses protested again, "God, I am just not the right guy for this job. I'm not a smooth talker. I don't think well on my feet." God answered, "Moses, who made your mouth in the first place? I'll give you the words you need!" Then Moses said, "You've got to find someone else to do the talking." This annoyed God and He said, "Fine Moses, I'll send your brother Aaron with you. You tell him what to say and he'll say it." So Moses headed to Egypt. He had some marriage problems on the way. His wife left him and went back to Midian. When Moses and Aaron got to Egypt, they appeared before the Elders of Israel. Aaron showed the signs and delivered the message. The people believed they would be saved from slavery and they worshipped God.

Exodus 5:1-7:6 *First meeting with Pharaoh and the results*
Then Moses and Aaron appeared before Pharaoh. They asked for the three-day leave. Pharaoh said, "God who? I don't know this God you speak of. No way; you and your people aren't going anywhere." Then Pharaoh addressed his own officials and said, "These darn Hebrews must have a lot of time on their hands if they're listening to this religious nut. We normally provide straw for the brick-making operation. Now they'll have to find their own straw, but their daily quota will stay the same. That should get their minds off this Moses kook and his God." When the Hebrews got the bad news they realized it was because of Moses's audience with Pharaoh; they were pretty upset with Moses and Moses was pretty upset with God. "What have you done to me God? Now your people's condition is worse!" God answered, "I told you he was going to say no. Now you will see the things I'll do to get you all out of Egypt. Go tell the people this: The God of their father Abraham, Isaac, and Jacob has heard their prayers and is going to use His strength and power to deliver them back to the land I promised their fathers." Moses told the Hebrews what God said. They were so down hearted and tired from the extra work they didn't even care.

Exodus 7:7-25 *Snake and blood*

Moses and Aaron went back to Pharaoh. Again, they said God wanted the Hebrews to take the three-day retreat. Pharaoh said, "Why should I even listen to this God you speak about, show me something to make me believe." Moses instructed Aaron to throw the stick on the ground. It turned into a snake. Pharaoh's magicians were also able to create snakes from sticks, but Moses's snake ate their snakes. Still Pharaoh held his ground and would not let the people go.

God told Moses to meet Pharaoh the next morning on his daily trip to the river. Aaron said to Pharaoh, "You aren't listening to the Lord! Now you will learn who the Lord is. The waters of the Nile will be turned to blood, the fish will die and you won't be able to drink the water from the Nile." Then Aaron took Moses's staff and touched the Nile. It turned into blood. Pharaoh's magicians were also able to turn water into blood. Pharaoh remained stubborn and would not let the people go.

Exodus 8 *Frogs and insects*

Seven days later God gave new instructions to Moses. He and Aaron appeared before Pharaoh again, "This is what God says to you Pharaoh. Let my people go or I will smite all Egypt with frogs. There will be frogs everywhere, in your house, in your bed and on your cooking utensils." Aaron took Moses's staff and touched the Nile. Up came the frogs. They covered all Egypt. Pharaoh's magicians were also able to create frogs but they sure couldn't do anything about getting rid of them. Pharaoh called Moses and Aaron, "Tell your God to get rid of the frogs and I'll let the people go." So Moses asked God to clear them out. The next day dead frogs were piled all over Egypt! There was significant odor in Egypt for many days. Since there was some relief, Pharaoh decided to go back on his word. He wouldn't let the people go, just as God had said.

Then God told Moses to have Aaron strike the ground with the staff. When he did, gnats came up from the ground and covered everything in Egypt. Pharaoh's magicians were stumped this time. The next day, God had Moses meet Pharaoh on his way to the river, "Pharaoh, you're stubborn. God is going to add all kinds of insects to the gnats already plaguing Egypt, but there won't be any insects in Goshen where the Hebrews live. You will see how God views his people differently from Egyptians." When the insects came, Pharaoh called for Moses, "OK fine; you all can sacrifice to God right there in Goshen." Moses insisted they be allowed to leave. Pharaoh agreed. Moses warned him not to go back on his word again. But, as soon as the insects were gone, Pharaoh went back on his promise. He would not let the people go!

Exodus 9 *Dead livestock, boils on the Egyptians, and hail*

Moses and Aaron went to Pharaoh again. "God says if you don't let the people go all your livestock will be destroyed. The Hebrews' livestock will be spared. This will happen tomorrow morning." The next morning all the Egyptian livestock was dead, not a single Hebrew animal was even sick. Pharaoh still wouldn't let the people go, so God told Moses to go before Pharaoh with some soot from a kiln and to blow it in the air in front of Pharaoh. The soot would become a fine dust all over Egypt that would cause boils and open sores on all living things in Egypt. The Pharaoh and all the Egyptians including Pharaoh's magicians had sores and boils. Pharaoh's heart stayed hard. He did not let the people go!

God told Moses to say this to Pharaoh: "Let My people go! You keep saying no, so there is more punishment in store for you. You don't seem to realize that if I wanted, I could destroy you and your nation quickly and completely. The only reason I'm not doing that, is to show you My power and to let the whole world know who I am. Tomorrow, Egypt is going to see the biggest hailstorm ever. My advice would be to bring your things and yourselves in from outside. Those who don't will be destroyed". Some of the Egyptians were beginning to fear the Lord, and they did prepare for the storm. God told Moses to point his staff at the sky, when he did, the hail started. There was thunder, lightning, hail and even fire coming out of the sky! It was the worst storm any one in Egypt had ever seen. Pharaoh summoned Moses. "I have had enough of God's hail. Ask Him to stop it and I'll let you go!" Moses answered, "I know you don't fear God yet, but I will ask Him to stop the hail." When God stopped the hail, Pharaoh hardened his heart again! He did not let the people go.

Exodus 10 *Locusts and darkness*

God said to Moses, "Go back to Pharaoh, I have hardened his heart again because I want you, your sons and your grandsons to know how I made a mockery of the Egyptians and how I worked all My signs to free you. You will know I am the Lord." So Moses and Aaron went back into Pharaoh and said, "This is what the God of the Hebrews says to you, 'How long are you going to be stubborn? Let My people go. If you refuse, tomorrow I will bring locusts to Egypt. More than you've ever seen. They will eat everything that's left in Egypt.'" Moses and Aaron left Pharaoh but were called back because Pharaoh's advisers said to him, "How much longer are we going to have to deal with these two? Egypt is already destroyed!" Pharaoh tried to negotiate with Moses, "Who is going on this retreat?" Moses answered, "Men, women, children, livestock...the works." Pharaoh replied, "Oh I'm sure...you guys would never come back. Just take the men and go worship." Moses rejected the deal and was driven from

Pharaoh's offices. God told him to lift his staff. The locusts ravaged Egypt, but Goshen didn't see a single locust. Moses was quickly summoned back to Pharaoh' office. "Moses, I have sinned against your God. Please ask Him to stop these killing locusts." When the locusts were gone, God hardened Pharaoh's heart again, and he did not let the people go.

God told Moses to lift his staff. A darkness came over Egypt. It was a darkness that could be felt. It was dark for three days. The Egyptians were paralyzed because of the darkness. There was light in the homes of the Hebrews. Pharaoh summoned Moses again. "You can go with everything but the livestock." Moses answered, "We won't know exactly what to sacrifice until we're away. We have to take all the livestock." Pharaoh was livid. "Get out of here. I won't have you here again. If I ever see you again I will have you killed!" Moses replied, "You're right Pharaoh, we will never see each other again."

Exodus 11:1-12:36 *The last plague and the first Passover*
Then God said to Moses, "I've got one more plague for Egypt, then Pharaoh will let you go. About midnight I am going out into Egypt, all the first born in the land of Egypt will die: from the palace, to the slave quarters, to the barns. There will be a cry in Egypt like never before and never again. Israel will be spared, so that you will understand how I love you above the Egyptians."

"From now on this month is the first month of the year for Israel. On the 10th of the month I want every house in Israel to take a prime male lamb, or goat, without any blemishes, into their homes for a few days. On the 14th of the month you will slaughter the animal. Take a hyssop branch and dip it in the blood. Put the blood on the top and two sides of the doorway. The Lord will see the blood and will pass over your house when the destroyer goes through Egypt. Then roast the animal with fire, don't boil it. Don't break any of the animal's bones. Eat the meat with no-yeast bread, garlic and bitter herbs. Eat the meal standing up, with traveling clothes on. Then eat only no-yeast bread for the next seven days. This is something you'll do every year from now on. When your children ask you why you're doing it, you will be able to explain how I delivered you from your Egyptian slavery! It will be called the Feast of Unleavened Bread. You'll start it with a service on the first of the month and again on the seventh. On the 14th you'll have the Passover meal and then you'll stay away from yeast for seven more days. This feast is for Israel. Your circumcised slave and circumcised visitors can eat the meal too, no one else. You will also dedicate your first born to Me, your sons and your livestock. When your sons ask you about this you will tell them about your deliverance from slavery that I accomplished at the expense of the Egyptians."

That night the Hebrews ate the first Passover meal and the Angel of Death passed through Egypt. All the first-born were killed. Pharaoh sent word to Moses and Aaron to take the people and go. The Egyptians everywhere gave the Hebrews whatever they asked for. The Hebrews left Egypt packed with silver and gold from the Egyptians.

Exodus 12:37-13:22 *The exodus and consecration of first born*
There were about 600,000 Hebrew men who left Egypt, not including the women and children. God lead the way. God instructed Moses about how import it was for all this to be remembered through a solemn practice of consecrating all first born offspring in Israel. He appeared before the people as a pillar of cloud by day and pillar of fire by night. The Hebrews followed the pillar. He took them on a wilderness route towards the Red Sea. They stayed away from populated areas.

Exodus 14:1-15:21 *Red Sea parted and songs of celebration*
The Hebrews hadn't been gone two days before God hardened Pharaoh's heart again. Pharaoh and his advisors felt the loss of more than a million slaves. Pharaoh headed after Israel with 600 select chariots and with all the other chariots of Egypt along with thousands of soldiers. They found the Hebrews camped in front of the Red Sea. The Hebrews complained to Moses. "So you decided there weren't enough graves in Egypt! You've brought us out here to be killed by the Egyptians!" Moses told the people to hang on and watch God work. The pillar of cloud, which was just turning into fire because it getting to be evening, went from in front of Israel to the back. It was between the Hebrews and the Egyptians. There were no confrontations that night. Early the next morning God commanded Moses to raise his staff and create a dry lane through the Red Sea for the Hebrews to go through. The waters parted and the Hebrews walked through on dry ground. The Egyptians followed them. As soon as the last Hebrew was out of the sea, the waters closed in on the Egyptians! When the Hebrews saw all these great works, they finally started to trust Moses and believe in God. They were all excited and relieved. They sang songs and celebrated.

Exodus 15:22 -16:36 *Manna from heaven*
Soon after the celebration, the Hebrews complained again saying, "Moses has brought us out here to die of thirst!" They found some undrinkable water. God showed Moses a tree to throw in the water to purify it and the people drank. God directed them into a wilderness call Sin, down on the Sinai Peninsula. They'd been gone a few weeks by

now. The Hebrews complained to Moses about food, "It would have been better if we stayed in Egypt as slaves. In Egypt we ate till we were full every night! Have you brought us out here to starve to death?" God said to Moses, "Every night I will rain bread down from heaven for the Hebrews. They are to go out in the morning and collect a day's ration. On the morning before our end of the week rest day, they should gather enough for two days. This way I can see how obedient they are. Each evening I'll fill the camp with quail and they'll have meat to eat as well."

The next morning the Hebrews were amazed at how the fields were filled with what they called "manna" (which translates: what is it?). It appeared each morning like dew. It evaporated after they did their gathering. It was flaky and tasted like a wafer with honey. If they tried to keep it over night (many did at first) it would be spoiled the next day, except for their rest day, then it would last two days. They called their rest day "The Sabbath." God wanted the Hebrews to take one day a week to relax and worship Him. They took a jar of the manna and kept it so they would remember how God fed them each day in the wilderness. God gave them manna and quail six days a week for the entire 40 years they wandered in the wilderness.

Exodus 17 *Water and war*

It wasn't long before the Hebrews started complaining about water again. Moses went to God and said, "These people do nothing but complain!" God instructed Moses to take the Elders to an area called Horeb. Moses used his staff to strike a rock and water flowed out for the people to drink.

About this time a king named Amalek came out to fight against Israel. Moses commanded Joshua to put together an army. Moses stood on the hillside above the battle with his staff. When Moses had his staff up Israel prevailed. If he dropped his hands, Amalek got the upper hand. They gave Moses a rock to sit on. Aaron and an assistant, named Hur, helped him keep his arms and his staff up. The Hebrews beat the army of Amalek that day.

Exodus 18 *Jethro's counsel*

When Jethro, the priest of Midan and Moses's father-in-law, heard about Israel's deliverance, he came out to see Moses in the wilderness. Moses's wife, Zipporah, and Moses's two sons came with him. They had a nice time talking in Moses's tent. Jethro said, "After all I've heard and seen, I now believe the Lord is greater than all the gods!" He offered sacrifices to the Lord. The next day Jethro watched Moses work. All day long the people came to Moses with their problems, big and small. Moses handled problems from sun up to sun down. That night Jethro took Moses aside and said,

"Moses, you're on an unhealthy pace. Please listen to some advice. Pick out men who are wise and hate dishonest dealings. Teach them the law. Put them in charge of judging groups of a thousand, or one hundred, or ten. Let them handle the everyday duties. They will share your burden. When they have a complex problem, they can bring it to you. You and the people will be better off. Moses did everything Jethro advised him. Jethro went back to Midan

Exodus 19:1-15 *At the foot of Mt. Sinai*
Three months to the day, after they left Egypt, the Hebrews camped at the foot of Mt. Sinai. Moses went up on the mountain. God talked to him, "Talk to the people of Israel and tell them I am ready to enter into a national contract with them. They've seen who I AM and what I can do. If they will follow My instructions I will be their God and make them a nation of kings and priests." When Moses talked to the elders of Israel, they agreed and said, "Whatever God says, we will do!" Moses went back up on the mountain. God said, "Moses, I will come to you in a thick cloud so the people will see that you are the leader I've chosen. Go back down and tell them to take three days to get cleaned up. I want clean clothes and clean minds. The people should not come close to the mountain and certainly not touch it or they will die."

Exodus 19:16-20:21 *The Ten Commandments*
After three days Moses took the Hebrews closer to the mountain. There was smoke and fire all over the mountain. There was thunder and lightning. The mountain shook and trembled with violent earthquakes. Moses called out to God and He answered Moses with awesome thunder. God warned Moses not to let anyone get too close. God instructed Moses to come up the mountain with Aaron. God gave Moses "The Ten Commandments": "I am the Lord and your God. I brought you out of Egyptian slavery. You cannot have any other God but Me. I don't want you to make and worship idols that represent things I've created. I am a jealous God. You will worship only Me. Folks who hate Me will be judged. Those who love Me will receive My love in return. Don't use My name lightly or in jest. Anyone who uses My name in vain will surely be punished! Have a Sabbath day every week. I made the world and all that is in it in six days and then rested the seventh. I blessed that day so don't forget it. Be obedient to your father and mother, it is the key to a long successful life. You are not to commit murder. You are not to have sex outside of marriage. Don't steal. Don't lie about your neighbor. Don't feel like you have to have everything your neighbor has."

Down in the valley all the people were trembling because of the smoke, fire, lightning and noise. They told Moses, "You can say anything you want to us from God but don't let Him talk directly to us. It would probably kill us." Moses answered, "Try not to be too scared. God's playing up the light show a bit because He wants you to see how powerful He is, so you won't sin."

Summary of the Law Given to Moses

Exodus 20-23
Moses went back up on the mountain with Joshua his servant and spent a good deal of time up there. He told the elders to stay behind and wait. Aaron was left in charge. The people could see the Glory of God as it rested on Mount Sinai. God called Moses from the glorious cloud. Moses remained on the mountain for 40 days. God gave Moses the Law He wanted the people to follow while he was on the mountain and at various other times while the Hebrews were in the wilderness.

The conquest of Cannan was a major part of the contract between God and Israel. God identified the borders of the land. It was very important that Israel destroy all of the idols the current inhabitants of the land worshipped. The law that God gave was state of the art for its time. Our laws today have their roots in the law God gave Moses.

The law not only gave specific rules it also gave general principles. The Law came in these categories:
Civil and criminal law: laws concerning how to treat neighbors and visitors.
Ceremonial Law: laws about how the priests would conduct the ceremonies that would allow the people to commune with God.
Personal Law: covered how to handle certain diseases, personal hygiene, good foods, vows, and even some guidelines on how to dress.
The Tabernacle: this was a very special tent were all the religious ceremonies were conducted.
Special Holidays (Feasts) God wanted his people to get away from the day-to-day cycle a few times a year.

The basis for the criminal and civil elements of the law are contained in the last six Commandments: Honor your Father and Mother, this is a key to long and successful life. Do not murder. Do not commit adultery. Do not steal. Don't lie about your neighbor. Don't wish you had everything your neighbor has."

There were many civil laws about how to respect and obey parents. The law prescribed punishments for those who didn't. Related to these laws were laws about marriage, divorce, adultery and other moral issues. Some marriages were deemed unacceptable; brothers and sisters were not to marry. A son was not to marry his dead father's wife. Sexual practices ranging from sex with animals, homosexuality and prostitution were forbidden.

The law had provisions for the elderly. They were to be respected and revered. There was consideration for the poor, handicapped, widows and orphans. Farmers were instructed not to harvest the corners of their fields so the poor could glean the leftovers. The law had special regulations for land management. Fields were to be left unused every seven years so the soil could rebuild itself. Every 50 years was a jubilee year for the land, it would not be planted. Eating fruit while passing through a neighbor's field was permissible. Carrying fruit out of a field was stealing.

There were laws about slavery and long contract labor. If a Hebrew fell on hard times he could sell himself to cover debts. He would be freed after six years unless he wanted to seal a lifetime contract with his boss. This could be desirable because his needs would always be met. He would punch a hole in his ear in front of witnesses and that made him a lifetime servant to his employer. Slavery of foreigners was permitted but regulated. Slaves were to be cared for and shown mercy. If a slave lost a tooth or an eye on the job he was to be freed as compensation. The law was designed so owners would want their slaves to stay safe! Having one hurt in an accident was meant to be a financial blow.

Criminal law followed the general principle of an eye for an eye, a tooth for a tooth. Arson, slander and fraud are covered in these sections. If someone murdered accidentally or in a fight, he could flee to a "city of refuge", until he got a fair trial. If judged innocent he'd have to stay in the city of refuge until the High Priest died. A person convicted of murder was put to death very quickly compared to today's standards.

The law also covered business practices. Interest rates on loans and fair weights and measures were regulated. Gift giving and excessive entertaining was warned against. Laws about inheritance of property were included. The law meant to protect family property. Property could be sold, but it was always returned to the original owners during the year of Jubilee, which happened every 50 years. If someone bought property, the price was based on how many years until Jubilee. If there were only five years before Jubilee, land prices would be way down because any transaction would only last five years. This allowed family property to stay with the family as an everlasting inheritance.

There were laws designed to protect the longevity of families. If a man died with no sons, the widow was to marry one of his brothers so his family line could continue. The law also provided for the humane treatment of animals. Witches, false prophets and heretics were severely dealt with. The law also had rules for kings. They were not to become rich at the expense of the people. Visitors were to be dealt with kindly. God wanted his people to remember that they were not dealt with kindly by the Egyptians.

There were many laws covering hygiene and health-related matters. Women having their period had certain rules. There were a number of regulations regarding leprosy and quarantines. Certain foods were prohibited.

Some Hebrews felt compelled to make vows and there was a body of law concerning these. The Nazarite vow was a vow of separation. The person who made this vow would not cut his hair, nor drink any alcohol. A Hebrew could make the vow for as long as he wanted. If he broke his vow he'd have to start again from the very beginning. There were other vows in which objects or land could be dedicated to God for certain periods. All of these vows were voluntary and made only as a sign of devotion and love for God.

Exodus 24

Moses went back down the mountain to conduct a ceremony with the elders and the people. They erected twelve pillars, one for each tribe of Israel. Moses read all the law he had received so far and the people agreed to follow the law. Then they offered sacrifices. Then Moses went back up into the cloud that covered the mountain

Exodus 25-31 *More law summary*

God gave Moses very specific instructions for building the Tabernacle. Each of the materials was specifically identified. It was made with Acacia wood, gold, silver, animal skins and fine cloth. The Tabernacle was 45 feet long, 15 feet wide and 15 feet high. It had two rooms; one was 30 feet long, 15 feet wide and 15 feet high. This area was called the Holy Place. The other room was in the rear of the tent. It measured 15 feet long, 15 feet wide and 15 feet high; it was called the Holy of Holies. Surrounding the Tabernacle was a seven and a half foot fence that created an area around the Tabernacle called the court. It was 150 feet long and 75 feet wide. There was one veiled entrance to the court. Any Hebrew who had prepared himself with the proper rituals could go in the court. Only the priests could go into the Holy place to perform ritual duties. Only the High Priest could go into the Holy of Holies, just once each year on the Day of Atonement. The Holy of Holies was separated from the Holy place by a linen curtain. It was woven of four colors of fine twined linen, blue, purple, scarlet and white, with angels embroidered in it. The tabernacle had important pieces of furniture in it. The ark, a chest-like box, 45 inches long, 27 inches wide and 27 inches tall, was located in the Holy of Holies. It was made of Acacia wood and overlaid with gold. On the top of the ark was a slab of gold called the Mercy Seat. Two angels faced each other on opposite sides of the Mercy Seat. Their wings touched over the ark. God's glory dwelled in the area between the seat and the wings. A jar of manna and the two stones with the Ten Commandments on them were kept in the ark. When it was time to move the ark, the Levites put poles in gold rings attached to the ark and carried it on their shoulders.

The "table of show bread" was located in the Holy Place. It was 36 inches long, 18 inches wide and 27 inches tall. It was covered with gold and had rings so the Levites could carry it. Each day, 12 loaves of bread were placed on the table with a number of other golden utensils. There was also a gold lamp stand. It had seven oil lamps, one in the center and three on each side. Also in the Holy Place was the altar of incense, which was gold. The sacrificial altar was located in the court. It was 7 1/2 feet long, 7 1/2 feet wide and 4 1/2 feet tall, overlaid with bronze; a bullhorn came up from each corner. The altar had rings for the Levites to pole and carry. There was a golden washing bowl near the altar, which the priest used to ceremonially cleanse themselves before a sacrifice.

Priests were the only ones actually allowed in the Tabernacle. Aaron was the first priest. His sons and their descendants were the only priests for quite awhile. The priest's job was to be a representative between God and His people. Ceremonies conducted in the Tabernacle were designed to allow a Hebrew with faith to approach and commune with a very loving, yet fearful God. The Priest did his job in a specific uniform. The main part of the outfit was called an ephod. It was an apron that hung over the priest's shoulders. On the shoulder pieces there were two precious stones, one on each shoulder. Engraved in the stones were the names of the tribes of Israel, 6 on each side. On the front of the ephod was a breastplate that was nine inches square. The breastplate had 12 precious stones. Each stone had the name of a tribe engraved on it. The breastplate also had two other stones of judgment called the Urim and Thummin. These stones were used occasionally as sacred dice to determine God's will in certain matters.

The nuts and bolts of the priest's job were to preside over ceremonies conducted at the tabernacle. The bulk of these were offerings and sacrifices of various kinds. A Hebrew could express his religious devotion and gain forgiveness of his sins by offering something of real value to him. For this reason there were a number of rules about what could be sacrificed. A sacrificial animal could only be a domesticated variety. Trapping a deer and bringing it in to sacrifice didn't cut it. An animal had to be at least 8 days old and no older than three years, when it was in the prime of usefulness and value to its owner. Bringing an animal that was just taking space in the barn wasn't considered a sacrifice. Vegetable offerings were roasted corn, flour or no-yeast bread. Yeast was thought of as a sign for sin in any ritual.

Vegetable offerings were pretty simple. The Hebrew would bring them in and the priest would take them up to the altar to be burned. Drink offerings, always wine, would simply be poured out on the altar. Animal sacrifices followed this general pattern: The offerer would bring the animal to the altar and would place his hands on the animal's head. This would transfer himself to the animal in a symbolic way. In a private ceremony the offerer would then slaughter the animal. The priest handled that chore in the public ceremony. The blood of the animal would be sprinkled in certain areas around and on the altar. Then certain parts of the animal would be burned. Sometimes, the offerer, the priest, and the poor would eat parts of the sacrifice. There were different names for the offerings. There was a "burnt offering" made everyday by the priests for all the people. This was a male lamb without any defects. They would offer more than one on special days. This sacrifice stood for Israel's devotion to God. There was a "Peace or Thank offering." This was an offering that signified everything was OK between the offerer and God. Everybody ate afterward, which made the people feel like they were sitting at the same table with God. A "Trespass offering" could be made when a particular sin had been committed. The offerer couldn't eat any of this one.

Then there were "Sin offerings". The most important Sin Offering was made on the Day of Atonement, which fell in the midst of the autumn feasts. Early in the day the High Priest would get cleaned up and put on a special white outfit. He would sacrifice a young bull for himself. He would then carry coals from the burnt part of the offering through the veil, which separated the Holy Place from the Holy of Holies. Then he came back out and he'd carry in some of the blood from the sacrifice. He'd sprinkle that in front of the Mercy Seat. Then he'd come back out to the court where the altar was and sacrifice the first of two goats. He would carry the blood from the first goat back into the Holy of Holies and sprinkle it on the Mercy Seat. This blood would atone for the people's sins the same way the bull's had for the High Priest. Finally some of the blood from the first goat would be put on the head of the other goat (the scapegoat). The Scapegoat would then be sent off into the wilderness bearing on its head the collective sin of all Israel. This signified that sin had been removed for another year. Then the High Priest would clean up and put his regular uniform back on.

Religious days and feasts were very important for Israel. Every week they had the Sabbath. Once a month they had a special day for the New Moon. The Feast of Unleavened Bread started with the Passover meal, the Feast of Trumpets announced the start of the autumn festival season, and the Feast of Tabernacles came right after the Day of Atonement. The people would camp out for a week during this feast to remember their time in the wilderness. The Feast of In-gathering came right after the Tabernacles Feast. The Feast of Weeks happened during the summer time and celebrated the harvesting of early crops.

Exodus 32:1-14 *God intends to destroy the disobedient people, but changes His mind*

God wrote the law on two tablets of stone for Moses to take to the people. During the long period that Moses was on the mountain the people were beginning to think he was never going to come back. So they went to Aaron and said, "We don't know what's happened to Moses. Make us a god who can go before us." Aaron instructed the people to bring him their gold earrings. Aaron crafted a golden calf from the rings. Then he put it on an Altar and said, "This is your god, who brought you out of slavery in Egypt!" All the people celebrated and worshipped the golden calf. The next day they offered sacrifices to the golden calf and had a wild party.

Up on the mountain, God said to Moses, "You're not going to believe this Moses, the people have already forgotten you and Me. They have made an idol. They are worshipping it and offering sacrifices to it. They are actually saying it brought them out of Egypt! I think I've had about enough. I'm going to destroy those obstinate people!" Moses interceded and said, "Hold on God. What will the Egyptians think? They'll say that you brought this people out here into the wilderness just to kill them. You also need to remember your promises to Abraham, Isaac and Jacob! You said, 'I will give their descendants the land and make them as numerous as the stars of heaven.'" God cooled down and decided not to destroy the people.

Exodus 32:15-33:6 *Consequences*

Moses went back down with Joshua. He carried the stone tablets that God himself had engraved with the law. When he saw the wicked party that was going on he was very angry. He threw the two tablets on the ground and they broke in pieces. Moses commanded that the golden calf be burned in a fire, ground into dust and thrown into a lake. Moses made the people drink the water. He said to Aaron, "What have you been doing down here! You have allowed a terrible sin to come on the people!" Aaron began making excuses, "They didn't think you were coming back so they asked me to make them a god. They brought me their gold. All I did was throw it in the fire and out popped this calf!" Moses called out and said, "Anyone who is for God come to me." All the sons of Levi came to him. He told them to take their swords and go through the camp cutting and slaying. Three thousand of the people were killed.

The next day Moses said to the people, "You have committed a terrible sin. I'm going to try to work this out with God." So Moses went back to the Lord and said. "God, if you will just forgive these people, You can take my name out of the record You have written." God said, "The ones who have sinned against Me will be blotted out of the book. I am not going to dwell with these people any longer. They are an obstinate people." When the Hebrews heard this, they were very sad. They took off all their jewelry and kept it off for the rest of the time they were in the wilderness.

Exodus 33:7-23 *God stays with Israel*
Moses had a special tent where he met with God. He called it the "Tent of Meeting." When he'd enter the tent, the pillar of cloud would come down at the door. The people knew that Moses was talking to God. They would worship at the entrance to the tent. God talked to Moses just as a man would speak to his friend. Joshua stayed in the tent constantly while Moses was in camp.

Moses said to God, "Lord, there's no reason for Israel to continue if You're not with us. The fact that Your presence is with us is what sets us apart from any other nation! Please teach me Your ways and I'll pass them on to the people." God answered, "All right Moses, I will stay and go with you. Because of you Moses, I will keep my presence with the people." Then Moses said, "Lord, I want to see Your glory." God replied. "I will make My goodness pass before you, but you can't see My face. If any man saw My face he would surely die. Make two more stone tablets and meet Me in the morning."

Moses did as he was instructed. When he got to the mountain, God passed close in front of him and proclaimed His goodness, "I am the Lord, the Lord God, compassionate and gracious, slow to anger and abounding in loving kindness and truth. I keep My loving kindness for thousands. I forgive transgression and sin, yet I do not let the guilty go unpunished!" Moses immediately bowed down low and worshipped. He said, "Lord, if I have found favor with You, please go along with us and be in our midst. I know this is an obstinate people but we need You to forgive us and take us as Your own people." God answered, "Yes I am going to stay with you. We are going to enter into a contract. I will give you possession of the land. You have to make sure you destroy all the idols and temples when you get in the land, or I'm sure these people will end up worshipping other gods. Nothing makes Me angrier than that! I am the only God who deserves your worship! You need to follow the laws that I give you."

Exodus 34-40 *Building the Tabernacle (Quite a bit of this is Law...see summary)*
Moses stayed up on the mountain with God another 40 days. God wrote the law on the tablets again and gave them to Moses. When Moses returned to the people his face was shining from being in God's presence. He had to wear a veil when he spoke to the people. His aura was so bright the people were afraid of him.

Moses then brought all the people together. God chose two men to supervise the building of the Tabernacle, Bezalel who was from the tribe of Judah and Oholiab from the tribe of Dan. God anointed them with His spirit so they would be able to complete the work exactly as God had commanded Moses. Moses took up a collection to get all the materials that would be needed to build the Tabernacle. The people came with everything that was needed. They gave from their hearts. Even after everything needed was collected, they still came wanting to give more! Then Bezalel, Oholiab and all the skilled craftsmen went to work building the tabernacle.

When the project was completed Moses inspected the work and saw it met all the specifications God had given him. God told Moses to wait for the first day of the year to set up the Tabernacle. On dedication day, Aaron and his sons dressed in their Priestly clothing and were officially anointed. When the Tabernacle was fully assembled with all the furniture in place, the pillar of cloud settled on the Tabernacle. From that day on in the wilderness the people would stay where they were until the pillar of cloud lifted from the tabernacle. Only then would they go forward, following the pillar of cloud.

Numbers

Numbers 1
Moses was then instructed by God to take a complete census of the people. He got numbers for each tribe based on men older than 20 who could go to war. The total was 603,550 The only tribe left out was the tribe of Levi. Their job was to take care of the tabernacle. Whenever the Hebrews set out it was the Levites who handled taking down the tabernacle and setting it up again when they arrived at their new camp. Each family in the tribe of Levi had responsibilities for certain parts of the tabernacle.

Numbers 2-10 *Mostly law and these bits of narrative*

The Hebrews camped in a specific order around the tabernacle. They also broke camp in a regimented fashion. The Levites camped close to the tabernacle. On the east side of the tabernacle the tribes of Judah, Issachar and Zebulun camped. They were the first to break camp when the pillar of cloud lifted from the tabernacle and a silver trumpet was blown to signal the move. The silver trumpets were also used to signal meetings of elders, meetings of the whole congregation and during feasts. On the south side of the tabernacle the tribes of Reuben, Simeon and Gad camped. They would go out behind the east side tribes when camp was broken. When the Hebrews moved out, the tribe of Levi, with the tabernacle, would follow the south side tribes. On the west side, the tribes of Ephraim, Manasseh and Benjamin camped. They would set out right after the Levites. Finally on the north side, the tribes of Dan, Asher and Naphtali camped. They would take up the rear when Israel set out.

When the first anniversary of the Passover arrived, the people celebrated it on the 14th of the month just as God had instructed. The next month the cloud that rested on the tabernacle was lifted and the Hebrews made their first move according to the instructions and marching orders God had given Moses. The cloud settled again in an area called the wilderness of Paran. As the cloud led them away Moses proclaimed: "Rise up God! Let your enemies be scattered, let those who hate you, flee before you!" When the cloud stopped, Moses shouted out: "Return now, oh God, to the many thousands of Israel!"

Numbers 11 *More complaining*

As soon as they made camp, the people started to complain about the lack of meat and they murmured concerning the monotony of manna. God and Moses were very displeased. Moses spoke to God and said, "I have had it with these whiners! Just kill me now God, I can't go on with these cry babies!" God announced a new help for Moses. "Moses, I want you to select 70 elders from among the people. Bring them here to the tent. I will put the same spirit I have placed on you, on them. They will truly be able to share your burden. Then I will give these people so much meat they'll be sick of it!" The next day the Elders were anointed and the Spirit came to rest on them. That night a wind blew in from the sea; it brought more quail than the people could ever eat. The greedy ones who had done the most complaining got deathly ill as soon as they began to eat the quail. Many of them died.

Numbers 12 *Aaron and Miriam rebel*

After this, Aaron and Miriam rebelled against Moses. They believed Moses had made a mistake by marrying one of the local girls. They said, "The Lord doesn't only speak through Moses. He speaks through us as well." God immediately spoke from inside the cloud. He said, "Hold your tongue out there Aaron. Moses is no ordinary prophet. He doesn't get visions or dreams. I talk to him face to face. He understands who I am. He has been absolutely loyal to Me. You should be afraid to say anything bad about him!"

When God finished talking, Miriam became covered in leprosy. Aaron begged Moses to forgive them. Moses forgave Aaron and asked God to cure Miriam. God was forgiving, so Miriam was healed, but she was banished from camp for seven days.

Numbers 13:1-14:25 *Spies sent into the land Caleb and Joshua get it right*

After this, God instructed Moses to select one man from each tribe to go into Canaan to spy out the land. They were to report on these issues: What kind of people lived in the land? Were they strong or weak, few or many? How was the land, was it good or bad? What kind of cities did it contain? Was the land fat or lean? Were there a lot of trees? Moses instructed them to try and get some of the fruit of the land to bring back.

The spies set out and spent 40 days on their totally successful mission. They were able to spy out the entire land and bring back fruit. Ten of the 12 spies gave this report: "It's true, Cannan is a great place to live. It would easily support us. There is ample area and it is abundantly fertile. This is a land that literally flows with milk and honey! Unfortunately the people who live in the land are too strong for us to defeat. Not only are they numerous, they're big! These people seem like giants compared to us. All the cities have walls and gates. Many strong nations inhabit the land. We could never get it away from them."

The people were upset when they heard this. Caleb stood to speak. He and Joshua were the two spies that felt differently than the first ten to report. He said, "We can take these people because we have the Lord on our side!" The other ten disagreed and said, "No way we can win, it would be like grasshoppers against giants." All the people cried that night. The next morning the Hebrews started to complain against Moses saying, "Why did he bring us out here? It would have been better to die in Egypt. Let's select a new leader and he can lead us back to Egypt." Moses and Aaron fell on their faces before the grumbling crowd. Joshua stood up and addressed the assembly. "Don't you understand that God is with us? The people in the land will fall before us in terror. God is much more powerful than anything I saw in Canaan! Don't sin by doubting, trust God!" All the people were getting ready to pick up stones to kill them when the cloud started to thunder. The glory of the Lord was present in the cloud.

God spoke to Moses from the cloud. "My patience is wearing pretty thin with this group. How many miracles do they have to witness before they get the idea straight about who I am! I am going to kill them with pestilence, then we'll start over with you Moses!" Moses replied, "God, I don't think you want to do that. What are all the nations going to say? They'll say you brought them out here, but weren't able to get them into the land You promised. You are a very forgiving God, slow to anger, I pray God, please forgive these whiners!" God said, "All right, because of you Moses, I will not wipe them out right here and now. I will say this; the whole generation who have seen My mighty works with their own eyes and not believed or trusted in Me will not go into the land. Every one of them will be buried here in the wilderness. They will not go into the land I've promised. The only ones from this generation that will go in will be Joshua and Caleb, because they understand who I am and they believe in Me."

Numbers 14:26-15:41 *Botched attempt, Sabbath breaking, tassels*
When Moses announced this verdict to the people, they all decided they would try to take the land. Moses warned against this but they went anyway. The ark and the tabernacle stayed in camp with Moses. The Hebrews marched into the hill country in the very southern part of Cannan. The Amalekites and Cannanites who lived in the area beat them soundly.

While Israel was in the wilderness a man was found gathering wood on the Sabbath. God instructed Moses to have the man taken outside the camp and stoned. God also instructed Moses to have the people place tassels on the corners of their garments. This would be a reminder for them to follow the laws He had given them.

Numbers 16 *Korah rebels and the aftermath*
A man named Korah, who was from the tribe of Levi, began an insurrection against Moses and Aaron. He came before Moses with three other leaders named Dathan, Abiram, On, and 50 other prominent Hebrews. They said, "Moses, you've gone too far. You are the master of self-promotion! We have the same authority as you and Aaron. We should be able to serve as priests just as well as Aaron and his sons." Moses replied, "So you think God hasn't done enough for you already. You already have the distinction and privilege of the family of Levi, but now you want the priesthood too? Tomorrow morning we'll see who should be favored by God to serve as priest. Bring your censors, put fire in them and bring them in front of the tabernacle." Then Moses

said to Dathan and Abiram, "You all come along with them." They answered, "Moses you're nothing but talk. You told us we'd be leaving Egypt and going to a land God promised. You said we'd inherit vineyards we didn't plant. Instead you've brought us out into the wilderness to die! We won't be doing anything you say."

The next morning Korah and 250 others came to the tabernacle with their censors. God said to Moses, "Get away from this sinning congregation. I'm going to destroy the whole lot." Moses and Aaron fell on their faces and said, "God, you can't kill everybody! Only some of them have sinned." Then God said, "Tell the people to get away from the tents of Korah, Dathan and Abiram." After Moses relayed the message, he yelled over to Dathan and Abiram, who were standing in the doorways of their tents along with their families, "You will now see whom God has chosen to serve before Him as priests." At that moment the ground opened up and swallowed the dwellings of Dathan and Abiram. Fire also came out from the tabernacle and consumed Korah and the 250 "priests" holding the censors. God told Moses to have Aaron's son, Eleazar, take the censors from the ashes and use them to make plating for the Altar. The Hebrews would be reminded every time they saw it that Aaron and his sons had been set aside for the priesthood by God.

The next day all the Hebrews complained to Moses. They blamed him for all that occurred the previous day. God was angered again. He said, "Moses, move away from these people. I am starting a plague now to consume them this instant." Moses and Aaron fell on their faces. Moses looked over at Aaron and said, "Get your censor and put fire from the Altar in it and carry it among the people so you can stop the plague God has started. Aaron did as Moses instructed and the plague was stopped, but not before 14,700 people died.

Numbers 17 *Aaron's rod blossoms*
God spoke to Moses the next day, "Tell each of the twelve tribes to bring the staff of their chief leader to the tabernacle. Aaron's staff will represent the tribe of Levi. These people need to see clearly that Aaron and his sons are the men I have chosen to be priests. Moses put the 12 staffs in the Tabernacle for the night. The next morning 11 of the staffs were not changed. Aaron's staff had living buds on it. It produced blossoms and it bore ripe almonds! God told Moses to put the staff in the Tabernacle as a constant reminder. Just after these things the people who came anywhere near the Tabernacle were dying. God firmly established the connection of Aaron and his sons as priest and the tribe of Levi as their helpers in the tabernacle.

Numbers 20:1-13 *More water problems and complaining*

There was a water shortage near a place called Meribah. The people came before Moses complaining. "This is about as far from 'flowing with milk and honey' as you can get. Why did you even take us away from Egypt! This is a terrible place. We're going to die of thirst." God told Moses to take Aaron's staff and go to the rock of Meribah. He instructed Moses to speak to the rock and tell it to bring forth water. When Moses gathered the people around the rock he yelled at them, "You are a rebellious group. Even so, here's your water!" He then hit the rock with the staff and water flowed out. God was upset with Moses because he didn't follow his instructions exactly, so He told Moses that he would not lead Israel into the Promised Land.

Numbers 20:14-21 *Edom denies pasage*

Moses wanted to cut through the land of Edom to get further north and to the east of Cannan. He sent messengers to the Kings of Edom. "Please remember our shared family roots, (the nation of Edom came from Esau, Jacob's older twin brother). Please let us pass through your land. We won't take anything we don't pay for." The Edomites not only denied the passage, they sent a large military contingent to the border to dissuade any idea Moses might have had to go against their edict.

Numbers 20:23-21:3 **Aaron dies, Arad defeated**

Miriam and Aaron died around this time. Aaron passed the torch of the High Priesthood to his son Eleazar. As they were heading towards the Red Sea, to go around Edom, the king of the area, named Arad, made a raid against the Hebrews. Some Hebrews were captured, but the people rallied and they asked God to help them. They defeated Arad and destroyed all his cities.

Numbers 21:4-35 *The bronze serpent, and cities captured*

As the journey around Edom lagged on the people started to complain against God and Moses with the same old tired lament: "Why did Moses bring us out to the wilderness to starve and die." God was tired of hearing this. He sent snakes into the camp and many were dying from their bites. The people came to Moses and said, "We have sinned against you and God. Please pray that God would deliver us from these snakes!" God instructed Moses to make a post with a bronze snake wrapping itself around the top. When the people were bitten, they were to look at the snake on the top of the post and they would not die from the bite.

As the Hebrews continued their journey around Edom they came to a region ruled by a king named Sihon. He ruled the Amorites who lived in the area. Moses requested passage through the region. Not only was it denied, the Amorites came out against the

Hebrews. God helped Israel defeat Sihon and the Amorites. The Hebrews stayed for quite awhile and lived in the region, in the cities that Sihon had governed. Then a king named Og made the mistake of trying to fight Israel. He was also defeated and the Hebrews lived in his cities as well.

Numbers 22:1-24:25 *The talking donkey and prophecies of Balaam*
Finally the time to leave the captured cities came. The cloud led them to the east of the Promised Land in the plains of Moab. Balak, the king of Moab, saw the mighty hordes of Israel camped out next to his country and was very concerned. He sent a message to a highly regarded prophet named Balaam. The message said, "Come here to Moab. A huge group of Hebrews is camped next to my country. I want you to come pronounce a curse on them so I can go out and defeat them. I know whoever you curse is cursed and whoever you bless is blessed." Balaam told the messengers he needed to sleep on it, to see what God would instruct him to do. The next morning he announced to the messengers, "Sorry fellows, you can head on back to Moab. I won't be coming with you. God's made it very clear to me that He does not want the Hebrews cursed. As a matter of fact they are exceedingly blessed!"

When Balak heard Balaam wasn't coming, he sent a bigger more dignified group of messengers down to Balaam. Their message from the king was more emphatic, "Please, let nothing stop you from coming to me. This is going to be a very lucrative engagement for you. We need these people cursed and are willing to pay dearly to have the job done." Balaam replied to the messengers, "Money is irrelevant here, if God tells me not to curse those people, I'm not going to curse them. Stay here tonight, I'll let you know tomorrow. The next morning Balaam said, "God said I can go, but I'm not going to say anything He doesn't tell me."

On the way to Moab God sent an Angel to meet Balaam and make sure he had his attention. As Balaam was riding his donkey along the road, the Angel stood with his sword drawn before Balaam. The donkey saw the Angel, Balaam didn't. The donkey left the road to avoid the Angel so Balaam beat his donkey. Later they were in a narrow area at the edge of a vineyard when the Angel appeared. The donkey pinched Balaam's leg against the vineyard wall as he tried to avoid the Angel. Balaam still didn't realize what was happening and beat the donkey again. Finally they were traveling on a narrow ridge with no room for the donkey to divert when the angel loomed in front of them. The donkey lay down in front of the Angel, with Balaam on top of him. As Balaam was beating the donkey again, the Lord opened the donkey's mouth. It said to Balaam, "Why do you keep beating me?" Balaam replied, "Because you keep making a fool of me, laying here in the road. If I had a sword with me I'd kill you right now!" The donkey answered, "I have been your donkey my whole life, have I ever acted this way before?" Balaam replied, "No." Then he finally saw the Angel with his drawn sword and bowed quickly to the ground. The Angel said, "Why do you keep beating your donkey? She has protected you from me. As a matter of fact if she hadn't laid down just now I would have killed you and let her live!" Balaam replied, "I am sorry, I felt I had a green light to go on this trip. If you want me to go back home, I am on my way right now!" The Angel said, "Go, but be very careful to say only what God tells you!"

When Balaam arrived, Balak was miffed about having to send two groups of messengers, but they got right to work. They went to a hill overlooking just a small portion of the hundreds of thousands of camped Hebrews. They set up seven altars and sacrificed seven rams. Then Balaam went to a bare hill by himself and returned with a prophecy. "How can I curse what God has blessed? I see before me a nation that has separated itself from the Nations to be God's special people. I wish I were a Hebrew!" Balak of course was not pleased. "Real nice curse there Balaam! You could at least try not to bless them!" Balaam replied, "I told you I was going to say what God told me to say!"

Balak decide to try from a different vantage point so they went to a different hill. Again, Balak heard a blessing for Israel, not a curse so they went to another area with the same result. Finally Balaam prophesied again and said that Israel would be a major force in the world. A king would come from Israel who would be a star! He would prevail on all the nations, not just Moab. Finally, Balak and Balaam both returned to their homes.

Numbers 25 *Phinehas shows zeal*
After some time in Moab the Hebrews began to act like Moabites. They worshipped their gods and had sex with the Moabite temple prostitutes. Moses ordered the elders to execute anyone who was worshipping the Moabite gods. A killing plague swept through Israel. One man of Israel took a prostitute into his tent right in front of Moses. Phinehas the son of Eleazar the High Priest took a spear and killed the man and the prostitute with one thrust. The plague stopped and the Hebrews began to behave themselves. God expressed his pleasure with Phinehas. He said he was a good priest because he was zealous for his God.

Numbers 26-36 *Additional law and final events concerning Moses*
God then came to Moses and said, "I've got just a few more things for you to do before you are finally buried with your ancestors. Commission Joshua to be your successor. I want the nation of Midian destroyed. Muster an army with 1000 soldiers from each tribe. Phinehas will accompany them. Take the holy vessels and the silver trumpets." So Israel went out against Midian and they killed every male. They also killed Balaam, who was a Midianite. They took all the Midianites' possessions, but they did not kill the women and children. Moses was upset by this and said, "Don't you remember that these are the very women who can seduce Israel to prostitute themselves to the local gods? Kill every male child and every woman who is not a virgin." They divided all the Midianite wealth as God directed.

During the Hebrews' stay east of the Jordan River the tribes of Reuben, Gad and the half tribe of Manasseh became very comfortable. They approached Moses requesting that they be allowed to settle east of the Jordan, build cities and make the region their inheritance from God. At first Moses was upset because he felt they were jumping ship. The leaders of the tribes of Reuben, Gad and Manasseh assured Moses that their army would help take the land. Only when the conquest was complete, would their army would return to the land east of the Jordan. Moses approved of this plan.

Leviticus
Leviticus contains Law, except for the 10th chapter, which tells the story of Nadab and Abihu.

Not long after Aaron and his sons had been anointed as priests, two of Aaron's sons named Nadab and Abihu made offerings before the Lord that were not in accordance with the rules God had given Moses. Fire came from the presence of the Lord and consumed them. Naturally, Aaron was upset. Moses told Aaron and his two surviving sons, Eleazar and Ithamar, not to display too much sorrow. After all God was the one who consumed Nadab and Abihu. It wouldn't be to smart to second-guess God! Then God himself talked to Aaron and said, "From now on no priest should drink wine or hard liquor when performing priestly duties." Moses told Aaron and his surviving sons to make some sacrifices with regard to this situation. There was even a little confusion about that, but it was worked out with no further trouble.

Deuteronomy

Much of Deuteronomy reviews the history of Israel to this crucial point. It also restates many portions of the Law. Moses promises that God will raise up another prophet like him. God said, "I will raise up another prophet like Moses and I will put my words in his mouth. Whoever does not listen to him, I will require it of him." (Duet 18:18-19) The rest of the book reads like a contract between God and Israel. It delineates the benefits of fulfilling God's requirements and the curses for non-fulfillment.

Moses gathered all the people together and spoke to them. "You have seen all the incredible things God has done. Yet it still doesn't seem like you get it! He led you out of Egypt with many signs and wonders. For 40 years He has provided food for you here in the wilderness. He's settled us temporarily here, east of the Jordan, because He helped us defeat the people who were living here. Our brothers in the tribes of Reuben and Gad and Manasseh will come back and keep this land as an inheritance from God."

"You've seen the idols in the nations we've come through so far. Don't have anything to do with these false gods. The Lord is the real God. He is the one who created the world. He is the one who has led you from Egypt and will lead you into the Promised Land! Worship only Him. When you take the land, destroy all the idols. If one of you begins to turn his heart towards an idol, treat him like a poisonous plant. God will not have His people worshipping statues made of wood."

God said, "If you follow all these laws and commandments God has given you, you will be blessed more than you can imagine. You will be blessed wherever you are, in the city or the country. You will prosper in every way. You'll have big families, full barns and large healthy cattle in your pastures. Every nation will see that you are My people. They will be afraid of you because they will see that you are My people. They will see all My good works for you because you have chosen Me!

"But if you disobey these laws and worship other gods, things will go disastrously for you. Nothing you touch will prosper. Rain will seem like dust to your crops. You'll lose every war you fight. Nations will come and plunder your families in the country and the city. Those of you they don't kill they will carry away as slaves. You will be scattered over the whole earth. You will be a laughing stock of the whole world. Your name will be used like a nasty word.

Moses continued, "The Lord knows you will turn away from Him. When you do, curses will fall upon you. You will see plagues and famine. You will be driven from your land. You will live in nations hostile to you. People will see how poor and afflicted you are and they will say, 'It's turned out this way for them because they didn't keep their contract with God.' God says, 'I will bring you back to your land. I will bring you back from all the areas where you are scattered around the Earth. I will restore you and prosper you again.'"

"Today you have been given a choice. You can have good or bad. I, Moses, have led you these 40 years and I have seen myself how you tend towards bad more than you tend towards good. I'm afraid once I'm gone, it will only get worse! Take the good path. Follow these laws. You've seen what God can do, both good and bad. You've seen manna fall from heaven everyday. You've also seen Dathan and Abiram get swallowed into the ground. You know it's better to be on God's good side. Oh what a good side that is. To have the creator of the entire universe loving and blessing you is a sure-fire recipe for success and happiness! He has all the power. You saw what he did to Pharaoh. He counts powerful kings as mice. He can keep His promises to you. You also know how angry God gets when you cross Him. You know the thing He hates most is when you give fake gods credit that only He deserves. I repeat, follow the good path!

"I am 120 years old. God has told me I won't be crossing the Jordan with you. God has chosen Joshua to lead you now. Be strong and courageous. Don't be afraid of the nations across the river. They will fall before you because God will be there with you!"

Then Moses commissioned Joshua as the Hebrews' new leader. He gave the Book of the Law, which he had written, to the Levites and told them to keep it next to the Ark as a testimony of all God had instructed His people. Moses had no doubt that the people would fail once they were in the land because he'd seen them in action.

God told Moses to walk up a mountain in the land of Moab. From there he could see the land God had promised Abraham, Isaac and Jacob. He died there on the mountain and was buried. Nobody knows exactly where. Even though Moses was 120 years old when he died, he never lost a step; he was as sharp in his last day as he was when he appeared before Pharaoh. He was the most powerful man Israel had ever seen.

Joshua

Joshua 1 *Be strong and courageous*
After Moses died God spoke to Joshua, "It's time for you to lead the people into the Promised Land. No one will be able to stop you. I will be with you. Be strong and courageous. Follow the laws I've provided. Stay on the course I've set, don't go to the right or to the left. Study the book Moses has left for you. Then you will be prosperous and have good success!"

Joshua instructed the people, "Take three days to get all your provisions organized, because the time has come to cross the Jordan and take the land God has promised us." He reminded the tribes of Reuben, Gad and the half tribe Manesseh of their commitment to Israel. They replied, "Count us in. We will follow your commands the same way we followed Moses. Any one of us who doesn't will be executed. Be strong and courageous!" About 40,000 men of war from these three tribes accompanied their brothers to help take the land.

Joshua 2 *The spies and Rahab*
Joshua then sent two spies into Jericho. The king of Jericho heard the spies had come and had gone to a brothel out by the city wall. He sent men to investigate. Rahab the proprietor of the establishment told the king's officers that two men had been there, that she hadn't realized they were Hebrews, and that they had left in time to make it out of the city gate before it had closed for the night. She advised the officers to pursue them immediately; perhaps they could overtake them on the road.

Actually, Rahab had hidden the spies on her roof under some neatly piled straw. She said to them, "I know God has given you this land. Everybody is totally frightened of you. We have heard the stories of how God parted the Red Sea for you when he led you from Egypt and we've heard about your conquest on the other side of the river. Your God is obviously the real God! I ask you to please deal kindly with my family and all who are connected with us because I've helped you on your mission." The spies replied, "You have been a big help. Don't tell anyone about this conversation. When we come to take the city, tie this scarlet thread in your window. Stay in your house. If anyone leaves the house we are not responsible. But if anyone is hurt inside the house, their blood is on our heads."

Rahab told them to camp stealthily in the hills for three days to let their pursuers run out of steam. Then she let them out a window on the city wall. (Rahab's house was right on the wall.) The spies escaped to the hillsides where they eluded their pursuers for three days before heading back to Joshua. Their report to Joshua was simple: "We can take the land. The inhabitants are scared to death of us!"

Joshua 3-4 *The people cross the Jordan*
So the Hebrews came to the edge of the Jordan River. Joshua sent the priests ahead of the congregation carrying the Ark. Joshua said to the people, "Watch the power of God. With him on our side, we have nothing to fear from the Canaanites, Hittites, Hivites, Perezites, Girgashites, Amorites, or Jebusites whom we will be conquering to get the land God promised us!

When the feet of the priest carrying the Ark touched the banks of the Jordan, the water began to stop in a heap up the river. So the Hebrews made their crossing on dry ground. The priest stood in the middle of the Jordan with the Ark. When everyone was across, a leader from each of the twelve tribes went down into the middle of the Jordan, where the priests were still standing. Each leader collected one large rock, one for each tribe. They made a monument out of the stones so they would remember and tell their young ones how God had helped them cross the Jordan on dry ground.

Joshua 5 *Circumcision and the first Passover in the land*
God commanded Joshua to circumcise all the men in the camp. (While they were in the wilderness the children were not circumcised). So that operation was undertaken and completed. None of the men moved around much for the next few days. On the 14th of the first month of the year they observed the Passover meal. This was the first meal where they ate food from the Promised Land. From that day onward they ate only from the land. The manna that had sustained them for 40 years in the wilderness ceased. Joshua saw an Angel of God while they were camped by Jericho. The Angel announced that he was the Captain of the Lord's army. Joshua removed his sandals because the Angel informed him he was standing on holy ground.

Joshua 6 *The march around Jericho, Rahab spared*
Now it was time to take Jericho. The Hebrews were instructed not to take anything from the city. Every living thing was to be killed. (Except for Rahab and her family, they would come and live peacefully with the Hebrews from that day forward). All the gold and precious metals were to be added to the treasury of the Lord. Everything else was said to be "under the ban" and had to be destroyed.

The walls of Jericho were shut tight against the Hebrews. Joshua instructed seven Priests to carry the ark around the city each day. They blew seven trumpets made from rams' horns. The army of Israel marched before and after the Ark for six days. On the seventh day they marched around the city seven times. On the seventh time as the Priest blew the horns, all the Hebrews shouted as one voice. The walls of Jericho fell in a flat rubble. Then the Israelites stormed the city and killed every living thing, (except Rahab and her family). They burned the city and kept only the gold and precious metals for the Lord's treasury. Joshua swore an oath saying, "Cursed is the man who rebuilds this city. If a man does rebuild, he will lay its foundation with the loss of his first son. He will finish the gates with the loss of his second son. News of this spread through the region. Joshua was infamous in the land!

Joshua 7-8 *Trouble at Ai*
There was a small town called Ai not far from Jericho. A couple of spies were sent to check it out. They came back and said, "The city is small, and we can take it with 3000 men. So 3000 Hebrew soldiers went to defeat Ai. The men of Ai defeated the Hebrews and chased them out of their area! Joshua tore his clothes and fell before the Lord, "Oh God, what is happening? Why did You even bring us over? Now that the inhabitants of the land have heard that Israel has turned and run from its enemies, they will all take courage and be too strong for us! What will You do to protect Your great name?" God answered, "Joshua, get up off the ground. Someone has taken goods from Jericho that were prohibited under the ban. This is why Israel had to run away from their enemies! Have the people prepare themselves. Tomorrow you will identify the guilty party by drawing lots. Throw the names of the twelve tribes into the pot. When a tribe is pulled out, take all the names of the tribes' families and put them in. When a family is pulled out, put in the names of all the households. When a household's name is pulled, put in all the names of the men. You will find the guilty party."

The next morning the lots were drawn. The tribe of Judah was drawn, then the family of Zerahites, then the household of Zabdi, finally the lot fell on Achan. Joshua implored him to honor God and not lie. Achan answered, "I have sinned against the Lord. Here's what I did. I saw a beautiful mantle, 200 shekels of silver and a 50 shekel gold bar. I took them and hid them under the ground inside my tent." Joshua sent men into the tent to bring out the property taken under the ban. Achan, his sons, daughters, all his cattle, his tent and the banned items he took were taken into a valley. Achan and his family were killed with stones. The possessions were burned. The ashes were covered with a large pile of stones. The Valley is called the Valley of Trouble to this day.

Then God told Joshua, "Now you'll have no problems taking Ai. This time you can take the cattle and precious metal for yourselves, but kill all the people and burn the city just as you did with Jericho. Use an ambush from behind to take the city." So Joshua selected 30,000 valiant warriors to defeat Ai. Joshua stayed with 5000 men in front of Ai and the rest went behind Ai to create the ambush force. Joshua and his 5000 went up against the city and allowed themselves to be chased off again. All the men of Ai left the city in spirited pursuit. When they were all out of the city, the ambush force easily overtook the city and set it on fire. When the men of Ai saw the smoke they knew they were dead men. The ambush force came in behind them with Joshua in front of them. None escaped the swords of Joshua's army. They hung the King of Ai on a tree while the mop-up operationwas being conducted. That evening they pulled his carcass down and threw it towards the old gate of the city. They covered it with a pile of stones. Israel took only the cattle and spoil for themselves. Then Joshua had an altar built with the whole Book of the Law copied on the stones. He read the whole Book of the Law to the congregation of Israel. He read the blessings and the curses. Everybody heard it, the men, the women, the children, and the strangers who were living with them.

Joshua 9 *The Gigeonites trick*
All the Kings in Canaan began to hear what Israel was doing. They made alliances to fight against Israel. One group of people living in a place called Gibeon created their own deceitful strategy. They sent messengers on a short trip to meet Joshua. They dressed the messengers in worn-out sandals and clothes. The bread in their sacks was old and crumbly. When they got to Joshua they said, "We have heard about your exploits from our far-away country. We have traveled far to come to you. Our clothes were new when we started off and the bread was fresh from our ovens when we began our journey. Oh, it has been a long trip! We want to make a treaty with you." Joshua and the leaders of Israel saw the old clothes and dry bread. They reasoned the Gibeonites lived outside the boarders of the Promised Land. Without asking God, they made a treaty with the men from Gibeon. Then the Gibeonites took the one-day trip back to their homes.

Three days later Joshua learned the truth. He was forced to keep his promise because he had sworn in the Lord's name. So the men of Gibeon were put to forced labor. They sawed wood for the Altar and hauled water for the Hebrews. Joshua called for them and said, "Why have you deceived us when you knew you lived in the land God has given to us?" They replied, "We have heard that the Lord your God has given you all this land. We tried only to save our lives. You own us now, we will do what you command."

Joshua 10 *Five kings align against Israel and are destroyed*
When the king of Jerusalem heard that Joshua had destroyed Jericho and Ai, and that Gibeon had made peace with Israel and was in service to them, he was very distressed. Gibeon was a big city and had a substantial army! He solidified an alliance with the kings of Hebron, Jarmuth, Lachish and Eglon to fight against Israel. Their first move was to go against Gibeon. The men of Gibeon sent quick word to Joshua, "Please do not abandon your servants. All the kings of the Amorites are coming against us." When Joshua got the message, God assured Joshua, "Don't fear this Amorite coalition, I will drop them right in your lap!"

So Joshua and the entire army of Israel marched all night to Gibeon and met the five kings in battle. Israel prevailed quickly. Then God decided to get into the battle Himself. As Israel's enemies ran before them, God hurled hailstones on them from heaven. God's barrage of hailstones was very effective. More Amorites were killed by hailstones than by the swords! Joshua was so intent on completing the total slaughter of the Amorites that he asked the Lord to stop the sun in the sky, so the battle could continue. The sun stayed in its place, extending daylight, while God fought powerfully for Israel.

During the battle, the five kings hid in a cave. Joshua ordered that the cave be sealed with a boulder until the battle was over. Then Joshua had the kings removed from the cave. He called for the chiefs of his army to come to him. Joshua said, "Come here and put your feet on the necks of these kings. Don't be afraid or worried; instead, be strong and courageous. God will put all your enemy's necks under your feet just as these are!" The five kings were hung from trees till evening, and then the corpses were thrown back into the cave. Joshua completely destroyed all of the cities of the five kings.

Joshua 11-12 *Hazor burned and further conquests of Joshua*
Then the king of Hazor organized a coalition of kings from all over the land to fight against Israel. The numbers of soldiers they assembled were too many to count. They also had many horses and chariots. God told Joshua: "Don't worry about this large army amassed against you. By this time tomorrow the battle will already be over. Hamstring their horses and burn the chariots."

Joshua and his army attacked the assembled forces of Hazor and defeated them. They burned the city of Hazor, but left the other cities standing. They killed all the people in the cities and kept the cattle and precious metals for themselves. Joshua conquered a good deal of the land God promised. He destroyed all the peoples he came against, except the Gibeonites. God hardened the hearts of the inhabitants of the land to come against Joshua, so that Joshua could totally defeat them and wipe them off the face of the land. Finally the land was at rest from war.

Joshua 13-21 *Land is apportioned to each tribe*
Joshua was old. God said to him, "Joshua you're old and still much of the land needs to be won. Apportion the land to the various tribes so they'll have a motivation to win it." God told Joshua all the areas he wanted each tribe to inhabit. The only tribe not to get any land was the Levites. The Lord himself was their inheritance. Caleb, Joshua's only partner in the spy business who also trusted God like Joshua, was given a special area of land in Hebron. Each of the tribal regions had cities that were listed and given to particular tribes according to the region that was to be their inheritance. Cities of refuge, as prescribed by the law, were assigned regionally. The Levites were given cities in each of the regions, where they could live and raise cattle.

Joshua 22 *The eastern tribe return to their inheritance*
Then Joshua summoned the Reubenites, Gadites, and the half tribe of Manasseh. He said, "You have done all you promised Moses you would do. It's now time for you to return to your land on the east part of the Jordan. Be very careful to follow all the law and love the Lord your God. God bless you on your journey!" When they got close to the Jordan they built a large altar to God. The rest of Israel felt they built the altar on the west side of the Jordan to lay claim to land that wasn't theirs. They sent Phinehas the priest, along with ten leaders from the other tribes, to confront the men of Reuben, Gad, and the half tribe of Manasseh. "Why have you done this? It seems to us you are rebelling against the Lord by building this altar for yourselves. You don't want to end up as an enemy of the Lord!" The Eastern tribes answered, "In no way do we want to rebel against the Lord, or our brothers. We've built the altar out of concern. We're afraid as time passes your children will see us on the other side of the Jordan and say, 'Those people don't have a portion from the Lord!' So we built this altar as a witness between us and you, that we are brothers!" Phinehas and the Elders were pleased by the eastern tribes sincerity.

Joshua 23-24 *Joshua's farewell address, and burial*
Joshua was now very old. The wars had ceased for the moment. Joshua called the people before him, "You have seen all the things God has done to help you get the land we have so far. We have apportioned all the rest of the land you need to conquer as

your inheritance. You need to be very careful to stay firm and follow all the laws God has given us. Do not associate with the nations we have not defeated. Do not intermarry with them or have anything to do with their gods. If you do, God's blessing will no longer be with you. He won't drive your enemies before you. God's a good God; He's done everything He said He would to this point. Take heed to worship only Him and this good trend will continue! If you go against God, you'll lose the land you have. So be careful to follow God."

Then Joshua called all the people to an area known as Shechem. He said, "Here's what God says: 'Your father Abraham started east of here. He and his family followed other gods, but I called him away. He had faith in Me and I made a promise to him that he would get this land. I repeated my promise to Isaac and Jacob. The people went to Egypt where they were made slaves. I heard their cry and sent Moses to lead them from Egypt. I lead them out with great works and miracles; Pharaoh's army was finally destroyed when I covered them with the Red Sea. You wandered in the wilderness for 40 years. I brought you up to the east part of the Jordan and gave you that land. Then you crossed over and I drove your enemies from this land. Now you live in cities you haven't built and harvest vineyards you haven't planted.'" Joshua continued, "Now because of all these things, I implore you to choose the Lord. He has done all He said He would. As for as me and my house, we choose to serve the Lord." The people answered, "Far be it from us to forsake God and serve other gods. We will serve the Lord." Joshua answered, "I like the sound of it, but I'm afraid you won't keep your promise. Remember God will do harm to you when you forsake Him." Again, the people answered, "We will serve the Lord!"

So Joshua added these words to the Book of the Law and made a covenant there with the people by putting up a monument. He said, "This monument will stand as a witness. It has heard these words, that you will serve the Lord." Joshua died and was buried. They also buried Joseph's bones in a plot that Jacob had bought almost 500 years before. Eleazar the High Priest died, and his son Phinehas took over as High Priest.

Judges

Judges 1-2 *A pattern develops*
After Joshua died there was still land to conquer. The tribes of Judah and Simeon helped each other in their battles against the Canaanites. They took possession of

their lands. The tribe of Benjamin did not drive out the Jebusites who lived in their lands. The house of Joseph took possession of their land. The tribes of Ephraim, Zebulun, Naphtali and Asher did not fully drive the Cannanites out of their territories. Some Canaanites were subjected to forced labor, but they were never completely driven out of the land. The tribe of Dan did not prevail against the Amorites. They only took part of their possession.

The Hebrews were very loyal and reverent during the days of Joshua and his Elders. But soon after Joshua's death, they began to forget about God. They began worshipping other gods. A pattern began to develop where the people would worship other gods, and then the Lord would punish them by allowing a foreign nation to defeat them; then the Lord would lift up a leader (called a Judge) to deliver them from their enemies. As soon as the Judge died, the Hebrews would quickly go after the local gods and be even more wicked than their fathers before them. So the nations that inhabited the land were never driven out. God allowed them to stay and act as tormentors to his non-compliant children. The nations that were left included the Philistines, the Canaanites, the Moabites, the Sidonites, the Perizzites, the Hittites, the Jebusites, and the Hivites.

Judges 3 *Othneil and Ehud*
The Hebrews married foreign women and worshipped their gods. It made the Lord angry, so he allowed the king of Mesopotamia to come and defeat the whole land. The people cried out to God and he heard them and raised up the first Judge, whose name was Othniel. He was a relative of Caleb. He defeated the king of Mesopotamia and judged Israel for 40 peaceful years. When he died, the people went immediately back to their sin. Then God allowed the king of Moab to come and rule them harshly for 18 years. The Hebrews cried out to God and He heard them. Ehud rose up as the next Judge of Israel. Ehud was a left-handed fellow. He took a sword, bound it to his right thigh and went to present a tribute to the very fat Eglon, king of Moab. After Ehud presented his tribute, he told Eglon he had a private message for him. Every one left the room except Ehud and Eglon. Ehud said, "Here is a message to you from God." Then he took his left hand, reached to his right side and unsheathed the sword. He thrust it into Eglon. The handle of the sword disappeared into his fat. When Ehud withdrew his hand he left the sword. As he left the chamber, he locked the door. Eglon's servants came to the locked door and reasoned, "He must be in the bathroom because he's locked the door." Soon they became unsettled and unlocked the door. They found Eglon dead on the floor. Ehud escaped during the interval and hurried back to the Hebrews. He rallied the troops and they returned to battle the Moabites.

10,000 Moabites were slain that day. Israel lived in relative peace for the next 80 years.

Judges 4-5 *Deborah*
Again the Israelites worshipped the local gods. The Lord allowed a king named Jabin and his general named Sisera to oppress Israel for twenty years. Sisera's army had 900 chariots. Deborah was a prophetess in Israel at this time and became a Judge in Israel. God instructed her to summon Barak, a man of influence and strength. She said, "Take 10,000 men from the tribes of Naphtali and Zebulun, march to Mount Tabor and God will draw Sisera out to you. God will deliver him into your hand!" Barak replied, "I'll go only if you come too." Deborah replied, "All right, I'll come too, but the honor you would have won won't come to you, because God will be delivering Sisera into the hands of a woman."

So they marched to the mountain. When Sisera heard of their movement, he came out against them with all his chariots. Deborah cried out, "Rise up, God has preceded us and will deliver Sisera to us today!" God blessed Barak as Deborah predicted, so Sisera was routed. Sisera fled from the battle on foot. He came to a tent of a man named Heber. Heber's wife, Jael, was at the door of the tent. She said to Sisera, "Come in, I'll hide you." So Sisera went in and Jael covered him with a rug. He was thirsty so she opened a container of milk, gave it to him and covered him with the rug again. He told her not to tell anyone he was there, and he went to sleep, exhausted from the battle. Jael took a tent peg and set it on his temple, as he laid under the rug. She hammered the peg through his head into the ground. When Barak came by in his pursuit of Sisera, Jael called to him, "Here is the man you are seeking." Barak entered the tent to find Sisera's head pegged to the ground. So Jabin and Sisera were both defeated that day at the hands of two women! Israel lived in peace for the next 40 years.

Judges 6-9 *Gideon*
Israel forgot God again and did the wrong thing by worshipping idols called Baals and statues of wood called Asherah. God used the Midianites to punish Israel this time. At every harvest, the Midianites would come in droves as numerous as locusts. They and their livestock would destroy Israel's crops, so everyone in Israel went hungry. It went on like this for seven years, and the people were crying out to the Lord. God sent a prophet who said, "This is what God says, 'I am the Lord who led you out of Egypt and gave you this land, yet you have disobeyed Me by worshipping false gods."

An angel of the Lord came to a man named Gideon who was working hard at the time beating out wheat to save it from the Midianites. The angel said to Gideon, "The Lord is with you, oh valiant warrior!" Gideon replied, "I don't think God's with us; He certainly isn't doing any miracles now like He did when he led our fathers out of Egypt." The Lord answered, "I am appointing you to be Israel's deliverer from Midian." Gideon reasoned, "I don't think You have the right guy. I'm from the smallest family in the tribe of Manasseh and I am the youngest of the family. How am I going to deliver Israel?" God replied, "You are the one I have chosen. I will be with you."

Gideon brought an offering of a slaughtered kid, bread made without yeast, a bushel of flour, and a pot of broth. God said, "Lay the offering on this rock." When Gideon did, the angel of the Lord touched the rock with His staff. Fire sprang from the rock and consumed the offering. Then the angel disappeared. Gideon was afraid he would die because he'd seen the Lord. God assured him he would not die.

That night God told Gideon to tear down his father's shrine to Baal. He was instructed to build an altar in its place and sacrifice a bull as a burnt offering. He was to use the wood from the idol for the fire. Gideon got ten servants to help him. He did it late at night because he was afraid. The next morning all the people of the city realized Baal's shrine was destroyed. When they found it was Gideon's doing, they spoke to his father, Joash, saying, "Bring Gideon out to be killed. He has destroyed Baal's shrine." Joash answered, "If Baal is a god, shouldn't he be able to speak for himself? Let Baal handle his own affairs."

The Midianites and the Amalekites started massing for war in the valley of Jezreel. Gideon began to gather an army from the tribes of Asher, Zebulun and Naphtali. Gideon said to God: "If you want me to lead this army, I need to see a sign. I will put a fleece of wool out on my threshing floor. Tomorrow morning if there is dew only on the fleece and the ground is dry, I will know you are with me. The next morning the fleece was wet with dew and the ground was dry. Gideon prayed again and said, "God, I don't want you to be mad, but I need to know for sure. Tonight I'll set the fleece out again. If you are truly with me, keep the fleece dry but let the ground collect the dew." The next morning Gideon found the fleece dry and the ground wet with dew.

Gideon and 32,000 soldiers camped to the south of the Midianite\Amalekite force. God told Gideon his army was too large. Gideon announced to his army, "Anyone who is afraid can leave!" 22,000 soldiers went home. God told Gideon to take the remaining soldiers to the river for a drink. Only the ones who drank the water from their cupped hands were to go with Gideon. Only 300 drank the water out of their hands. All the rest put their mouths right in the water. God said, "300 is just right!" The rest were sent home.

That night God said to Gideon, "The camp of the Midianites and the Amalekites will fall before you and your 300. If you have any doubts, go down secretly to the enemy camp tonight and listen to what they're saying." Gideon took his servant, Purah, down near the camp under cover of darkness. He heard two men talking. They were predicting their own defeat at the hands of Gideon! Gideon bowed in worship to God as he heard the words of the doomed men.

The next night Gideon separated the 300 men into sections of 100 each. They all had torches covered with clay pottery pitchers and each of them carried a trumpet. Once they had surrounded the camp Gideon broke his pitcher showing the light of his torch. All Gideon's men did the same around the camp. Then they blew their horns and yelled, "For the Lord and for Gideon!" The army in the enemy camp was so frightened and confused they began to kill each other as they fled. Gideon sent messengers to the tribe of Ephraim instructing them to pursue the Midianites. The Ephraimites did and routed them completely killing two of their kings, Oreb and Zeeb. The Ephraimites complained to Gideon saying, "Why didn't you call us when you started this engagement?" Gideon replied, "God has delivered Oreb and Zeeb into your hands! What have I done that compares to that?" These words made the Ephraimites feel much better.

Gideon and his men went after two other Midianite kings named Zebah and Zalmunna. He passed by two towns on the way, Penuel and Succoth. Neither of these towns would help provision Gideon and his men. Gideon vowed to return and repay them for their unfriendliness. Finally Gideon caught up with Zebah and Zalmunna. He captured them and headed back towards home. On the way he disciplined the men of the towns who had not helped him. Then he turned to Zebah and Zalmunna announcing they must die for the sons of Israel they had killed. Gideon ordered his oldest son Jether to kill the kings. Jether was afraid because he was still young. Zebah and Zalmunna then said, "Get up Gideon and kill us; show us what you've got." Gideon showed them the last thing they saw, a sharp sword slicing towards their necks!

When Gideon returned to the land, the Hebrews wanted to make him king. He said, "God is your King. He will rule over you, not me or my sons. I would request that each of you give me a gold earring that you took from the people we defeated." The Hebrews were happy to give the rings. Gideon ended up with 1700 shekels of gold! Gideon took the gold and made an Ephod that he put in his hometown. The people started worshipping the Ephod! This became a snare to Gideon and his family. Gideon had 70 sons with many wives and mistresses. One of his sons, Abimelech, was born to one of Gideon's mistresses, not to one of his wives. The mistress was from the town of Shechem.

Judges 9 *Abimelech, Jotham, and Gaal*
When Gideon died at a ripe old age, (the land had peace 40 years under Gideon), the people went back to worshipping Baal. Abimelech went to his mother's relatives in Shecham and said, "What's better for you, that 70 kings, all sons of Gideon, rule over you or that I, your own relative, rule over you." The people of Shechem agreed they'd prefer Abimelech as king. They gave him 70 pieces of silver. Abimelech used it to hire a mob of worthless and reckless fellows. They went to Gideon's hometown of Ophrah and killed every one of Abimelech's brothers except the youngest, named Jotham, who was able to escape.

Abimelech was made king. Jotham, Gideon's only surviving son, stood on top of a hill and yelled down to the men of Shechem and Abimelech, "You are a selfish and evil group. You chose a king who is the son of one of Gideon's mistresses, just because he is related to you. Then you gave him the means to kill all his brothers except me! If this has been done through integrity, then may all go well with you and Abimelech. If this has been done treacherously, then let fire come from Abimelech to consume you and may fire come out from you and consume him!" Jotham hid himself in the mountains because of Abimelech.

Things did not go well for the people of Shechem or Abimelech. The people of Shechem rebelled against Abimelech by taking a new leader named Gaal. Abimelech's lieutenant, Zebul, heard of the defection and warned Abimelech. Abimelech came and fought against Gaal and the men of Shechem. He defeated the town. The people remaining alive holed up in the town tower. Abimelech grabbed an ax and cut a branch from a tree. He instructed all his men to do the same. They took the wood to the bottom of the tower and set it on fire. So all the men and women in the tower were killed, about 1000!

Abimelech then went against a town called Thebez. He got all the people of Thebez into their town tower. When he went to burn this tower one of the women of the city dropped a millstone on his head, crushing his skull. Abimelech called his armor bearer. "Draw your sword and kill me, or it will be remembered that I was killed by a woman!" So the young man killed Abimelech with his sword. The story of Abimelech dying at the wall was remembered anyway. So God repaid the wickedness of the men of Shechem and Abimelech, just as Jotham the son of Gideon had said.

Judges 10 *More years same pattern*
Two judges provided leadership in Israel over the next 45 years, Tola from Ephraim and Jair from Gilead. When Jair died, the Hebrews forgot the Lord and worshipped Baal. God allowed the Philistines and Ammonites to plunder Israel for 18 years. They started on the tribes east of the Jordan and then came over and fought against Judah, Benjamin and Ephraim west of the Jordan. The Israelis cried out to God. And God said, "I'm the God who led you out of Egypt. I'm the God who delivered you from the Midianites and the Amorites. Yet all you people do is forsake Me and worship false gods! Go cry to the gods you've chosen instead of Me. If they're so great, they should have no problem delivering you from your enemies!" Then the sons of Israel stopped the wrongs they were doing, destroyed all the false idols and worshipped God. So God decided to deliver them. The Ammonites began to gather east of the Jordan. The Hebrews in Gilead began to assemble themselves for battle.

Judges 11:1-12:7 *Jephthah (and his unfortunate daughter)*
There was a man named Jephthah who was from Gilead, who was a valiant warrior. His mom was a prostitute; his dad was named Gilead. After Jephthah's birth, his father took a wife who bore him two sons. When they became men they drove Jephthah out saying, "No son of a prostitute will share in our inheritance". Jephthah went to live in a place called Tob. He assembled an army made up of worthless and reckless fellows. When Ammon gathered against Israel in Gilead, the men of Gilead went to Jephthah asking him to lead them against the Ammonites. Jephthah didn't feel too beholden to the men of Gilead. So he said, "I will fight for you against the Ammonites but I will also be the leader over all of you." The Israelis in Gilead agreed to make Jephthah their leader.

Jephthah sent a message to the Ammonites asking why they were gathered for battle against him. They told Jephthah they were trying to get the land back that Moses had taken from them. Jephthah replied, "When Moses came into your land he simply asked if Israel could pass through. Not only would you not let us pass through but also you came out to fight against us! The Lord delivered your father's land to us. When your god, Chemosh, gives you land, isn't it your land? Consider Balak from Moab, we lived next to him for years but he never came out to fight us, so he still has his land. We'll let the Lord settle this between you and us....Let's Rummmble!"

Jephthah made a vow to the Lord. "If You will deliver the Ammonites to me, I will sacrifice the first thing I see when I return home." Jephthah and his army went out against the Ammonites and defeated them soundly with a great slaughter! When Jephthah returned home, his only child came out to meet him dancing with her tambourines. Jephthah cried out, "Oh my precious daughter you have made me terribly sad today because I have made a vow to sacrifice what I saw first upon my arrival!" His daughter answered, "Let it happen as you promised, because God has delivered the Ammonites to you. Only let me go away with my friends for two months so I can mourn the fact that I will never marry and have children." It became a custom in Israel for all the young girls in Israel, once each year, to spend a few days away as a group to remember Jephthah's unfortunate daughter.

The men from Ephraim came to Jephthah saying, "Why didn't you call us to help defeat the Ammonites? We will burn your house down with you in it!" Jephthah replied, "I did call you and you didn't come! I had to act quickly. Why are you threatening me?" So Jephthah fought the Ephraimites and beat them. Jephthah captured the crossing areas of the Jordan. Whenever an Ephraimite tried to pass, his men would say to them, "Pronounce the word: Sh-ibboleth". The Ephraimites couldn't pronounce it correctly; they would say S-ibboleth, so 42,000 Ephraimites died because of their accent!

Judges 12:8-15 Fifteen years, *two more Judges*
Jephthah judged Israel six years. Then Ibzan, from Bethlehem, judged seven years. He had thirty sons who married outside his family and thirty daughters who were given in marriage outside the family. The next judge was Elon, who was from the tribe of Zebulun, he judged for ten years. Then Abdon judged for eight years. He had 40 sons and 30 grandsons and each of them had their own donkey.

Judges 13-16 *Samson*
Soon after the death of Abdon, Israel forgot God and began worshipping false gods again. God allowed the Philistines to rule Israel for 40 years. A man named Manoah and his wife were not able to have children. One day an angel of the Lord appeared to Manoah's wife. He said, "I know you've been having trouble getting pregnant. Not to worry, you will have a son. Do not drink any alcohol or eat anything unclean during your pregnancy, and never cut his hair or let him drink alcohol. He is to be a Nazirite from the moment he is born. He will deliver the Israelites from the Philistines."

When Manoah's wife told him what transpired, he prayed and asked God for more details. God appeared to the woman again. She ran and got her husband. The angel told Manoah to do all he had already told his wife. Manoah asked the angel his name. The angel explained that his name was incomprehensible and wonderful. Manoah prepared a burnt offering. When he laid it on the rock the angel performed wonders in front of Manoah and his wife. Fire consumed the sacrifice and the angel went up into heaven with the smoke. Manoah figured they were going to die because they had seen God. Manoah's wife said, "I don't think the Lord would kill us if He wants us to complete these instructions."

The woman had the baby boy and named him Samson. When Samson was grown he went down to Timnah in Philistia. He saw a girl he liked down there and went to his parents asked that they arrange a marriage with this Philistine girl. They would have liked Samson to take a Hebrew girl. They didn't understand that God was preparing an opportunity for Samson to hurt the Philistines. On their way down to Philistia, Samson took a sidetrack from his parents. He saw a lion. The Spirit of God came mightily on Samson and he killed the lion. Later he passed by again and went aside to see the carcass of the lion. Bees had gotten into the carcass and made honey. Samson scooped some out. He ate some and gave some to his parents, but they didn't know where it came from.

Samson's father set up the marriage. They had the customary feast. Thirty young Philistine men came to be with Samson at the feast. Samson made a bet with them. If they answered a riddle, Samson would get them each a new set of clothing. If they weren't able to guess in the seven feast days, then they would give Samson 30 changes of cloths. This is the riddle: "Out of the eater came something to eat, out of the strong came something sweet." After three days the Philistines had not guessed the riddle. They went to Samson's new Philistine wife and said, "Thanks a lot for inviting us to your feast so we could become poor providing clothes for this Hebrew. Entice your husband to tell you the answer or we'll burn your house and your fathers house!"

Samson's wife cried to him that evening, "You don't love me, and you have propounded a riddle to my brothers but have not told me the answer." Samson's reply: "I haven't even told my mom and dad the answer, why should I tell you?" She cried to Samson every night during the last four nights of the feast. Finally he broke down and told her the solution to the riddle, which she quickly shared with her Philistine friends. The final day of the feast the young men "solved" the riddle. Samson was pretty upset. He knew where they'd gotten the answer. He went to a town called Ashkelon in Philistia and killed 30 Philistine men. He brought the young men their clothes and went home in a huff, without his new wife. His new father-in-law gave her to Samson's best man!

After a while, during the time of the wheat harvest, Samson took a young goat for a present and visited his estranged wife. His father-in-law wouldn't let him visit. He said, "I really thought you hated her, so I gave her to your best man. Why don't you take my younger daughter, she's even prettier than the older girl." Samson angrily replied, "I am not responsible for the harm I will now inflict on you Philistines!"

So Samson caught 300 foxes and tied their tails together with a torch attached to each pair. He lit the torches and set the foxes loose in the Philistine wheat harvest. The entire harvest was destroyed and all the vineyards and groves as well. When the Philistines heard how it happened, they took their revenge on Samson's wife and father-in-law. They burned their homes and killed the family. Samson came back into Philistia and slaughtered a great many Philistines. Then he went down and lived in a small cave in Judah.

The Philistines came to Judah in force to collect Samson. 3000 of Judah went to Samson's cave and said, "Samson don't you realize the Philistines are our rulers. You can't be wiping out their towns like this!" Samson answered, "Hey, they started it! You can take me to them if you promise not to kill me." The Judeans replied, "We won't kill you, but we are going to tie you up and hand you over to the Philistines." So they tied Samson with two new ropes and handed him over. The Philistines shouted with joy as they saw their bound enemy before them. At that moment, the Spirit of the Lord fell on Samson mightily. He broke the new ropes like threads. He picked up a donkey's jawbone and attacked the Philistines. 1000 Philistines died with a blow from Samson's donkey bone! After the slaughter Samson was very thirsty. He said, "God, have you empowered me to kill 1000 Philistines, only to die of thirst and fall into the hands of these uncircumcised gentiles?" God opened a rock and water came out. Samson drank and his strength was renewed. Samson went on to judge Israel for 20 years.

One day Samson was on a road trip and stopped in Gaza along the coast of Philistia. He saw a prostitute there and got a room with her. The Gazites, perceiving an opportunity to kill their enemy, plotted amongst themselves, "Let's lie in wait at the gate until morning. Then we will all rush him and kill him." Samson stayed with the whore until midnight. When he got to the gate, he ripped the entire gate assembly from the wall and carried it to the top of a mountain in Hebron. The Gazites canceled the ambush.

Samson then found another Philistine woman he loved named Delilah. The five lords of the Philistines came to Delilah and said, "Delilah, find out were Samson gets his strength so we can capture him. We will each give you 1100 pieces of silver for your trouble." So Delilah asked Samson, "Please tell me where your strength comes from; how can you be captured?" Samson answered, "If you bind me with seven new cords that have not been dried, I will be just like any other man." When he was asleep, she bound him with seven new cords. Then she yelled, "The Philistines are upon you Samson!" He broke the cords like threads. So the secret of his strength was still safe. The next night Delilah said, "Samson why have you lied to me? Tell me were your strength comes from." Samson answered, "If you tie me with new ropes that have not been used I will be like other men". When he slept, she tied him up with new ropes and yelled as before. Again he broke them easily. The next night she asked again. Samson told her if she would weave seven locks of his hair and bind them with a pin then he would be like other men. As Samson slept, she followed the new instructions and again Samson was as powerful as ever.

The next night Delilah said, "How can you say you love me Samson? Do you deceive the one you love?" She kept after him day after day to the point that Samson could endure it no longer. He finally said, "I have been a Nazirite from my birth. No razor has touched my head. If my hair was cut, I would lose my strength." Delilah could tell this was the truth so she called the lords of the Philistines. They brought her the 5500 pieces of silver and waited in a side room. That night Delilah had Samson fall asleep in her lap. A man came in and shaved Samson's head. He lost his strength. The Philistines overtook Samson. They gouged out his eyes, bound him with bronze chains and put him to work as a grinder in their prison.

They were very pleased with themselves. They believed their god, Dagon, had delivered Samson to them. Later on, they had a big party where they offered sacrifices to Dagon, and they had Samson brought out so they could make sport of him. Samson was lead into the courtyard between the pillars supporting the entire building. Samson prayed, "God, please give me my strength back just long enough to avenge these Philistines for gouging out my eyes." God heard his prayer. Samson used his strength to pull down the pillars and the entire building collapsed. It was a big party; all the lords of the Philistines and their guests were there. So Samson killed more Philistines with his last revenge than he had killed in his entire career!

Judges 17-18 Micah (and his priest)

There was a man named Micah from the hill country in Ephraim. His mother took some money she thought was lost and paid to have an idol built. It was delivered to Micah's house. Micah made an ephod and assigned one of his sons as priest to the idol. Later a Levite man from Bethlehem was coming through the area looking for work. Micah paid him a salary and took care of his living expenses to have him serve as a real Levite priest for his shrine. Micah thought, "Now that I have a Levite priest, God will certainly bless me!"

In those days the tribe of Dan, who had not yet taken their inheritance from the land, were seeking land to possess. They sent out five spies to find a place to conquer. The spies passed through Ephraim and Micah's property. They recognized Micah's Levite priest! When they heard he had become Micah's priest they asked, "Tell us if this mission we are on will be blessed." Micah's priest said that God was with them and they went off encouraged. They came to an area called Laish and found it to be a very pleasant region with people living in peace, not having dealings with anyone else because all they needed was right there.

When they returned home they made this report: "We need to take Laish now. It will be easily defeated. It has all we need!" So off they went with 600 men, fully outfitted for battle. When they went through Ephraim they stopped by Micah's place. They went into his shrine and robbed the idol and implements. When the young Levite priest stumbled on the burglary, the Danites asked, "What's better for you, to stay here and be a priest for one family or go with us and be a priest and father to a whole family of Israel?" It sounded like a great promotion for the young priest so he went happily with the Danites. Micah pursued them but was quickly turned back by the Danites. Micah was happy to have lost only his idols and priest, and not his life! The Danites fell on Laish with their swords and easily conquered the area. They established a new city named Dan and set up Micah's idols and shrine with the young Levite serving as priest.

Judges 19 *With no king everyone did what they thought was right in their own mind*

This was the time when Israel didn't have a king. Everybody did whatever they thought was right in their own mind. There was a Levite living in the hill country of Ephraim whose mistress cheated on him. She returned to her father's house in Bethlehem. After four months the Levite decided to go down there, talk kindly to her and hopefully get her to come back with him. When he got to Bethlehem his mistress's father was really pleased to meet him. They ended up partying every day and night for several days because the father-in-law just wouldn't let them go.

In the late afternoon of the fifth day, his mistress's father was still trying to get them to stay one more night. The Levite prevailed and they were finally on their way in the late afternoon. The Levite wanted to get close to Jerusalem, in the region of Benjamin, so they wouldn't have to stay in a Gentile city. They made Gibeah, in Benjamin, in the early evening. They were setting up camp in the city square because no one was willing to take them in. An old, hardworking fellow came by. He had lodging available and took the Levite, his mistress, his servant, and two donkeys into his house.

That evening the men of Gibeah came by. They wanted the old man to send out the Levite so they could have sexual intercourse with him. The owner said, "Please stop this foolishness. Let me send out my young daughter or this man's mistress, you can have your way with them." The men would not be swayed. Finally the Levite took his mistress and sent her out. The men of Gibeah raped and abused her till dawn. Finally, she fell in front of the doorway to the old man's house. When the Levite got up to leave, he opened the door and there she was. He tried to rouse her, but she was dead. So he put her on his donkey and went back to Ephraim. When he arrived he took a knife and cut her into twelve pieces. He sent a piece to every region of Israel with a report of what had happened in Gibeah. All the people who heard the report agreed, nothing this terrible had ever happened in Israel!

Judges 20-21 *Resolution to punish the guilty*
The people gathered together in Mizpah. They had 400,000 men with swords. The Levite told the story about what happened to him. They determined not to return home until the wickedness had been repaid to the men of Gibeah and the tribe of Benjamin. They sent word to Benjamin's Elders, "What is this horrible thing that has occurred in your region? Deliver the men of Gibeah to us so we can repay this evil." The sons of Benjamin did not listen. They gathered their army together to go against Israel. The Benjaminites had 700 men who were left-handed and could sling a stone at a hair and not miss!

The first day of the battle Israel sent the army of Judah to meet Benjamin. Benjamin's army killed 22,000 Judean soldiers that first day. The next day Israel lost another 18,000 men to the Benjamites. That night Israel fasted and offered sacrifices to the Lord. God said, "Tomorrow I will deliver them to you." The next day they set up an ambush to the rear of the main force. When the battle began, the Benjamites came out of Gibeah and began to defeat the Israelites as before. They left Gibeah un-defended as they pursued Israel. Then the ambush force easily took the town and set it on fire. The Benjaminites realized they were doomed and tried to escape. When all the dust settled only 600 Benjaminite soldiers were still alive. They holed up in the wilderness for four months.

The people of Israel were sad because the tribe of Benjamin was in danger of being totally wiped out. They were in a fix because when they first gathered at Mizpah they had all taken an oath not to give any of their daughters to the men of Benjamin. But they also had said if any family did not come to Mizpah they would be cursed. They checked the roll call and found that none had come from the city of Jabesh-gilead. So they sent 12,000 soldiers to destroy the city. They killed everyone in Jabesh-gilead except 400 virgins. These were given to the remaining Benjamites. Because there were not enough virgins for each Benjaminite, they allowed the Benjamites to take 200 more virgins from among the dancers at a festival that happened once each year at Shiloh. So all the Benjamites got wives and went back to their land to rebuild their cities.

This was a time in Israel when there was no king. Everybody did what they thought was right for them.

Ruth

During the time of Judges in Israel there was a drought in the land. A man named Elimelech, his wife Naomi and his two sons Mahlon and Chilion went to Moab to escape the famine. The two sons married two Moabite women named Orpah and Ruth. Then Elimelech died. A few years later both of his sons died as well.

Naomi heard things were going better back in Bethlehem, her hometown. She decided to return to Israel. She advised her daughters-in-law to stay. Orpah elected to stay in Moab. Ruth said, "Naomi, I love you too much to be separated from you. Where you go, I go. Where you die, I die. Your God will be my God." Together, the two women went to Bethlehem.

When the people of Bethlehem saw Naomi, she said, "Don't think of me as you once did. I am different, I left full. I return empty." Barley was being harvested, so Ruth went to pick up harvest scraps as allowed in the law. She happened to be gleaning in a field owned by Boaz, a relative of Elimelech, Naomi's dead husband. Boaz was a wealthy gentleman.

Boaz visited the harvest operation and asked the harvesters who the young woman was gleaning behind them. They reported that it was Ruth, the daughter-in-law of Naomi, Elimelech's widow. Boaz went to Ruth and said, "Listen carefully my daughter, stay in this field and glean here. My harvesters will leave you alone. When you are thirsty drink with my servants." Ruth fell to the ground and said, "Why are you being so nice?" Boaz replied, "I have heard about how faithful you have been to your mother-in-law. The Lord, whom you have chosen as your God, is protecting you!" Boaz then invited her to lunch with the servants. Boaz instructed the harvesters to leave plenty behind when Ruth was following them. At the end of the day Ruth had a very large amount of barley!

That evening Ruth told Naomi all that had transpired. Naomi told Ruth that she was related to Boaz and advised her to stay in Boaz's field through the harvest. Late in the harvest Naomi advised Ruth. "Ruth, I think you have an opportunity to secure a future for yourself. Listen to me and do as I say. Boaz is going to be processing barley at his winnowing plant this evening. Clean up, put on your nicest dress and wear some perfume. Go down to Boaz's winnowing plant, but don't let him know you're there. Let Boaz finish his work for the day. Then let him have his dinner. When he lays down for the evening, go take the cover at his feet, lie down and see what he says."

Ruth did just as Naomi advised and covered herself at Boaz's feet. About midnight Boaz woke up and found Ruth there. He said, "Ruth, may God bless you. You have shown yourself to be a wise girl by not going after a young man, rich or poor. Everybody in town has seen that you are a woman of excellence! I am going to do the right thing by you. I have the position according to the law of being able to redeem the possessions of Elimelech and legally take you as my wife. But there is one relative ahead of me according to the law." When they woke up the next morning, Boaz gave Ruth some barley and said, "I'll not have you go back to Naomi empty handed." Ruth went home and told Naomi all that happened. Naomi said, "Wait here my dear; Boaz will not rest till he gets this matter settled."

That day Boaz went into town and sat at the gate with the elders of the city. The person who had first rights of redemption to Elimelech's estate was there. Boaz said, "I would like to use my right of redemption to Elimelech's estate to purchase his field. You have first rights, do you want to purchase the field?" The man said, "Yes, I will purchase it." Boaz replied, "Keep in mind that according to the Law you will also have to acquire Ruth the Moabitess in order to keep Elimelech's name going." The man answered, "Well that kills the deal. I won't put a legal hold on my own inheritance.

The Story Bible for Adults

You are free to redeem it." The custom at that time was that when a transaction like this took place, to confirm the matter before witnesses, the man passing the right of redemption would take off his sandal and hand it to the one gaining the right of redemption. So the man took off his sandal and handed it to Boaz. The men of the city acted as legal witnesses to a proper negotiation and placed their approval on the transaction.

Ruth and Boaz were married. Then Ruth gave birth to a boy and named him Obed. Naomi became the child's nanny. Boaz was a descendent of Perez, one of the twins that Tamar bore to Judah. Obed grew up and had a son named Jesse. Jesse grew up and had a son named David.

The First Book of Samuel

I Samuel 1:1-11 *Samuel's birth*
There was a man named Elkanah who lived in the hill country of Ephraim. He had two wives named Peninnah and Hannah. Peninnah had children, but Hannah had none. Every year Elkanah and his family would go to Shiloh to offer sacrifices to the Lord. Elkanah would give double portions for the sacrifice to Hannah because he loved her so much. Peninnah's habit was to provoke and irritate Hannah because she was not able to have children.

During one of the trips to Shiloh, Hannah was so upset she was crying and would not eat. Elkanah saw her and said, "Hannah, please don't be upset. Aren't I as good to you as ten sons?" So Hannah got up to have a meal. Then she went to the tabernacle and prayed to the Lord, "God, if You will remember me and give me the child I pray for, I will dedicate him to You. He will never have his hair cut, and he will never drink alcohol. I will turn him over to You, for Your service." As Hannah was praying, Eli the priest saw her lips move, although she made no sound. He went to her and said, "Woman, put the wine away; stop making your self drunk!" Hannah explained that she was praying and told Eli what she was praying about. Eli said, "Go in peace and may God grant your petition!" So Hannah left happy.

Soon after this, Hannah and Elkanah had a son. They named the child Samuel. When he was old enough to be weaned, Hannah took him to Eli in Shiloh along with a bull to sacrifice. After the sacrifice Hannah said to Eli, "I am the woman you saw praying. God has answered my prayer. I promised God I would dedicate my son totally to the Lord. So here he is." Then Hannah worshipped God with a song of praise! Every year Hannah went to see Samuel. She always brought along a new robe for his duties in the Tabernacle. Eli blessed Hannah and said, "May this woman have many children." Hannah ended up having three more sons and two daughters.

I Samuel 2:12-36 Eli's evil sons
Eli's own two sons were worthless men. They were priests, but they cheated and lied to the people they were supposed to be serving. They took portions of the sacrifice not intended for the priest. They even had sex with women who were serving at the gate of the tabernacle. Eli was very old at the time. He approached his sons and said, "This evil mustn't continue. If you sin against man that's one thing but sinning against God has no remedy." The sons paid no heed and continued their practices. A man of God came to Eli and said, "This is what the Lord declares, 'You know I honor those who honor Me. That's certainly not happening with your two sons. Your house will be cursed because of them. In generations to come you won't have a single man in your family who will live to old age. This is the sign you will see to know this is true. Both of your sons will die in one day. I will raise up a priest who will be faithful. I will build him an enduring house and he will always walk before Me."

I Samuel 3:1-18 *Samuel's vision and calling*
Samuel was ministering before the Lord daily. During this period getting a word from the Lord was very rare. One night Samuel was resting in the temple where the ark of God was. The Lord called Samuel. Samuel answered, "Here I am." He ran to Eli, because he thought Eli was calling him. This happened three times. Each time Eli told Samuel to go lie down since Eli had not called. The fourth time Eli perceived it must be the Lord calling Samuel, so he said, "When it happens again say, 'Yes Lord, I'm listening!'" When God called Samuel the fourth time, he answered as Eli advised. God said, "I am about to do a thing in Israel that will make the ears of all who hear about it tingle. Eli has sinned by allowing his sons to continue to cheat the people and me. His house is coming under judgment soon. There isn't a sacrifice that can be made to clear the sin of Eli's house." Samuel went back to sleep. The next morning Eli compelled Samuel to tell him what God had said. Upon hearing the news, Eli's only comment was, "It's the Lord, let him do what seems good to Him."

I Samuel 3:19-4:22 *Israel defeated, the Ark taken, Eli and his sons die*
Samuel grew in favor before God and men. At this time Israel went out against the Philistines in Ebenezer. Israel was defeated in the battle and 4000 Hebrews died. The

Israelites decided to take the ark of God with them into the next battle. So Eli's two sons went with the ark to the army camp. There was a great cry of joy when they arrived. When the Philistines heard it they were afraid. But they gathered their courage and became determined to fight like men. They defeated Israel again, captured the ark, and killed both of Eli's sons. A man from the battle ran back to Shiloh and reported the news. There was a great cry from the city. Eli was sitting near the road when he heard the uproar in the city and was very concerned about the ark. The runner came and reported the ark's capture to Eli. When Eli heard it, he fell backward from his seat and broke his neck. He had judged Israel for 40 years. When Eli's pregnant daughter-in-law heard about the ark's capture, the death of her husband, and the death of her father-in-law, she began to have labor pains. As soon as her child was born she said, "The glory has departed from Israel because the ark of God has been taken." Then just before she died, she named her son Ichabod.

I Samuel 5:1-7:2 *The Ark in the keeping of the Philistines*
The Philistines took the ark and put it in the shrine of Dagon, their god, located in the city of Ashdod. When they awoke the next morning Dagon was laying face downward in front of the ark. So they lifted him up and put him back on his stand. The next morning Dagon had fallen again and this time his head and hands were cut off. Then the Lord began to ravage the people in Ashdod and its territories with tumors. The people realized the ark of the Hebrews was causing the tumors so the lords of the Philistines decided to take the Ark to Gath. It caused a great uproar and confusion in the city and many men were slain, while numerous others got tumors. Then the ark was sent to Ekron. The same things happened there.

The priest and diviners in Philistia were summoned after seven months of havoc. They prescribed an offering of five gold tumors and five gold mice, one each for the five lords and cities of Philistia. The ark was placed on a cart with two nursing cows pulling it. They reasoned that if the cows headed straight back towards Israel, then the ark had caused all the plagues. But if the cows went back to the barn to nurse their calves, then the ark wasn't the problem. When the cows were released with the cart, they headed straight back to Israel! They stopped in a field owned by a fellow named Joshua, near the town of Beth-shemesh. All the Bethshemites celebrated the return of the ark. They used the wood from the cart to build a fire so they could offer the cows as a burnt offering. The Levites set the ark on a large stone, which still stands in Joshua's field. Some of the Bethshemites looked inside the ark. So God caused a great slaughter in Beth-shemesh to punish them for looking inside the ark. After the problems in Beth-shemesh, the ark was taken to Kiriath-jearim where it stayed for 20 years.

I Samuel 7:3-17 *Philistines defeated*
The Hebrews were still worshipping Baals. Finally Samuel said, "If Israel will stop worshipping false gods, the Lord will defeat the Philistines." So Israel removed the false idols and worshipped the Lord again. A short time after they had gathered together in Mizpah, the Philistines came against them. Samuel offered sacrifices and the people fasted. When the Philistines were about to attack, God confused them with a great thunder and they were defeated that day. Israel took back all the cities they had lost, and the Philistines were kept inside Philistia while Samuel judged Israel.

I Samuel 8 *The people ask for a King*
As Samuel got older he appointed his sons as judges. They didn't follow Samuel's ways. They took bribes and profited in many dishonest ways. The elders of Israel approached Samuel and said, "Samuel, you're getting old and your sons aren't worth a quarter shekel. We want you to appoint a king over us like the other nations." Their words didn't set well with Samuel. The Lord said to Samuel, "Samuel these people aren't rejecting you; they're rejecting me. They've done this and served other gods from the time I took them out of Egypt. We'll give them a king, but they need to understand that the king will tax them, draft their sons into the army, take the best of their daughters and confiscate their good fields. He will take the best of everything, and then they will cry to Me because we gave them a king!" Samuel told the people the facts. But they didn't listen; they wanted a king just like all the other nations.

I Samuel 9 *Samuel finds Saul*
There was a man named Saul who was a Benjamite. He came from a family of valiant men. Saul was a very handsome man and about a head taller than any man in Israel. One day his father told him to go and look for some lost donkeys. Saul and his servant searched through much of the land. After a while, Saul said to his servant, "We better head home, or Dad's going to stop worrying about the donkeys and start worrying about us! There is a town on the way where a man of God lives. Let's stop and have him tell us if we'll ever find those donkeys." When Samuel saw them, he knew who they were becasue God told him the previous evening, "The man I have chosen to be king will come into town tomorrow afternoon, looking for you." Saul came to Samuel and said, "Do you know where the seer is?" (At that time they called prophets seers). Samuel answered, "I am the seer. Eat with me tonight and I'll let you go tomorrow. As for the lost donkeys, don't worry, they have already been found. God has only the best in store for you and your family." Saul wondered, "Why is he talking to me like that? I am a Benjamite, the smallest tribe in Israel and my family is the smallest family in Benjamin." Samuel led him up to the house for their supper. He instructed the

servants to give Saul the best piece of meat. Samuel said, "See, I have set aside the best for you." That night Saul slept on the roof.

I Samuel 10 *Saul becomes King*
The next morning Samuel sent Saul's servant ahead so he could give his word from the Lord to Saul. He poured oil on Saul's head to anoint him as king. Then he gave Saul a word from God: "Today the Lord has anointed you as king over His people. When you leave here, as you approach Rachel's tomb in the territory of Benjamin, you will meet two men. They will inform you that your donkeys have been found. They will also inform you that your father is concerned about your well being. When you get to the old oak at Tabor, you will see three men carrying three kids, three loaves of bread, and two jugs of wine. They'll give you two loaves of bread. When you get to the Philistine garrison, you'll see a group of prophets. They will be singing and playing their tambourines. The Spirit of the Lord will come upon you. You will become a changed man and you will prophesy with them. You'll see at this time that God is with you. Then go down to Gilgal. Wait seven days for me. I'll tell you what to do when I get there." So Saul went on his way. Everything happened as Samuel said. When Saul got home he met his uncle, who asked about the trip. Saul mentioned Samuel and the recovered donkeys, but said nothing about his being anointed as king of Israel!

Samuel called all the people together at Mizpah. He proclaimed the word from the Lord to them: "I am the God who led you from Egypt and the God who delivers you from your enemies. But today you reject Me by saying, 'Give us a king.' Separate yourselves into tribes and families." Samuel then drew lots. The first lot fell on the tribe of Benjamin, the second lot identified the family of Matrite and finally the lot fell on Saul, the son of Kish. But Saul could not be found. The Lord revealed that he was hiding in the baggage. When he finally stood before the people, and they saw that he was a head taller than anyone, Samuel said, "See who God has chosen; there's no one else like him among you!" All the people shouted, "Long live the king!" Some worthless men said, "Who is Saul, that he can deliver us?" They didn't join in the celebration. Saul kept silent about them, and everyone returned to their homes.

I Samuel 11 *Saul acts like a King*
Then Nahash, the Ammonite, besieged the town of Jabesh-gilead. The Jabesh-gileadites said to Nahash, "Make a covenant with us and we will serve you." Nahash replied, "Instead of killing you I will gouge out one eye from each of you and then you will serve me." The men of Jabesh said, "Give us a week, perhaps we can find someone in Israel to deliver us. If no one comes, then we'll have to come out.

Saul was coming up from the field behind two plowing oxen when he got the message from Jabesh-gilead. When he heard the specifics of Nahash's proposal, the Spirit of the Lord came upon Saul powerfully. He slaughtered the plowing oxen and cut them in pieces. He sent the pieces to all the territories in Israel with this message, "Whoever does not come up and help me deliver Jabesh-gilead, will have his oxen cut up like these!" Every man who got the message came because they feared Saul. Saul had 300,000 men from Israel. 300,000 additional men came from Judah. They went up and delivered Jabesh-gilead from Nahash. The few Ammonites that were not killed were so scattered that no two of them were left together.

After the battle the people said to Samuel, "Let's get the worthless men who said, "Who is Saul, that he can deliver us?" and kill them. But Saul said, "No one will be executed today because God has helped us!" Then they all went to Gilgal and Saul was properly ordained king. They offered sacrifices. Saul and everybody in Israel were rejoicing.

I Samuel 12 *Samuel's speech to the people*
Samuel said to all the people, "I have done as you've asked. Now you have a king. I'm old, and I have walked honestly as your leader all these years. I have never taken a bribe or gained dishonestly from my position." All the people agreed that Samuel would go down in history as a great leader. Samuel continued his speech, "The Lord has always been your deliverer. He brought you out of Egypt. Then when you got into trouble with Sisera or the Philistines or the King of Moab, He sent deliverers like Gideon, or Jepthah or me to save you. The reason any of these nations are allowed to come against you is because you constantly forget the Lord and worship false gods! You want a king to rule over you, well here he is. God has set him before you. Now both you and your king need to follow the Lord! If you don't follow the Lord, He will be against you and your king. God is angry that you have rejected Him by asking for a king." Then rumbling thunder and rain came upon the land, even though it was summer! The people asked Samuel to pray for them. They thought they might die, because they had asked for a king. Samuel said, "Don't be afraid. Serve the Lord with all your hearts. Don't follow after gods who can't deliver you. False gods are a waste of energy." Samuel assured them that he would always pray for them. He finished by saying, "Respect the Lord and serve Him, consider all He has done for you. But if you do wickedly both you and your king will be swept away." Saul was 40 years old when he began his reign. He was king in Israel for 32 years.

I Samuel 13 *War with Philistines and Saul's missteps*

Saul put together a standing army. He chose 3000 men from Israel. 2000 of them were with Saul in the hill country of Bethel. 1000 were with Saul's son, Jonathan, at Gibeah. Jonathan victoriously lead his men against the Philistine garrison at Geba. Saul blew the trumpet throughout Israel about the victory. He called the people together in Gilgal. The victory angered the Philistines so they assembled an army of 30,000 chariots, 6000 horsemen and countless foot soldiers. They camped at Michmash, east of Beth-aven. The people of Israel were frightened. Many hid in caves. Some fled east of the Jordan. Those remaining with Saul in Gilgal were trembling.

Obedient to Samuel's instructions, Saul waited seven days in Gilgal, but Samuel didn't show. Saul's army was starting to scatter, so Saul went ahead and conducted a burnt offering, hoping to gain God's favor in the battle. As soon as he was finished Samuel showed up. Saul went out to greet him. Samuel said, "What have you done?" Saul answered, "The people were scattering from me and you hadn't shown up yet. The Philistines are all assembled and I hadn't asked for God's favor in the battle, so I conducted a burnt offering!" Then Samuel proclaimed, "Saul, instead of establishing your kingdom, you have acted foolishly. God is looking for a man who follows His direction. Because you have not followed the Lord's instructions, your kingdom will not endure."

Samuel left Gilgal and went to Gibeah. Saul counted those who were left; he had 600 men. Meanwhile the Philistines started maneuvering their forces. Saul's disadvantage was exacerbated because only he and Jonathan had iron weapons. The Philistines had forbidden anyone in Israel to work as a blacksmith. They didn't want Israel to have advanced weapons. They even charged exorbitant rates for blacksmith work they did on farming tools in Israel!

I Samuel 14 Jonathan's exploits

Then Jonathan and his armor carrier stealthily left Saul and the main group. They approached a Philistine garrison between Michmash and Geba. Jonathan said to the young man, "Let's advance on this garrison of uncircumcised Philistines. God can save with many or few." The armor bearer replied bravely, "I'll go where you go!" Then Jonathan said, "We'll make ourselves visible to them. If they say, 'Wait where you are, we'll come meet you', then we'll stand our ground. If they say, 'Come up to us', it will be a sign to us that the Lord has delivered them into our hands!" When the Philistines saw Jonathan and his armor carrier they said, "Look at this, the Hebrews are coming out of the rocks!" They yelled down to Jonathan and his armor bearer, "Come up here, we want to say something to you!" Jonathan and his bearer went up and killed about twenty men in a swath two feet wide and about 100 yards long! Jonathan was killing in front and his bearer killed some behind Jonathan.

This victory caused a fear to fall on the Philistines. Then God sent an earthquake in the Philistine camp, and they became even more unsettled. Saul's watchmen reported that the Philistine multitude was beginning to scatter. Saul ordered a role call and realized Jonathan was missing. When Saul called the priest to bring the ark to him, word arrived that the Philistine confusion was continuing. Then the Hebrews rallied and engaged the Philistines in battle. Distraction continued in the Philistine camp, and they were killing each other. Some Hebrews who had defected to the Philistines also began fighting for Israel. The men who had scattered from Saul heard about the Philistine disorder and came back to join the battle. So the Philistines were badly beaten that day.

The Hebrews were fatigued because Saul had prescribed an oath: "If anyone eats before evening they will be cursed." So the soldiers were tired and ineffective for lack of nourishment. When they chased the Philistines into the woods, there was honey available in many places, but no one ate. Jonathan wasn't in camp when Saul required the oath so he ate honey and his eyes brightened because of the food. Israel would have killed many more Philistines that day if everyone had eaten!

The people rushed greedily onto the Philistine spoil. Some of them ate raw meat. Saul was upset because this was against the ritual. He built an altar and the animals were sacrificed correctly. Saul wanted to keep fighting all night so he asked God if they would be successful, but God did not answer. Saul cried, "Who has sinned and caused God to not answer me?" Saul ordered lots drawn to find out who had eaten and the lot fell on Jonathan, who confessed to taking the honey. Then Saul ordered Jonathan executed! But the people wouldn't hear of it, because of all Jonathan had done for Israel that day.

Saul fought against the Philistines during his entire reign as king. He also fought against the Ammonites, the Edomites and the Zobahites. He inflicted punishment against all of his enemies. His family included his sons; Jonathan, Ishvi and Malchishua, his daughters, Merab and Michal, and his wife was Ahinoam. His cousin, Abner, was his general. If Saul saw a man who was mighty or valiant, he was drafted into the army.

I Samuel 15 *God rejects Saul*

Later, Samuel called Saul and said, "Hear the word of the Lord; 'I will punish Amalek for attacking Israel when they came out of Egypt. Go and strike Amalek and utterly destroy all he has. Do not spare him. Kill everything that breathes. Leave nothing alive." Saul gathered an Army of 200,000 foot soldiers and 10,000 men of Judah to fight against Amalek. The Kenites were warned to leave the area so they wouldn't be killed with the Amalekites. All the people were killed except Agag the king and the choice livestock.

That night God spoke to Samuel, "I'm sorry I made Saul king. He doesn't follow Me or My commands." Samuel was distressed and cried out to God all night. The next morning he went to meet Saul. At Carmel he was told Saul had made a monument to him self and gone on to Gilgal. Samuel headed towards Gilgal. Saul came out to meet him. "Blessed are you of the Lord, Samuel! I have done all God commanded!" Then Samuel answered, "If you did all God commanded why do I hearing the bleating of sheep and the lowing of oxen?" Saul said, "Oh, well yes, we did save some of the best animals to sacrifice to the Lord, but everything else we totally destroyed." Samuel replied, "This is what God says; 'I chose you, Saul, even though you were little in your own eyes and I made you king over Israel. Then I sent you on a mission with specific commands and you did not obey. Instead your army fell quickly upon the spoil that I said was to be totally destroyed. Why do you not obey the Lord?" Then Saul cried, "But I did obey, the only one I've brought back is Agag. The people brought back the animals to sacrifice." Samuel answered, "God wants obedience, not sacrifice! Disobedience is sin. Because of this, God has rejected you as king!" Saul confessed, "I have sinned. I listened to the people and not God when I did not totally destroy Amalek. Please forgive me and return with me so I can worship the Lord." Samuel turned away and said, "No, I will not return with you. You have disobeyed the Lord, and He has rejected you from being king." As Samuel was turning away, Saul reached out and grabbed his cloak, tearing it. Samuel said, "And so the kingdom has been torn from you and will be given to your neighbor. God will not change His mind!" Saul still pleaded, "Please come back with me so I can be honored by the people and worship the Lord!" Finally Samuel relented and went back with Saul.

Samuel had King Agag brought to him. Agag appeared before Samuel saying cheerfully, "Certainly everything is behind us now!" Samuel replied, "I don't think so. As you have killed the sons of many mothers, so will your mother be childless today." Samuel then hewed Agag to pieces. Samuel went back to his home in Ramah and did not see Saul again until the day of his death. The Lord regretted that He had made Saul king.

I Samuel 16 *David and Saul*
Then the Lord said to Samuel, "How much longer are you going to grieve over Saul? I have rejected him. Go to the House of Jesse, in Bethlehem. I have selected a king from among his sons." Samuel said, "Hold on, if Saul hears about this he's going to have me killed." God answered, "Just go down and say you want to make a sacrifice and invite Jesse's family to the service." So Samuel went down to Bethlehem. When he arrived, the elders of the town came trembling to Samuel asking if he was coming in peace. Samuel said he was there to conduct a sacrifice. Jesse's family was invited. When Samuel saw Eliab, Jesse's oldest son, he was sure he must be the one. God said, "Keep looking. I see not only the appearance of a man but also the attitude of his heart." All the rest of Jesse's sons were brought out. Samuel asked, "Are these all your sons?" Jesse answered, "No, my youngest is in the field." Samuel sent for him. When David came, he appeared tanned from the sun, with excellent eyes and very handsome. God told Samuel to anoint him. The Spirit of God came heavily upon David from that day on but the Spirit of God left Saul and he became terrorized by an evil spirit from God.

When Saul's handlers saw how troubled he was they suggested that Saul allow them to find a skilled harp player to soothe him with music. One of Saul's servants knew David. He reported that David was a gifted musician; a man of valor, a warrior, prudent of speech, handsome, and the Lord was with him. So David was summoned. Jesse sent him to Saul with a donkey laden with gifts. When Saul was oppressed, David's harp playing did the trick. Saul loved David and made him his armor carrier. He sent word to Jesse that David had a job.

I Samuel 17 *David and Goliath*
Then the Philistines mobilized their forces at Socoh. Saul and his army gathered across the valley. The Philistines had a champion named Goliath, he was nine feet tall, his armor weighed 125 pounds, and the head of his spear weighed 15 pounds. Each morning he stood in the valley yelling up at the Hebrews, "Hebrews! Send someone down to fight me! If he wins, we Philistines will serve you, but if I win, Israel will serve us!" This caused concern for the Hebrews since none believed Goliath could be beaten.

Three of David's brothers were soldiers for Saul. One day Jesse called David, "Take these supplies of food to your brothers. Also take these cuts of cheese to their commanders and find out how they're doing." David headed for the front lines. When he got there, Goliath was making his 40th consecutive daily challenge. After Goliath made his provocation, the men all clamored, "Man, that guy is huge! The king has said that any man who goes out and beats him will be given one of his daughters in marriage, and his family will never have to pay taxes again!" David replied, "To take the reproach from Israel would be reward enough. Who is this uncircumcised Philistine to mock the army of the living God?"

Eliab, David's oldest brother, reprimanded David, "What are you doing here piping up like you could do anything about it. You should be home tending sheep." David turned away and said, "I was just asking an honest question!" When Saul heard about David's comments, he sent for him and said, "David, there's no way you could beat Goliath. You're just a youth and that giant has been a soldier since he was your size!" David replied, "I've been in the wilderness tending my flock and have been attacked by lions and bears. None have escaped; I've killed them all. This uncircumcised Philistine won't be any different to me than a lion or bear because he has taunted the armies of the living God. It was God who delivered me from the lion and bear. He will certainly deliver me from this uncircumcised Philistine!" So Saul clothed David with armor and provided both spear and sword. David felt uncomfortable with all the gear. He explained that he would feel more comfortable without it. Then he went to the brook and gathered five smooth stones for his sling and put them in his shepherd's bag.

As David approached the giant and his armor bearer, Goliath mocked him, "Who am I, a dog? Why have they sent a little wimp like you with sticks and rocks against me? Keep coming little boy, I'm going to rip you to pieces!" David yelled back, "You have your sword and spear, but I come in the name of the Lord of Hosts, the God of the armies of Israel, whom you have taunted. Today, God will deliver you into my hand. I will remove your head from you, and the birds and wild animals will eat the bodies of your Philistine soldier friends up on the hill. Everyone on earth will know the God of Israel is the real God and all those assembled on these two hills will know God doesn't need a big sword to deliver His chosen people. This isn't my battle, it is the Lord's!" At this, the giant began his charge on David and David ran to meet him. As he sprinted towards the giant, he pulled a stone from his bag and slung it at the giant with his sling. The stone struck Goliath and sank into his forehead. He fell forward, dead on the ground. David ran and stood over him. He took Goliath's sword and cut the giant's head off with it. The Philistines panicked and fled with the Hebrews in hot pursuit. There were dead Philistines all the way back into Philistia.

I Samuel 18:1-5 *David and Jonathan*

From this time on, David was a soldier for Saul. Saul's son, Jonathan, and David became very special friends. They loved each other like brothers and had deep respect for each other. When David went out against the Philistines he always returned victorious. The women would come out singing and dancing on his return with this song: "Saul has slain his thousands, and David his ten thousands!" This made Saul angry. He feared that David would take the kingdom from him.

I Samuel 18:6-30 *David marries Michal*

One day Saul was oppressed, so David was playing music to calm the king. Saul took a spear and tried to kill David, but David escaped. David spent most of his time in the field fighting the Philistines. He commanded 1000 men and his exploits were always successful because God was with him. He continued to gain favor with the people of Israel and Judah. At this time Saul offered his oldest daughter to David for his wife. Saul was actually plotting that David would be a better target for the Philistines if he was the king's son-in-law. David turned down the offer saying, "What am I or my family that I should be the son-in-law of the king?" Because his younger daughter, Michal, loved David, Saul offered her. David responded as before. Saul realized that David was humbled because he was poor and would not be able to pay a dowry. Saul had his servants tell David that the dowry was the foreskins of 100 hundred Philistines. This was an assignment David felt comfortable with. He went out with his men and returned with 200 Philistine foreskins. So David and Michal were married. Saul observed how much God was blessing David and how his own daughter loved him. He hated David even more.

I Samuel 19 *Saul repeatedly tries to kill David*

Saul instructed Jonathan and his servants to kill David. Jonathan first warned David and then talked to his father. He said, "Father, how can you want David killed? He is a hero of Israel and has done nothing wrong." So Saul made a pledge not to kill David. David continued his normal schedule. A few days later, he was playing music for Saul when the king repeated his spear attack and David skillfully escaped again. Then Saul sent men to David's house to kill him, but his wife, Michal, learned about the plan and helped him escape.

David fled to Ramah and told Samuel about Saul. Before long, Saul learned David was there and sent men to kill him. When Saul's men approached, they were overcome by the Spirit of God and began to chant uncontrollably. Saul came later. The Holy Spirit also overcame him. So David was able to flee to safety.

I Samuel 20 *Jonathan helps David*

Then David returned to the palace to meet with Jonathan. David said, "Your father is set on having me killed! What on earth have I done to offend him?" Jonathan answered, "David, my father doesn't do anything, great or small, without talking to me. He swore he would not hurt you!" David said, "Jonathan, I'm telling you, as far as your father is concerned I'm a dead man." Jonathan replied, "Tell me what you want me to do." David then said, "Tomorrow is the beginning of the new moon feast. Normally I'd come and sit at the king's table. If your father questions you about my absence, tell him I was called to Bethlehem to be with my family. If he's angry with this, then you'll know he means to kill me. If he is calm about it, then I will know that I have misjudged him." Jonathan replied, "I love you David. I will do as you say. If my father wants to kill you, I will come and tell you. But remember, you and I will always be friends. I know that God will always deliver your enemies to you. Always think of my family kindly because of our great friendship!"

On the first night of the feast, Saul said nothing about David's absence, assuming he was detained. On the second night, he asked Jonathan about David. When Jonathan explained that David was in Bethlehem with his family, Saul became very angry with Jonathan. He yelled, "Jonathan, don't you know that as long as David lives you will never be king! He must die!" Jonathan said, "How can you want to kill a man who has done you no wrong?" At this Saul hurled his spear into the wall just past Jonathan. Now Jonathan knew his father was very serious about having David killed. So he met David at a secret place. They both wept bitterly, but David wept more than Jonathan. They again remembered their vow to one another: that God would be between them and their descendants forever. Afterward, David fled and Jonathan returned to the city.

I Samuel 21-22 *David on the run*

David came to Nob where the tabernacle was. He met Ahimelech the priest. David told him Saul had sent him on an urgent mission that was so important he was not able to pack properly. Ahimelech agreed to let David have the showbread from the table in the Holy Place. Goliath's sword was stored there, and David took that as well. Saul's chief shepherd, named Doeg, was nearby and overheard David and Ahimelech's transaction.

David left Nob and journeyed to Gath in Philistia. The servants of Achish, the king of Gath, warned him, "Isn't this David of whom it is sung, 'Saul kills his thousands, and David his ten thousands'?" David was afraid and as a ploy, began to act irrationally. He let his spit roll down his beard. The king said, "Don't I have enough insane people here already? Take this one out of my country!" So David escaped to a cave near

Adullam. His family heard he was there and came to him. So did any man in Israel who owed taxes or was discontented or in debt. David became their captain. He now had 400 fighting men with him and went to Moab. The king of Moab allowed David to leave his family there in safety. The prophet Gad instructed David to go into Judah. So he and his men made their way into the forest of Hereth.

Saul heard of David's army and asked his servants, "Why do none of you help me? My own son has conspired with the son of Jesse to lie in ambush against me. He's out there right now with a band of rebels!" Doeg, Saul's servant, was standing nearby and said, "King Saul, I saw David just a few days ago in Nob. Ahimelech gave him food and Goliath's sword." Saul sent for Ahimelech and said, "Why have you conspired against me by helping the son of Jesse?" Ahimelech answered, "My king, David is your trusted servant. When I helped him, I thought I was helping you. I don't know anything about a conspiracy!" Saul ordered his servants to slay Ahimelech and the other priests of the Lord, but they refused to kill the priests. Then Saul ordered Doeg to do the killing. Doeg killed 85 priests that day. Then the people of Nob were killed including women and children. One person escaped: Abiathar, Ahimelech's son. He fled to David and told him about the massacre. David grieved because he felt he had brought this on them. He assured Abiathar that he would be safe.

I Samuel 23 *David saves Keilah and Saul pursues*
When David heard that the Philistines were fighting against Keilah, he inquired to God, "Should I go down there and deliver Keilah?" God answered, "Yes, go down and you will win." Because his men were fearful, David asked God again. God assured David he would be victorious, so they went down and defeated the Philistines at Keilah.

When Saul heard David was there he was glad because he felt he had David in a trap. David learned that Saul was on his way and asked God if he should stay or flee. God said, "Flee, because the people of Keilah will give you to Saul." David fled with an army that had grown to 600 fighting men.

Saul continued to pursue David through the wilderness. Jonathan caught up with David and said, "David, it is clear to me that God is with you, and you will be the king in Israel. I will stand with you, and my father knows it!" So David and Jonathan renewed their promises to each other. Saul came very close to David in the wilderness of Maon. At one point Saul's group was on one side of the mountain, and David's on the other. David always tried to keep some obstacle between his army and Saul's. Saul was about to close the trap on David when he received word that the Philistines were making a raid on Israel. He was forced to break off pursuit of David, to fight the Philistines. David was delivered again.

I Samuel 24 *David spares Saul's life*
David moved into the caves of Engedi. When Saul finished with the Philistines he put together a group of 3000 of his finest fighters and went after David again. When he arrived in the Engedi area he pulled off into one of the caves to rest. David and his men were back in the recesses of the same cave! As Saul rested, David stealthily approached and cut off a piece of Saul's robe. When Saul woke up, David followed him out of the cave and yelled down at him, "Saul, how can you say I am your enemy? You were lying in the cave. I could have easily killed you. Instead here is the piece of your robe I cut off. Would your enemy spare your life? Now you must know I am not your enemy. Who am I? I am just a flea, a dead dog to you. How could I hurt you?" Saul answered, "Now I know, I am wrong. I also know God has given you this kingdom. I only ask that you remember my family and me. I'm going home, I won't chase you anymore."

Israel's last judge, Samuel, died after these events, and all of Israel went to Ramah to mourn Samuel's passing.

I Samuel 25:2-44 *David and Abigail*
David went to the wilderness of Paran. There was a man named Nabal running a sheep ranch there. He was sheering sheep in Carmel. David had been protecting Nabal's operation from robbers and Philistines. When the sheering was about complete, David sent ten of his young men to receive a token payment from Nabal for the protection of his operation. Nabal said, "Who is David that I should give anything to him? Go back and tell David he'll get nothing from me!" When David got this message, he was agitated. He instructed 400 of his men to put on their swords. They would teach foolish Nabal what trouble was really about! As they were on their way, one of Nabal's men rushed to Abigail, Nabal's wife, to warn her that David and his men were coming. Abigail hurriedly prepared a generous offering for David and his men. She loaded two hundred loaves of bread, two jugs of wine, five prepared sheep, five measures of roasted grain, one hundred clusters of raisins and two hundred fig cakes on donkeys. She sent all these provisions ahead and followed behind. David was saying, "Nabal will not have a living servant, nor will he be breathing when the sun rises!"

When Abigail saw David, she threw herself face down before him and cried, "Please David, do not carry out this plan! It's my fault; I didn't see the young men you sent. I would have dealt differently with them. Nabal is a foolish and evil man. You are the future king. The Lord is with you and fights your battles because you fight his enemies. Please accept these items and spare my household. I'm afraid you might be troubled in heart if you shed blood today." David replied, "Well, bless your heart Abigail. I will accept these gifts and we will kill no one today, which was my intention. I'm happy I won't have to!"

When Abigail went back to her house, Nabal was there drinking and eating in celebration of his successful shearing. He was so drunk Abigail didn't tell him about what had transpired with David. The next morning Nabal was hung over. When Abigail told him how close he was to being killed and having his ranch ransacked, his heart went numb. He died ten days later.

When David heard about Nabal's death, he thought kindly of Abigail. Not only was she very beautiful, she was wise. She had kept David from doing a great evil. He sent a proposal of marriage to Abigail, which she happily accepted. David also had a wife named Ahinoam. Saul had given Michal, his daughter and David's first wife, to a fellow named Paltiel.

I Samuel 26 *David spares Saul's life again*
Saul received fresh intelligence on David's location and he gathered his best fighters and headed back out. After Saul had made camp near a hill for the night, he and Abner, his chief general, and all his men slept very soundly. David and Abishai (Joab's brother) crept into the camp, right up to where Saul was sleeping. Abishai wanted to kill Saul but David forbade it and took Saul's spear and water jug. He said, "Killing Saul is not my job. When God wants him, God will take him, probably in battle." The next morning David yelled down into Saul's camp, "Abner, wake up! I could easily have killed the king last night. I have his spear and water jug! A general like you ought to be put to death." Saul recognized David's voice and yelled back, "David, you've done it again. I have played the fool coming against a man who refuses to hurt me. Certainly God is with you and you will accomplish all he has in mind for you!" David answered, "Saul, I can't understand why you would come after me. Why would the king of Israel hunt for a flea or a small bird in the forest! Send one of your young men up here and we'll return your things. Leave me alone, and know I will not harm the king of Israel!" Saul returned home, and David went back into his camp in the wilderness.

I Samuel 27 *David goes to work for the Philistines!*
David finally said to himself, "One of these days Saul is going to be successful with his desire to kill me. Better for me to go into Philistia and create an allegiance with the

Philistines. So David and his men went into Gath to meet with King Achish, who gave them refuge. Saul had no interest in pursuing David into Philistia.

After a time David requested clearance from Achish to take a city for himself and his men. Achish authorized settlement in Ziklag. David went into the south territory and slaughtered the Geshurites, Girzites and the Amalekites who lived in the land. He wiped out all the inhabitants, every man and woman. He took all the livestock and went back to Achish.

King Achish ask David whom he had gone out against. David answered; today I have fought against the people in the south country of Judah; Jerahmeelites and the Kenites. I killed every man and woman. Achish felt that these actions would make David Israel's enemy and that David had basically made himself a permanent servant to Achish's kingdom.

I Samuel 28 *Saul consults a medium, sees Samuel again*
Then the Philistines began to assemble themselves to go out against Israel. Achish said to David, "David, you and your men will come with us." David replied, "Achish, you know very well what I can do." Achish answered, "Very good, I will make you my body guard for life."

When Saul learned the Philistines were gathering for war, he became very frightened. He asked God what the outcome would be, but the Lord did not answer him. Saul had banished all mediums from the land, but he needed one now. His servants found one. Saul dressed in a disguise and went to the woman. She said, "You know what Saul has said about mediums, I could get killed for this." Saul replied, "I swear by the Lord, no punishment will come to you. I want you to bring Samuel up for me." So she conjured up Samuel. Samuel said, "Saul, why are you disturbing me by bringing me up from the grave?" Saul answered, "I am in big trouble. I've got the Philistines coming out against me. God doesn't answer me any longer. I need to know what to do." Samuel gave this answer, "It's just like I said when I was alive; God is taking the kingdom from you and giving it to David because you didn't follow orders in regard to your mission against Amalek. You're going to lose this battle with the Philistines. Both you and your sons will be with me by this time tomorrow." Saul fell on the ground at this news. He laid there and refused to eat for hours. Finally the medium was able to get him to take some food. Saul and his servants left that night.

I Samuel 29 *David is released from his commitment to the Philistines*
The Philistines continued their muster. When the other kings of Philistia saw that Achish had brought David, they disagreed with the strategy. They felt David could very easily turn on them in the heat of battle. They reminded Achish about the song, "Saul has killed his thousands and David his ten thousands", and said, "The song is about David killing Philistines!" This counsel convinced Achish to send David home.

I Samuel 30 *David defeats the Amalekites who raided Ziklag*
When David got back to Ziklag, he found that the Amalekites had come and made a raid on the city. They didn't kill anyone, but they carried everyone away, including David's two wives, Abigail and Ahinoam. All David's men were so angry with him for leaving the city un-defended; there was open talk of rebellion. David asked God if he should pursue the Amalekites. God assured David the mission would succeed, so they set off. When they got to the brook at Besor, 200 of his men were too exhausted to continue so they stayed behind with the baggage.

David and the remaining 400 met an Egyptian who was near death with hunger. They fed him and he revived. David asked where he was from. "I am a servant of the Amalekites. They left me three days ago when I got sick. We were coming back from raiding Ziklag." David asked if he would lead them to the Amalekites. "Yes I will take you to them as long as you promise not to return me to them." The Egyptian lead them straight to the Amalekite camp where a victory celebration was under full steam! Then David and his men slaughtered the Amalekites from early morning till twilight. Only 400 Amaekites who had camels escaped; David killed everyone else. David recovered everything; nothing was lost. When they got back to the brook at Besor, worthless men said, "Let's not share the spoil with these slackers. Let's just give them their wives back and send them away." David answered, "Far be it from us to do this. It was the Lord who delivered the Amalekites to us. So we will share equally with those who stayed with the baggage." Sharing victories, with even support personnel, has been the custom in Israel ever since this incident. When David got back to Ziklag, he made a point of distributing some of the spoil from their exploits to many of the towns in Judah. David and his men were honored in Judah.

I Samuel 31 *Saul and Jonathan killed*
Meanwhile, up in Israel, things were going just as Samuel had said they would. Saul's sons, Jonathan, Abinadab and Malchi-shua, were all killed in the battle. An arrow wounded Saul. When he saw how close the Philistines were to him, he ordered his armor bearer to put a sword through him so the Philistines would not have an opportunity to torture him. His armor bearer would not kill his king, so Saul fell on his

own sword and killed himself. The armor bearer then fell on his sword and died with Saul. The Israelites fled from the Philistines. Later, the Philistines cut Saul's head off and hung his body along with the bodies of his sons, on the wall at Beth-shan. Some valiant men from Israel went the next night and recovered the bodies for proper burial. They mourned and fasted for seven days for Saul and his sons.

The Second Book of Samuel

II Samuel 1 *David learns Saul is dead*
Three days after David's return to Ziklag, a man came into town with torn clothes and dust on his head. He had come from Israel's battle with the Philistines. David asked him how it went for Israel. "The Israelite camp is fleeing from the Philisitines. Many have been killed, including Saul and Jonathan." David asked him how he could be sure that Saul and Jonathan were dead. "I was there at mount Gilboa when I saw Saul leaning on his sword. He asked me to kill him. I knew he could not survive his wounds so I struck him and killed him. I took off his crown and bracelet for you." He handed them to David.

When David and his men heard the news, they tore their clothes, mourned, wept and fasted until evening. David called the young man who brought the news. "Where are you from?" The man answered. "I am an Amalekite." David continued, "How can you be so brave to lift your hand to kill the Lord's anointed?" David turned to one of his young men. "Fall on this Amalekite and slay him." So the young man struck him and the Amalekite died. David mourned Saul and Jonathan with the "Song of the Bow" that is still remembered in Israel.

II Samuel 2:1-11 *David becomes King in Judah*
David asked God if he should go up to Judah and if so, where. God told David to go to Hebron. The people of Judah quickly anointed David as their king. David then sent messengers to Jabesh-gilead because they had retrieved the bodies of Saul and Jonathan. His message: "God bless you for your kindness to Saul and his family. The Judeans here have already anointed me as king." Abner, Saul's General, had taken Ish-bosheth, Saul's surviving son and made him king over Israel in Gilead. Ish-bosheth was king in Israel for two years. The people of Judah always followed David. In time, David produced a number of sons in Hebron. One of the sons was named Absolom.

II Samuel 2:12-32 Abner and Joab

At this time Abner and his army met with David's general, Joab, and his army at the pool in Gibeon. Joab's brothers, Abishai and Asahel, were with him. What started as a tournament to test soldiering skills, turned into an all-out battle! The battle went well for David's men. Asahel was the fastest man in the land. He was chasing Abner when Abner yelled back at him, "Asahel, don't pursue me any longer, turn and pursue one of the younger men and take your spoil from him because I don't want to kill you today." But Asahel kept chasing Abner. When he got close, Abner stopped abruptly and Asahel was impaled on the back of Abner's spear. All the men who saw it stood still at the spot were Asahel was killed, but Joab and Abishai continued to pursue Abner into the countryside. All the available men of Benjamin joined Abner. They turned and faced Joab and Abishai as one band. Abner cried down to them: "Let's stop this killing between brothers!" Joab and Abishai stopped the chase and each group returned home. Asahel was dead, but the forces of David had killed 360 of Abner's men.

II Samuel 3 *Abner defects, Joab murders him*

During this entire period there was fighting between David's army and the army of Ish-bosheth. David was becoming stronger and the house of Saul weaker. Abner was increasing his influence. When Abner took one of Saul's mistresses, Ish-bosheth confronted him about it. Abner answered Ish-bosheth angrily, "Am I the head of a dog that you speak to me this way about this trivial issue. I've had it with you Ish-bosheth, I am going to see God's will completed. He has promised the kingdom to David. I have the power to see this accomplished!" Ish-bosheth couldn't say a word because he was afraid of Abner.

So Abner sent word to David indicating his desire to help unify the two kingdoms. David was receptive but insisted that Michal, his wife, be returned to him before Abner could hope for a successful summit meeting. David sent a message to Ish-bosheth, who immediately had Michal delivered to Abner for his meeting with David. Michal's husband, Paltiel, followed along crying for Michal until they met Abner. Abner ordered Paltiel to return home; humiliated, Paltiel complied. On the way to see David, Abner had meetings with the elders of Israel. He oiled Israel's political machine by reminding them that God had said David would deliver Israel from their enemies.

Abner's summit with David was successful. Abner left Hebron to make final arrangements for the coronation of David as king over all Israel. Meanwhile Joab returned from a raid and heard what had happened between Abner and David. He went to David and said, "What have you done? Abner is up to no good. He's down here spying on us to find a weakness!" Then Joab left David and sent messengers to Abner telling him to return to Hebron. When Abner got back into Hebron, Joab met him in private. He stabbed him in the belly, killing Abner. This is how Joab avenged the death of Asahel, his brother.

David was livid when he heard about it. He told Joab, "This kingdom is innocent of killing Abner. What you've done is cowardly. Take off your sword, and we will all mourn Abner's death." David wrote a song about how Abner was killed in an evil fashion. So all the people knew David was not responsible for Abner's death.

II Samuel 4 *Ish-bosheth murdered*
When Ish-bosheth heard about Abner, he and all Israel were frightened. He was taking a mid-day nap in his home when two of his commanders, Baanah and Rechab, came into the house pretending they were collecting wheat. They went into Ish-bosheth's room and killed him in his bed. They cut off his head, and then rode all night to Hebron where they presented the head to David saying, "Here is the head of the one who sought your life." David answered, "A couple of years ago a man came to me in Ziklag to report the death of Saul, assuming it would be good news for me. I had him killed for his news. How much more will I require your blood today for killing an innocent man in his bed?" Baanah and Rechab were killed, their hands and feet were cut off and they were hung up beside the pool in Hebron. Ish-bosheth's head was buried in Abner's grave.

II Samuel 5 *David becomes king of all Israel*
All the elders of the tribes of Israel came to David at Hebron and said, "We are your relatives. Even when Saul was king, it was you who troubled the Philistines. God has said that you should be the king over Israel." So David became king over all Israel. He was 30 years old. He reigned seven years in Hebron and 33 in Jerusalem.

Now all of Saul's sons were dead. The only son of Jonathan still living was Mephibosheth. When he was five years old, he became crippled in his feet because his maid dropped him as they were fleeing from the Philistines on the day Saul and Jonathan were killed.

When David fought to capture Jerusalem, it was heavily fortified. The Jebusites who lived there taunted David saying, "If we were blind and crippled you could not take the city." David offered an enticement to his men, "Whoever kills the first Jebusite will become the chief commander of the army. Joab found a way through a water tunnel into the city. He earned the position as chief commander. David developed Jerusalem and made his residence there. The city became the Capitol of Israel, and it was called the City of David. He became greater and greater because the Lord was with him. Hiram, the king of Tyre, sent craftsmen and materials to build David a palace. As David became more comfortable as king, he took additional wives and concubines into the palace who bore sons and daughters.

The Philistines began to assemble for war in the valley of Rephaim. David asked God if he should go out against them. God said, "Go out, I will make you victorious over them." David broke through their lines with such ease he called the place "Master of Breakthrough." David also captured the Philistine idols in this engagement. Once more the Philistines gathered in the valley and David asked God if they should go out against them. God said, "Don't go directly out, circle around and attack from the woods." In this battle David drove the Philistines completely out of Israel and into Philistia.

II Samuel 6 *David retrieves the Ark*
David wanted to bring the ark of God into Jerusalem. He gathered all Israel together and they went to Abinadab's house in Kiriath-jearim where the ark was kept. They removed the ark on a new cart. Abinadab's two sons, Uzzah and Ahio, walked beside the cart. All the people and David went with them, dancing with tambourines and all kinds of instruments. When the cart hit a bump, the ark nearly fell off. Uzzah reached out to steady it and was killed. David was angry and afraid. He wondered if he could ever get the ark to Jerusalem. They left the ark in Obed-edom's house. God blessed Obed-edom the three months it stayed there.

Then David realized that only Levites should carry the ark according to the law. They tried again with Levites carrying the ark and offered regular sacrifices as they went along. This proved successful. David marched and danced with all his might along the whole procession. Michal, David's wife and the daughter of Saul, saw David, who had removed his robes, dancing with the people as the ark entered the city. She felt embarrassed by David's display. David had a special tent set up for the ark. (The tabernacle was still in Gibeon with Zadok serving as head priest.) The people offered burnt offerings and a peace offering. David distributed cakes of raisins and dates to all the people. When David got back to his palace, Michal rebuked him for dancing with the people. David replied, "God has lifted me up over your father's house and appointed me ruler over Israel. If I want to celebrate before the Lord, that's my business." David rarely saw Michal after this incident.

The Story Bible for Adults

II Samuel 7 *David plans the Temple, God replies*

David was comfortable because his enemies were pretty well whipped. He brought the Prophet, Nathan, into his office and said, "Here I am living in this fancy house and God's house is still a tent." Nathan replied, "You're thinking along the right track. Carry out your plans. God is with you."

That night Nathan heard from the Lord, God said, "This is what I want you to say to David: 'Are you the one to build My house? I haven't had a house from the time I brought Israel out of Egypt. I have been moving about with them in the tabernacle. In that entire time have I ever instructed anyone to build Me a house? As for you David, when I called you, you were a shepherd, leading sheep. Now you lead Israel. I have been with you and delivered your enemies to you. You have become one of the most powerful people in the world! I have established a place for My people and they aren't being harassed. I will build you a house! When you die, I will raise up one of your descendants who comes after you and I will establish his kingdom. He will build a house for My Name and I will establish his kingdom forever. I will be his father he will be My son. He will receive My correction from the beating of men. I will never take My loving kindness from him like I took it from Saul. In this way your kingdom will be established forever.'"

The next morning Nathan returned to David and relayed the exact words the Lord had given him. David prayed before the Lord. "Who am I God? What is my house that You have brought me this far? It is a wonderful thing You have done, revealing things to me about my lineage. What can I say to You, Lord; You know all that's in my heart. You are showing how very great You are by showing us all these things ahead of time. What nation is like Israel, whom You have chosen, brought out of Egypt, made Your own people and established in this land You have given us. God, let Your word be established: My house will endure forever before You. May You be greater and greater as a result of this promise."

II Samuel 8 *Victories*

David went into Philistia and captured the chief city. He defeated Moab, and they paid taxes to David. David defeated Hadadezer out by the river and established his rule there. The Arameans came to help Hadadezer, and David defeated them as well. All these new areas of conquest paid regular taxes to David. God was helping David wherever he went. David brought large quantities of gold and bronze into Jerusalem. Toi, the king of Hamath came and paid a large tribute of silver and bronze because David had fought against Hadadezer his enemy. David dedicated the entire tribute to the Lord. In addition, David put garrisons all over the land. David ruled with righteousness and justice in Jerusalem. Joab was his general, Jehoshaphat was the recorder, Zadok and Ahimelech were the priests, Seraiah was secretary, Benaiah was in charge of the king's personal guard, and David's sons were ministers.

II Samuel 9 *Kindness to Jonathan's son*
Then David said, "Is there anyone left from the house of Saul that I can show kindness to because of my great love for Jonathan?" His staff found a man named Ziba who had been a servant to Saul. Ziba came before David and told David about Jonathan's crippled son Mephibosheth. He was living with a man named Machir. David had Mephibosheth brought to the palace. Mephibosheth prostrated himself in front of David. David said, "Don't be afraid Mephibosheth. I am going to show you kindness because of my deep love for your father, Jonathan, and your grandfather, Saul. You will eat at my table regularly." Mephibosheth replied, "Who am I, that you would think of a dead dog like me?" David then said to Ziba "I am returning all that belonged to Saul, to his grandson, Mephibosheth. You and your servants will take care of the land for him and care for his needs. He shall come and eat at my table regularly, like my own son." Ziba answered, "I will do all you've said." Mephibosheth had a son named Mica. They moved to Jerusalem. Ziba and his entire house were servants to Mephibosheth.

II Samuel 10 *More victories*
At this time Nahash, the king of the Ammonites, died. His son, Hanun, took over. David said, "I will show kindness to Hanun just like his father showed me." David sent messengers to Hanun, to console him during his period of mourning. When the messengers arrived in Ammon, Hanun's counselors advised him, "Do you think David has sent these men to console you? No, he has sent them to spy and devise an attack plan." Hanun agreed with this evaluation. He cut off the messenger's beards, cut their robes off at the hip and sent them away. When David heard it, he told the humiliated messengers to stay in Jericho until their beards grew back. When Hanun saw he had angered David, he hired a mercenary army from the Arameans, a total of 33,000 soldiers. David sent Joab and his army to Ammon. When Joab saw the strength of the combined force he split his army in two. His brother, Abishai, commanded the second group. Joab said to his brother, "I'll go against the Arameans, you take the Ammonites; if one of us gets in trouble, the other will come to aid his brother. Let us be strong and courageous for the sake of our people and for the cities of God. May the Lord do what is good in His sight." Joab and his group went up against the Arameans and were prevailing. When the Ammonites saw this they retreated into the city, with Abishai pursuing them. With the battle won, Joab and the entire army returned to

Jerusalem. When the Arameans realized how badly they were defeated, they consolidated all their forces. When David heard this, he mustered his army and crossed the river to fight them. He destroyed 700 chariots, killed 40,000 horsemen and killed Shobach, the Aramean general. The Arameans made peace with Israel and paid taxes. They never again collaborated with the Ammonites.

II Samuel 11:1 - 12:25 *David and Batsheba, Uriah murdered, and the consequences*

Kings normally go out to battle in springtime. But that spring David sent Joab to besiege the city of Rabbah in Ammon, while he stayed in Jerusalem. One evening David was out on his roof. He saw a beautiful woman bathing. Her name was Bathsheba, the wife of Uriah, one of David's most valiant warriors. David had Bathsheba brought to the palace and he had sexual relations with her, then she returned to her house. Soon Bathsheba realized she was pregnant and notified David.

David sent a message to Joab: "Send Uriah to Jerusalem." When Uriah arrived, he and David discussed the state of the war. Then David told him to go home. A gift from David was sent after him. But Uriah did not go home, he slept out in front of the palace with the other servants. When David found out, he asked Uriah why he had not gone home. Uriah said, "The ark of the Lord and his army are out camping in the field. Is it right for me to eat, drink and sleep with my wife, while they sleep on the ground? I don't think so!" David replied, "Stay here tonight. Tomorrow you can return to the battle."

That night David got Uriah drunk, hoping he would lose his resolve, but he still slept with the servants. The next morning David wrote a letter to Joab. Uriah carried it with him as he returned. The letter said, "Place Uriah in the fiercest part of the battle and then withdraw from him so he will be killed." Joab sent Uriah to an area near the wall where valiant men were known to be stationed. Uriah was killed along with some other Hebrew soldiers. Joab sent the daily report back to David. He told the messenger what to say if David became angry and asked why men went near the wall. (The story of Abimelech, the evil son of Gideon, who was killed by a woman throwing a millstone down from the wall was common knowledge. Any private in Israel knew not to send soldiers close to the wall). The messenger's response to this line of questioning was to be: "You're servant Uriah died in the engagement." When David got the message he was not angry. He told the messenger, "Encourage Joab. Tell him many die by the sword; be strong and courageous." When Bathsheba heard her husband had died, she mourned him. When her time of mourning was completed, David took her as his wife.

God instructed Nathan, the prophet, to meet with David. Nathan told David this story: "There was a rich man and a poor man. The rich man had many flocks of sheep. The poor man had one ewe lamb that he and his family loved like part of the family. One day the rich man had a visitor, and he did not want to prepare one of his animals, so he took the poor man's lamb, and prepared that for his visitor."

When David heard the story he was angry. He said, "That man should die, and he should have to compensate the poor man fourfold for his lack of compassion." Then Nathan said, "You are that man! This is what God says to you, 'I am the one who delivered you from Saul and anointed you king of Israel. I have given you a palace with plenty of wives. Why have you done this wicked thing? You have killed Uriah and taken his wife. Because you have done this, the sword will not leave your house. I will raise up trouble for you from your own house. I will take your wives from you and give them to someone you know, and he will have sex with them in broad daylight. You did your evil secretly, I will do this thing publicly.'" David said, "I have sinned against the Lord. Nathan replied, "God has removed your sin. You will not die, but the child that is coming will not survive."

When the child was born, it was weak. David fasted and would not listen to anyone during the child's short life. On the seventh day, his servants were afraid to tell him the child had died. They thought he might kill himself. When David saw them whispering to themselves, he asked if the baby had died. After receiving the news, David got up, washed himself and had his servants bring him some food. They wondered why he fasted while the baby was alive and now was eating after it was dead. David said, "When the baby was alive I fasted and prayed, hoping God would be gracious to me and spare the child. Now that he has died, can I bring him back? Can I go to him?" David comforted his wife Bathsheba. He continued to have relations with her, and she had another son. They named the boy Solomon and God loved him.

Joab finally got the upper hand against the fortified city of Rabbah. He sent word to David. "The city is ready to fall into our hands. You should come and finish it; otherwise I'll get the glory, not you." So David went out and defeated Rabbah. They took a large amount of spoil and killed all the inhabitants. They did the same thing to all the smaller cities as well and returned to Jerusalem.

II Samuel 13 *Amnon and Tamar, Absalom's revenge*
David's son Absalom had a beautiful sister named Tamar. Another of David's sons, Amnon, had a crush on her. He was so infatuated with Tamar; he almost made himself

ill with frustration, because she was a virgin. Amnon had a cousin named Jonadab. He asked Amnon what was wrong. Amnon told him how crazy he was about Tamar. Jonadab gave Amnon a plan, "Act like you're sick. Ask your father to send her to your place and cook you a special meal." So Amnon lay in his bed, acting sick. When David came to visit him, he made the request. David sent for Tamar. She came to Amnon's bed, made dough and kneaded it in front of Amnon. When the cakes were ready she presented them to Amnon. Then Amnon sent all the servants from the room. He asked Tamar to feed him the cakes in his bed. As she was giving him the cakes, he took her hand and said, "Make love with me my sister." Tamar replied, "No, this isn't proper. It is a disgraceful thing. Please do not violate me, I would be humiliated, and you would be looked at in disgrace. Ask the king and he will probably give me to you." But Amnon wouldn't listen and forced himself sexually on Tamar.

When Amnon was finished, his hate for Tamar was as complete as his infatuation had been. He told her to go away. She said, "This is worse than what you've already done." He wouldn't listen to her and had his servants remove her. She put ashes on her head and removed the sleeves from her blouse because only virgins wore long sleeves. Her brother, Absalom, tried to comfort her. When King David heard about the incident, he was angry. Absalom hated Amnon because of the rape but said nothing to Amnon.

Two years later at the end of his shearing season, Absalom had a party in Ephraim. He invited all of David's sons. Considering the burden to Absalom, David didn't want to send them, but Absalom persisted. Peculiar as the invitation sounded, David finally sent all his sons. Absalom's servants killed Amnon during a cocktail party and all the rest of David's sons fled.

Back in Jerusalem the first report David received was that Absalom had killed all his sons. David ripped his clothes and lay on the ground wailing. Jonadab, Amnon's cousin, said, "Take comfort my king, surely Absalom has killed only Amnon because of the incident with his sister Tamar." As Jonadab was speaking, some of David's sons were entering the city, and David was comforted. Absalom fled to Geshur. David longed to go out to Absalom. He wasn't angry about the death of Amnon.

II Samuel 14 *Joab intercedes, Absalom recalled*
Joab could see how King David missed Absalom. He formulated a plan. He sent a woman into the king for a hearing. She reported a domestic issue that was similar to David's situation with Absalom. The story moved David. He perceived Joab had sent her; she did not deny it. David said, "I will send for my son Absalom." Joab was very

pleased that his plan worked and went to Geshur to get Absalom. David instructed Joab to take Absalom to his own house in Jerusalem, but did not request him to be brought to the palace.

Absalom was the most handsome man in Israel. His hair was thick and heavy. He had three sons and one beautiful daughter named Tamar. Absalom had been in Jerusalem for two years, and he had still not seen David. Absalom sent two messages to Joab that went unanswered. Finally, he told his servants to burn one of Joab's fields, which was next to Absolom's property. This got Joab's attention, so he came to Absalom. Absalom said, "I have left messages for you, but you have not answered. As it is, I should have stayed in Geshur. Go to the king and ask him to send for me." Joab arranged a meeting between Absalom and David. Absalom prostrated himself before the king, and David kissed him.

II Samuel 15:1-18 *Absalom's conspiracy*
Later, Absalom provided himself a chariot and horses and 50 messengers. He made a habit of going to the city gate each morning. He would speak to people coming in to have an audience with the king for judgment on certain issues. Absalom would listen to their issues and say, "Yes, you're right about this. Unfortunately, the king won't listen. Oh, that I would be made king, and we could really get some things done!" After a few years of this course, the people of Israel felt more loyalty to Absalom than they did to David.

One day Absalom said to David, "When I was hiding from you in Geshur, I made a vow to the Lord, that if he brought me back to Jerusalem, I would go to Hebron and serve him. Please let me go fulfill my vow." David said, "Go in peace." Absalom sent spies to all the areas of Israel were he had allies, (the fruits of all his promises at the gate). The spies spread this message: "As soon as you hear the trumpet, announce; 'Absalom is king in Hebron!'" Absalom's conspiracy was very strong. David's approval rating was plummeting, while Absalom's was growing quickly.

II Samuel 15:19 16:14 *David quits town*
A messenger came to David, "The hearts of the men of Israel are with Absalom." David was fearful and said, "We need to leave the city because he could attack us quickly, and we are not properly prepared." His advisors agreed and they all fled Jerusalem, except for ten concubines David left to care for the palace. He took the elite palace militia and all his faithful men who were with him in Gath and Ziklag. One of David's old war buddies, named Ittai, had just come to visit David in Jerusalem. David encouraged him to return to his home. No one would associate Ittai with David, so he would be in no

danger. But Ittai said, "As God lives and you live, where you go, I go; if you die, I die." So Ittai and his whole household left with David's group. Everybody in the group had heavy hearts, many shed tears.

Zadok and Abiathar, the priests, wanted to follow David with the ark of God. But David said, "Take the ark back; hopefully God will return me to Jerusalem. Maybe He's removed His favor from me. It's up to Him now. At any rate I can use your help. Your sons can be messengers between us. I'll wait by the fords of the Jordan until I get word from you."

As David was heading up the Mount of Olives, he was told that Ahithophel, one of his trusted counselors, had defected to Absalom. David commented, "I hope his wisdom is turned to foolishness!" At that time another of his trusted advisors, Hushai, met him with torn clothes and dirt in his hair. David said, "Hushai, I want you to return to Jerusalem. Tell Absalom that you will serve him as you served me. Then you can be my eyes and ears and possibly thwart Ahithophel's counsel. I already have Zadok and Abiathar in Jerusalem to provide the communication link between us." So Hushai, David's friend, returned to Jerusalem at about the same time Absalom was arriving back in Jerusalem from his trip to Hebron.

Meanwhile Ziba, the servant of Jonathan's son, Mephibosheth, came to David with two saddled donkeys. He had two hundred loaves of bread, a hundred clusters of raisins, a hundred summer fruits and a jug of wine. David said, "What is all this? Where is Mephibosheth?" Ziba answered, "The food and drink is for your journey. Mephibosheth stayed in Jerusalem saying, 'Today the house of Israel will return the kingdom of my father to me.'" The king replied, "Ziba, today all that belonged to Mephibosheth has become yours."

As David and his group continued their march, a man named Shimei came out on the hill beside them and started cursing David. He threw rocks and dirt down on the procession and yelled, "Get out of here you worthless fellow, you man of bloodshed. The Lord is returning on you all the wickedness you have done." Abishai, one of David's valiant men said, "Why should this dead dog be allowed to continue cursing the king. I'll go up and put a permanent end to his babble!" David didn't let Abishai kill Shimei. He said, "Let him wail. He's probably right. My own son has rebelled against me; why shouldn't this Benjaminite feel the same? Perhaps God will see all this horrible trouble I'm in and help me."

II Samuel 16:15-17:14 *David's exit strategy works out well*

Back in Jerusalem, Absalom, David's rebellious son, Ahithophel, the counselor who deserted David, and Hushai, David's friend who was risking his life on a critical mission, had their first meeting. Absalom said to Hushai, "So this is how you repay your friend, by serving me?" Hushai replied, "My job is to advise the king of Israel. You're the king of Israel now, not David." Absalom turned to Ahithophel and asked for his take on things and his advice. Ahithophel said, "Go have sex with your father's concubines in the royal palace. All the people who are with you will see that you have taken what was your father's, and they will have more confidence in you. Furthermore, let me muster 12,000 good men tonight, to pursue David. I'll come upon him when he and his people are tired. When David is dead, your kingdom will be quickly established."

Absalom liked the plan. A tent was pitched on the roof of the palace and Absalom went into David's concubines in the sight of all Israel. He returned to Hushai and said, "What do you say about Ahithophel's advice to pursue David?" Hushai answered, "Taking David and his men tonight is not wise. You know your father and his men. They are all proven warriors. Are you sure David is with them? How many times did David escape Saul? Those 12,000 men would go out with only a chance to catch David and a very good possibility of being defeated by the most valiant men in Israel. That's not a very good way to start. I advise you to consolidate your power here and assemble a force so large you'll fall on David and his men like the dew falls on the ground. You will personally lead this army. Even if David withdraws into a city you will have enough force to destroy it. You will make a name for yourself." So Absalom did not follow Ahithophel's entire plan. When Ahithophel saw that not all his counsel was followed, he knew his position was weak. He returned to his hometown, put his house in order and hung himself.

II Samuel 17:15 - 18:5 *David receives counsel*

Hushai sent word to David through Zadok and Abiathar's sons, Ahimaaz and Jonathan. They were almost caught but eluded capture by hiding in a well, and the help of a woman who misguided their pursuers. Hushai's advice was for the royal party to head across the fords of the Jordan, out of Israel. David followed Hushai's counsel. Meanwhile, Absalom was also following Hushai's advice. He sent a large force after the king. He put one of David's cousins, Amasa, in charge of the mission. Absalom went along as well. Meanwhile David was being fully provisioned on the east side of the Jordan by the people of Rabbah, the people of Ammon, and by Barzillai of Gilead.

David organized his men. He separated them into three groups lead by Joab, Abishai, and Ittai. The king said, "I will surely fight with you." This idea met with protest. They all said, "If you fight, you will be the target. They'd rather kill you than ten thousand of us." So David relented and stayed out of the battle. But David ordered his men to deal kindly with Absalom.

II Samuel 18:6-33 *Outcome*
The battle took place in the forests of Ephraim. David's forces prevailed and killed 20,000 of Absalom's troops. Actually, the forest killed more that day than the sword. When Absalom was riding through the forest, his head got caught in some oak branches. Word got to Joab that Absalom was caught. Joab told the messenger, "If you would have killed him I would have given you ten pieces of silver and a belt!" The man replied, "I wouldn't take 1000 pieces of silver. We both heard the king say: 'Deal kindly with my son.' I would have done the deed, and you would have let me take the punishment!" Joab said, "I will not waste my time here with you." He went straight to where Absalom was hanging, still alive, and struck him with a spear. Joab's ten armor bearers also participated in the killing.

Joab blew the trumpet and the fighting stopped. They dug a grave for Absalom and erected a great heap of stones over it. Absalom had already erected a pillar to himself because he had no sons. It's called Absalom's Monument. Zadok's son, Ahimaaz, wanted to run to the king with the news. Joab dissuaded Ahimaaz and sent word to David by a Cushite. Ahimaaz convinced Joab to let him run after the Cushite and overtook him. Now David was sitting by the gates of the city and a watchman called out, "Runner coming in!" David thought, "If it's only one, it must be good news!" Then the watchman cried out again, "I now see a new runner; the first runner looks like Ahimaaz." David reasoned, "If it is Zadok's son Ahimaaz, it is surely good news!" Ahimaaz arrived at David's feet and cried, "Blessed be the Lord for He has delivered your enemies to you today!" David replied, "What about Absalom? How did it go for him?" Ahimaaz answered, "There was a lot going on so I can't tell you about that." Then the Cushite finally arrived and announced, "God has defeated all those who rose against you!" David asked, "Is Absolom OK?" The Cushite answered, "Let all of your enemies meet the same end he has met!" At this David was deeply moved, "Oh my son Absalom, my son, my son, Absalom, I wish I could have died instead of you!"

II Samuel 19:1-8 *Joab's disapproval*
When Joab heard David was grieving for Absalom, he was livid. He felt a day that should have been celebrated as a victory was turning out to be a day of mourning for a

slain enemy. All of David's people returned to their homes, like people who had been humiliated in battle. Joab burst into the house where King David was staying. "Today you have made people ashamed, who should be proud. These people risked their lives to save you and your family and your concubines! Now you mourn the death of the one who started the whole thing! Today we all know that if we were dead and Absalom alive you would be happy! I promise you, if you don't get back to the gate and act like a king, you won't be king tomorrow." So David went out to the gate and the people came out to him.

II Samuel 19:9-43 *David's return*
All the people in Israel spoke to each other this way, "David delivered us from all our enemies. Then he fled from his own son Absalom. We anointed Absalom king over us and now David has defeated Absalom. Shouldn't we invite the king back?" Then David sent a message through Zadok and Abiathar to the elders of Judah saying, "I am your relative. Why have you not invited me back to my house? Today, I will take the command of my army from Joab and give it to Absalom's general, Amasa." So all the men in Judah followed David. They came to escort David back to Jerusalem.

As they were crossing the Jordan, Shimei, the one who cursed David, Ziba the servant of Jonathan's son Mephibosheth, and 1000 other Benjaminites came to David. Shimei fell at David's feet asking forgiveness. Abishai said, "Shouldn't we kill this guy now?" David answered, "You and your brother Joab always seem ready to kill someone! No one will be killed today. Don't I know I am king in Israel again?" Then Mephibosheth came to David. He looked terrible. He hadn't taken any care of himself at all. David asked, "Why didn't you come with us?" Mephibosheth answered, "Ziba has deceived you. I wanted to come, but he left me. You know I'm crippled. You're the king. Like an angel, nothing is hidden from you; do what you think is right. Who am I but a dead dog and who is alive in my family? How could I have eaten at your table...." David interrupted, "Don't go on talking about your affairs. I have decided that you and Ziba will divide Saul's estate."

Barzillai, the Gileadite, who had helped provision David when he had crossed the fords, accompanied David to the Jordan. David invited him to come to Jerusalem. He declined saying he was too old. He wanted to die in his own hometown. Once they crossed over the Jordan the people of Israel and the people of Judah had some words because the people of Judah were accompanying David and the rest of Israel had not been invited. The words of Judah were harsher than the words of Israel.

The Story Bible for Adults

II Samuel 20 *Revolts and murder*

There was a worthless fellow named Sheba from the family of Benjamin. He blew the trumpet and cried, "We don't have anything to do with David! He's not our king! Everyone leave him and go to their tents!" So all of Israel left David, but the tribe of Judah remained loyal.

David returned to Jerusalem and put the ten concubines he left there under house arrest. Their needs were taken care of but they couldn't come or go, so they lived like widows for the rest of their lives. The king instructed Amasa, his new general, to call the army together within three days to deal with Sheba. After three days Amasa still hadn't mustered the whole army. Then David called Abishai, Joab's brother. "Take the palace militia and go after Sheba or he'll find a fortified city and we'll have a serious problem." Abishai took Joab with the palace militia and all David's valiant warriors to deal with Sheba. Along the way Amasa met them with the army he had assembled. Joab approached Amasa as if he were going to greet him and instead sank his sword into Amasa's stomach. His guts spilled to the ground. One of Joab's men, who was with Amasa, yelled, "All who are with David and Joab, follow Joab!" But the men who had come with Amasa didn't seem to be responding because Amasa was lying in his blood in the middle of the road. So Joab's man moved him into the field and covered his body. Then all the men followed Joab.

When Joab and his men found Sheba, he was holed up in a fortified city called Abel Beth-maacah. Joab and his men began the hard task of building a mound against the wall, so they could storm the city. Within a short time, however, a wise woman came to the wall and called down to Joab, "Joab, this is a peaceful city. As you know Abel is reputed as a place to come to settle disputes. Why destroy a city like this?" Joab replied, "Ma'm, I don't want to destroy Abel, but you have within your walls a man who has committed treason by starting a rebellion against the king. If you deliver him, I will not destroy Abel!" The woman responded, "Very soon you will see his head come to you over the wall." She went back and explained the situation to the people of Abel. They cut Sheba's head off and threw it over the wall. So Joab blew the trumpet, they collected Sheba's head, and returned to Jerusalem.

So, Joab was still commander of the army. Benaiah commanded the king's elite palace militia, Adoram was over the forced labor, Jehoshaphat was recorder, Sheva was scribe and Zadok and Abiathar remained as priests.

II Samuel 21-22 *Famines and wars*

Now there was a famine in Israel that lasted three years. When David asked God why, the Lord said, "It is because Saul killed the Gibeonites." (The Gibeonites deceived Joshua by pretending they had traveled a long distance. Believing they didn't live in the land, Joshua made a treaty with them.) Saul had sought to wipe them out because of his zeal for Israel and Judah. So David said to the remaining Gibeonites, "What can we do for you to make amends for the brutality of Saul?" The Gibeonites replied, "We aren't concerned about money. Give us seven male relatives from the man who sought to destroy us and we will hang them." David spared Mephibosheth because of his oath with Jonathan. He gave the Gibeonite sons from two of Saul's daughters, Rizpah and Merab. The Gibeonites hanged them. Rizpah stayed by the bodies through the whole barley harvest until it rained, keeping any birds from eating the corpses. When David heard about Rizpah's acts, he had the bones of Saul and Jonathan taken from Jabesh-gilead. (The brave men from there had retrieved their bodies from the Philistines.) He brought them to Saul's family grave in the territory of Benjamin. He also put the seven men hanged in the same grave. Then rainfall returned to normal.

At this time the Philistines came back to fight against Israel. David went out to fight with the army. A descendant of Goliath named Ishbi-benob came against David on the battlefield to kill him. David had been fighting all day and was tired, so Joab's brother, Abishai, came to David's aid and killed the giant. The army wouldn't let David on the battlefield anymore after that. Goliath had four sons who fought against Israel. Sibbecai killed one, Elhanan killed another and Jonathan, David's nephew, killed one who had six fingers on each hand and six toes on each foot!

II Samuel 23 *David's Hall of Fame*

David had some very mighty men who fought with him. There were three who stood out. First was Josheb-basshebeth, they called him Adino for short, because he killed 800 men in one day! Next there was Eleazar. In one battle he struck down Philistines all day long until he couldn't lift his sword. Israel won the battle because of him. Next was Shammah. He became trapped in a field full of Philistines because all the men around him fled. He stood his ground, struck the Philistines, and Israel won a great victory. When David was fleeing Saul, there was a camp of Philistines who were holding the well near Bethlehem. David had a craving and said, "I could sure use a drink from the Bethlehem well!" So these three mighty men went down, defeated the Philistines, and brought David the water. David poured it out because the men had risked their lives. These are examples of exploits these three had throughout their careers.

The Story Bible for Adults

There were thirty very mighty men in David's guard. Abishai was the most honored of them. He killed 300 in one day with his spear. He was most honored of the thirty but he was not honored among the top three. Benaiah did many mighty deeds. He fought against the two most honored heroes of Moab and beat them. One snowy day, Benaiah went down into a pit and killed a lion. He also killed a mighty Egyptian who had a spear. Benaiah went after him with just a club. He was able to take the spear from the Egyptian and killed him with it! Benaiah was honored right up there with the three but not as highly as they were. Some other prominent names among the thirty included: Asahel, Joab's brother, who Abner killed. The three who killed the giants were members of the thirty: Elhanan, Shammah and Jonathan. Ittai, who joined David when Absalom rebelled, and Uriah, the brave warrior whom David had killed in the siege of Rabbah, were also counted with David's mighty men. There were 37 in all.

II Samuel 24 *misguided census and an altar*
At this time David hit a low in his life by deciding to take a census in Israel. He brought Joab into his office and told him about his plan. Joab replied, "I hope God adds one hundred to each person who is in Israel; but David, aren't they all your servants? Why take a census? This seems like a bad thing to me, a thing that will cause guilt to come on Israel." David held fast and charged Joab with the task of going through the land and numbering the people. Joab took over nine months to finish the job. He didn't count any Levites or any from the house of Benjamin because he disagreed with the whole census idea anyway. There were over a million warriors in Israel, and about five hundred thousand in Judah.

David began feeling guilty about taking the census. He prayed to the Lord, "God, this is a bad thing I've done, please take this sin from me!" God sent Gad, the prophet, to see David. Gad said, "God will give you three choices about how to pay for this evil. You can see three years of famine in the land, or you can flee while your enemies pursue you for three months, or you can have three days of the Lord's judgment in Israel." David answered, "This is horrible! I choose to fall into the hand of the Lord, rather than the hand of man. Perhaps God will grant me some mercy." So pestilence came upon Israel and 70,000 died. As the Angel of God was coming up to Jerusalem to destroy it, God finally relented. The Angel of the Lord was standing by the threshing facility owned by a man named Ornan. David saw the angel. Then David and the elders fell on their faces wearing burlap clothes. Gad was instructed by the Lord to tell David to construct an altar by the threshing facility owned by Ornan. So David went to Ornan, "Let me buy this facility and the land it's on, so I can build an altar to God." Ornan, who had seen the angel too said, "David, you take the facility and the land."

David protested, "It won't be from me if you give it; I need to pay for it." Ornan received full price for the property and David built an altar where sacrifices were offered.

The Kings and Chronicles

Kings and Chronicles present the story of the kings of Israel. In this telling the two perspectives are joined as they occur chronologically. The books of Kings will be primarily listed on each page. Chronicles will be listed when it fills in a part of the history not covered in Kings. I Chronicles reviews Israel's history and records genealogy and detail about priestly service. The story continues in the 22nd chapter of I Chronicles.

Many books in the Bible that are not history related were written during this period in Israel: Psalms, Proverbs, Ecclesiastes, Song of Solomon, and many of the Prophets. Short samples of these writings are inserted into the story line chronologically.

I Chronicles 22:14-19 *David instructs and helps Salomon*
King David knew he was not to build a temple for God. But, he did accumulate large stores of building materials for the construction: iron, bronze and cedar timbers. David spoke to his son, "Solomon, I had intended to build a house for the name of the Lord. But he said, 'You shall not build a house for me because you have been a man of warfare and bloodshed. You will have a son who will build my house. I will give him peace on every side, and he will build my house. I will be his father and will establish his kingdom forever.' I believe he was speaking of you, my son, so you've got a big job to do. Be strong and courageous. Don't be discouraged. Follow all of God's laws and you will prosper. I have, with great pains, set aside one hundred talents of gold, one million talents of silver and more bronze and iron than you can weigh. I have timber and stone in storage. I have collected a pool of skilled workers. May the Lord be with you in this project." David commanded all the leaders of Israel to help Solomon.

I Chronicles 28:1- 29:30 *Plans and David's prayer*
David brought Israel together in Jerusalem, all the dignitaries and mighty men were present. David made a speech about his desire to build a temple but said that God had chosen Solomon for the task. He presented Solomon with the exact plans that God had helped him create for the temple with its porches, storehouses, upper and inner rooms and the room for the mercy seat. These plans also included lists of all the utensils for

service and worship and the weight of gold for various items. He prayed a blessing over the entire project.

I Kings 1 *Salomon made King*

David was very old. His servants covered him with blankets, but he could not get warm. They searched the land for a beautiful virgin to be David's companion. They found a very attractive young lady named Abishag. She would lie with David and keep him warm but they were not lovers.

Adonijah, a very handsome man and one of David's sons, felt he was rightful heir to the throne, not Solomon. He put together a personal guard. David never dissuaded him. Adonijah also conferred with Joab and Abiathar and they joined him. Zadok, Benaiah, Nathan and the mighty men were not with Adonijah. Adonijah invited all the king's sons, along with Joab and Abiathar to offer sacrifices before anointing himself king. Zadok, Benaiah, Nathan and the Mighty Men were not invited.

Nathan went to Bathsheba and said, "Go immediately to David and say, 'Isn't Solomon supposed to be the next king? Why is Adonijah becoming king' I will follow you into the king and confirm what you've said." So Bathsheba went in to David and bowed respectfully, "My lord, you swore that Solomon would be king, but now Adonijah is making himself king. Abiathar and Joab are with him. I'm afraid Solomon and I will be in danger if he successfully steals the throne." Nathan followed Bathsheba. "Did you say Adonijah should be king?...I don't think so, but he's down sacrificing oxen and is surrounded by all your sons and they are saying to Adonijah: Long live the king!"

David said, "Take Solomon and bring him to Gihon on my own mule with Zadok the priest. Anoint him there with Benaiah and Nathan and all the mighty men. Blow the trumpet and say, 'Long live king Solomon.' Then bring him back to Jerusalem and he will sit on my throne here in my palace." Benaiah said, "We will do it and may the Lord be with Solomon even more than he was with you!" When they did these things the whole city broke into celebration. When Adonijah heard what had happened and how the people were celebrating, he and those with him became terrified and split up in different directions. Adonijah went to the altar and put his hands around the horns of the altar. King Solomon heard about it and said if there was no evil intent in his actions, he could go home. So Adonijah was spared that day.

I Kings 2:1-12 *David dies*

As David's time to pass away came near, he called Solomon to him, "I will die soon. Be strong and courageous. Show yourself as a man to Israel. Be careful to follow the whole law of God with all your heart. A king who loves God and follows Him is like a beautiful sunrise. If you follow the law, the promises God has made about always having a man on this throne will be sure. You know that Joab has shed much innocent blood, Abner and Amasa, to name two. See that he does not die in peace. Show kindness to Barzillai from Gilead, as he did to me when I fled from Absolom. Shimei, the Benjamite who cursed me as I fled Absolom has been spared as I lived, per my promise to him. After I'm dead do not let him go unpunished. David died and was buried in Jerusalem.

David was a skilled musician and songwriter. The words of his songs are found in the book of Psalms. David wrote nearly half of all the songs in Psalms. One of David's first and most famous songs was probably written out in the fields where he worked as a shepherd. It is the 23 Psalm (All these Psalms are quoted from the New American Standard Bible):

Psalms

The Lord is my shepherd,
I shall not be in want
He makes me lie down in green pastures
He leads me beside still waters
He restores my soul
He guides me in the paths of righteousness
for His name's sake
Even though I walk trough the valley of the shadow of death
I will fear no evil for You are with me
Your rod and Your staff, they comfort me
You prepare a table before me
in the presence of my enemies
You anoint my head with oil
my cup over flows
Surely goodness and mercy will follow me all the days of my life
and I will dwell in the house of the Lord forever!

The prophet Nathan told David about a great King who would be a descendant of his that would have an everlasting kingdom. Psalm 2 looks forward to his reign:

Why do the nations conspire and the peoples plot in vain?
The kings of earth take their stand and the rulers gather together against the Lord and against His anointed one.
"Let us break their chains", they say, and throw off their fetters.
The one enthroned in heaven laughs, the Lord scoffs at them.
Then He rebukes them in His anger and terrifies them in His wrath, saying,
"I have installed my King, on Zion, My holy hill."
I will proclaim the decree of the Lord:
He said to Me, "You are My Son; today I have become Your father.
Ask of Me, and I will make the nations Your inheritance, the ends of the earth Your possession.
You will rule them with an iron scepter, You will dash them to pieces like pottery."
Therefore you kings be wise, be warned, you rulers of the earth.
Serve the Lord with fear and rejoice with trembling.
Kiss the Son, lest He be angry and you be destroyed in your way,
for His wrath can flare up in a moment.
Blessed are all who take refuge in Him.

Some of the Psalms also seem to speak of one who would suffer. Psalm 22: 1-18:

My God, my God, why have you forsaken me?
Why are you so far from saving me, so far from the words of my groaning?
Oh my God I cry out by day, but you do not answer, by night and am not silent.
Yet you are enthroned as the Holy One, you are the praise of Israel.
In you our fathers put their trust, they trusted and you delivered them.
They cried out to you and were saved, in you they trusted and were not disappointed.
But I am a worm not a man, scorned by men and despised by the people.
All who see me mock me, they hurl insults, shaking their heads:
"He trusts in the Lord, let the Lord rescue him.
Let him deliver him, since he delights in him.
Yet you brought me out of the womb, you made me trust in you,
 even at my mother's breast.
From birth I was cast upon you, from my mother's womb you have been my God.
Do not be far from me, for trouble is near and there is no one to help me.
Many strong bulls surround me, strong bulls from Bashan encircle me.
Roaring lions tearing their prey open their mouths wide against me.
I am poured out like water and my bones are out of joint.
My heart has turned to wax, it has melted away within me.

My strength is dried up like potsherd, my tongue sticks to the roof of my mouth,
You lay me in the dust of death.
Dogs have surrounded me, a band of evil men has encircled me,
they have pierced my hands and my feet.
I can count all my bones, people stare and gloat over me.
They have divided my garments among them and cast lots for my clothing....

Most scholars believe that Job was the first book written in the Bible. In the Bible it appears before Psalms.

Job

There was a man named Job, who was upright and turned away from evil. He had seven sons, three daughters, and was the richest man in the east. One day, Satan appeared before the Lord with the rest of the sons of God. He talked with the Lord about Job. Satan alleged that Job would curse God if he lost his wealth and family. So God allowed Satan to work against Job and test him. Soon, Job lost his entire estate to natural disasters and his family was killed by an overwhelming band of Chaldeans, all in a single day. Through it all Job never cursed God, but said, "Naked I came from my mother's womb, naked I will return. The Lord gives and the Lord takes away, blessed be the name of the Lord."

In Satan's next meeting with the Lord, he claimed Job would curse God to his face if he lost his health. So God allowed Satan to inflict illness on Job. The next day Job was covered with oozing boils. He sat scratched at himself with a broken piece of pottery in the ashes of one of his ruined buildings. His wife challenged him to curse God. But, Job did not sin with his lips.

Three friends of Job decided to visit him in his adversity. They all sat with out saying a word for seven days. Job finally spoke; he cursed the day he was born. Job spent the next part of the day defending himself against his friends' assertions that he was to blame for his afflictions because of some un-defined sin. No specific accusations were leveled. Long dissertations were delivered regarding the characteristics of God, but the consensus among the three was that Job had a problem with God that he wasn't willing to talk about. Job continued to hold his position; he was fully aware of who God was, and that he had been true to his beliefs. He expressed how much he hated his life in the midst of this horrible trial and how additionally hurtful this conversation with "friends" had made it.

A young man who had listened the entire afternoon felt compelled to put his position on record. He chastised the older men for not bringing any specific charge against Job. He urged Job to confess his sin, because he must be sinning to have all this adversity befall him. He rebukes Job for not confessing and justifies God's use of affliction against Job.

Then the Lord addressed the group from a whirlwind. God speaks about their ignorance of how creation was accomplished and His work in nature. Job answers by simply saying he was speechless in the presence of God. God continued to explain how his work in creation and nature illustrated his character. Job agreed and acknowledged his humble position before God.

Then God blesses Job and rebukes Jobs friends for their incorrect attitudes about Job and God. He instructs Job's friends to offer sacrifices with Job so that he could pray for them.

Job's riches were re-established so that he was twice as rich as before. He had seven more sons and his three new daughters were the finest looking in the land. He died a happy old man.

<>

I Kings 2:13-46 *Salomon's first actions as King*
After David died, Adonijah approached Bathsheba. He asked her to go to Solomon and request that Abishag, David's beautiful companion, be given to him as a wife. When Bathsheba made the request to Solomon, he replied, "Why are you asking me this? You might as well say, 'Give the entire kingdom to Adonijah.' Adonijah, my older brother, along with Abiathar and Joab conspired to take my throne! This is the last attempt at my throne he will make." Benaiah, the captain of the palace guard killed Adonijah by direct orders from Solomon. Solomon also called for Abiathar and sent him away to his own house. So Abiathar was no longer a priest in Israel. He was the last of the house of Eli to be a priest in Israel.

When Joab heard about these events he went to the Tabernacle and held fast to the altar. When Solomon heard of it, he sent Benaiah to kill him. Benaiah went to the tabernacle and called for Joab to come out. Joab said, "You'll have to kill me in here." Benaiah sent word back to Solomon and Solomon instructed Benaiah to go into the temple and kill him. Joab was buried at his country home. Benaiah took charge of the entire army.

The king then called for Shimei, the man who had harassed David when he fled from Absolom, and put him under house arrest in Jerusalem. He said, "Stay here in your house in Jerusalem. If you leave town you will pay with your life." Three years later two of Shimei's servants ran away into Philistia. He went after them and brought them back to Jerusalem. When Solomon heard of it, he had Shimei brought in. He said, "Shimei you agreed not to leave the city. Now the evil you did to my father will finally be returned to you." Solomon ordered Benaiah to kill him.

I Kings 3 *Salomon's wisdom*
Early in his reign, Solomon established an alliance with the Egyptian Pharaoh and he took one of Pharaoh's daughters as his wife. At this time the people didn't have the temple, so they offered sacrifices at various high places. Solomon loved God and walked according to the law. He went to the tabernacle in Gibeon to offer sacrifices. He offered 1000 burnt offerings. God appeared to Solomon in a dream and said, "Whatever you wish, I will give it to you." Solomon answered, "You have been very good to my father David. You have put me on his throne. I feel overwhelmed by the task of being king. Israel is a great nation with countless people! I need wisdom to be able to handle this job correctly. Please give me wisdom."

God was pleased that Solomon had made this request. "Because you have asked for this, not a long life and great riches, I will give you the wisdom you have requested. You're going to be the wisest person who has ever ruled and there will be none like you again. I am also going to give you the things you have not requested, riches and honor like no king has ever received. If you walk according to my instruction, I will also give you a long life.

When Solomon returned to Jerusalem, two prostitutes came to him for judgment on a dispute. They both lived in the same house and had small infants born three days apart. One of the babies was killed because his mother had rolled on him in her sleep and suffocated him. She took her dead baby and exchanged it with the live baby sleeping with the other mother. In the morning one woman woke to find a dead baby. As she inspected it in the light of morning, it became clear it wasn't hers. The other woman would not return the living child claiming it was hers. After Solomon had heard the story he said, "Give me a sword. I will divide the remaining child in two pieces so each can have half." The child's real mother said, "Oh no, don't kill the child, give him to the other woman." While the other woman said, "Divide him, he will be neither yours or mine." Then Solomon said, "Give the child to the first woman, she is the mother." When the people of Israel heard about how Solomon judged with such wisdom, they respected the king.

I Kings 4 *Salomon wealth (and wisdom)*
Israel was a prosperous and happy place in the days of Solomon. All the regions paid taxes to Solomon. Solomon had 40,000 stalls for his horses and 12,000 horsemen. Solomon had many servants who saw to his every need, and they were all happy and fed. Solomon continued to get smarter; he was the wisest king in the world at that time. He wrote 3000 proverbs and 1005 songs. He knew all about nature and could identify all the plants and animals.

Proverbs

Here is a sampling of the proverbs of Solomon quoted from the New American Standard Bible:

The Lord gives wisdom.
From his mouth come knowledge and understanding
Trust in the Lord with all your heart.
Do not lean to your own understanding.
In all your ways acknowledge Him,
and He will make your paths straight.
Do not be wise in your own eyes.
Fear the Lord and turn away from evil.
It will be healing to your body
and refreshment to your bones.
Honor the Lord from your wealth
and from the first of all you produce,
then your barns will be filled with plenty,
your vats will overflow with new wine
Do not reject the discipline of the Lord
Or loathe His reproof.
For whom the Lord loves, He reproves,
even as a father, the son in whom He delights.

Solomon also wrote the book of Ecclesiastes. Solomon, who was able to fulfill any fantasy of wealth, power or love came to the end of his life and realized any benefit that life could provide was hollow. His final conclusion: "Fear God and obey His commands."

Solomon is also credited with the authorship of the Bible's most romantic tale, The Song of Songs. It is a story of the deep love between a young country girl and the king of Israel.

I Kings 5-7 *The Temple (and Salomon's house) built*

When Hiram, the king of Tyre and David's friend, heard of Solomon's succession he sent messengers to Solomon. Solomon told Hiram about his plans for the Lord's temple. Hiram and Solomon cut a deal. Hiram sent down cedar wood and skilled workers in return for wages from Solomon. Solomon had 30,000 laborers who went to Lebanon in 10,000 man relays, one month in Lebanon, two months in Israel. He had 70,000 stone transporters and 80,000 stonecutters. There were 3300 foremen. Solomon started the project during the fourth year of his reign. This was 480 years after God had brought the Hebrews out of Egypt.

The dimensions of the temple were all carefully established and built. All the stones were prepared at the quarry. There was never the sound of hammer or iron tool in the temple while it was being built. The stone was completely overlaid with finely carved cedar, so there was no visible stone inside the temple. The temple had a Holy Place and a Holy of Holies similar to the tabernacle. It took seven years to build the temple. Solomon also built a palace and throne room for himself that took thirteen years to build. Solomon brought a man from Tyre named Hiram, (not the king). This man was a widow's son who was skilled in all kinds of craftsmanship, particularly with bronze work. He did much of the detail work in both buildings. Because of the massive quantity, the weight of the bronze in the project was never completely tabulated. The altar, the table for the showbread, all the lamp stands, snuffers and implements were pure gold. Solomon filled the treasuries of the temple with the items David had set aside for that purpose.

I Kings 8 *Dedication of the Temple*

Finally, the temple was finished. It was time to bring in the ark. The ark contained the two tablets that Moses put there at Mount Horeb. There were many sacrifices and offerings during the dedication weeks. The dedication took 14 days. When they placed the ark in its place, the glory of the Lord filled the building. Solomon stood up to offer his prayer of dedication, "The Lord has come to inhabit His house!" Then he turned and blessed the people, "God is a wonderful God. David wanted to build this temple, but God told him his son would come after him to build it. This has been fulfilled just as

God said! He has kept all the promises He made to His people. God is so big that even the heavens can't contain Him, yet He has chosen this city and this house, to place His name here. Now God, please look on this house and keep Your spirit here and with Your people. If a man sins (there is not a man who doesn't sin) let him come to this house and make himself right with You again. If Your people are defeated in battle or if there is a drought or famine because we have sinned against You, let us turn to You here in this place and pray to You in heaven. Hear our prayer and answer with victory or rain from heaven or healing from our diseases. If a foreigner hears about You, which I am sure they will, listen to and answer his prayer that he makes to You here, so all the earth will know about how great You are, as we do in Israel. Wherever we go in battle or carried away with defeat, let us be able to look back towards this place and make our prayer to You. Hear us and grant us deliverance or victory. Whenever we stray from Your path, help us to return to You with our whole hearts. You have separated Israel from all the peoples to be Your people. Please listen to us when we call upon You!" Then Solomon blessed the congregation, "Now, may we always follow God with our whole hearts because He has called us to be His people. He has kept His promises and delivered His inheritance to us. May He continue to provide for us each day so the whole world will know that the Lord is God, there is no other. Dedicate your hearts completely to Him and follow His instructions."

After this they offered many sacrifices and worshipped and celebrated seven more days. On the eighth day Solomon sent the people home. They went with happiness in their hearts for all God had done for David and for Israel.

I Kings 9 *God sees the Temple, settlement with Hiram, and Salomon's fleet*
After this, God appeared to Solomon again and said, "I have heard your prayers and supplications concerning the temple, and I will keep My eyes on the place perpetually and My name will be on the place forever. Now as for you, if you will walk before Me as David did with uprightness and integrity, then I will establish your throne. But if you or your sons turn away from Me and worship other gods, then this nation will be cut off and this temple will be a pile of ruins. People will say, 'It is because they have forsaken the Lord that these adversities have come upon them.'"

So, Solomon had been king twenty years. Solomon gave 20 cities in Galilee to Hiram in payment for all the cedar and gold he had sent down to Israel. Hiram came out to see the cities Solomon had given him. He wasn't very pleased with them but still sent Solomon many thousand pounds of gold.

Solomon had thousands of men in forced labor from among the peoples David had conquered. He built many cities. He also improved the wall around Jerusalem. King Solomon continued to do business with Hiram. They built ships and staffed them with sailors from Tyre and from Israel. They got tons of gold from the expeditions these ships made.

I Kings 10:1-13 *The Queen of Sheba*
When the Queen of Sheba heard about Solomon's wisdom, she decided to come see for herself and ask him some difficult questions. She came with a large caravan and tons of goods. Solomon did not disappoint her. He answered all of her questions completely. She was also very impressed with the sophistication of the servants and cupbearers. She found the temple facility awe inspiring. She said, "When I heard about you I didn't believe half of what was told me. Now I realize, being here myself, that I hadn't heard half of what is true! What a fortunate nation! The servants here in the palace are exceedingly blessed, to be able to listen to your wisdom each day! She gave the king tons of gold. She delivered more spices and almug trees than have ever been seen in Israel. She also presented musical instruments. Solomon gave Queen Sheba all that she desired from his riches.

I Kings 10:14-29 *More wealth*
Now Solomon was bringing in over 20 tons of gold a year! He made 200 large shields and 300 smaller shields from pure beaten gold. His throne was made of ivory overlaid with gold. There were six steps with lions on each side up to the throne with two large lions on each side of the throne. There wasn't a throne like it in the world. In Solomon's house all the drinking cups were gold, none were silver. Silver wasn't considered valuable in the days of Solomon. He kept getting greater and greater. Every one in the world hoped to be able to see Solomon and hear the wisdom that God had given him. All who came brought gifts for the king.

I Kings 11 *The last days of Salomon and the introduction of Jeroboam*
Solomon had a penchant for foreign women. He took wives from the Moabites, Ammonites, Edomites, Sidonites and Hittites. These were all nations God had warned against because a foreign wife would tempt her husband to worship false gods. Solomon loved these women. He had 700 wives and 300 concubines and they did lead him into worshipping false gods. He built high places for worship to the gods of these foreign wives. So God said to Solomon, "Because you have not followed Me with your whole heart like your father David, I will take the kingdom from you. I will not take it during your lifetime because of My promise to David. I will leave one tribe for your son, so David's lamp will not burn out in Jerusalem." God rose up adversaries against

Solomon. Hadad the Edomite, Rezon, who had a marauding band, and Jeroboam, who rebelled when Solomon improved on the wall around Jerusalem. All these caused problems for Solomon.

Jeroboam was a valiant warrior. He was also industrious and Solomon appointed him head of all forced labor in the house of Joseph. One day Jeroboam was traveling outside Jerusalem when the prophet Ahijah found him on the road. Ahijah wore a brand new cloak. They were alone in the field when Ahijah took the cloak and ripped it in twelve pieces. He said to Jeroboam, "Take ten pieces for yourself because the Lord says: 'I am taking the kingdom from Solomon and giving it to you. Solomon has forsaken Me, by worshipping false gods. He no longer follows My laws. I am leaving his son with one tribe because of his father David. If you follow Me and My laws like David, then I will build an enduring kingdom from you in Israel. I will afflict the descendants of David but not always.'" When Solomon heard of this, he sought to put Jeroboam to death. But Jeroboam fled to Egypt and stayed there until Solomon died. Solomon reigned in Jerusalem for 40 years. He was buried in Jerusalem, the city of David. His son Rehoboam reigned in his place.

I Kings 12: 1-24 *Rehoboam runs into immediate trouble*
When Jeroboam heard from Egypt that Solomon had died, he returned to Israel. All of Israel gathered in Shechem to make Rehoboam king. The Israelis called upon Jeroboam to be their spokesman before Rehoboam. He addressed the new king with this message: "Your father made our burden hard. We worked hard and paid exorbitant taxes. If you lighten our burden, we will certainly serve you." Rehoboam replied, "Leave for three days and then come back."

Rehoboam consulted with the elder counselors who had served Solomon. "How should I answer the people?" They said, "If you will speak kindly to the people and lighten up the tax burden just a bit, they will serve you forever." This didn't sound appealing to Rehoboam. He asked his young counselors who had grown up with him and served him, "How would you answer the people?" They replied, "Say to those cry babies, 'My little finger is thicker than my father's loins. My father gave you a heavy burden; I will give you an even greater burden. My father disciplined you with whips. I will discipline you with scorpions.'" Rehoboam listened to his young counselors' advice.

When the people heard Rehoboam's harsh reply, they said, "What do we have to do with the house of David? Look after your own house Rehoboam." Everyone left Shechem and went home. The people living in the region of Judah stayed with Rehoboam. Those who left Rehoboam stoned Adoram, the manager of Rehoboam's forced labor, to death. When Rehoboam heard about this he hurried back to Jerusalem. Then the Northern tribes made Jeroboam their king. From this time forward there were two kingdoms: Israel in the North, and Judah in the South.

When Rehoboam arrived back in Jerusalem, he mustered the army of Judah and Benjamin to make war against the North in hopes of reuniting his kingdom. A prophet named Shemiah warned Rehoboam not to proceed. "Remember Rehoboam, this was already predicted by Ahijah the prophet. If you fight against your brothers you will lose."

II Chronicles 11:13 – 23 *Rehoboam fortifies Judah*
Rehoboam stayed in Jerusalem and fortified Judah. He built defenses around key strategic cities and supplied them with ample provisions. Most of the priests and Levites in Israel moved to Judah, because Jeroboam excluded them from serving as priests in Israel. All the people up in Israel whose hearts wanted to seek God followed the Levites and priests to Judah as well, this strengthened Rehoboam's kingdom. He took a wife and she bore him a number of sons. His son, Abijah, was the leader of his brothers because Rehoboam intended for him to become king after him. The other brothers were wisely stationed in all the territories of Judah and Benjamin. They also had many wives.

I Kings 12:25-13:10 *The beginning of Jeroboam's reign in Israel*
In Israel, Jeroboam built up the city of Shechem and lived there. He began to realize that if the people of his kingdom continued to go to Jerusalem for feasts, as they always had, eventually Rehoboam would be perceived as the true king and Jeroboam would be killed. To discourage this possibility he built two holy cities, one in the south of his kingdom called Bethel and one in the north called Dan. He set up altars with golden calves and appointed priests from among the people. (The Levites had returned to Jerusalem.) He established a feast on the 15th day of the eighth month of the year. (A day he thought of on his own.)

A man of God from Judah was called by God to go to Jeroboam and deliver a message. When he got to Bethel, Jeroboam was burning incense at the altar he had set up. The prophet then called out, "Oh altar oh altar, one day human bones of your own priests will be burned on you. This will be the sign, the altar shall be split apart and the ashes which are on it will be poured out." When Jeroboam heard this, he stretched out his hand and said, "Seize him!" Then his hand dried up, and he couldn't bring it back to his body. He called to the Man of God and said, "Please pray and have God restore my hand." The prophet prayed and Jeroboam's hand was restored to normal. Then Jeroboam said to the man, "Come home with me and I'll give you a nice meal and a reward." The man replied, "If you gave me half your estate, I would not go with you. God told me not to eat anything and to leave a different way than I came."

I Kings 13:11-34 *A disobedient prophet*
An old prophet, who lived in Bethel, heard from his sons about all that had taken place. He got on a donkey and went after the man of God. He found him under an oak tree. He said, "Come back with me to my home to eat and drink." The man of God said, "No, I have been commanded not to eat and drink here." The old prophet replied, "I am also a prophet. An angel of God has told me to have you come eat and drink at my home." He lied when he said this because no angel of the Lord had appeared to him. So the man of God went with him and ate and drank in the old prophet's house. As he was eating the old man cried, "I have just heard from the Lord. He has said you will not be buried in the graves of your fathers because you have disobeyed and eaten here!"

They put the man of God on a donkey and sent him on his way. Outside the town a lion attacked and killed him. When the old prophet heard about it, he went out with his donkey. He saw the lion had killed the man and not hurt the donkey. He said, "God only punished the man." He picked up the body, put it back on the unhurt donkey and took them home. He buried him in his own grave and told his sons, "When I die bury me next to the man of God, because what he said concerning the altar will come to pass." Even after these events Jeroboam continued to worship at his un-approved shrines and encouraged the people to do the same. This became the great sin of Jeroboam.

I Kings 14:1-20 *Jeroboam's demise*
At this time Jeroboam's son, Abijah, got sick. Jeroboam sent his wife, in disguise and with gifts, to Ahijah, the prophet who had told him he would become king of Israel, to see what would become of his son. Ahijah, the prophet, was old and blind. God revealed to him that Jeroboam's wife was coming to inquire. When he heard her feet in his doorway he said, "Hello, wife of Jeroboam, why are you pretending to be someone else? You must know that I have a bad message for Jeroboam. Say this to your husband: "This is what the Lord says to Jeroboam, 'I took the kingdom from the house of David and gave it to you. Yet you have not followed me like David. You have done worse than all before you because you have not followed my commands and you have created molten images to worship. Therefore, I am going to sweep your family from Israel like dung is swept from a stall! Those of your family that die in the city, the dogs

will eat. Those that die in the field, birds will pick away at.'" Ahijah continued, "Now go to back to your house. When your feet enter the city your son will die. He is the only one of Jeroboam's house that will be properly buried. Inform Jeroboam that Israel will be uprooted from this good land God has given to them. He will scatter them out of the country because of the idols they have chosen to worship. God will give up on Israel because of the sins Jeroboam." Jeroboam's wife went back to the city and Abijah, Jeroboam's son died as Ahijah the prophet said. Jeroboam died after a 22-year reign in Israel. His son Nadab reigned in his place.

I Kings 14:21-31 (II Chronicles 12-1-16)
Meanwhile back in Judah, Rehoboam continued as king. He was 41 years old when he became king and reigned 17 years. After his relatively good start, the people began to forsake the Lord and worship idols. There were male cult prostitutes in the land. The Judeans did all the evil things the people in the countries surrounding them did.

In the fifth year of Rehoboam's reign, king Shishak of Egypt made war on Jerusalem. The prophet, Shemaiah, came to Rehoboam. He said, "God says, 'Because you have forsaken Me, I have forsaken you into the hands of Shishak.'" When Rehoboam and his leaders heard this, they humbled themselves before the Lord. Then God said through Shemaiah his prophet, "Because they have humbled themselves, I will save Jerusalem, but Judah will serve Shishak. They will learn the difference between serving Me and serving a foreign king.'" Shishak ransacked the temple and took the gold shields Solomon had made. Rehoboam replaced them with bronze shields. In time things did improve in Jerusalem. Rehoboam and Jeroboam had skirmishes throughout their reigns. Finally, Rehoboam died and his son Abijam became king. This happened during the eighteenth year of Jeroboam's reign in Israel.

II Chronicles 13 *Abijam's war with Jeroboam*
Abijam sinned as much as his father. The only reason he was allowed to reign was because of David, who always walked in God's ways. (Except in the case of Uriah.) There were battles between Abijam and Jeroboam throughout Abijam's reign. Abijam mustered Judah (400,000 chosen men) to go to battle with Jeroboam in Israel. Abijam delivered this word to Jeroboam and his 800,000 warriors: "God gave the house of David rule over Israel with a covenant of salt. Yet Jeroboam rose up and rebelled. Worthless men gathered around him. They proved to be too strong for Rehoboam because he was young and inexperienced. Multitudes have gathered around the golden calves that Jeroboam has made for you. You have driven out the true Levites and priests. In Jeroboam's kingdom anyone who sacrifices a young bull and seven rams can become a priest of what are not gods. In Jerusalem the sons of Aaron serve in the

prescribed manner, offering daily sacrifices to the Lord. God is with us, we have the priests here to blow the trumpets, and we will prevail over you."

Jeroboam set an ambush from the rear and the front, surrounding Judah. They cried out to God and the priest blew the trumpets. The Judean warriors raised the war cry and routed the greater army of Jeroboam. 500,000 of Jeroboam's men were slain. The army of Judah pursued them into Israel and captured some of their cities.

II Chronicles 14 *Asa fights Ethiopia*
After three years Abijam died. His son Asa became king of Judah in his place. Asa was a good king. He followed God like his great grandfather David. He put away the male cult prostitutes and destroyed all the idols his father had made. Because his mother made a heathen idol, her title of Queen Mother was removed and he burned the idol. But the people did continue to offer sacrifices in the high places. Asa filled the temple with dedicated silver and gold utensils.

Zerah the Ethiopian came out against Asa with 1,000,000 men and 300 chariots. Asa had fewer than 600,000 warriors. Asa called out to God and said, "There is no one like You to help in battle when the strong come against the weak. We trust in You to help us prevail against this multitude. It wouldn't be right for anything to overcome You." Judah won, and pursued their enemies out of the country. They were able to carry away a great amount of plunder. They also captured a large number of livestock.

II Chronicles 15 *Revival in Judah*
Azariah, the prophet, came to Asa and said, "Listen Asa and all Judah: God is with you when you are with Him. Without Him there is no joy or peace, only confusion, distress, and darkness. Nations come against nations and there is destruction. Be strong and courageous because your faithfulness will be rewarded." When Asa heard these words, he created a revival in Judah. All the false altars were destroyed. He and the people entered a renewed agreement with God that they would seek only Him. They sacrificed 700 oxen and 7000 sheep the day they entered the agreement. They blew the trumpets and it was a great day in Judah. There was peace in the land for many years after this.

I Kings 15:25-32 *Baasha kills Nadab*
Meanwhile back in the North, Jeroboam's son, Nadab, became king. He was in a battle with the Philistines when a man named Baasha who was an Israelite killed him and

Baasha became king. He killed all of Jeroboam's family just as God said through Ahijah his prophet. Baasha reigned 24 years. He did all the same evil as Jeroboam by honoring the worship of Jeroboam's idols in Bethel and Dan. Baasha built fortifications in Ramah on the border between Israel and Judah, to prevent travel between the two countries.

II Chronicles 16 *Baasha's reign, Asa's mistake*
Asa sent a sizable gift of gold and silver, which he took from the temple treasury, to Ben-Hadad, the king of Aram. He proposed an alliance between Aram and Judah, where Ben-Hadad would make war with Baasha on Israel's northern border. This would draw Baasha away from the project in Ramah to the south. The strategy worked. With Baasha forced to fight Ben-Hadad, the Judeans were able to disassemble the fortifications. They carried the stones and timber into Judah to build the town of Geba in the territory of Benjamin.

Hanani the prophet came to Asa and said, "You were wrong to seek the help of Ben-hadad instead of God. Didn't God help you with the Ethiopians when you sought Him? His eyes are always looking over the entire earth to help those who trust Him." Asa was angry at the rebuke of Hanani so he imprisoned the prophet. Asa began to oppress some of his people at this time. In the 39th year of his reign, Asa became lame in his feet. His condition was severe. Even then, he did not seek the Lord; he only sought the help of doctors. He died in the 41st year of his reign. His son Jehoshaphat became king in Judah.

II Chronicles 17 *Jehosaphat starts his reign*
Jehoshaphat strengthened Judah. He was careful to follow the Lord and seek Him with his whole heart. He made sure all the strategic cities where fortified and provisioned. He sent officials into the cities to teach the law. He had close to 1,000,000 warriors on the ready in the various territories in Judah. The Philisitines and the Arabians paid taxes to Jehoshaphat. All the neighboring countries were afraid of the power Judah possessed, so there was peace in the land.

I Kings 16 *A quick run of kings in Isreal*
Up in Israel the prophet Jehu spoke from the Lord against Baasha. "God says you're as bad as Jeroboam. So He will deliver the same judgment on you and your house as He did with the house of Jeroboam. In the 26th year of Asa's reign in Judah, Baasha died in Israel. His son Elah became king. He only reigned two years. Zimri, who commanded Elah's chariots, conspired against Elah. One day Elah was on a drinking binge in Tirzah with some friends. Zimri came in and killed him so Zimri became king.

His first act was to put the entire house of Baasha and Elah to death. So God's judgment was delivered against Baasha and his family. Zimri only reigned seven days. When the people heard of his conspiracy, they made Omri, the commander of the army, king. Omri besieged Tirzah. When Zimri, heard what was happening he committed suicide by going to the king's house and setting it on fire with himself inside.

Some of the people wanted a man named Tibni to be king. Omri and his people prevailed and Tibni died. So Omri became the un-contested king of Israel. He was king 12 years. For six years he reigned in Tirzah. He bought a hill from a man named Shemer for 200 pounds of silver. He built a city there and named it Samaria. He made Samaria the capitol of Israel and reigned there for the last six years. Omni was as bad as Jeroboam and Baasha. He sinned in all the same ways. And all the people in Israel sinned along with him.

Omri died during the 38th year of Asa's reign in Judah. His son, Ahab, became king. He reigned 22 years in Israel. He was even more evil than his predecessors. He married Jezebel, the daughter of Ethbaal, king of Sidon. He worshipped their god, Baal. He built a temple to Baal in Samaria and he put up all kinds of idols. He did more evil than any of the previous kings. God was very angry about all his sinning.

At this time a man named Hiel began to rebuild Jericho. His first son died when he laid the foundation. He lost his second son when he finished the gates. This happened just as Joshua said when he destroyed the city hundreds of years earlier!

I Kings 17 *Elijah begins*

Elijah, the Tishbite, was a man of God. He went to king Ahab and said, "As the Lord, the God of Israel lives, there shall be neither dew nor rain these years except by my word." After he delivered the message, God told Elijah to go east past the Jordan to a creek called Cherith. God added, "I have commanded the ravens to provide for you there." Elijah arrived at the creek and drank from it. Every morning and evening the ravens would come with meat for Elijah. After a while the creek dried up. God said, "Go into Sidon, there is a widow there whom I have commanded to provide for you. When he got to Sidon and found the widow he said, "Could you please bring me some water, and while you're at it bring me some bread too." She replied, "As the Lord your God lives, I have no bread. I was just going to take this last bit of flour and oil I have, make bread, eat it with my son as a last meal and then die." Elijah answered, "Don't worry, and just do as I have said. Make me a cake from what you have and bring it to me, and then you can make some for yourself and your son. The Lord says, 'The bowl of flour will not be exhausted, nor will the jar be empty until rain is sent back to the land.'" She did as he said and they all ate for an extended period.

Some time after this, the widow's son became sick. It was so severe that he stopped breathing. The widow cried out, "How is it that God is cursing me with this man Elijah here, I want nothing more to do with him!" Elijah said, "Give me your son." Elijah took the boy to his room and laid him on the bed. He called out to God, "How can you let the child die with me here?" He laid on top of the boy and prayed three times. "Oh God please give the boy his life again." God answered, and the boy revived. Elijah took the boy to his mom. She said, "I am confident that you are a man of God now!"

I Kings 18:1-16 *Elijah goes to Ahab (via Obadiah)*
The period of drought lasted three years. God told Elijah to go to Ahab and he would send rain. Elijah started on his way to Samaria. Meanwhile in Samaria, Ahab called the head of his household staff, Obadiah, to the palace. Obadiah had maximum respect for the Lord. There had been an incident when Ahab's wife, Jezebel, had sought to destroy the prophets of the Lord. Obadiah had personally hidden 100 of them in caves and provided food for them, so they were saved. Ahab said to Obadiah, "Let's survey the land to see if we can find some grass in valleys. Perhaps we can save some cattle. You go this way, I'll go the other." Obadiah ran into Elijah as he was on his way. He bowed when he saw Elijah. Elijah instructed Obadiah to tell Ahab he wanted to see him. Obadiah replied fearfully, "I have a problem with that. Ahab has been looking for you for three years. If I go to him and say Elijah is here and then suddenly, the Spirit of the Lord carries you to a different place, he'll have me killed even though I have loved God from my youth. Certainly you heard about how I protected the prophets from Jezebel!" Elijah replied, "Obadiah, as the Lord of Hosts lives, before whom I stand, I assure you, I will see Ahab today!" So Obadiah found Ahab and arranged the meeting.

I Kings 18:17-40 *Elijah posts up on false prophets, and the drought ends*
When Ahab saw Elijah he said, "So here is the one who troubles Israel." Elijah answered, "You're the one who troubles Israel because you worship false gods! Send for all the false prophets who sit at Jezebel's table, 450 of Baal and 400 of the Asherah, and have them meet me at Mount Carmel." So they all came to Mt. Carmel. Elijah said to the people, "How long will you hesitate between two opinions. If the Lord is God then follow Him. If Baal is true, follow him. I am the only prophet of the Lord here; there are 450 prophets of Baal. Bring us two oxen. Let them cut one up and place it on their wood. I will prepare the other and place it on my wood. The God who brings down fire from heaven, He is the true God!" The people all replied, "That's a good idea."

So the prophets of Baal went first. They prepared their offering and spent the whole morning calling out to Baal to send fire. They were jumping all around their altar. Around noon Elijah began to mock them, "Call louder, you know Baal's a god. Who knows, maybe he's just busy, or in the bathroom, or maybe on a journey. Maybe he's asleep and needs to be wakened." Baal's prophets got all the more agitated and began cutting themselves with swords and lances, as was their custom, until they were all quite bloody! They kept it up all afternoon. No one answered; their god paid no attention. Bottom line, there was no fire from heaven.

Finally Elijah called the people to him. He repaired the proper alter with 12 stones according to the number of tribes in Israel. He dug a trench around the altar. Then he prepared the wood and the offering. He ordered barrels of water to be poured over the whole sacrifice so it filled the trench he had dug. Then he had them pour the same amount over the whole thing twice more. Then Elijah prayed, "Oh Lord, now let everyone know who You are and that I am Your servant, so this people will turn their hearts back to You!" Then fire came down from heaven and consumed the entire sacrifice with the stones and the water. The people all fell on their faces and said, "The Lord is God. The Lord is God!" Then Elijah said, "Capture all the prophets of Baal, and let none escape!" They were all rounded up and killed down by the Kishon brook.

Elijah said to Ahab, "Go get something to eat because a big storm is coming." Elijah went off by himself and put his head between his knees. He told his servant to check if there were any clouds coming from the sea. After checking, the servant reported that the sky was clear. Elijah told him to check again....nothing, and again....nothing. Finally on the seventh try, he saw a small cloud heading in. He reported back, telling Elijah a small cloud about the size of a man's hand was floating in. Elijah said, "Go tell Ahab to hurry to Jezreel so he can beat the storm. The sky grew dark and there was a heavy shower. Elijah became full of the Spirit of the Lord. He pulled up and tightened his pants. Then ran to Jezreel himself, beating Ahab and his chariot!

I Kings 19 *Elijah's hears God, and meets Elisha*
When Jezebel heard what Elijah had done to her 450 prophets, she sent this message to Elijah: "May my gods kill me if I don't take your life in the next 24 hours!" This frightened Elijah, and he hurried from the area. He went down into Judah, left his servant there and continued on by himself. He went a day's journey and rested under a juniper tree. He prayed, "God, just go ahead and kill me, I'm no better than any other prophet." Then he went to sleep. When he awoke there was an angel touching him. There was a nice loaf of bread baked on hot stones and a jar of water set before him.

The angel told him to eat. After he'd finished, he went back to sleep. The angel woke him up a second time and said, "Get up and eat because the journey is too difficult for you." He ate and that food was enough to sustain him 40 days while he traveled to Mt. Horeb, the mountain of God.

When he got there he found a cave to live in. God asked, "What are you doing here Elijah?" Elijah answered, "I have worked hard for the Lord. Israel has forsaken God, broken their agreement with Him, torn down His altars and killed God's prophets with swords. I am all that's left and they are after me now." God said, "Go stand on the mountain. I will pass by." Elijah arrived at the mountaintop. A great and powerful wind roared against the mountain. It was breaking up the stones, but the Lord wasn't in the wind. After the wind there was a powerful earthquake, but God wasn't in the earthquake. After the earthquake came a fire, but God wasn't in the fire. After the fire came a gentle blowing wind. That's when Elijah heard God's voice saying, "What are you doing here Elijah?" Elijah repeated his previous reply about being the only follower of God left. Then God said, "Go down to Damascus in Aram and anoint Hazael king of Aram. Then go anoint Jehu as king of Israel. Next find Elisha, who will take over for you when you're gone. Whoever escapes the sword of Hazael will be found by Jehu's sword. And by the way, there are 7000 in Israel, in addition to you, who have never bowed the knee to Baal, or kissed him.

So Elijah went down and found Elisha plowing in a field behind 12 oxen. Elijah threw his mantle on Elisha. Elisha said, "Let me go back and kiss my parents, then I will follow you. He went back, sacrificed two oxen and gave the meat to the people. Then he followed Elijah and ministered to him.

I Kings 20:1-21 *Ben-Hadad takes a crack at Israel*
Ben-Hadad, the king of Aram, gathered up his army and besieged Samaria. He sent this message to Ahab: "All you have: silver, gold, wives and children, they all belong to me now." Ahab sent messengers back saying, "Just as you say Ben-Hadad, they are all yours now." Then Ben-Hadad sent another message, "Tomorrow my servants will come to your palace. Anything they see of value they will bring here to me." Ahab then called in the elders and described Ben-Hadad's actions. They said, "Don't give him anything!" So Ahab sent a message saying, "Sorry, you can't have my possessions." Ben-Hadad sent a message back, "You will see now how I destroy Samaria." Ahab sent a final message back to Ben-Hadad, "So far all we've heard is talk!"

When Ben-Hadad got this final message he was drinking in his tent with some of his captains. He gave the command to go to battle stations against Samaria. Back in the city a prophet had come to Ahab and said, "This is what God says, 'You see the multitude gathered against you. Well, I am going to deliver them into your hand today, and you will know that I am the Lord!'" Ahab asked, "Who will accomplish it?" The prophet answered, "God says by the young rulers of the provinces." Then Ahab asked, "Who will start the battle?" The prophet answered, "You." So Ahab collected the 232 young rulers and the rest of his army, which numbered 7000.

At noon Ben-Hadad was drinking heavily in his tent when he heard Israel's 232 rulers and 7000 Israelite soldiers approaching. He commanded they be taken alive. As it turned out, Ben-Hadad was the one who was fortunate to survive! Israel routed Aram that day with a great slaughter. Ben-Hadad narrowly escaped on a horse.

I Kings 20:22-34 *Ben-Hadad fails again*
The prophet warned Ahab that by the end of the year Ben-Hadad would try to again do battle with Israel. Sure enough, Ben-Hadad's servants said, "Israel's God is a god of the mountains. If we fight them on the plain we shall prevail against them. We'll go out with the exact size army as before and beat them in the plain." So they mustered themselves in the flat area of Aphek. Israel looked like two flocks of goats compared to the multitudes of Ben-hadad. The prophet assured Ahab, "Because they think the Lord is only a god of the mountains, I will give this great multitude into your hand, so you will know I am the Lord!" They camped seven days before the battle was joined. Israel killed 100,000 Amonite foot soldiers. Another 27,000 fled into the city where they were killed when a fortification collapsed on them. Ben-hadad and his entourage were in an inner chamber in the city. His servants said, "Kings of Israel are generally forgiving. We should beg for mercy!" They dressed in sackcloth and sent word to Ahab begging for their lives. Ahab sent for Ben-hadad with a friendly reply, so he came to see Ahab. Ben-hadad said, "I will restore all the cities my father took and even give you Damascus." So, Ahab let him go.

I Kings 20:35-43 *Ahab chastised*
There was a charismatic group called "the sons of the prophets." One of the sons of the prophets told another, by the word of the Lord, to strike him. The other refused so the first prophet said, "Because you have not listened to the voice of the Lord, a lion will kill you as soon as you leave here". When the prophet who refused to strike went on his way, a lion killed him! Then the first prophet asked another, "Please strike me." This prophet complied with the odd request. The blow wounded the prophet so he wrapped his head wound and waited for the king by the city gates. When the king passed by the prophet said, "When I went out to battle one of the captains told me to hold a man and

not let him go, or I would be killed. Well, I got a little busy with something else and the man is gone." The king replied, "Your punishment has already been established, you should be killed!" Then the prophet took off the bandage from his wound and the king recognized him as one of the prophets. The prophet said, "God says, 'Because you have let Ben-haddad go, who I had devoted to destruction, you and your people will be destroyed.'" The king entered Samaria very sullen and sad.

I Kings 21:1-16 *Naboth's vineyard*
There was a vineyard beside Ahab's palace in Jezereel owned by a man named Naboth. Ahab asked Naboth if he could buy the land. Naboth wouldn't sell, which upset Ahab. When Ahab's wife, Jezebel, saw how sullen he was over the matter, she conspired against Naboth by having lies told about him. Her lies were successful and Naboth was stoned to death. When the deed was done she went into Ahab and said, "Go take possession of the vineyard. Naboth is dead".

I Kings 21:17-29 *Ahab denounced*
The word of the Lord came upon Elijah and he met Ahab in the vineyard. Ahab greeted Elijah, "So my enemy finds me again." Elijah answered, "Yes, I've found you because you've sinned again, by allowing this evil to fall on Naboth. You will be swept away like so much dung out of a stall. Your wife will also be killed and eaten by dogs. Your whole household will be destroyed." When Ahab heard this he ripped his clothes, put on sackcloth and fasted. He went about despondently. Then God spoke again to Elijah, "See how Ahab has humbled himself before me. Because of this, the curse will not fall on him but on his family after him."

I Kings 22:1-28 *Micaiah's prophecy*
For three years there was no war between Aram and Israel. During this time, Jehoshaphat the king of Judah, who had married a relative of Ahab's, came to visit Ahab. As they were talking the king of Israel said, "Aram still holds Ramoth-gilead, which rightfully belongs to us. Jehoshaphat, will you help me win it back?" Jehoshaphat replied, "I sure will, but first let's inquire of the Lord as to how we will fare." Ahab brought in his prophets, about 400 of them, and they all agreed the battle would go well for the new alliance. Jehoshaphat said, "Isn't there a prophet of the Lord we can inquire with?" The king of Israel answered, "There is a prophet of God but he always prophecies bad against me." Jehoshaphat replied, "He's got to like the fact that Judah and Israel are working together again, call him in!" So they sent for Micaiah the prophet of which Ahab had spoken. The two kings were both finely arrayed in their robes and sitting on their thrones at the entrance to the city. Before Micaiah arrived one of Ahab's 400 prophets named Zedekiah made horns of iron and said, "Thus says

the Lord, 'With these you shall gore Aram until they are consumed!'" All the other prophets were prophesying in the same tone. The messenger sent to retrieve Micaiah advised the prophet like this: "All the other prophets are being favorable towards this new alliance, so you should be too." Micaiah replied, "My job is to say only what God tells me."

When Micaiah arrived, the king of Israel asked, "So Micaiah, how will we do in our quest to win back Ramoth-gilead?" Micaiah replied, "Oh sure you'll do fine. You've got 400 prophets here telling you there will be no problems." Ahab shot back, "Don't mess with me, Micaiah, just give me what God says." Micaiah replied, "I saw all Israel scattered on the mountains, like sheep with no shepherd. God said, 'These have no master, let them all return home in peace." Ahab looked over at Jehoshaphat and said, "What did I tell you, this guy is gloom and doom all the way." Then Micaiah said, "Hear what God says, I saw the Lord sitting on His throne, all the host of heaven surrounding Him and God said, 'Who will entice Ahab to go up and fall at Ramoth-gilead?' There was a bit of a stir, then a spirit came forward and said, 'I will entice him.' God asked, 'How?' The spirit replied, 'I will go out and be a deceiving spirit in the mouths of Ahab's prophets.' God said, 'Good plan, go and you will succeed.' Ahab, God has allowed a deceiving spirit to enter the mouths of these prophets, so you will be destroyed in Ramoth-gilead." At this point Zedekiah, the "prophet" who made the iron horns, struck Micaiah and said, "How is it that the Spirit of the Lord has passed from me to you?" Micaiah answered, "You'll see when you have to hide yourself in an inner chamber."

I Kings 22:29-40
Ahab ordered Micaiah to be imprisoned and be fed sparingly until he returned safely. Micaiah said, "If you return safely, then God has not spoken through me." So the two kings went out against Ramoth-gilead. Ahab said to Jehoshaphat, "I will disguise myself as I go to battle but you wear your royal robes." Now, the king of Aram offered a bonus for who ever killed the king of Israel. When the Amorites saw Jehoshaphat royally arrayed they started after him. He yelled out, "I am the king of Judah, not Israel!" Meanwhile an arrow shot at random in the battle found a small opening in Ahab's armor inflicting a critical wound! King Ahab was propped up in his chariot as they pulled him from the battle.

At sunset the order was issued for each soldier to return to his own country. Ahab died as the blood was running down onto the floor of his chariot. Dogs came and licked up his blood just as the Lord had said. His son Ahaziah took over as king of Israel. He was every bit as bad as his dad. He worshipped Baal and did evil during the two years he reigned as king of Israel.

II Chronicles 19 and 20 *Judah saved*

Jehoshaphat returned safely to Jerusalem. At this time he wisely appointed judges for all the regions of Judah. He instructed them to fear the Lord and judge according to his law and word, also to judge faithfully and wholeheartedly. They were to show no partiality or accept any bribes.

A report came to Jehoshaphat about a large army consisting of Moabites, Arameans and Meunites being allied and coming against Judah. Jehoshaphat immediately sought the Lord. He gathered all the people in Jerusalem and prayed this prayer to God: "God, You are the God of the heavens. You have authority over all the kingdoms of the earth. No power on earth can prevail against You. You gave us this land by driving out all the nations that lived here before us. We have lived here and built a house where You have put Your Name! We are praying for deliverance from a great multitude that is coming against us. They are the very same nations that we did not destroy when we came into the land. This is how they repay; they are trying to take our inheritance! We are keeping our eyes on You for deliverance; You are our only hope against so great a threat!

All Judah, women and children were assembled listening when the Spirit of the Lord fell on Jahaziel, the prophet, who said, "Listen all Judah and Jehoshaphat, this is what God says: 'Don't worry about this great army coming against you. This battle is Mine, not yours. You won't even have to swing a sword. Tomorrow just go down against them and you will see My power prevail for My people!" So with joy and gladness, singing and praising, they headed off the next day against their enemies. When they got to the wilderness lookout they saw nothing but dead men in the valley. The Lord had caused confusion amongst Judah's enemies and they had fought against each other and totally wiped each other out. Jehoshaphat and the people took three days collecting all the plunder! On the fourth day they returned to Jerusalem singing and praising God. All the nations feared Judah and there was peace in the land.

I Kings 22:41-53 *Jehoshaphat's navy*

Jehoshaphat aligned himself with Israel latter in his reign to put together a fleet of trading ships like the one that succeeded for Solomon. The prophet Eliezer told Jehoshaphat he was wrong to align himself with Israel and that his venture would fail, and it did fail. The ships did not make one successful trip. When Jehoshaphat died after his 25-year reign his son, Jehoram, took over as king of Judah.

II Kings 1 *Ahaziah and Elijah*

Late in Ahaziah's evil reign in Israel, he fell through a lattice on his roof. His injuries made him very ill. He had messengers travel to Ekron in Philistia to inquire of Baal-zebub, the god of Ekron, as to whether he would recover from his illness. An angel of the Lord came to Elijah and said, "Get up and meet the messengers the king of Israel has sent to Ekron and say, 'Is it because there is no God in Israel that you are traveling to Ekron to inquire to Baal-zebub? This is what the Lord of Israel says to the king, 'You will not get out of your bed, you will die.'" So the messengers returned to Ahaziah and delivered the message. Ahaziah asked, "What did the man who said this to you look like? The messenger replied, "He was a very hairy man and he wore leather pants." Ahaziah said, "That's Elijah all right." So Ahaziah sent a captain and 50 men to go collect Elijah and bring him in.

They found him on top of a hill. The captain called up, "Man of God, the king says come down." Elijah replied, "If I am a man of God, let fire come down from heaven and consume you and your fifty." Fire came down and consumed the captain and his men. Ahaziah sent another captain and fifty men. The same exchange occurred between the captain and Elijah, with the same results. The third captain sent by King Ahaziah approached Elijah carefully. He bowed down on his knees and said, "Please do not kill me and my men as you have the others. Let our lives be more valuable to you." An angel of the Lord said to Elijah, "Go on down with them, do not be afraid." So Elijah went to the king and said, "You seem to think the god of Ekron, Baal-zebub, is able to give you information the Lord can't. You must think there is no God in Israel. Because of this you will not get up from your bed, you will die." Ahaziah died just as Elijah said. He had no son, so Joram, the son of Ahab, became king.

II Kings 2 *Elisha takes over*

It was about time for God to take Elijah from the earth. As Elijah was getting ready to leave Gilgal, where they were lodged, he said to Elisha, "Please stay here, God has told me to go to Bethel." Elisha replied, "As God lives and you live, I will not leave your side." When they got to Bethel, a contingent of the "sons of the prophets" came out to meet them. They said to Elisha, "Do you know that the Lord will take your master from you today?" Elisha said, "Yes, now pipe down." Then Elijah said to Elisha, "Please stay here for the Lord has called me to go to Jerico." Elisha replied, "You will not go without me!" So they went to Jerico. At Jerico the sons of the prophets came to Elisha again and said, "Do you know the Lord will take your master from you today?" Elisha said, "Yes, now keep still." Then Elijah said to Elisha, "I've been called by God to go beyond the Jordan, please stay here." Elisha replied, "As sure as you and the Lord live, I will not leave your side." So off they went with the sons of the prophets following at a distance.

When they made the Jordan River, Elijah took off his mantle, folded it and struck the waters with it. The water divided and he and Elisha crossed over on dry land. When they got across, Elijah said to Elisha, "What can I do for you before I am taken from you?" Elisha replied. "I want a double portion of your spirit on me." Elijah replied, "Well, that's going to be tough, but if you see me when I am taken up, then you will receive a double portion. If you miss it, it won't happen for you." As they were walking along talking, a chariot of fire and horses of fire separated them and Elijah was taken up into heaven in a whirlwind. Elisha saw it and cried out, "My Father, My Father, the chariots of Israel and its horsemen!" After this he didn't see Elijah again. He took his own clothes and ripped them. Then he took Elijah's mantle, which fell off Elijah and he struck the water at the Jordan and said, "Where is the God of Elijah?" As he said this, the waters separated again and Elisha walked across on dry land. When the sons of the prophets saw it they proclaimed, "The spirit of Elijah has certainly come upon Elisha." They bowed down before him.

Then they said to Elisha, "We have 50 strong men here perhaps they should go look for Elijah. Perhaps God has just taken him, and cast him onto some mountain or valley." Elisha said no. They kept after him until finally he said, "Fine, go look for him." After three days of looking the 50 returned, having found nothing. Elisha engaged in a bit of "I told you so."

They were staying in Jerico and the men of the city commented to Elisha, " You can see this is a great city but our water supply is always poor." Elisha told them to bring him a jar of salt. He took it to the town spring and threw in the salt saying, "Now God says this water is pure." The waters of Jerico have been fine ever since.

The next day Elisha left for Bethel. Along the way a group of teenage thugs mocked him saying, "Keep on walking bald head! Keep on walking bald head!" Elisha looked back at them and cursed them in the name of the Lord. Two bears fell on the group and they tore up 42 of the mockers. Elisha finally ended his journey in Samaria.

II Kings 3 *Moab rebels and is defeated*

Joram was king in Israel. He wasn't as bad as his father Ahab. He actually removed the sacred pillar of Baal, which his father had made. But he still supported the false religion Jeroboam had set up with the altars in Bethel and Dan.

The king of Moab was a sheepherder. When Ahab was king, Moab paid 100,000 lambs and the wool from 100,000 rams to Israel every year. When Ahab died Moab stopped paying. King Joram mustered all of Israel and sent word to Jehoshaphat in Judah asking if he'd help deal with the rebelling Moabites. Jehoshaphat was happy to help with all his military assets. So they traveled through the wilderness of Edom towards Moab. The king of Edom joined them. It was a seven-day journey and they ran out of water. Joram complained, "It seems God has led three kings out here just to be defeated by the Moabites!" Jehoshaphat replied, "Isn't there a prophet of the Lord here?" Joram's servants mentioned Elisha and the three kings went to see him.

When Elisha saw them he said, "What have I to do with you, Joram? Go to the prophets of your father and mother." Joram answered, "No. Why has God called three kings to be delivered into the hands of Moab?" Elisha replied, "If Jehoshaphat of Judah weren't here with you, I would have nothing to do with you. Bring me a singer." When the singer started to play and sing the spirit of God came on him and he said, "Dig trenches throughout this valley. No wind or rain will come but the trenches will be filled with water for you and your animals. This is no big thing for the Lord, but He will also deliver Moab into your hands. You will plunder all their fine cites and cut down every choice tree."

The next morning, around the time for the morning sacrifice, water did come into all the trenches. The Moabites meanwhile began to muster themselves for battle. The next morning they assembled at their border and looked down into the valley. All the water shone up at them as if it were red as blood. So they said to themselves, "Look, the kings have fought against each other and are dead! Let us march to victory and the spoil!" When they reached the valley, the three kings rose up and smote them completely. They went forward into the land of Moab and destroyed the cities and ruined the land. When the king of Moab saw that his position was hopeless; he mounted a desperate charge with 700 strong swordsmen to kill the king of Edom, but was unable to break through. Finally he sacrificed his own son as a burnt offering at the city wall. The Israelis were all so disgusted they withdrew and returned to their homes.

II Kings 4:1-7 *Widow's oil*

One of the sons of the prophets had a wife. She came to Elisha and said, "My husband is dead. You know he feared God. We have some outstanding debts and our creditors want to take my two boys in payment." Elisha replied, "What do you have in your house?" The woman answered, "Only a jar of oil." Then Elisha said, "Go borrow as many containers as you can find from your friends and neighbors, do not get just a few. You and your boys go into your house with the containers and start filling them from your jar of oil." She did as Elisha instructed. Her jar of oil continued to pour. Finally all the containers she had collected were full! She went to Elisha and reported what had happened. He said, "Go sell the oil and pay your debt. You and your boys live off the rest."

II Kings 4:8-37 *Elisha raises the dead son*

One day Elisha came through the town of Shunem. There was a prominent woman living there and she persuaded Elisha to eat at her house. He ate at her home anytime he passed through town. Eventually she said to her husband, "I know this is a mighty man of God. Let's make a room for him in our attic. We can furnish it with a bed, table, chair and lamp stand. When he comes through he can lodge with us." One day while Elisha was staying there, he said to his servant, Gehazi, "This woman has been very good to us, bring her to me." When he saw her he said, "What can I do for you, can I mention you to the king or to the commander of the army?" She said, "No, I live here with my own people." So Elisha asked Gehazi, "What can I do for her?" He said, "She has no son and her husband is very old." So Elisha called her to the doorway and said, "This time next year you will have a son." She answered, "Man of God, you should not lie to me in this way!"

She did have a son the next year. When the child was a boy, he went with his father to watch the reapers. The boy complained about having a headache, his father had a servant carry the boy back to his mother. The boy sat on his mother's lap all morning and at noon he died. The woman took him up to Elisha's room and laid him on the man of God's bed, shut the door and left. Her husband arranged for a servant and a donkey to take her directly to Mount Carmel, where Elisha was. When he saw her approaching, he sent Gehazi ahead to see what was up. She told him, "All is well." When she met Elisha she fell at his feet. Gehazi started to push her away, but Elisha stopped him saying, "She is troubled and God has not told me what the problem is." She cried, "Did I ask for a son? No, I told you not to lie to me!"

Elisha said, "Gehazi, take my staff, go to the boy and lay it on his face." So Gehazi set off. The woman and Elisha followed. When Gehazi did as his master instructed, the boy did not awaken. When Elisha and the woman arrived, he gave them the news. Elisha went up to the room and closed the door. He prayed to God, then he laid right on top of the boy with his mouth and eyes touching the boy's mouth and eyes. The boy's skin began to feel warm. He went out of the room and walked through the house. Then he returned to the room and laid on the child again. This time the boy sneezed seven times. Elisha called for Gehazi to summon the woman. When she came into the room she fell at Elisha's feet, then she took the boy and went out of the room.

II Kings 4:38-44 *Poison stew and multiplied loaves*
When Elisha returned to Gilgal there was famine in the land. The sons of the prophets sat before him, and he said to his servant, "Put on a large pot and boil a stew for the sons of the prophets. Herbs were gathered from the field. They also found a vine of gourds that they cut up and put in the stew, but they didn't know what it was. When they began to eat the sons of the prophets said, "There is death in the pot!" and they couldn't eat it. So Elisha said, "Now put some meal in the pot." This made the stew fine for eating.

A man came from Baal-shalishah. He brought twenty loaves of barley and some fresh ears of grain. Elisha said. "Give these to the people to eat." The attendant said, "There are 100 men here! This isn't close to enough food." Elisha replied, "Give it to them! God say's they'll be full and there will be leftovers." They all ate and there was plenty left, just as the Lord said.

II Kings 5 *Naaman*
There was a man in Aram named Naaman. The king of Aram loved Naaman because Naaman was the head of Aram's army and God had blessed him with many victories. He was also a mighty warrior in his own right, but he was a leper. During a raid in Israel a young Hebrew girl was taken captive and became a servant to Naaman's wife. She said to Naaman's wife, "I wish Naaman could go to the prophet who is in Samaria, because he could heal his leprosy!" When Naaman heard this, he went into the king and told him what the young Hebrew girl had said. The king replied, "I'll send a letter to the king of Israel and get you an appointment with the guy!" So Naaman headed down to Israel with close to 1000 pounds of silver and a few hundred pounds of gold. When the king of Israel received the letter he tore his clothes and said, "Am I a god? Can I heal this Naaman fellow? The king of Aram is obviously trying to start something here." When Elisha heard the king had torn his cloths he sent a message, "Why have you torn your clothes? Send the Aramite to me, and he will know there is a prophet of God in Israel!"

So Naaman and his whole company came to Elisha's house and stood outside. Elisha sent a messenger out. He told Naaman to dip himself in the Jordan River seven times to be healed. Naaman was furious; "This prophet doesn't even come out here himself and call upon the name of his God, wave his hand over the place and heal the leper? Aren't the rivers in Damascus better than the Jordan? If I wanted to get wet, I'd start there, not here!" He turned and left in a rage. One of his servants caught up with him and said, "Master, if the prophet had ask you to do some mighty deed, you certainly would have done it. Why don't you just give a few dips in the Jordan a try?" So Naaman dipped himself in the Jordan seven times and came out with perfect skin like a child.

He returned to Elisha's house. He stood before him and said; "Now I know there is no God in all the earth except here in Israel. Please accept a gift from me." Elisha wouldn't accept a gift. Naaman said, "Please let me take two donkey loads of earth from here so I can return to Aram and build an alter to sacrifice to your God. I will no longer sacrifice to any other god. Also, I ask that I be granted a pardon. Because of my official duties, I sometimes have to go into the house of Rimmon, Aram's god. I have to bow there occasionally. Will you please pardon me in this matter?" Elisha said, "Go in peace." So Naaman started his journey back to Aram.

Elisha's servant, Gehazi, thought to himself, "That was quite a bit of silver and gold Elisha sent back to Aram. I will run after Naaman and take something from him." Gehazi caught up to Naaman's company. Naaman asked if everything was all right. Gehazi said, "Oh sure everything's fine, but Elisha asked me to come and make a request. There are two sons of the prophets who need a little help. He asked that you provide 100 pounds of silver and a few changes of clothes." Naaman was happy to oblige and had a servant deliver the merchandise to Gehazi's house. When Gehazi appeared again before Elisha, Elisha asked, "Where have you been?" Gehazi said, "I haven't been anywhere." Elisha replied, "Gehazi, I know exactly where you've been and what you've done. Now the leprosy that was upon Naaman will fall upon you and your family forever." Gehazi left Elisha's presence white with leprosy.

II Kings 6:1-7 *Floating ax*
One day the sons of the prophets approached Elisha and said, "The place where we live is too small. We would like to go to the Jordan and cut down trees so we can build ourselves a bigger place. Elisha said, "Go ahead." And he accepted their invitation to join them. They were cutting trees by the river when one man's ax head fell into the water. He cried out, "Master, master, the ax head has fallen into the water and it was

borrowed!" Elisha replied, "Where did it fall?" When the man showed him the place, Elisha cut a stick and threw it in the water. The ax head floated to the surface!

II Kings 6:8-23 *Opened eyes*
The King of Aram was conducting skirmishes against Israel at this time. He would set up camp in various areas. Elisha knew, in advance, every movement the king of Aram's army made. He warned the king of Israel each time, so the king of Aram was never successful. The king of Aram called in his advisors. "Who's the spy? Someone is informing the king of Israel of every move we make!" One of his servants replied, "None of us, O lord my king, but Elisha, the prophet of God in Israel, can perceive the things you say in your bedroom and he relays it to the king of Israel." The king replied, "Find out where Elisha is." The king received intelligence that Elisha was in Dothan. So the king of Aram sent a large army there and surrounded the city.

When Elisha's servant awoke and went outside he saw the large army surrounding the city. He ran back to Elisha and said, "My master, what shall we do?" Elisha answered, "Don't be afraid. There are more with us than there are in that army." Then Elisha prayed, "God, open my servant's eyes so that he will see." Then the servant saw that the mountains around the city were full of horses and chariots of fire, to protect Elisha. So Elisha went into the city and prayed, "Lord blind the army of Aram." The whole army was blinded just as Elisha had prayed. Elisha went out and said to the army, "This isn't the right place, follow me and I will take you to the man you seek." He led them to Samaria.

When they got to Samaria, Elisha prayed that they would regain their sight. Aram's soldiers saw they were right in the middle of the capital city of Israel. The king of Israel said to Elisha, "Shall we fall upon them with swords and kill them?" Elisha replied, "Would you kill those you have captured? No, feed them well and send them back to their master." The king gave them a great feast and sent them off. Marauding bands of Arameans no longer pestered Israel.

II Kings 6:24-7:20 *Arameans besiege Samaria*
But after this Ben-hadad, king of Aram, gathered his entire army and besieged Samaria. There was a great famine in Samaria. It was so bad during the siege that inside the walls of Samaria, a donkey's head was being sold for almost 40 ounces of silver and two quarts of doves' dung cost two and a half ounces of silver. The king of Israel was walking on the wall around the city when a woman called up to him, "Help me O King!" He answered, "How can I help you? There is nothing for me to give." She

answered, "A woman said to me, 'Let's eat your son today and tomorrow we will eat mine.' Well, we cooked and ate my son. Now she is hiding her son!" When the king heard this, he tore his clothes, and the people saw that under his clothes he was wearing sackcloth. He cried out, "I will have Elisha's head removed from him today!"

Elisha was sitting at his house with the elders. He knew an officer and men from the king had been sent to bring him in for execution. He instructed his people to block the door. He said, "This evil attempt is from the Lord, I will wait no longer. So he called out to the captain of the band who had come to collect him, "Tomorrow a full measure of fine flour will be sold for a half ounce of silver and double the portion of barley will be sold for the same amount." The captain yelled back, " It would be easier for God to make windows into heaven, than for this to happen." Then Elisha answered, "You will see it, but you will not taste it."

That night there were four leprous men outside the gate of Samaria. They said to each other, "Why go into the city? We know there is nothing to eat and we will die. Let's go into the camp of the Arameans. If they kill us, well, we would have died anyway! But maybe we can get some food and live." In the breaking dawn they went towards the Aramean camp. No one was there! During the night the Lord has caused the Arameans to hear the sound of chariots and horses. They thought the king of Israel had hired the Hittites and the Egyptians to come and route them from Samaria. So they fled for their lives and left everything in the camp, including the donkeys and horses.

When the lepers got to the first tent they entered and ate a meal. Then they took the gold and silver from the tent and hid it. Next they went into another tent and got all the loot from it too. Then they said to one another, "Hold on, this isn't right. We've got to share this news or we will certainly be judged. We'll go straight to the house of the king of Israel. When they got to the gate they announced what they had found, "We went to the camp. We found the horses and donkeys tied and the tents like normal, but not a voice anywhere."

When the king heard the news, he thought it must be a trick by the Arameans. "They have left the camp only to lure us out and then ambush us." One of his servants said, "Let's take the five horses we have left in the city and go check it out. If our horses and their riders are killed, they'll just be the first casualties in Israel, because we're all doomed anyway." The king replied, "Check it out." They sent out two chariots, when they got to the camp, it was as the lepers had said. They followed a path of clothes and equipment that the Arameans had discarded in their haste to escape that ran towards the Jordan. They returned and told the king. The officer who had been sent, the previous day, to arrest Elisha was put in charge of the gate. He was trampled to death as the citizens of Samaria riotously charged out of the city towards the Aramean camp. That day the prices for barley and fine flour dropped to a half an ounce of silver just as Elisha had predicted. The royal messenger who doubted Elisha's word and was trampled at the gate, did see it, but did not eat of it.

II Kings 8:1-7 *Property restored*
One day, Elisha said to the Shunammite woman whose son he had restored to life, "Leave the land with your husband and all your household, because there are seven years of famine coming on Israel." She went to live in Philistia with her family for seven years. When the drought ended, she returned to Israel and went to the king to appeal for her property to be restored to her. As she approached the throne, Gehazi, the servant of Elisha, was there relating to the king some of the miracles Elisha had performed. He was telling the story about the woman's son being revived from death. Gehazi looked over, saw the woman and declared, "Behold the woman and her son!" She verified the story for the king. He restored all her property and all the proceeds from the property since the day she left.

II Kings 8:8-15 *Ben-Hadad murdered*
Elisha went to Damascus where Ben-hadad was ill. When Ben-hadad heard Elisha was in town he told Hazael, (the man God had instructed Elijah to anoint as king of Aram years earlier), to take gifts and ask Elisha if he would recover from his illness. Hazael loaded 40 camels with the best products in Damascus. He asked Elisha if Ben-hadad would recover from his illness. Elisha replied, "Go tell him: 'You will certainly recover.' But the Lord has shown me he will certainly die." Elisha continued to stare hard at Hazael until Hazael had to look away. Then Elisha began to cry. Hazael said, "Sir, why are you crying?" Elisha answered, "Because I know all the evil you will inflict on Israel, you will set their forts on fire, you will kill their young men and you will kill women and children." Hazael said, "Who am I? I'm just a dog, how could I do all these things?" Elisha replied, "God has shown me you will be king over Aram." So Hazael went back and gave Ben-hadad Elisha's story that he would recover. The next day Hazael used a wet towel to suffocate Ben-hadad. Then Hazael became king of Aram.

II Chronicles 21:1-22:6 *Letter from Elijah*
In the fifth year of the reign of king Joram in Israel, King Jehoshaphat of Judah died and his son, Jehoram, took over. Jehoram was 32 years old when he became king. His reign lasted eight years. He was like the kings in Israel. He even took Ahab's daughter

as a wife. When Jehoram was secure, he killed all his brothers and some of the leaders in Judah. God did not destroy Judah, because of His promise to David. Edom revolted against Jehoram and appointed their own king. Jehoram tried to put a stop to it but was unsuccessful. At the conclusion of that engagement he had to cut through the enemy lines at night to make his escape. He did make it back to Jerusalem. But Edom never ceased rebelling against Judah. Libnah also revolted from Judah at this time. Jehoram put up idols in the high places and Judah worshipped them.

A letter written by Elijah came addressed to Jehoram. It said: "This is what the Lord says: 'Because you have not walked the same way as your fathers, Jehoshaphat and Asa, did but have acted the same way the kings of Israel have, putting up idols and leading the people astray and killing your own brothers, who were better than you, I am going to strike your people, your wives, your sons and all your possessions with a great calamity. You will suffer a sever sickness in your intestines until they come out day by day.'"

God stirred up the Philistines and Arabs to come against Jerusalem. They sacked the city and carried away all Jehoram's family and possessions, except for his youngest son. Then Jehoram became ill with and incurable and painful disease that ate away his intestines. He suffered for 2 years before it finally killed him. He was buried with little or no ceremony.

When Jehoram died, his youngest son, Jehoahaz, who was also called Ahaziah, became king. He was as evil as Ahab, his father in law. The house of Ahab was Ahaziah's counselor. Ahaziah helped Joram, king of Israel, when he fought against Aram. Joram was wounded in a battle and returned to Jezreel to heal. Ahaziah went to visit him while he was recovering.

II Kings 9 *Jehu punishes Ahab and Jezebel*
Elisha called one of the sons of the prophets and said; "Go to Ramoth-gilead with this flask of oil. Look for Jehu. When you find him with his brothers, call him into a separate room and pour the oil over his head, saying, 'God says, I have anointed you king of Israel.' Then open the door and run! Do not wait around." So the young servant of Elisha went to Ramoth-gilead. When he got there, the captains were sitting together. The prophet announced, "I have a word for you, oh captain." Jehu said, "For which one of us?" The prophet replied, "For you." They went into the house and the prophet poured the oil on Jehu and said, "This is what the God of Israel says, 'I have anointed you as king over Israel. You will completely destroy the house of Ahab and

kill Jezebel to avenge all the evil they have done!'" When he finished he left the house and ran back to Elisha, as instructed.

When Jehu came out of the room all the others wanted to know what the crazy prophet said. When Jehu told them, they all said, "Jehu is king!" They went to Jezreel where Joram was recovering from the injuries he sustained fighting against Hazael the king of Aram. Ahaziah was still there visiting. When the watchman saw the approach of Jehu and his band, he reported to Joram who ordered a horseman to see if his approach was peaceful. When the horseman reached Jehu and asked if he had peaceful intent, Jehu replied, "What have you to do with peace? Fall behind and follow me." So the horseman stayed with Jehu and did not return to Jezreel. The watchman reported this to the king who ordered another rider deployed. The same thing happened; the horseman joined Jehu. When this was reported to the king, Joram and Ahaziah took their own chariots and approached Jehu.

When they reached him Joram asked, "Are you coming in peace?" Jehu replied, "How can there be peace with all the prostitutions of your mother Jezebel?" So Joram reined his chariot around and fled yelling as he went, "Turn back Ahaziah, this is treachery!" Jehu took aim with his bow, pulled it back with all his strength and shot at the fleeing Joram. The arrow pierced Joram right between the shoulder blades and went all the way through him, piercing his heart. He fell dead in his chariot. Jehu ordered Bidkar, his officer, to deposit the body of Joram in the field of Naboth, saying, "I remember the word of the Lord spoken against Ahab when you and I were in his service: 'The blood of his family would be required because he allowed Jezebel to kill Naboth.'" Ahaziah fled also. Jehu ordered him killed but he was only wounded. He made it back to Megiddo before he died. He was returned to Jerusalem and buried there with his fathers.

When Jehu got into Jezreel, Jezebel put on makeup and looked out the window to see Jehu and called, "Is all well with you, who kills his master." He looked up at the window and yelled, "Are there men up there on my side?" Two or three officials came to the window. Jehu commanded, "Throw her down." So Jezebel was thrown down. She hit the wall and left some blood on it. She also splattered some blood on the horses as she hit the pavement. The horses trampled her body as Jehu continued on his way to lunch. After his meal, he issued the order that Jezebel be buried. When the men arrived at her carcass to do the job, dogs from around the neighborhood had eaten her. All that was left was the skin on her hands and her skull. When it was reported back to Jehu he said, "Isn't that exactly what Elijah prophesized about her!"

II Kings 10:1-15 Jehu finishes the house of Ahab

The late King Ahab still had 70 sons living in Samaria. Jehu wrote letters to the sons and their masters in Samaria and to the rulers and elders in Jezreel who were guardians of Ahab's sons saying, "Now that you've received this letter, you're sitting in a fortified city, you have chariots and weapons, choose the strongest of you to sit on his father's throne and fight for his master's house." When they received the letter, they were afraid and said. "This Jehu prevailed over two kings. He can certainly prevail over us!" They returned a letter. "We will appoint no king, we are your servants, do what is good in your sight."

Jehu's return message: "If you are with me, at this time tomorrow I want the heads of all Ahab's sons delivered to me here in Jezreel." The great men of the city who were rearing Ahab's sons received the second letter. They slaughtered all 70 of Ahab's sons, put their heads in baskets and delivered them to Jezreel. Jehu had them piled in two heaps at the gate of the city till the next day. In the morning he went out and announced to the people, "You are innocent. I have conspired against my master and killed him. Who has killed all these? Everything the Lord spoke against Ahab and his family, through his prophet Elijah, will be fulfilled." Jehu proceeded to kill all the other relatives of Ahab in Jezreel. He also killed all his priests and acquaintances until there was none associated with the house of Ahab left alive.

Then Jehu traveled down to Samaria. He passed some relatives of Ahaziah, the late king of Judah. When Jehu asked who they were, they answered: "We are relatives of king Ahaziah. We have come to visit the sons of the king of Israel and the queen mother, Jezebel. Jehu ordered his men, "Take them alive." They were taken alive to a pit and then killed.

II Kings 10:15-36 *Baal worshippers killed*

As Jehu continued on his way he met Jehonadab, (a man whose family never drank wine and always lived in tents). Jehu greeted him, "Is your heart as right towards me as my heart is towards you?" Jehonadab replied, "It is." Jehu invited him into the chariot. "Come with me and see my zeal for the Lord!"

The first thing Jehu did when he arrived in Samaria was to order the death of Ahab's remaining relatives and friends. Then he gathered the citizens of Samaria and announced: "Ahab served Baal a little. Jehu will serve him much! Now gather all the worshipers of Baal and all his priests and prophets, for I am preparing a great sacrifice for Baal! Let none who love Baal be absent or they will die." (Jehu did this as a trick. He was preparing a trap to kill all those who worshipped Baal.) When all the worshipers were gathered, Baal's house was filled from end to end. Jehu had all the garments of worship distributed, then asked Jehonadab to accompany him into the house to make sure no servants of the Lord were in there for any reason. Jehu stationed 80 men outside with these instructions, "When the command is given, slaughter every worshiper in the house of Baal. If any escape, the one who allows it will pay with his life." Jehu went in and offered a sacrifice. Then he went out and delivered the order. After the slaughter, they pulled out the idols and burned them. Then they tore down the house and built a public bathroom on the site. So Jehu eradicated Baal from Israel. The Lord promised Jehu his family would reign in Israel to the fourth generation, because he had been His instrument in fulfilling His wishes against the house of Ahab. But Jehu was not careful to follow the laws of the Lord with his heart and he never stopped the cult religion of Jeroboam, which made Israel sin by worshipping the golden calves in Bethel and Dan. During his days Jehu lost parts of Israel to Hazael, king of Aram.

II Kings 11 *Trouble in Judah*

Back in Judah, when the late king's mother, Ahab's sister, Athaliah, heard Ahaziah was dead, she killed all the royal offspring. But Jehosheba, the daughter of king Jehoram and sister to Ahaziah, took Joash, one of Ahaziah's son's, and stole him from the palace. He was an infant and was hidden for six years while Athaliah was reigning over Judah. In the seventh year, Jehoiada, the wise High Priest, brought the captains of the palace militia, who were still loyal to David's lineage, into the temple. He made them swear an oath. Then he showed them Joash, the true heir to the throne. They laid out a plan where the mighty royal captains would protect the young king with David's weapons from the temple armory, while Jehoiada would present Joash to the people, hand him the testimony and crown him king. When the plan was successfully executed, all the people rejoiced enthusiastically when they saw the rightful king being anointed by the high priest and the elite palace militia protecting him.

When Athaliah heard the commotion she cried, "Treason! Treason!" And she tore her clothes. Jehoiada commanded the guards to capture Athaliah and take her to the gates for execution. He made a covenant with the people and the king that they would follow the Lord. Then they all went to the house of Baal and destroyed it and they killed the priests of Baal.

II Kings 12 (II Chronicles 24:15 - 24:22) *Temple restored in Judah*

The people rejoiced because the city was quiet and the king was on his throne. Joash was seven years old when he began his reign. He was king for 40 years. Joash was a good king all the years Jehoiada was alive to instruct him. Sacrifices were made at the high places. Joash said to the priests, "Take the money that comes into the temple from assessments and from whatever any man's heart prompts him and bring it into the treasury. Also go out to your acquaintances and try to raise money. We'll use this money to completely renovate the temple." After many years passed and the work hadn't even begun, Joash called for Jehoiada and the other priests and said, "Why hasn't this project begun? Stop raising money and begin the work with what you have." The priests agreed to stop their solicitations but also decided to cancel the renovation!

Jehoiada brought out a chest. All the money from the treasury of the temple was put into it. After they counted it and put it in bags they realized they had quite a bit of money, so skilled craftsmen were hired for the work. Strict accountings of payments were not kept, because the workers were honest men. The temple was repaired and new utensils for the service in the temple were made with the left over silver and gold. Proper temple service was conducted all the days of Jehoiada the high priest.

After the death of Jehoiada things went down hill fast in Judah. Asherim and idols were put back up and Judah rebelled against God. Prophets were sent to bring them back to the Lord but they wouldn't listen. The Spirit of the Lord came upon Zachariah, the son of Jehoiada, and he announced, "This is God's question. Why do you disobey the commands of the Lord and do not prosper? Because you have forsaken the Lord, he has also forsaken you." At the command of King Joash, a false trial was conducted and Zechariah was stoned to death. As he died he said, "May the Lord see and avenge."

Joel

Joel prophesied in Judah during these days. He saw a final judgment coming on the earth. "The Day of the Lord" would be a fearsome time of judgment for all nations. God would keep all his promises to the house of Jacob. After judgment had passed, God would show His loving kindness to Israel and the earth. God said through Joel: "When all is done you will know that I am the Lord, and there is no other. My people will never be put to shame again. I will pour out My Spirit on all mankind. Your sons and daughters will prophesy. Your old men will dream dreams. Your young men will see visions."
-<>-

II Kings 12:17-21 *Hazael bought off*
Meanwhile Aram's king, Hazael, was conducting some successful military campaigns. He conquered Gath and decided to come down to take control of Jerusalem. They

defeated Jerusalem with a smaller army than Judah. Then Joash took all the sacred things Jehoshaphat, Jehoram and Ahaziah had stored, added his own sacred things and gave it all to Hazael. Joash was very sick by the time the Arameans left. Two of Joash's servants: Jozacar and Jehozabad, made a conspiracy against Joash. They assassinated him and he was buried with his fathers. His son, Amaziah, became king.

II Kings 13:1-19 *Kings and a visit to Elisha*
In Israel, during the 23rd year of Joash's reign in Judah, Jehu the king of Israel died. His son, Jehoahaz became king in Israel. He ruled the same way his father did, following the sins of Jeroboam, with the golden calves set up in Bethel and Dan. God stayed angry with Israel and He allowed Hazael to defeat them and take their cities. After Hazael, king of Aram died; his son Ben-hadad became king in Aram. He also came against Jehoahaz.

Jehoahaz prayed to God for deliverance from the Arameans and God sent a deliverer. But conditions were never very good. The people of Israel lived in tents like they did in the old days. They never turned away from their sins. They continued to follow the false religion Jeroboam set up and they also had idols set up in Samaria, the capitol of Israel. Jehoahaz's army consisted of only 50 horsemen 10 chariots and 10,000 soldiers. The king of Aram destroyed everything else.

When Jehoahaz died, his son, Jehoash, became king in Israel. He was like his father. He continued to follow the religion Jeroboam set up in Israel. Elisha became very sick at this time. Jehoash went down to him and wept over him and said, "My father, my father, the chariots of Israel and its horsemen!" Elisha said, "Get a bow and arrows. Put your hand on the bow and open the east window." Elisha put his hands on the king's hands and said, "Shoot." When he did Elisha said, "The arrow of the Lord's victory! You will defeat the Arameans until you have destroyed them. Now take the arrows and strike the ground." King Jehoash struck the ground three times. Elisha became angry and said, "You should have struck the ground five or six times, now you will only defeat Aram three times."

II Kings 13:20-25 *Elisha dies*
Elisha died and was buried. In the spring bands of Moabites came to raid the land. A burial was being conducted near Elisha's grave. When the burial party saw the marauding Moabites, they threw the body of the man they were burying into the grave of Elisha. When he touched the corpse of Elisha, his body revived and lived again!

Ben-hadad and Jehoash fought continually. Three times Jehoash defeated him and took back cities that had been lost to Ben-hadad's father, Hazael.

II Chronicles 25:1 - 25:16 *Amaziah*
In Judah, Amaziah was a good king, not as good as David but at least as good as his father. Sacrifices were still being offered outside Jerusalem at the high places. When Amaziah had his kingdom firmly in hand he killed both Jozacar and Jehozabad, the servants who killed his father. He did not kill their sons, in accordance with the law.

Amaziah decided to make war against Edom. He did a census and found 300,000 men able to handle a spear and a shield. He also hired 100,000 men from Israel. A prophet of the Lord advised Amaziah to send the Israelite soldiers home, because God was not blessing Israel. Amaziah wanted to know what was going to happen to the 900 pounds of silver he had paid for the Israelite mercenaries. The prophet advised that God would have much more than that for the king. So Amaziah sent them home. They were angry at the insult, so they ransacked a number of Judean cities on their way home. Amaziah's campaign against Edom was successful. But he brought the Edomite gods home and began to worship them. God sent a prophet to Amaziah saying, "Why is it that you are worshipping gods who couldn't even deliver their own people from you?" Amaziah replied to the prophet, "Who made you a royal counselor?" The prophet answered, "I know that God has planned to destroy you because you have not listened to my counsel."

Then Amaziah sought other counsel. He sent a message to Jehoash in Israel saying, "Let us fight each other in battle." Jehoash responded, "You have defeated Edom, and it has made you proud. Stay home. Enjoy your victory. If you fight me, you will fall and Judah with you." Amaziah wouldn't listen. He met Jehoash in battle and was defeated. Jehoash came into Jerusalem, destroyed 200 yards of city wall, looted the temple, and the king's house. He took hostages and went back to Samaria.

When Jehoash died, his son Jeroboam became king of Israel. Amaziah, king of Judah, lived another 15 years after Jehoash died. Late in his life, he completely stopped seeking the Lord. There was a conspiracy against Amaziah, and he fled Jerusalem, but he was pursued and killed in Lachish and buried in Jerusalem.

Hosea

At this time a man named Hosea prophesied in Israel. God instructed him to take a wife, so he married a girl named Gomer. She had three children. The first was a son named Jezreel because God was soon to punish the house of Jehu for the bloodshed that started in Jezreel. The second was a daughter named "No Compassion" because God had lost his compassion for Israel. The third was another son named, "Not My People" because God was ready to abandon Israel because of their sins.

Hosea's wife left him and became a prostitute. God was showing Hosea and the people of Israel that this was exactly what they were doing. They left the God who loved and provided for them. They were prostituting themselves with idols that were not real, just beautiful craftsmanship. God told Hosea to take his cheating wife back because he would also take Israel back. Hosea also spoke against the fake religious system Jeroboam set up. He said the golden calves would be broken in pieces.

-◇-

II Chronicles 26:1 - 26:21 *Uzziah begins in Judah*
In Jerusalem Uzziah, Amaziah's son, became king of Judah. He was 16 years old and reigned 52 years in Jerusalem. He was a good king, following the ways of David during his early years. He built up Judah to a point of great strength. He rebuilt the fortifications of Jerusalem. He built towers and water storage. On the towers, he commissioned skillful men to design and build state of the art weapons of war that could shoot many arrows and hurl large stones. He loved the soil. He developed farmland and vineyards throughout Judah. Still the high places remained, so his reign wasn't perfect by any means. When he had made himself strong and secure he became proud in his heart. He decided to go into the temple himself to burn incense to the Lord. Azariah, the high priest, went with 80 brave priests to oppose Uzziah's being in the temple, where only priests were supposed to be. Uzziah was very angry with them. As he began to burn the incense, he was struck with leprosy. Azariah and the rest of the priests hustled him from the temple. Uzziah himself was in a hurry to get out, because God had struck him. He was a leper the rest of his life. He lived in a separate house and his son Jotham handled the day-to-day duties of king.

Amos

At this time a man named Amos came up to Israel from a town south of Jerusalem to prophesy in Israel. He was a shepherd. His time of prophesying began and ended quickly. He never considered himself an "official" prophet. He announced: "Like a lion,

God has roared. Does a lion roar in the wilderness if he has no prey? Do two men walk together if they haven't made an appointment? Does a young bird fall into a trap if there is no bait? Surely punishment is coming from God upon this wicked people. They make themselves rich on the backs of the poor. They live in large comfortable houses while the poor starve. They rub themselves with fine oil while the poor suffer. They recline on beds of ivory and sprawl on their couches. They eat lambs from the flock and improvise to the sound of the harp. They drink wine from sacrificial bowls. Yet they don't grieve over the moral demise of their nation. God says, 'If they would seek good and not evil, they would live. They offer me sacrifices I don't want. They sing songs I can't hear because they carry along their own little images with them, the star of their gods, which they make for themselves. Therefore Israel will go into exile ahead of the exiles. The partying will pass away.

"The fallen tent of David will be restored. Israel will be renewed. I will keep my promises to Israel...but not before judgment has come." When Amos had completed his message to Israel he returned to Judah. Jeroboam and his high priests were happy to see him go. There was a huge earthquake in the land two years after Amos's ministry in Israel.

II Kings 14:23 – 14:28 *Another Jeroboam in Israel*
King Jeroboam of Israel continued in the sins of his namesake by keeping the false religion the first Jeroboam set up; it caused all of Israel to sin. He did restore some of the old borders of Israel lost during Jehu's reign. Jeroboam was king 41 years in Israel. When he died his son, Zechariah became king of Israel.

Jonah

Jonah was a prophet in Israel during this period. He predicted through the word of the Lord many of Jeroboam's successes. At one point God told Jonah to go Nineveh to proclaim his judgment against that great city. Jonah didn't want to do it. He went to the coast and paid for passage on a ship out of the area. At sea, a great storm came upon the craft. The sailors threw cargo overboard to lighten the load. Jonah was sleeping below deck. The sailors cast lots to see who brought such a storm on them. When the lot fell on Jonah. He explained how he was trying to get away from God so he wouldn't have to go to Nineveh. He advised them to throw him overboard so the storm would cease. They tried to row to shore but the wind was too strong. They reluctantly followed Jonah's advice. The storm subsided as soon as Jonah was off the boat. Jonah was close to drowning when a whale swallowed him. He spent three days in the fish's stomach before he was vomited up on a beach.

God came to him again with the order to go to Nineveh. This time Jonah obeyed. Nineveh was a massive metropolis. It took Jonah a full day to walk through the city proclaiming that in 40 days the Lord would destroy it. When the king of Nineveh heard the news, he and the whole city repented from the evil they were engaged in and prayed earnestly for forgiveness. God decided not to destroy the city! This made Jonah angry. He prayed, "Isn't this exactly why I didn't want to come here? I know you are a very compassionate God. You don't want to bring calamity on folks, so now I look like a fool. I would be better off dead!"

Jonah went east of town and waited to see what might happen. God caused a plant to grow up over Jonah and it provided shade so Jonah would be comfortable. Jonah was extremely happy about the plant. The next day God caused a worm to eat the root of the plant so it withered. The sun shown down on Jonah and he was close to heat stroke. God said to Jonah, "Do you have reason to be angry about the plant?" Jonah answered, "I have reason to be angry, I want to die!" God said, "So, you're sad about the death of a plant that you did not cause to grow, yet you would have me destroy Nineveh where there are 120,000 children and many animals as well!"

-◇-

II Kings 15:8-38 *Bad years in Israel*

The next few years were turbulent for royalty in Israel. Zechariah was king for six months. He continued in the sins of Jeroboam that made all Israel sin. A man named Shallum conspired against Zechariah and killed him in a public place. So the word of the Lord to Jehu was complete, four of his generations reigned in Samaria. Shallum reigned as king for just one month. A man named Menahem killed Shallum and reigned in his place. Menahem reigned 10 years in Samaria. He did the same evil as all the kings of Israel by following the false religion set up by Jeroboam and this made all Israel sin. He also struck the city of Tiphsah and killed all the pregnant women there. The king of Assyria came against Israel during Menahem's reign. Memahem gave him close to 75,000 pounds of silver. He also made each of the rich men in Israel give over a pound of silver to the king of Assyria so the king of Assyria would not stay in the land.

When Menahem died, his son Pekahiah took over as king of Israel. He reigned two years. He followed the same path as his father and the religion Jeroboam set up stayed in place. One of his officer's sons, named Pekah, conspired against him and killed him. Pekah reigned 20 years. He followed all the same patterns as his fathers. Jeroboam's false religion was still the official religion of the land and it made all Israel sin. The king of Assyria, Tiglath-pileser, came against Israel during the reign of Pekah. He defeated much of Israel and took many captives back to Assyria as slaves. A man named Hoshea made a conspiracy against Pekah and killed him. Then Hoshea became king in what was left of Israel.

In the second year of Pekah's reign in Israel, Uzziah the king of Judah died and his son Jotham took over. Jotham was a good king like his father. Of course he elected not to enter the temple as his father had. Still the high places remained and people would take sacrifices to them instead of Jerusalem. Jotham did some repair work to the temple during his reign. He also did some extensive building that strengthened Judah strategically. He went out against the Ammonites and defeated them. They paid heavy tribute to Jotham for three years after their defeat. Rezin the king of Aram and Pekah king of Israel began to fight against Judah during Jotham's reign. When Jotham died his son Ahaz became king in Judah.

II Chronicles 28 *War between Israel and Judah*
Ahaz did not follow the ways of his fathers or of David. He went the same direction the kings of Israel had gone. He even sacrificed some of his own sons in the fire! There were idols everywhere. King Rezin of Aram and King Pekah of Israel came down and besieged Jerusalem, but were not able to capture it. Many Judean warriors were killed. King Rezin of Aram did capture Elath and drove out all the Judeans. The warriors of Israel carried away 200,000 captives to Samaria.

Obed, the prophet, went out to meet them and said, "God raised you up to do great harm to Judah because they have deserted the Lord, but you are going too far. Do not subjugate your own brothers into slavery. Return these people to Judah, or God's anger will burn against you. The heads of the house of Ephraim met the group returning with the captives and made the order for them to be returned. The Judean prisoners were clothed, fed, and lead off to Jerico as a drop off point for them to return to the land of Judah.

With all the problems he was facing, Ahaz sent a message and a large sum of money to Tiglath-pileser king of Assyria, that said, "I am your servant and your son, come and deliver me from King Resin of Aram and Pekah the king of Israel, who have made war against me." The king of Assyria listened to Ahaz because of the large gift and went against Aram. He captured Damascus and carried away prisoners. He also killed King Rezin.

II Kings 16:10-20 *New altar with Damascus design*
Ahaz, king of Judah, went to Damascus to meet Tiglath-pileser. While he was there he saw the altar in Damascus and wanted one like it in Jerusalem. He sent plans for the altar to Urijah, the head priest, with instructions to build it. Urijah had the work done before Ahaz got back from Damascus. When the king arrived in Jerusalem he offered all his sacrifices on the new altar. He had the bronze altar, which had been used previously, moved to the north side of the temple where he could "inquire" by it. The new altar was used for all the regular sacrifices. Ahaz also changed many of the features of the temple from their original design. He used gold and silver from the temple to make his idols and altars! He did all this to copy Tiglath-pileser, the king of Assyria. When Ahaz died his son Hezekiah reigned as king of Judah in his place.

Isaiah

God called Isaiah to be a prophet the year king Uzziah died. He saw and recorded the decline of morality in Jerusalem during the days of Ahaz. He saw a Day of Judgment coming: "God has abandoned his people, the house of Jacob. They are filled with influences from the east. There is great wealth in Jerusalem today. The land is filled with silver and gold, horses and chariots, treasure abounds. God says, 'Yet the land is also filled with idols that are manufactured with hands. The people worship them instead of me! So I will bring it all to ruin. The rich man will be in the same boat as the poor man. His proud look will be humbled. The loftiness of man will be humbled. Men will hide in caves. All that they thought could save them will be swept away; the high towers, the mighty warriors, the ships, and all the beautiful craftsmanship will be ruined. The Lord alone will be exalted in that day.'"

"Israel has become like Sodom and Gomorrah. The people are proud of how much they can sin! Their only remembrance of Me is with meaningless ceremony. They bring multiple sacrifices in which I take no pleasure. They trample through My courts with pious procession that is empty tradition. I am tired of people raising their hands to Me in prayers meant only for religious display."

"Israel is a mess. The men become heroes because they can mix a strong drink. The women find their beauty only from the way they appear, with seductive eyes and stride. A day is coming when God will take away their anklets, headbands, crescent ornaments, dangling earrings, bracelets, sashes, perfume boxes, finger rings, nose rings, fine robes, fancy underwear and money purses. That day, instead of a belt they will wear a rope, instead of well-set hair they will have plucked scalps, instead of fine clothes they will wear burlap rags. Their men will be killed in war. All their mighty heroes fallen. In that day seven women will take hold of one man and say, 'We'll eat our own bread and wear our own clothes, just let us be called by your name to take away our shame.'"

Isaiah presented this analogy: "Let me tell you about God's vineyard. He planted it in a fertile valley, carefully chosen. He dug it up, removed all the stones and planted it with the finest vine. He built a tower in the middle and built a large vat for all the wine it would produce. Instead of producing good grapes it produced worthless fruit. What else could God have done to His vineyard? Because it is not producing, He will tear down its hedges and leave it to waste. He will no longer hoe and prune. He will also cause no more rain to fall on it."

These warnings were mostly ignored in the days of Isaiah. He also spoke of the redemption of Israel: "A virgin will become pregnant with a boy she will name "God is with us." He will be a light in the darkness. The government will rest on his shoulders. He will be called: Wonderful Counselor, Mighty God and the Prince of Peace! He will rule from the throne of David. His kingdom will never end. He will be a king who judges righteously. The wolf will lie down with the lamb, the leopard with the kid, and the calf with the young lion. A nursing child will play with the cobra. In those days the world will be full of the knowledge of the Lord as the water covers the sea."

The Lord proclaimed through Isaiah, "Everybody wants to worship fancy idols! An idol is made in a craftsman's shop. He carefully selects the materials that will last a long time. He nails it in its place so that it won't fall over, then people come and worship it! I am not like an idol. Tell Me, what idol announces what will happen in the future as surely as if it were history. I will tell you now what will happen. I will put a hook into a king from the east. Cyrus is his name. I will use him to teach My children. He like any other earthly king can do nothing unless I sanction it. He worships other gods. No problem, I can still use him. When I'm done using him to chastise My people, then his mighty and beautiful kingdom will be destroyed."

"No one believes My message. I will raise up a servant who will grow up like a tender shoot. He doesn't appear great on the outside. He was despised and rejected by men. Our grief's He surely bore and our sorrows He carried. He was pierced for our transgressions. He was crushed for our iniquities. We have all gone astray like sheep, but He has paid for our sins. He was oppressed and afflicted; yet He did not open His mouth in protest. Like a lamb being led to slaughter, like a sheep is silent before its shearers, He did not open His mouth. He was killed with wicked men, yet His grave was with the wealthy. He had done no violence; there was no deceit in His mouth. God was pleased that He was crushed! Because He was offering Himself as a guilt offering, He will see His offspring because of what He's done. He will be allotted greatness because He bore the sins of many."

-◇-

Micah

Micah was another prophet who saw the doom of Israel and Judah. While Samaria seemed like an indestructible city, Micah announced that it would be made into a pile of ruins. Destruction would come because of all the idol worship and greed in Israel. Even though God had kept every promise, the people still seemed to want nothing to do with Him. Israel's leaders pronounced judgment for a bribe, her priests instructed and her prophets prophesied only for money.

God said through Micah, "O little town of Bethlehem, One will go forth from you who will be ruler in Israel. He started long ago, even from eternity. He will come and be a shepherd to His flock. He will become the peace of the whole world!" Micah said that eventually God was going to throw the sins of Israel into the depths of the sea. God would keep all His promises to Abraham.

-◇-

II Kings 17 *End of Israel*

When Pekah, the king of Israel, died, his son Hoshea became king. He was the worst of all the kings of Israel. Shalmaneser, the king of Assyria, came against him and Hoshea paid tribute to him. One year the king of Assyria found treachery in Hoshea. Instead of paying tribute, Hoshea had contacted the King of Egypt, named So, attempting to get some help against Assyria. The king of Assyria put Hoshea in prison and came up against the whole land of Israel. He defeated them, captured Samaria and carried all the Israelites into captivity in Assyria. Israel never returned to the land. Only Judah remained.

Now this all happened to Israel because they did not follow the laws God had given them. Not only did they not follow the laws but also they went after the gods from the nations the Lord had driven out of the land. They did things in secret, which were not right. They had idols under every green tree. They did all kinds of evil things to provoke the Lord. They even made their children walk through the fire, just like the evil nations that surrounded them. Jeroboam set up a false religion with the calves in

Bethel and Dan and this made all Israel sin. Judah wasn't much better, but the Lord rejected Israel first and gave them into the hand of Assyria.

The king of Assyria brought people from Babylon to live in Samaria and the other cities of Israel. At the beginning of their living in Israel, they did not fear the Lord. God sent lions amongst them and many of them died. The settlers sent a letter to the King of Assyria that said, "We do not know the ways of this local god down here in Israel, so he's sending lions among us. Send someone to teach us this god's customs." So the king chose one of the priests from among the Israelites in Assyria and sent him down to teach them to fear the Lord.

They did learn to fear God, but they kept offering sacrifices to their own gods. To this day they have a mixed-bag religion. They do some of what the Lord commands yet still follow their own customs as well.

II Chronicles 29:1 - 30:21 *Revival in Judah*

It was during Hoshea's third year as king in Israel that Hezekiah became king in Judah. He was 26 years old and reigned 29 years in Jerusalem. He did what was right in God's eyes, just like his father, David. The first thing Hezekiah did was order the cleansing of the temple. He called the priests and the Levites and said, "The doors of the temple are shut, and the lamps are not burning. We have turned our backs on the Lord, and we're paying the price. Many of our people have been carried away captive. Many have died in battles. It's in my heart to renew our covenant with God so He'll turn His anger away from us. Cleanse the temple as prescribed by the law. Do not be negligent. You priests and Levites are the ones God has called to serve in the temple."

So the priests and Levites went to work. It took more than two weeks to complete the work according to the instructions prescribed in the law outlined by Moses. When they notified Hezekiah the temple was ready, he assembled the princes of Judah. They went to the temple and ordered the priests, the sons of Aaron, to sacrifice seven bulls, rams, lambs, and male goats as a sin offering for the kingdom. Hezekiah then ordered the Levites to assemble with their musical instruments. The priests got ready with their trumpets. When everything was ready the burnt offering started, and the priests played their trumpets along with the Levites playing their cymbals, harps and lyres, the same type of instruments King David and Asaph had written Psalms to be played with. They continued until the burnt offering was finished they bowed and worshipped, then they started playing and singing again!

Hezekiah said, "Now that we've got the temple on line, all the people can start making offerings and sacrifices as they see fit." So Judeans from all over came to make sacrifices. There were so many that the priests couldn't keep up, so the Levites who had consecrated themselves helped with the work. This was because some of the priests were a little remiss in getting themselves ceremonially prepared to do the service. Jerusalem rejoiced because the regular service of the temple was suddenly available again.

Hezekiah sent messengers into the territory of Israel. They went all through Ephraim, Manasseh, and as far as Zebulun. Most of the people scoffed and laughed at them, but some did humble themselves and came to Jerusalem. Passover was celebrated. Many of the people who came from the north hadn't prepared themselves to be ceremonially clean. They ate the Passover anyway. Hezekiah prayed and asked God to give them a pardon. God granted a bye: if their hearts were right before God they could go ahead and celebrate the Passover. Everyone joined in the celebration. They started off with a seven-day feast. There was music and ceremonies every day for the seven days. Then the whole assembly decided to go another seven days. Hezekiah and the princes had contributed 2000 bulls and 17,000 sheep so there was plenty for the extension. There was great joy in Jerusalem! There hadn't been this much joy since the days of David, king of Israel.

When everyone went home, Hezekiah appointed priests and Levites for each region. They tore down all the false altars and idols throughout the whole land. They also broke into pieces the bronze snake that Moses had lifted up in the wilderness, because up to then the people had burned incense to it. It was called "A Piece of Bronze."

The priests and Levites in Jerusalem stayed busy with all the offerings people were bringing from all over. There was a large harvest that year and all the people brought in a tenth of the first fruits of the harvest, so the temple was filled to overflowing! Extra space was provided for all of it. Throughout Judah there were priests, sons of Aaron, doing their job as prescribed in the Law of Moses. King Hezekiah provided all he was instructed by the law to give. Judah was prosperous and joyous.

Hezekiah was a very good king. He trusted in the Lord his whole life; he never stopped following him and kept his commandments. The Lord was with him and prospered him in whatever he did. Hezekiah rebelled against the king of Assyria and didn't serve him. He defeated the Philistines all the way back to Gaza.

II Kings 18:9-12 *Israel in exile*

It was in the fourth year of Hezakiah, which was the seventh year of Hoshea in Israel, that Shalmaneser king of Assyria came against Samaria to besiege it. It took three years for them to capture it. So the Assyrians carried Israel away because they had never followed the Lord the way they should. They did not keep their side of the contract made with God when Moses led them.

II Chronicles 32 II Kings 18:13 *Assyria comes against Judah*

In the 14th year of Hezekiah, even after all the acts of faithfulness in Judah, Sennacherib the new king of Assyria came against the fortified cities in Judah and seized them. Hezekiah knew they wouldn't stop till they reached Jerusalem. He ordered the people to plug all the wells and cover all the springs, so Sennacherib would not have water when he came upon Jerusalem. Hezekiah sent a letter to the king of Assyria saying, "I have done wrong, withdraw your troops and I will do whatever you require." The king of Assyria demanded close to 30,000 pounds of silver and 300 pounds of gold. Hezekiah had to dig very deep to come up with the money. He cut off gold from the doors and doorposts of the temple to make the payment.

The king of Assyria sent some of his officials along with a great army to Jerusalem. When they came into the city, Hezekiah sent: Eliakim, his personal manager, Shebnah, the scribe, and Joah, the recorder, to meet with the officials from Assyria. Rabshakeh, one of the Assyrian officials, said, "The king of Assyria wants to know where Hezekiah gets his confidence. He says, (but so far all we hear are words), that he has counsel and strength for war. Now who could this be? Egypt? We can tell you this, if you lean against Egypt for help, you are relying on a crushed reed. If a man leans on Egypt's staff, it will pierce his own hand. Maybe you are trusting in your Lord. You're feeling confident because you have destroyed all the high places that he disapproves of. Now you just worship here in Jerusalem. Here's the truth: If I gave you 2000 horses, you wouldn't have the riders to put on them. If you're depending on Egypt, the least of the kings of Assyria's servants could beat him. If you're depending on your Lord, it seems we Assyrians have His approval to destroy you, because here we are!"

Now Eliakim, Shebnah and Joah said to Rabshakeh, "Speak to us in Aramaic, not in Judean. There's no reason for the people on the wall to hear our discussion." Then Rabshakeh yelled in Judean, "Has my master sent me to speak just to your king? We have been sent to all the people in Jerusalem who are doomed to eat their own dung and drink their own urine with you and your king! Hear the words of the king of Assyria: Do not trust Hezekiah. He will not be able to protect you from Assyria. He tells you to trust in the Lord, He will deliver you. Your God can't and He won't. The king of Assyria says come out peacefully, and he will give you a good land full of good things. Otherwise you will die. Do not listen to Hezekiah who says, 'The Lord will deliver us.' Have any of the gods of the other nations been powerful enough to stop us? No, not one! How do you think the Lord has the power to deliver you?" The people on the wall were silent, because the command of the king was to be silent and say nothing.

Then Eliakim, Shebna and Joah returned to Hezekiah with their clothes torn. When Hezekiah heard their report, he tore his clothes also. He ordered his staff to visit Isaiah to inform him how the Assyrians mocked God and to understand how God was responding to this terrible day.

Isaiah told them to return to Hezekiah and say: "This is what God says, 'Do not worry about the words you heard from the servants of the king of Assyria, blaspheming Me. I will put a spirit in him so he will hear a rumor and return to his own land.'" Rabshakeh did leave the area. He heard Sennacherib, the king of Assyria, had changed strategies. When he joined Sennacherib in Libnah they sent a letter back to Hezekiah that said, "Do not let the God that you trust deceive you. He will not protect Jerusalem from Assyria. You've heard about how we have defeated our enemies. None of their gods have been able to protect them. Judah won't be any different."

When Hezekiah got the letter he went to the temple and spread it before the Lord and prayed, "God, You are the God of Israel, the Lord of all the gods of the earth and You have created heaven and earth. Open Your ears Lord and hear these words of Sennacherib that are a reproach to You, the living God! Assyria has defeated all the other nations and destroyed their gods, but they weren't gods, they were just the work of men's hands, wood and stone. I pray that You will deliver Your people, so all the Nations will know that You alone are the Lord."

Then Isaiah sent word to Hezekiah, "This is what God says, 'Because you have trusted and prayed to Me about the king of Assyria, I have heard you.' This is what the Lord says to the king of Assyria: 'Well, don't you think you're just the special king of all time! You have no idea who you're fooling with. You have mocked Me through your messengers saying I can't stop you, because of all the great conquest you have accomplished! I was the one who allowed you your victories. I was the one who made it happen! I know when you wake up each morning and when you lay down. I have heard your raging against Me. Now I will put a hook in your nose and My bridle in your lips. I will turn you back the way in which you came. Hezekiah, be assured, I will protect Jerusalem. The king of Assyria will not come near the city with spear or shield. He will return by the same way in which he came. I will defend this city for My own sake and for the sake of my servant, David.'"

That night an angel of the Lord went into the camp of the Assyrians and killed 185,000 soldiers. When the few who were left woke up, all they saw were dead bodies, Sennacherib returned to Nineveh. One day he was worshipping in the house of Nisroch his god. Two men named Adrammelech and Sharezer killed him and were able to escape to the land of Ararat. Esarhaddon, Sennecherib's son became king of Assyria.

II Kings 20 *Hezekiah's life extended*
Soon after this victory, Hezekiah became extremely ill. Isaiah came to the palace and advised him to get his house in order because he was going to die. Isaiah returned to his own home. Hezekiah prayed to the Lord, "God, You know how I've followed You all the days of my life. I've always tried to do what You've wanted me to do." He wept bitterly. Isaiah wasn't even all the way out of the palace complex when God came to him and said, "Go back to Hezekiah and tell him I have heard his prayer and seen his tears. Tell him in three days he will be healed and will go up to the house of the Lord to worship. I will add fifteen years to his life."

Isaiah went back and told Hezekiah's servant to put fig on the boil that was making the king so ill. He told Hezekiah he would recover and worship at the temple in three days. Hezekiah asked, "What will be the sign by which I will know that I'll go to the temple in three days?" Isaiah replied, "What do you prefer, that the sun move up ten steps or back ten steps?" Hezekiah answered, "It's easy for the sun to go down ten steps, make the sun go up ten steps." Isaiah prayed to the Lord and the shadow of the sun moved up ten steps on the stairway of Ahaz.

Then Berodach-baladan the king of Babylon sent a letter and a present to King Hezekiah because he heard of his illness. Hezekiah became friendly with the king of Babylon's messengers and he showed them all his treasures and all the wealth of his kingdom. Hezekiah showed them everything worth seeing.

When Isaiah heard all this, he warned Hezekiah. "The days are coming when all that is in your house, all the things that you and your fathers have stored up will be carried to Babylon. Nothing will be left. Some of your own sons will be carried away and become officials in Babylon." Hezekiah thought this was a good word, simply because it meant there would be peace during the rest of his reign.

II Kings 21:1-18 *Manasseh*

When Hezekiah died, his son Manasseh became king of Judah. Manasseh immediately began to follow all the gods from the surrounding nations. All the high places were reconstructed. Baals and Asherah were erected. He built idols to the host of heaven in both courts of the temple. He made his son walk through the fire; he practiced divination and dealt with mediums. All these things made God angry. Manasseh put an Asherah in the temple, where God had said, "In this house, in Jerusalem, which I have chosen from all the tribes of Israel, I will put My name there forever. I won't make the people wander anymore from the land I gave their fathers, if only they will observe and do all that I have commanded them, and according to the law that My servant Moses commanded them."

Judah was as easily seduced by all this as Israel had been. Manasseh seduced them to be more evil than any of the nations that God had driven out of the land. Manasseh also shed much innocent blood. He filled Jerusalem with death. Assyria came against Manasseh and carried him away, humiliated. Manasseh humbled himself before the Lord at this time. God heard him and allowed him to return to Jerusalem. He took down some of the idols he'd erected, conducted proper sacrifices and fortified Jerusalem.

II Kings 21:19-22:27 II Chronicles 35 *Josiah's reforms*

Manasseh died. His son Amon became king. Amon was the same as Manasseh. He reigned two years. Conspirators from among his servants killed him. The Judeans tracked down all the individuals who had conspired against Amon and killed them. They made Amon's son, Josiah, king. Josiah was eight years old when he became king of Judah. He was a good king and acted like his father, David. In his eighteenth year he sent Shaphan the scribe to Hilkiah, the high priest, with this message: "Count all the money that the doorkeepers have gathered from the people and give it to the skilled workmen who take care of the temple, to make all the repairs needed. Don't worry about accounting because they will deal faithfully.

When Hilkiah, the high priest, conducted the counting he found the book of the law in one of the storerooms. He called Shaphan and said, "Shaphan, I have found the book of the law in the house of the Lord." He gave the book to Shaphan and he read it. Shaphan went before Josiah and reported that the work had begun and told him about the book, which he then read to the king. When King Josiah heard the words of the law he tore his clothes. He said to Shaphan, "Go inquire of the Lord for me and all Judah concerning the words in this book. The wrath of God must be heavy on us because our fathers have not listened to these words and have not done according to all that is written concerning us."

So Shapan, Hilkiah, Ahikam, Achbor and Asaiah went to Huldah who was a prophetess. She lived in the second quarter of Jerusalem. She said, "Tell the man who sent you to me, this is what God says: 'Behold I will bring evil on this place just as the book says. My people have forsaken Me to sacrifice and burn incense to false gods. They have provoked Me to anger.' But to the king of Judah, who has sent you to inquire of the Lord say, 'Because your heart was tender and you humbled yourself before the Lord when you heard the words written in the book and you have torn your clothes and wept before Me, behold I have heard you. You will die naturally. You won't see the evil that will come on this place.'" So they went back to the king with the message.

The king gathered all the men of Judah, all the inhabitants of Jerusalem, the priests, the prophets, and all the people both small and great. He read the Book of the Law to them. Then the king stood by the pillar and made a covenant with the Lord, to follow Him, keep all His commandments, and do it with his whole heart. The people also entered into the agreement. Josiah started a major idol destruction program. First he had the idols removed from the temple. He burned those outside the city. He killed all the idolatrous priests of Baal, the sun, the moon and the host of heaven. He destroyed the places of male cult prostitution that were found in the temple. He broke down all the high places where sacrifices were made to the Lord. The priests of these high places did not return to Jerusalem but ate bread without yeast among themselves. He destroyed the place where children were forced to walk through the fire for the god Molech. He did away with the horses that the kings of Judah had given to the sun, and he burned the chariots of the sun. He cut down every pillar and Asherah in the kingdom. Then he went to Bethel and destroyed the altar Jeroboam had installed there. He removed the bones from all the graves on the hillside and burned them on the idolatrous altars to defile them. He did not disturb the grave of the prophet who came from Judah to warn Jeroboam about his new religion. He removed all the high places around Samaria and burned the priest of those places on their own altars. Then he returned to Jerusalem.

The king commanded that a Passover be celebrated. They collected Passover sacrifices from all the people. King Josiah contributed 30,000 offerings, plus 3000 bulls. His officers of the house of the Lord, Hilkiah, Zechariah and Jehiel also contributed for the people, 2600 offerings from the flocks and 300 bulls. Some of the officers of the Levites, Conaniah, Shemaiah, Nethanel, Hashabiah, Jeiel and Jozabad got together and they contributed 5000 from the flocks and 500 bulls. The service was prepared, and they had a Passover like hadn't been seen since the days of Samuel! None of the kings of Israel or Judah had ever celebrated a Passover like this! Josiah was a great king, but the wrath of God was not removed against Judah, because of all Manasseh's provocations.

Nahum

Nahum, a prophet from the town of Elkosh, predicted the complete destruction of Nineveh, the capitol of Assyria. God made it clear that he was Lord of all the nations. Assyria had been a major power, but God's purpose for them was complete. It might seem that some had great power, but God was in charge.

Zephaniah

The prophet Zephaniah declared that the day of the Lord would be a day of judgment. All of Israel's neighbors would be judged along with Israel. Israel will ultimately inherit the land and the whole earth will gather around Jerusalem in peace. God himself will dwell there as a victorious warrior. Zephaniah said, "God will exult over you with joy, and He will be quiet in His love!"

Habakkuk

Habakkuk prophesied that God was raising up Babylon to be the new instrument of God's judgment against His rebellious people. Habakkuk was hard pressed to understand how God could use such a proud and sinful people against His own. The answer came in the fact that the Babylonians would also be judged. Habakkuk declared that people who had a real relationship with God did so through their faith. God would remember and keep those who loved and obeyed Him.

-◇-

II Kngs 23:28-37 *War with Egypt*

At this time Pharaoh Neco, the king of Egypt, fought the King of Assyria at the river Euphrates. Josiah went out to fight against Pharaoh. Pharaoh Neco told Josiah that Egypt was on a mission from God, against the Assyrians, but Josiah didn't listen. He disguised himself to look like a soldier but he was shot anyway and was taken from the battle fatally wounded. His body was returned to Jerusalem. His son Jehoahaz became king. Jehoahaz was king for three months. He went back to the ways of Manasseh his grandfather. Pharaoh Neco came back and imprisoned Jehoahaz. He made Eliakim, one of his brothers, king instead. He changed Eliakim's name to Jehoiakim. He took Jehoahaz back to Egypt where he died.

Pharaoh demanded a tax of about 9000 pounds of silver and 100 pounds of gold. Jehoiakim levied all the people to pay the tax to Pharaoh. Jeoiakim was evil like his fathers and reigned 11 years in Jerusalem,

Jeremiah

Jeremiah, the prophet, spoke these words of warning from the Lord: " What injustice did your fathers find in Me that made them go so far from Me? They knew I brought them out of Egypt and gave them this land. Yet the priests and the leaders never really encouraged the people to follow Me. The prophets prophesied by Baal. No one seems to know Me. As a thief is shamed when he's caught, so is the house of Israel shamed along with their leaders. Israel says to any tree, 'You are our father' and to a stone, 'You gave me birth.'"

"If a husband divorces his wife and she goes from him and gives herself to another man, will he return to her? Israel has acted like a prostitute under every green tree with every idol imaginable. I thought maybe Judah would come to her senses when she saw what happened to her northern sister. She did come back to Me with outward display, not with her heart, rather with deception."

The word of God to Jeremiah continued: "Yet if they would only return and put away these detestable things; if they would return with truth and in righteousness then they would again be blessed among the nations. I want them to have circumcised hearts, not just circumcised bodies. Amend your ways and your deeds and I will dwell with you in this place. Don't trust in empty words like, 'This is the temple of the Lord, the temple of the Lord, the temple of the Lord.' Practice justice; do not oppress the foreigner, the orphan or the widow. Do not shed innocent blood or walk after other gods. Then I will let you live in this land forever. How can you steal, murder, commit adultery, lie and offer sacrifices to false gods and then stand before Me in this house which is called by My name and say, 'We are delivered'?

God told Jeremiah, "Do not pray for this people any longer. Do not intercede to Me for them; I won't listen. Do you see what they are doing in every town in Judah? The children gather wood, the fathers kindle a fire, and the mothers bake bread for the queen of heaven, they pour out libations on their roofs to other gods, in order to spite Me. They have built altars to burn their sons and their daughters in the fire! I did not command this! This is something that never entered My mind!"

"Because they have done all these wicked things, I will bring a nation out of the north that will completely destroy Jerusalem. The cities of Judah will be destroyed and will have no inhabitants. I will make Israel a wasteland. Because they have forsaken My law and have not obeyed My voice or walked according to it: I will feed them wormwood and give them poisoned water to drink. I will scatter them among the nations whom neither they nor their fathers have known. They have not met the terms of our agreement. I brought them into this land flowing with milk and honey. I gave it to them. I told them through Moses that they needed to listen to me. They have done nothing close to that. They have gone after other gods. They have as many gods as they have cities. Therefore their sons will die by the sword and their daughters will starve in famine."

God told Jeremiah to take a pottery jar before the head priests and say, "Hear what God has to say, 'I am about to bring calamity on this place because Judah has forsaken me.'" After he said this, Jeremiah broke the jar and concluded, "This is how totally destroyed Jerusalem will be! God instructed Jeremiah to write his prophesies down to be read to the people. Jeremiah dictated his prophesies to Baruch, his secretary. They were taken to King Jehoiakim. When the king heard them he tore them up and threw them in the fire. Jeremiah and Baruch rewrote the scroll adding additional prophesies.
-<>-

II Kings 24 *Exile to Babylon*
Nebuchadnezzer, king of Babylon, came up to Jerusalem. Jehoiakim served him three years with taxes. Then he rebelled. Bands of Chaldeans, Arameans, Moabites and Amorites came against Judah, as the prophets had said, because of all the sins of Manasseh and all the innocent blood he had spilled throughout Jerusalem.

Jehoiakim died and his son Jehoiachin became king. The king of Egypt did nothing during the infraction of Babylon into the region because Babylon had already defeated him. Jehoiachin was evil, just as his father was. At this time one of Nebuchadnezzer's generals came against Jerusalem and besieged it. Then Nebucadnezzer came himself. Jehoiachin surrendered and was taken captive along with the officials, the mighty men, the skilled craftsmen and the smiths. They were taken to Babylon. Nebuchdnezzer also took the gold and silver from the temple and the king's house. The king of Babylon made Jehoiachin's uncle, Mattaniah, the governor of the Judean territory and changed his name to Zedekiah. All this occurred because of the anger of the Lord against Judah.

Ezekiel

During the summer of the 5th year king Jehoichin and the Jews were in Babylon, Ezekiel, one of the exiles who was a member of the priesthood, saw a vision. He saw a storm brewing from the north. In the middle of the brewing storm there was a glow. Inside of this, he saw figures that resembled four living beings. Each had four faces and four wings. They shone like polished bronze. Their wings touched each other and their faces didn't turn. They always appeared to be going straight, wherever they went. There were wheels for each of the living beings and these wheels went wherever they went. It seemed the spirit of the beings was in their wheels. Above this was a throne that was brilliant and beautiful. On the throne was a figure that had the appearance of a man. This figure was wonderful and dazzling. Ezekiel fell on his face before it.

A voice came out and said, "Son of man I am sending you to the children of Israel. They are stubborn and obstinate. They won't listen to you, but you will announce; 'This is what the Lord says' Whether they listen or not, they will know a prophet has been sent." Then Ezekiel was given a scroll to eat. He ate it. It tasted like honey. He was instructed to act as a watchman. He was to warn the people what was coming. God knew they wouldn't listen.

Ezekiel announced: "This is what God says, 'I put Jerusalem at the center of the nations. She has rebelled against My law more than the lands that surround her. Because you have defiled My sanctuary with your detestable idols and all your abominations, one third of you will die from hunger, a third of you will die by the sword and a third will be scattered to the wind. Jerusalem and my sanctuary will be totally destroyed. Robbers will come in and loot My holy place. Then My anger will be spent and you will know that I am the Lord. You will become a reproach among the nations. Those of you who survive and are scattered will remember Me among the nations where you are scattered. You will hate yourselves for how you rejected Me and turned away.'"

"Jerusalem has been filled with false prophets who say, 'This is what God says', when I haven't said anything to them. They say they see visions, but everything they see, they think up themselves. They say, 'This is what God says', then they hope it comes true, because they know I didn't say it. They cry out, 'Peace!' when there is no peace. They build shaky walls that will certainly tumble when I blow wind upon them. They will be gone with the wall!"

"Israel has been led by shepherds who worry about themselves and not the flock. They feed themselves but not the flock. I will demand My sheep back from these shepherds. I will gather them back together. I will gather them from all the nations where they have been scattered. I will feed the flock and lead them to rest. Then I will set before them one shepherd. My servant, David, will feed them himself and be their shepherd. I will make the land prosperous again. Then they will know that I am the Lord."

"I will gather you back to the land from the nations were you have been scattered. I will sprinkle clean water on you and cleanse the filthiness off you. I will put a new heart in you. I will put My Spirit in you and cause you to follow My statutes. You will be careful to follow My ordinances. I will save you from all your uncleanness. I am not doing this for your sake. My name will be vindicated. I will keep My agreements with Israel. I will live with them. I will be their God and they will be My people. Judah and Israel will no longer be separated, they will be one people."

<>

Back to a narrative portion of Jeremiah
Jeremiah 39:1- 40:6 *Jerusalem destroyed*
During the ninth year of Zedekiah's reign, he rebelled against Babylon. Nebuchadnezzer came against Jerusalem and besieged it. Zedikiah asked Jeremiah what fate God had for Jerusalem. Before Jeremiah received a reply from the Lord, the Babylonians packed up and left the area because they had heard that the Egyptians were coming north. Jeremiah then sent word that Jerusalem would certainly be destroyed and burned. Jeremiah came close to being killed as a traitor. He was thrown into prison. The Babylonians returned and continued the siege against the city. It took about two and a half years for them to finally break into the city. Zedekiah tried to escape but was caught. He was brought before the king of Babylon at Riblah. His family was killed in front of his eyes. Then his eyes were plucked out, and he was placed in bronze fetters and lead away to Babylon.

Jerusalem was burned to the ground. The temple, the king's house and every house in Jerusalem were burned down. The wall around the city was destroyed. All the remaining bronze in the temple was broken up and carried to Babylon. All of the king's officers were rounded up and killed. Jeremiah was given a choice by the Babylonians to go wherever he chose. He stayed with the people in Judah.

Obadiah

Obadiah, the prophet, delivered God's words concerning the fate of Edom. Edom (the descendants of Esau) stayed safe in their mountain dwellings during all this upheaval in the land. When Jerusalem was being destroyed, the people of Edom took part in the pillage of Jerusalem. They took everything. They seemed to be gloating over the judgment that had fallen on the house of Jacob. So God announced that they too would be judged. No nation was exempt. Israel was ultimately to be in possession of the land.

<>

Back to a narrative portion of Jeremiah and Kings and Chronicles
Jeremiah 40:7 - 44:30　II Kings 25:7-30　*Bad times in Judah*
The Babylonians appointed Gedaliah governor of those remaining in Judah. Gedaliah told everyone remaining, a few of whom were from the royal household (Ishmael, Johanan, Seraiah, and Jezaniah) that they should serve Babylon and everything would be fine. After seven months, Ishmael and ten men with him killed Gedaliah and all who were with him, Babylonians and Jews.

The people remaining asked Jeremiah if they should stay in Judah or go into Egypt. They promised that whatever God told him is what they would do. After ten days of prayer, Jeremiah told them God wanted them to stay and that He would take care of them. They didn't listen. They went off to Egypt and took Jeremiah with them. Jeremiah predicted the downfall of Egypt while he was there and also predicted that only a few of the Jews in Egypt would ever make it back to Judah because many of them began to worship Egyptian gods while they were there.

Meanwhile, back in Babylon Jehoiachin, the former king of Judah was released from prison. Evil-merodach, the king of Babylon at the time spoke kindly to him. Jehoiachin ate at his table regularly and was given a pension for the rest of his life.

While the Jews were in Babylon, many of them achieved prominence and wealth. They were able to help their countrymen in their eventual return to Judah.

Esther

The Story of Esther begins with a party at the palace of Ahasuerus, the king of Babylon. The party was the final banquet of an event, which lasted over half a year in Susa, the capitol of Babylon. King Ahasuerus and all the main princes of the land were drinking wine in one area of the palace and Queen Vashti, his wife, was having a banquet for the women. King Ahasuerus wanted to show off his beautiful wife and her royal crown, so he sent for her. She refused to come. The king and the princes were enraged. The princes advised the king that this could not be tolerated or all the wives in the kingdom would refuse to come when their husbands called. Queen Vashti was banished and a decree was issued that all wives must come when called by their husbands. This decree was translated into all the languages of the provinces king Ahasuerus ruled.

When things settled down, it became clear a new queen was required. Virgins from all over the kingdom were brought to Susa and put in the care of Hegai, the king's eunich. He oversaw a beauty program at the palace compound. Each virgin attended the program for one year, to be at their best when they went before the king for one evening. The one who pleased the king would become the next queen.

There was a Jew living in Susa named Mordecai. He was raising his orphaned niece, named Esther. She was summoned to the palace to take part in Eunich Hegai's program. Esther immediately gained the favor of Hagai. She was given seven maids from the king's palace, was provided with cosmetics and oils and lived in the best area of the facility. Mordecai would check in every day to see how she was doing. He had instructed Esther to keep her Jewish heritage a secret.

Each evening one of the virgins would go into the king. She was allowed to take anything in Hegai's inventory along with her. She went to the king in the evening and left in the morning. She would then be transferred to another facility and would not see the king again unless he called for her by name.

When it was Esther's turn, and she was to select what to take before the king, she asked only for Hegai's advice about how to appear. He advised her as to all the preferences of the king. The king fell in love with Esther and he placed the royal crown on her head, and she became queen. A wonderful banquet was held in Esther's honor.

Around this time a plot was hatched to assassinate the king. Mordecai became aware of the plot and was able to get word to the king in time to save him. An account was kept in the chronicles of the kingdom.

There was a man named Haman who king Ahasuerus had promoted to a high position. Haman was in charge of all the princes. When he went through the gates of the capitol everyone would bow down to Haman, except for one man, Esther's uncle, Mordecai. This enraged Haman. Haman was determined to destroy Mordecai. He decided the best way to do it was to destroy all the Jews living in the kingdom. He told the king that the Jews followed their own laws; they weren't concerned about the laws of the kingdom and it would be in the king's best interest to eliminate them from the land. The king approved of a plan: On a specified day, the Jew's enemies would be allowed to attack and kill them. The plunder would then be added to the king's treasuries. The decree was legally binding. The written order was translated into every language in the kingdom and distributed to every region.

When Mordecai heard about the decree he and all the Jews mourned in burlap clothes. Mordecai went wailing bitterly to the king's gate. Esther sent new clothes to him, but he did not accept them. She sent servants to find out just what was going on. Mordecai told them everything about the decree and even sent a copy back with them. Esther replied through her servants to Mordecai: "The rule of the palace is never to approach the king unless he has summoned you. To approach the king unsolicited can easily result in death. The king has not summoned me in thirty days!" Mordecai told Esther's servants to say this to Esther: "Do you think you will escape just because you are in the palace? If you stay silent, God will deliver us through some other means and you won't be included. Who knows whether you have attained royalty for this time?" Esther replied, "You and all the Jews here in Susa fast for three days and so will I. Then I will go before the king. If I die, I die."

After three days Esther dressed in her royal robes and went into the inner court in front of the king's rooms. The king was sitting on his throne. When he saw Esther he pointed his scepter at her to invite her into the throne room. He asked, "What is wrong with you queen Esther and what is your request? If it will cure your sadness, I will give you half of my kingdom!" Esther answered, "If it is pleasing to the king, may he please invite Haman to a banquet that I have prepared for him." The king had Haman brought quickly to the banquet Esther had laid out. As they were drinking wine, the king repeated his offer of half the kingdom to Esther. She requested that Haman join them again the next evening.

Haman left the palace that day very pleased with how things were going. As he passed the gate, Mordecai did not bow, as usual. Haman knew Mordecai's days were numbered so he didn't make a fuss. When Haman got home he was drinking with his wife and friends. He recounted all his successes up to that day. He complained that even with all his accomplishments, Mordecai's lack of respect put a pale on everything. His wife suggested he have Mordecai hung on a fifty-foot gallows the next morning so he could fully enjoy the banquet the next evening with the queen. Haman agreed and ordered the gallows made that very night.

That same evening the king could not sleep. He ordered that the official chronicles of the kingdom be read to him. The section was read recounting Mordecai's involvement in squashing an assassination attempt on the king. The king was just finding out that nothing had been done to honor Mordecai for this deed, when Haman appeared in the inner court. Haman was there to get the king's signature on the decree to hang Mordecai.

When the king found out Haman was in the inner court he had him sent in. The king asked Haman, "What could be done to a man the king wanted to honor?" Haman thought, "Who would the king want to honor more than me?" So he answered, "A man who the king wants to honor should wear robes that the king has worn and ride the royal horse through Susa. He would be led by one of the king's high princes who would announce as they went along, 'This is what is done for a man the king wants to honor!" So the king said, "Go immediately and do all these things for Mordecai, the Jew who sits at the gate. You, Haman, will be the high prince who leads the way. Go do it just as you've said to me!"

So Haman did it all. He got the robes and the horse, presented it all to Mordecai and led him through town making the announcement. When it was over, Mordecai returned to the gate. Haman covered his head and went home. When he had recounted all these things to his wife and the wise men present, there was a discussion about what dire scenarios might be playing out for Haman with this turn of events. They were still discussing this when the king's eunuchs arrived to hurry Haman off to the banquet with Esther.

As Haman, the king, and Esther were drinking wine; the king repeated his pledge to grant Esther any request, up to half the kingdom. Esther replied, "If I am pleasing to you and am in your favor, let me and my people keep our lives. We are to be killed and annihilated. If we were only being sold into slavery, I wouldn't have bothered the king."

Ahasuerus asked, "Who is he and where is he, who presumes to do this?" Esther replied as she pointed to Haman, "A foe and enemy is this wicked Haman!"

The king left the room in anger. Haman stayed behind to beg Esther for his life. Haman fell at Esther's feet to beg. When the king returned and saw him falling on his wife, he yelled, "Now he assaults the queen right here in my palace!" The guards had Haman in custody almost as soon as the king had finished his statement. One of the Eunuchs said, "Haman has just built a fifty foot gallows to hang Mordecai, the man who saved your life." The king said, "Hang him on it." After Haman was hanged, the king's anger subsided.

Mordecai was promoted into Haman's old position and given the ring Haman had. Queen Esther asked the king to show his favor for her again by allowing a new decree be made, to allow the Jews to defend themselves on the appointed day. Mordecai handled the administration of the decree as his first official function. The Jews received the news with jubilation. The people of the land dreaded the Jews because of this sudden change of royal sentiment. When the appointed day came, many enemies of the Jews were killed. Ten of Haman's sons were hanged. The Jews created a holiday to remember their deliverance called Purim. Mordecai went on to great accomplishments in his new job. These were recorded in the official chronicles of the kingdom.

The first 6 chapters of Daniel is mostly narrative.

Daniel

The Judeans taken into captivity by Nebuchadnezzer were of the royal class and professional people. Nebuchadnezzer had some of the young Jewish boys separated for palace service. The idea was to take smart, good looking young people and educate them in the ways of Babylon so they could be put to productive service in the king's court. They were delivered to a special facility where they ate special food and went to school for three years. After this they entered the king's service. Daniel was one of these, along with three of his friends that Nebuchadnezzer named: Shadrach, Meshach and Abednego.

Daniel did not want to defile himself with the king's food. He gained favor with the overseer of the program and made an agreement with him. Daniel and his friends would eat just vegetables and water. If they looked healthy after ten days, they would not have to eat the king's food. After ten days they looked better than everyone else and continued to excel. There were none more exceptional and wise than Daniel,

Shadrach, Meshach, and Abednego. When the king consulted them for wisdom, their answers were ten times better than any of the other wise men.

Nebuchadnezzar had a vivid dream. He called his conjurers, sorcerers, and master astrologers to interpret the dream for him. They asked him to tell them the dream, so they could interpret it. The king demanded they tell him the dream and the interpretation or they would die. The man who successfully completed this task would be greatly rewarded. The counselors hemmed and hawed as skillfully as they could, but no one could step forward and provide what the king wanted. So a decree was issued to have them all killed.

When the king's men came to Daniel, because he was one of the wise men, he acted with discretion and tact in dealing with the captain of the Body Guards. So Daniel was brought to the king. He requested a continuance, so he could receive the information the king wanted. Daniel went home. Daniel, Shadrach, Meshach, and Abednego prayed for wisdom. Then the dream and the interpretation were revealed to Daniel.

Daniel went to the captain of the guards and they quickly went before the king. Daniel addressed the king: "No wise man, or conjurer or astrologer is able to relate your dream or its meaning to you. But there is a God in heaven who reveals mysteries and He has revealed to you what will occur in the future, through your dream. God is using me, not because of my wisdom to reveal this to you, but so you may understand your dream and its interpretation."

"This is the dream: You saw a statue. The head was gold. Its breasts and arms were silver. Its belly and thighs were bronze. Its legs were iron. Its feet were iron and clay. While you were looking at it, a stone that was cut without hands, crashed against the feet, destroying them. Then the rest of the statue was crushed at the same time and blew away like dust in the wind. Then the stone that hit the statue became a large mountain that filled the earth."

"That was the dream. Now we will reveal the interpretation to the king: You, O king, are the head of gold because God has given you dominion over the whole world. There will arise after you kingdoms that are inferior to yours, but will rule over the whole earth. These are the silver and bronze. The iron represents a kingdom that will crush all things. The feet of clay and iron will be a divided kingdom, part brittle, part strong. Then the God of heaven will crush that kingdom and set up an everlasting kingdom! It will be established by the stone cut without hands."

Because he interpreted the dream, the king paid great homage to Daniel. Daniel was placed in charge of all the wise men. Shadrach, Meshach and Abednego were appointed as heads over administration of the provinces of Babylon.

Later, King Nebuchadnezzar built a statue of gold 90 feet high and nine feet wide. He established a law that required everyone in the kingdom to bow down and worship the statue when a certain piece of music was played by a band of varied instruments. Whoever disobeyed this law was to be thrown into a burning furnace.

Shadrach, Meshach and Abednego did not worship the statue according to the king's command. Their enemies told the king. The fact that officials in such high positions as these three did not obey: infuriated the king. When they were called before the king he gave them a chance to fall and worship the idol. They refused to even answer the king on the matter, saying that God was fully able to deliver them, but even if God didn't, they would never worship an idol of gold. The king's face was warped with rage. He ordered the furnace to be heated seven times hotter than normal. Valiant men were ordered to cast Shadrach, Meshach and Abednego into the furnace. The heat was so intense that flames consumed these brave warriors as they completed their mission. Shadrach, Meshach and Abednego, however, walked around in the furnace with a fourth person who looked to the king like a son of the gods!

Nebuchadnezzar called into the furnace to Shadrach, Meshach and Abednego, "Come out you servants of the most high God!" When they emerged everyone saw that the fire had not singed a single hair on their heads. They didn't even smell like smoke! Nebuchadnezzar said, "Great is the God of Shadrach, Meshach and Abednego! What other God can deliver His servants like this!" A decree was issued stating that if anyone said anything derogatory about the God of Shadrach, Meshach and Abednego that person would have his arms and legs torn off and his house would be reduced to rubble. Shadrach, Meshach and Abednego continued to prosper in the province of Babylon.

Nebuchadnezzar had another dream: A tree grew to be strong, fruitful and beautiful. Then an angel came from heaven and said, "Cut the tree down, leaving the stump. Let him wander with the wild beasts and have the mind of a beast. Let seven periods of time pass. This will be done so all will know that it is the Holy One who gives kings their power or takes it away."

When Daniel was summoned to interpret the dream, he was troubled because he perceived the dream bode ill towards the king. He said, "I sure wish this dream wasn't about you. But here's its interpretation; the tree is your kingdom that has grown so powerful and fruitful. You are to be cut off and wander with the beasts, so that you will know that it is God who has given you your power. My advice is to turn from any evil and be fair to the poor. Then perhaps your prosperity will be prolonged."

Twelve months later the king was walking on his roof, talking to himself about his great power and majesty. While the words where still coming from his mouth, a voice came from heaven, "King Nebuchadnezzar, your sovereignty is now removed from you. You will be chased from society until you realize I'm the real ruler of the earth." Immediately the word was fulfilled. Nebuchadnezzar became crazy and wandered in the fields like a wild beast for seven years. Finally his sanity returned and he acknowledged God's power.

When Nebuchadnezzar died, his son Bellshazzar became king. One evening he had a feast in the palace. He ordered the wine glasses that had been carried from the temple in Jerusalem to be brought in so all his guests could drink from them. They toasted the gods of gold, silver, iron, wood and stone. Suddenly a hand appeared and began writing on the plaster of the palace wall. The king was terrified. All his wise men were called in. The king made this offer: the one who could interpret the writing would be elevated to third in command of the entire kingdom. None were able to interpret. This frightened the king even more. His wife informed him of Daniel, who had served his father. And reminded him of Daniel's ability to interpret mysteries. When Daniel arrived, the king repeated his offer regarding a successful interpretation. Daniel responded, "Keep your gifts. Give your rewards to someone else. I will, however, interpret this writing. You have seen what God did with your father. How he was separated from men to wander with the beasts until he acknowledged God's power over the world. Even though you knew this, you've brought holy things in here and prayed to false gods. Because of this your kingdom will be taken from you. The message says; 'God has put your kingdom to an end. You have been found deficient. Your kingdom has been divided among the Medes and the Persians." That night Belshazzar was slain by Darius the Mede.

Darius appointed 120 regional leaders to manage the kingdom. Daniel was one of three commissioners who ruled the regional leaders. He distinguished himself above the other two commissioners. They and some of the regional leaders conspired to find a weakness in Daniel they could exploit to his undoing. They couldn't find any. They realized their only chance was to target his devotion to the law of his God.

The conspirators approached the king with this advice, "Oh great king may you live forever. We advise you to make a decree saying, 'Any man making a petition, before any god or man, besides the king, for thirty days, should be cast into a den of lions.'" This seemed right to the king so he issued the decree.

When Daniel heard the decree, he still went to his upstairs room, with windows facing Jerusalem, and prayed to God three times a day. When this news reached the king, he was forced by his own decree to carry out the sentence. He said to Daniel, "May your God, whom you serve constantly, deliver you."

Daniel was thrown into the den of lions. The entrance was shut and sealed. Darius didn't sleep all that night. Early the next morning the entrance was opened and the king yelled in, "Daniel, has your God been able to deliver you?" Daniel answered, "Yes, he sent an angel to protect me, because I am innocent of any crime."

The king gathered all those who had accused Daniel and had them and their families thrown into the lion's den. They were devoured even before the door was sealed. (The lions were hungry because they had missed their supper.) Darius issued a decree, that in his entire kingdom, the God of Daniel must be respected. Daniel prospered all the years Darius reigned and in the years of Cyrus after that.

These prophecies of Daniel begin in the 7th chapter and continue to the end of the book.

Daniel had a dream: Four powerful beasts were coming up from the sea. First a lion, second a bear, third a leopard and finally a monster with iron teeth and ten horns that devoured everything in its path. Then three horns were pulled out and a little horn with a boastful mouth and eyes like a man grew out. Then Daniel saw the "Ancient of Days" sitting on a glorious throne of judgment. The blaring of the little horn continued in the background. Finally the beast was destroyed and thrown into the fire. Out of the clouds came one who looked like a prince. He went before the "Ancient of Days" and was given an everlasting kingdom over all people of every language and nation.

The vision surprised and frightened Daniel so he asked one of the saints standing near the throne for some interpretation. He was told the four beasts represented four great kings and kingdoms that would come on earth. The fourth had ten kings. Three are taken out by the little horn with the big mouth. This little horn speaks out against God and makes new rules for the earth. At the end he is destroyed and judged.

Daniel saw another vision with a ram and a goat. Again, a little horn pops up at the end and claims to be as big as God. He is a shrewd operator with a smooth delivery. He causes all kinds of problems for God's people but is ultimately judged. An angel named Gabriel interprets this dream for Daniel. He informs Daniel that all these visions have to do with the far future, the end of the world. They won't be fully understood until then.

In further visions it's revealed that all these events are set up on a specified time line. The end times will be a very rough time on earth. The crafty little king, at the end, will deceive even some of God's people. But God is triumphant and delivers His people and sets up an everlasting kingdom at the end of time.

<>

Ezra

The chronology in the book of Ezra does not always follow the chapter and verse

Ezra 1:1 - 4 *Return to Jerusalem announced*
In the first year of his reign in Babylon, Cyrus the King sent a written proclamation throughout his entire Kingdom. This was done at the exact time Jeremiah the prophet predicted. The proclamation said: "This is what the king of Persia says: The Lord God of heaven has given me all the kingdoms on the earth. He has appointed me to build him a house in Jerusalem. Wherever His people are in my kingdom, let them go to Jerusalem and rebuild the house of the Lord. He is the God of Israel and He is in Jerusalem. The people in that region should support the project with silver and gold. A freewill offering can also be taken for building the house of God in Jerusalem."

Ezra 7:1-10 ***Ezra***
Ezra was a man who was very diligent in studying the Law of Moses. He was a scribe, which means he was authorized to make copies of the scrolls, which contained the Law of Moses and an expert in all the things pertaining to the law. Ezra possessed exceptional wisdom as well. The king trusted Ezra because of his wisdom. Ezra was the conduit between the king and the Jews as they began their return to Jerusalem to rebuild the temple.

Ezra 1:5-11 ***Funded***
An offering was taken from all the Jews living in the Babylonian empire. It was a substantial amount. Cyrus also brought all the articles that had been carried away

from the temple and returned them to the Jews. There were 5400 articles, including silver and gold plates and bowls, and various other articles.

Ezra 7:11-28 **Administration**
Ezra oversaw all these activities. The king also instructed Ezra to appoint leaders in the various regions of Judah that were well educated in the law of Moses so they could teach those who were not. Those who chose not to follow the law would be dealt with harshly by decree of the king of Babylon. Ezra chose leaders of the people to help him.

Ezra 2:1-70 *Registration*
They returned to Jerusalem to rebuild the temple. Each of the families was carefully registered by name. They all returned to their own cities of origin in Judah. People from some of the cities were not able to provide complete records as to their lineage. A complete check of all records was conducted. Without proper written support for their heritage, they were excluded from the priesthood. Around 42,000 Jews left Babylon. They also had many servants and livestock.

Ezra 8:15 - 36 **The trip**
Ezra didn't request the king's troops to accompany the people because he had said to the king that God protects those who seek Him and is against those who forsake Him. When they got to one of the rivers in Babylon on the way out, Ezra stopped the company for three days. He realized there weren't any Levites among the group so he sent a message to Iddo, a man living in a region of Babylon, who was able to help find over 250 Levites and people qualified by lineage to serve in the temple and they were added to the group. The Jews traveled and arrived in Judah and Jerusalem.

Ezra 9:1 – 9:15 **Problems**
It was brought to the attention of Ezra that many of the people, along with priests and Levites had married local girls in Babylon. Israel was supposed to be a separate people, dedicated to God. They were not supposed to intermingle with the other nations. The princes and leaders had intermarried more than any of the others. When Ezra heard this news, he tore his clothes, pulled hair from his head and from his beard. Then he sat down, appalled at the situation. Everyone was frightened at how seriously Ezra was taking the news. Ezra stayed in his place until the evening offering. Then he got up and fell on his knees and spread his hands to God. "God, I am ashamed to even lift my eyes towards you. We have been disobedient since the days of our fathers. We find ourselves in exile as a result. The only reason we are returning to Jerusalem is because you have caused our captors to allow it. Here we are, with this sin added to our list. You wanted us to be a separate people, but we have intermarried with people who do

The Story Bible for Adults

not worship you, but worship false gods. We are hopeless at this point to continue. We are before you in guilt. How can anyone stand before you like this?"

Ezra 10:1 – 10:44 *Solutions*
All the people were deeply moved and wept bitterly. A man named Shecaniah approached Ezra and said, "We have sinned by marrying these foreign women. There is still hope! Let's make an agreement with God. We will send our foreign wives and children back to Babylon." So Ezra made a decree that all the Jews would gather in Jerusalem in three days. Anyone who didn't come would be banished from the remnant that had returned from Babylon. So all the people were gathered in Jerusalem. They were sitting in the open square, trembling because of this matter (and also because it was quite cold and rainy). Ezra got up and said, "You all have been unfaithful by marrying foreign wives. Now make a confession and separate yourselves from these foreign wives." The people answered, "You're right, it is our duty to do this, but there are many of us who have transgressed in this matter. It will take us awhile to sort it all out. That won't be convenient out here in the rain. So let's set a date to investigate this matter completely, so God will turn His anger away from us." A date was set and the people went back to the warmth of their homes. A complete list of the people who had intermarried was compiled. Some on the list had produced children by their foreign wives.

Ezra 3:1 – 3:13 *Work Begins*
In the seventh month of the year, all the Jews gathered together from all the cities in Judah in Jerusalem as one man. Jeshua and Zerubbabel with all their brothers built an altar to God and offered burnt offerings on it as prescribed by the law given by Moses. Even though the people living in the land terrified them, they kept the offerings up anyway, every morning and evening. The people celebrated the feast of booths and began to observe all the fixed festivals. They were all giving of their freewill to the Lord and his house. But the foundation was still not laid for the temple.

They began the distribution of moneys to the workman and laborers. They had materials sent in, just as Cyrus had decreed. When the foundation was laid there was a significant celebration. Some of the older men who had seen the original cried. Many others shouted for joy. Between the weeping and yelling it was a loud noise that was heard far away.

Ezra 4:1 – 4:24 *Enemies*

When the enemies of Judah living in the land heard about the building of the temple they wanted to get involved. They approached Zerubbabel and the other leaders about it. They indicated they had been offering sacrifices to God ever since they were brought into the land by the kings of Assyria. The Elders of Judah answered, "You all have nothing to do with us and will not participate in building this house. We will continue as Cyrus has decreed." The people of the land then tried to discourage the Jews and frightened them from building. They continued this harassment through the reign of Cyrus and Darius, kings of Babylon. In the reign of Artaxerxes they wrote a letter to the king in Aramaic and it was translated for the king. Rehum, the governor of Judah, and Shimshai, the scribe, wrote the letter. This is what it said, "To king Artaxerxes: We are your servants and these Jews have come into this area where we live. They are rebuilding the city of Jerusalem. They are fortifying the city. When it is complete, they will rebel against you. We recommend that you search the records. You will see that these people are rebellious. They always rebel against anyone who tries to rule them. That's why the city was destroyed in the first place."

The king returned the letter. It said, "I read your letter which was translated for me. You're correct. After I searched the records, I found that this has been a trouble spot. Jerusalem has had some powerful kings. Many collected taxes from all over. So see to it that the work is stopped in Jerusalem. We don't need the trouble!" When Rehuma and Shimshai got the letter they went down from Samaria to Jerusalem and stopped the work by force.

Haggai and Zachariah

When the work on the temple stopped, God spoke to two prophets, Haggai and Zechariah concerning the matter. Haggai exhorted the Jews by asking how they could continue to live in the houses they had built when the temple was in such disrepair. They were planting much and reaping little. They were drinking wine without satisfaction. They were wearing clothes but not staying warm. What they brought home was being blown away. Why? Because God's house was desolate. Haggai encouraged them saying God would provide for them from the very day they renewed their effort on the building.

Zechariah also provided encouragement through the visions he saw. He also spoke of the King who would come: "Shout in victory! Behold your king is coming to you. He is just and endowed with salvation. He is humble and mounted on a donkey. He will speak peace to the nations. His dominion will be from sea to sea." He also spoke of a good shepherd whom God would send. A prophet would some day inquire of this good shepherd, "What are these wounds on your hands?" The shepherd will answer, "I was wounded in the house of those who love me." Zechariah proclaimed; "One day the Lord will be King over the whole earth. He will be the only one, His name will be the only name".

-◇-

Ezra 5:1 - 6:22 **Work continues**
With these words of encouragement the work began again. The new local leaders, Tettenai and Shethar-bozenai addressed the Jews: "Who issued you a decree to rebuild this temple?" The Jews gave them a complete report of the work Cyrus had decreed. They also continued the work while this correspondence with Babylon was being delivered and answered. This is the letter Tettenai and his colleagues wrote to Darius the king in Babylon: "To Darius the king, all peace. We want you to know that the Jews are hard at work, rebuilding the Temple of the great God. They are using large stones and giant timbers. They are taking great care in the process and it is succeeding. When we asked them who issued such a decree, they answered with a full report about how Cyrus had made the decree and all the other names and official transfers. We would like you to research your records and send back a decision about this matter."

Darius's return letter: "We have researched the matter and have found a complete record of king Cyrus's decree. It confirms all the claims the Jews have made to you. Therefore, Tettenai, you and your colleagues stay away from there and leave them to their work. Also, I decree that you assist them by providing the necessary funds from the regional treasury so the work can be completed. Also, provide any bulls or rams they need for sacrifices or any other need. Do this diligently and without delay. Any man who disobeys this command will have his house torn down and will be impaled on one of its beams."

Tattenai and his colleagues were quick to comply with the edict. Zechariah and Haggai had delivered a true message and the temple was completed as they said. They had a great dedication ceremony with many sacrifices. The priestly assignments were made. Regular services were conducted. Then the Jews who had returned from Babylon celebrated Passover for seven days. There was great rejoicing because God had turned the hearts of the kings to encourage them to finish the temple, the house of God, the God of Israel.

Nehemiah

Nehemiah 1:1-2:9 *Nehemiah goes to the king*
The temple was completed but Jerusalem still had no wall or gates, they were in ruins. Nehemiah was one of the Jews who had stayed in Babylon. His brother Hanani came back from Judah. He reported to Nehemiah that conditions in Jerusalem were poor, and the city defenseless. Nehemiah was grieved. He fell down and wept with mourning for days.

He refused all food. He prayed, "God, You always keep Your agreement with those who love You and keep Your commandments. Please hear me. I have been weeping and praying here before You on behalf of the sons of Israel, confessing our sins. We have not been faithful and You have scattered us as You said You would through Moses. You also promised You would return us to our land. Please be with me and make me successful today as I stand before the king". (Nehemiah was a beverage server for the king).

Later Nehemiah was in the presence of the king, serving wine. He had never been sad in the king's presence before. While he was serving, the king noticed his dreary countenance and said, "Why are you sad? They wouldn't let you in here if you were sick, this can only be a sad heart I see." Nehemiah said, "May the king live forever. How can I be happy when the city of my fathers lies in ruins?" The king replied, "What is your request?" Nehemiah breathed a quick prayer and said, "If it pleases you and I have your approval, I would like to return to Jerusalem and repair it." The king, who had the queen beside him asked, "How long will the journey be and when will you return?" Nehemiah and the king discussed his plans. The king agreed to let Nehemiah go to Jerusalem, and they agreed upon a specific time for his return to the palace. Then Nehemiah requested written commands of the king for the governors of all the provinces on his route to Judah and also a decree for the governor of Judah to help Nehemiah and provide supplies for the work. The king provided all Nehemiah requested because the hand of the Lord was on him.

Nehemiah 2:9-4:23 *Work begins trouble follows*
Nehemiah proceeded to Jerusalem with a substantial escort. His arrival in Jerusalem disappointed Sanballat, the governor of the region. He wasn't thrilled that a representative from the capitol was in the area to observe the Jews and their welfare. After three days in Jerusalem, Nehemiah still had not disclosed to the Jewish leaders his intentions. He went out on his mount, which was the only animal in the city, to get a fix on the magnitude of the project. The condition of the wall around Jerusalem was

terrible. It was rubble and the gates were ashes. When he returned from his inspection he said to the elders, "The wall is destroyed. Let's rebuild it." Then he told them about the written decrees he had from the king. The leaders enthusiastically agreed to begin work immediately. When Sanballat heard about the work, he harassed the Jews by saying, "Why are you rebelling against the king by fortifying Jerusalem?" Nehemiah answered, "God will cause us to succeed and you will have no part in this project."

The work began. Families from all over Judah were involved with the building. They worked on the wall, the towers, and the gates with all the appropriate hardware. The work was divided among the families. When Sanballat heard about the progress of the project, he and his counselors were angry. They spoke about how feeble the project was because the Jews had to use materials from the rubble in the work. They joked that even if a fox were to jump against the wall, it would crumble.

When the wall was completed to half its height around the entire city, Sanballat and his counselors decided to make a military attack against the work. Word got to Nehemiah and he took defensive measures. Nehemiah and his men prayed for God's help. Half of the workers had their swords and bows ready, while the others worked with their weapons close at hand. Trumpeters were stationed so that if an attack were made at any section of the wall, others would rush to support in the fighting. Nehemiah could see that there was still great fear among the people. He encouraged them with the fact that God was great and certainly able to deliver them. When the Jew's enemies heard their intentions were known, they decided to cancel the attack. Still the work continued at the high level of military preparedness Nehemiah established. The men wore their weapons, even when they visited the latrine.

Nehemiah 5 *Nehemiah sets an example*
A problem arose concerning Jews lending money to other Jews. Because the general economy in Israel was so bad, many had to borrow to make ends meet. The lenders were charging high interest. Many Jews were mortgaging property to eat. When Nehemiah became aware of the problem, he rebuked the lenders and warned them to not take advantage of their brothers. He commanded that all back interest be written off. He shook off the front of his cloak and said, "So may any household that does not return mortgaged property, be shaken out and emptied." All the people agreed to the terms of the order. Nehemiah was appointed governor of the people. He reduced local taxes. Nehemiah never took a salary and provided for as many as 150 others out of his own stores. He also worked on the wall and all of his servants were involved in the work.

Nehemiah 6:-7:4 *A plot, then the wall is finished and no one lives there*
When Sanballat and his people heard the wall was nearing completion and Jerusalem was close to being completely fortified, he sent a message to Nehemiah asking him to meet at an appointed place. Nehemiah knew Sanballat meant to harm him so he answered: "I am doing a big job here. Why should I interrupt the work to come see you?" Sanballat sent the same message four times and Nehemiah answered in the same way. The fifth time Sanballat sent this message: "I have heard that you and the Jews are planning to rebel, which is why you're building the wall. Also I hear you are to be appointed king. Further, that you are appointing prophets to say you will be king in Judah. I will be reporting this to the king in Babylon. We really need to get together to talk about this." Nehemiah replied, "You are fabricating these facts to try to discourage us from the project. It won't work. God will strengthen us despite your interference."

Then Nehemiah went to the house of Shemaiah, who was a prophet confined to his home. Shemaiah tried to coax Nehemiah into hiding in the temple because assassins where coming to kill him. Nehemiah answered, "Why should a man like me flee? If they wanted to kill me badly enough they could certainly get in the temple. The work will continue, I'm not hiding." Nehemiah perceived that Shemaiah's advice was not from God and that Sanballat had hired Shemiah to say this to him. The plan was to make Nehemiah appear as a coward by having him hide in the temple and use it to political advantage. Even after the wall was fully completed, Nehemiah continued to be harassed by Sanballat and Tobiah, his associate.

Nehemiah appointed his brother Hananiah, who was already in charge of the defense of Jerusalem, as head of the city. Hananiah was a faithful man and feared God. The gates of the city were opened at certain times for commerce with outside merchants. Still, few people lived in Jerusalem and only a few houses had been built, even though there was plenty of room.

Nehemiah 7:5-8:18 *Grand opening*
God put it in Nehemiah's heart to assemble all the people of Judah in Jerusalem. Ezra, the scribe, brought out the law and read it to the entire assembly. A group of priests also read and explained all the stories and statutes that were in the law so the people understood. The people started weeping because they knew how disobedient both they and their ancestors had been. Nehemiah encouraged them by telling them it was not a

day to weep but a day to rejoice because of how God had brought them back to Jerusalem as he promised. So they feasted and celebrated.

The next day they gathered again to hear the law. They heard about the Feasts of Booths and how it should be celebrated to remember the time Israel spent in the wilderness. So they all went out to gather leafy branches to construct the booths and celebrated for the appointed seven days. The law was read publicly every day of the festival. On the eighth day they had a solemn assembly according to the ordinance.

Nehemiah 9:1-11:3 *Confession and obligation*
Towards the end of the same month the people assembled together again. They were all dressed in burlap and had not washed. They had gathered to confess their sins and to hear the reading of the law again. After half a day of hearing the law and confessing their sins to God, the Levites stood with Jeshua and prayed a detailed confession of the sins of the entire nation. They started by acknowledging God's promise to Abraham. They continued with the works God did when they were delivered from Egypt; the crossing of the Red Sea on dry land and the destruction of Pharaoh's army by the returning water, the pillar of fire, and cloud that lead them by night and day, the provision of manna and miraculous provision of water at key times. They confessed the sins of their fathers by rebelling against Moses and making a golden calf to worship while Moses was on the mountain. Still, God provided for them 40 years and even their clothes did not wear out. Then the Hebrews did enter and possess the land God had promised Abraham. There was a complete confession of all the times they had turned away from God while they lived in the land, even though He sent His prophets to turn them back to God. They acknowledged that their current condition, as mere servants to a foreign king in the land, was their own doing, because of all their disobedience.

Then they presented a document that was binding on the people to return wholeheartedly to God and the observance of His law in Judah. It contained the names of Nehemiah, and all his officials. Jeshua and all the leaders among the Levites were also listed on the document. All the people were bound by the document, to provide for the proper use of the temple and its support. They were not to intermarry with locals. They would observe Sabbaths and rest for the land every seven years. The descendants of Aaron were to serve as priests and the Levites were to care for the temple.

Lots were cast so that 10 percent of the Jews would live in Jerusalem, while the others would live in the other towns of Judah. The 90 percent that lived outside Jerusalem blessed all the men who had volunteered to stay in Jerusalem.

Nehemiah 11:3 13:30 *Dedication and following problems*

The wall was dedicated with full ceremonial circumstance. Choirs were positioned in certain places along a procession that was led by Ezra, the scribe. It was a grand parade with the people singing and rejoicing. Things were busy at the temple with many offerings being made to the Lord. The final assignments for temple service were made that day as well. The singers were also assembled officially and sang the Psalms. During the days of Zerubbabel and Nehemiah, support was laid aside for the needs of the singers, gatekeepers, priests, and Levites.

Nehemiah returned to Susa, the capitol of Babylon, per his agreement with the king. After a time there, he asked to return again to Judah. Upon his return, he found that conditions had worsened in Jerusalem and Judah. Regular temple services had been drastically cut and the singers and gatekeepers had all returned to their own fields for lack of support. Nehemiah restored each to his post and enforced the tithes necessary to return them to service.

Tobiah, Nehemiah's antagonist, was living in a room in the temple. It was read from the law that no Ammonite or Moabite should be able to join in the Assembly because they had not helped Israel as they entered the land. They remembered that the King of Moab had hired Balaam to prophesy against them but it had turned into a blessing instead. Nehemiah went into Tobiah's quarters and removed all the furniture from his room and ordered the whole area cleaned.

The people agreed to not mix with foreigners. Many had begun taking foreign wives again. Some of the children couldn't even speak Hebrew. Nehemiah was pretty rough on these citizens. He had to knock sense into some of them. He reminded them of the trouble King Solomon's foreign wives had caused the nation. The Sabbath was not being observed. The gates were open on that day and trading was taking place all over Judah and even inside Jerusalem. Nehemiah put an end to this practice. The gates were closed and guarded from sundown at the beginning of the Sabbath and not opened until it was complete. Some vendors camped outside the gate. Nehemiah put an end to that practice with threat of force.

Malachi

The prophesies of Malachi were delivered in the renovated city of Jerusalem. God could see that religiosity had replaced true worship again. "A son honors his father. Where is My honor? Why would you bring Me a blind lamb, or a lame goat as a sacrifice? What would the governor do if you brought him such an animal? I'm not anymore pleased than he would be! I simply won't accept this kind of offering. Cursed is the man who makes a vow with a strong male of his flock and then replaces it with a blemished animal that has no value to him! How can the priest allow such a thing? The true priest will only speak the truth. Unrighteousness will not be found in him. He will walk with me in peace and uprightness. He will turn many from iniquity."

"Yes I am going to send my messenger and he will clear the way before Me. He will be like a refiners fire, like a strong soap. Then those who respect the Lord will be entered into a book of remembrance. They will be Mine and I will spare them the judgment that is coming. Then you will be able to distinguish between the righteous and the ones who do not serve Him. I will send Elijah, the prophet, before the great and terrible day of the Lord. He will restore the hearts of the fathers to their children and the hearts of the children to their fathers."

There are four Gospels. Some events and things Jesus said are in all of them, some quotes and stories only appear in one (or two). This treatment catches them all in one telling.

The Gospels

Luke 1:5 - 25 *Gabriel appears to Zacharias*
When Herod was king, a priest named Zacharias and his wife, Elizabeth, lived in Judea. Both were of proper priestly lineage and strived to live blamelessly in regard to the Jewish Law. They were old and had no children. Zacharias won the priestly lottery and was chosen to go into the temple to burn incense. When he went into the Holy Place, an angel of the Lord appeared to him, standing by the altar of incense. Zacharias was gripped with fear, but the angel said, "Don't be afraid, Zacharias. You and Elizabeth will have a son, who you will name John. He will bring you much joy and will turn the hearts of Israel back to God. He will be great in God's eyes. He will not drink any alcohol and will be filled with the Holy Spirit even while he's in the womb. He will be the forerunner of the Lord in the power of Elijah." Zacharias answered, "How will I be sure this is true? My wife and I are quite old." The angel replied, "I am Gabriel, who stands in the presence of God. I wouldn't have been sent if it weren't true! Because of your unbelief, you won't be able to speak."

Everybody outside the temple wondered why Zacharias was taking so long in the Holy Place. When he came out unable to speak and making signs to them, they knew he had seen a vision. After he had completed his priestly service, he and Elizabeth returned to their home, and Elizabeth became pregnant. She kept it to herself for five months, even though she was quite pleased by the turn of events!

Luke 1:26 - 56 *Gabriel appears to Mary*
Six months after he was sent to Zacharias, Gabriel was dispatched to Nazareth to visit Mary, a young lady who was a descendant of David. "Greetings, Mary, God has chosen you to bear a son named Jesus. He will be great and will be called the Son of the Most High. The Lord will give him the throne of His father David. His kingdom will never end." Mary asked, "How can this be? I am a virgin." Gabriel answered, "The Holy Spirit will come upon you, and the power of the Most High will overshadow you. This is how your Holy Child will be called the Son of God! Your cousin Elizabeth has already conceived in her old age and is in her sixth month. Nothing is impossible with God!" Mary answered, "OK. Let it happen as you say."

Mary went to see Elizabeth. When Elizabeth saw her, her baby leapt in her womb and she said, "What an honor to have the Mother of the Lord come visit me!" They had quite a nice three-month visit and praised God about the wonderful things that were being accomplished. The folks around the area were talking about these things as well.

Matthew 1:18 -25 *Joseph deals*
When Joseph, Mary's fiancée, who was also a descendant of David, heard about her pregnancy, he was troubled, but decided to break off the wedding quietly, so as to not cause trouble for Mary. Then, one night in a dream, an angel appeared to him and said, "Joseph, son of David, don't be afraid to take Mary as your wife. She has become pregnant by a miracle of the Holy Spirit. She will have a Son whom you will name Jesus. He will save His people from their sins." Isaiah prophesied that a virgin would conceive the savior. Joseph did as the angel instructed. He didn't have marital relations with Mary until after she had given birth.

Luke 1: 57 - 80 *John born*
When Elizabeth gave birth to her son, their neighbors thought he should be named after his father. Zacharias, however, wrote a note saying, "His name is John." He regained his voice and proclaimed everything God had revealed to him about John and the coming of God's salvation. John grew up strong in spirit and he lived in the desert until he started his ministry.

Luke 2:1 - 40 *Jesus born*
In time, Caesar Augustus made a decree that the entire world should be counted in a census. Everyone had to go to his hometown to be counted. Being from the house of David, Joseph and Mary had to leave Nazareth and go to Bethlehem, David's hometown. Mary gave birth there. They were staying in a barn because there was no room anywhere else. They wrapped the baby in whatever blankets they had and laid him in a small feeding trough.

The night Jesus was born, just outside of Bethlehem, a group of shepherds were watching their flocks. Suddenly an angel appeared before them and the glory of the Lord lit the whole area. The shepherds were very frightened by this. The angel said, "Don't be afraid, I've got wonderful news; today, in Bethlehem, the Savior God promised through the prophets has been born! His name is Jesus. You'll find Him wrapped up, lying in a feeding trough." Then the angel was joined by a multitude of other angels all praising God. They said, "Glory to God in the highest and peace on

Earth among men with whom He is pleased". When the angels had gone, the shepherds went into town to see the baby. They found Him just as the angels had announced. They told Mary what had happened out in their pasture.

Eight days after His birth the child was circumcised and officially named Jesus, the name given by the angel. After the time for purification was completed Jesus was brought to the temple to be dedicated according to the law. There was a man in Jerusalem named Simeon who was full of the Holy Spirit. It had been revealed to him that he would see the promised Messiah before he died. When he saw Jesus, he knew the child was the future salvation of Israel. He told Mary how important Jesus was to Israel. An elderly widow who worked at the temple named Anna also came to see Jesus, she testified to all who were waiting for the Savior that He had indeed been born.

Matthew 2:1 - 18 *Wise men*
Wise men from a faraway country observed a new star in the heavens. Knowing the Jews were waiting for a Savior according to their prophecies, they came to Jerusalem to pursue it. King Herod was distressed by the wise men's inquiries about where this new king was to be born. The religious experts explained that Bethlehem was identified in the Prophets as His birthplace. Herod asked the wise men to report back when they found the baby, so he could worship Him too.

The star led the wise men right to Jesus. They gave Him gold, frankincense, and myrrh as gifts. They were warned in a dream not to go back to Herod, so they returned to their country by a different route. Joseph also received instructions in a dream to go to Egypt because Herod wanted to destroy this new king. Herod realized the wise men had eluded him, so he issued orders that all the baby boys in the Bethlehem area under two years of age should be killed. The prophets had spoken of all these things.

Luke 2:39 - 52 *Errant child?*
After Herod died, Joseph was informed in a dream that he could return to Israel. He settled his family in the city of Nazareth in the region of Galilee. (The prophets had also said the Savior would be called a Nazarene.) Every year Joseph would take his family to Jerusalem for the Feast of Passover. During a Passover trip, when Jesus was twelve, He became separated from His parents before they left the city. They thought He had joined the caravan back to Nazareth. When they became aware He was missing, they returned to Jerusalem to find Him. To their surprise, Jesus was in the temple surrounded by teachers who were questioning Him. They were amazed at His wise responses. Mary said, "Jesus, why have you done this? I was worried sick!"

Jesus answered, "Why were you looking for Me? Didn't you know I'd be in My Father's house?" They didn't understand what He was saying at the time. Jesus returned with them and remained a loyal son, growing in wisdom and stature. Mary, however, treasured all these things in her heart.

Mark 1:1 - 8 John 1:19 - 28 *John the Baptist*
John the Baptist started his ministry when Tiberius Caesar had been in power in Rome for 15 years, Pontius Pilate was governor in Judea and Herod was tetrarch of Galilee. The high priests in Jerusalem were Annas and Caiaphas. John preached in the wilderness of Judea, out by the Jordan River. His message was; "Repent, for the kingdom of heaven is at hand." Isaiah had prophesied, "I am sending a messenger before You who will prepare Your way. He'll be a voice in the wilderness proclaiming, 'Make ready the way of the Lord. Make His paths straight.'" John the Baptist preached a baptism of repentance and forgiveness of sins. Everybody from Judea and Jerusalem was going out to the Jordan River to see him and were confessing their sins and being baptized.

John wore a camelhair coat with a leather belt. He ate locusts and wild honey. He clearly said Someone was coming after him who was far greater than he. This Person would baptize the people with the Holy Spirit, not water. John said, "I'm not worthy to tie the shoestrings of the One coming after me." John had a confrontational relationship with the religious leaders. He called them a brood of vipers and down played their position as children of Abraham. He said, "God could turn these stones into children of Abraham. The ax is laid at the root of the trees, and any of them that do not bear good fruit will be cut down and burned!" The tax collectors and sinners were much more receptive to John's message than the religious leaders. John simply instructed them to live honest and generous lives. When asked, John was always clear about who he was. He never claimed to be the Christ, he said he was His forerunner.

Mark 1:9 - 11 *Jesus baptized*
Jesus came out to be baptized by John. John recognized Him as the Christ or Messiah and said, "You should be baptizing me, not me baptizing You!" But Jesus replied, "I will be baptized by you so all righteousness will be fulfilled." When Jesus came up from the water, the Spirit landed on Him like a dove. A voice came from heaven, "You are My Son and I'm very pleased with You."

Luke 4:1 - 13 *Temptation*
After Jesus was baptized, He was led by the Spirit into the wilderness to be tested by the devil. Jesus fasted for forty days and He was hungry. The devil said, "If you're the Son of God, tell these stones to become bread." Jesus answered, "It is written, 'Man shall not live by bread alone.'" Then the devil took Jesus to a high mountain and showed Him all the kingdoms of the world and all their glory. He said, "All of this has been given to me; I will give it to You, if You fall down and worship me." Jesus said, "It is written, 'Worship only the Lord and serve only Him.'" Finally he led Him to Jerusalem and had Him stand on the pinnacle of the temple and said, "If You're the Son of God, throw yourself off, because it is written, 'He will send His Angels to guard You. And They will bear You up with their hands.'" Jesus answered, "Take off, Satan; the scriptures say to not put the Lord to the test." So the devil left Him, to wait for a more opportune time. Soon, angels came and ministered to Jesus.

John 1:35 - 2:12 *First disciples, first miracle*
Some of Jesus' first disciples were those who had spent time with John the Baptist and were encouraged by him to follow Jesus. They were Andrew and John. They brought their brothers, James and Simon Peter, to meet Jesus. Jesus himself invited Philip and Philip invited Nathaniel to join their group.

After His new disciples had spent a few days with Jesus, they accompanied Him to a wedding party in Cana. During the party, the wine ran out. Mary, Jesus' mother, approached Him with a dilemma. Jesus said, "Woman, what am I to do with you, My time has not yet come." She said to the servants, "Do whatever He tells you." Jesus instructed them to take six stone water pots that the Jews used for ceremonial washing and to fill them up with water. Each held about 25 gallons. Next, they were to draw some out and take it to the headwaiter. When the headwaiter tasted the water that had been changed to wine, he called thebridegroom. He said, "Most folks serve the good wine first, then when everybody has a healthy little buzz going, they bring out the lesser wine. But You have saved the good wine until now!" This was the first sign Jesus accomplished. His disciples believed in Him because of it.

John 2:13 - 3:21 *First trip to Jerusalem*
After a few more days spent with His family, Jesus and His disciples traveled to Jerusalem to celebrate the Passover. When Jesus entered the temple and saw all the vendors selling animals for sacrifice and the currency exchange vendors, He made a whip with a leather cord, drove them out, overturned the tables and poured out the coin bags. He yelled, "Get these things out of here and stop making My Father's house a shopping mall!" The officials questioned Him as to where He received the authority

to do these things. Jesus answered, "Destroy this temple and I will raise it up in three days!" The Jews replied, "It took forty-six years to build this temple, how would You rebuild it in three days?" He was referring to the temple of His own body. The disciples didn't realize what He was saying at the time, but they remembered it after Jesus had risen from the dead.

Jesus was well received in Jerusalem and many believed in Him because of the signs He was accomplishing. Jesus, however, did not entrust Himself to the masses, because He knew the heart of man. He didn't need anyone to tell him what man was like. He already knew.

There was a Pharisee named Nicodemus who came to Jesus secretly at night. He said, "With all of your miracles, it seems clear You have come from God." Jesus answered, "If you're not born again, you can't see the kingdom of God." Nicodemus asked, "How can a man enter his mother's womb and be born a second time?" Jesus replied, "A man is born once the regular way, the second birth is spiritual. It's a bit like the blowing wind; you hear it, yet you don't know exactly where it came from or where it's going, so it is with those born of the spirit." Nicodemus said, "How can this be?" Jesus answered, "You're a teacher in Israel, yet you don't understand these things? I am telling you things that are true, and you can't accept them. I know they're true because I was sent from heaven. The Son of Man will be lifted up much like Moses lifted up the snake in the wilderness when people were getting sick. Whoever believes in the Son of Man will have eternal life. God loved the world so much, He sent His own Son, so that whoever believed in Him wouldn't die, but have eternal life. God sent His Son into the world to save it, not to judge it. The one who believes in Him won't be judged, but the one who doesn't believe is judged already, because he doesn't believe in the One God sent! God sent light into the world, but men loved the darkness more than light, because light exposes evil deeds. He who practices truth comes to the light because he's not ashamed."

John 3:22 -36 *John recedes*

Jesus and His disciples traveled back and forth between Galilee in the north of Israel to Judea in the south. When He was spending time in Judea, people came to Him more than to John, to be baptized. (His disciples did the actual baptizing). Word of these events got to John. John said, "A man can receive nothing except he receives it from heaven, and I said all along I'm not the Christ. I'm like the best man at a wedding, I don't get the bride, but I rejoice with the groom. Jesus must increase, and I will decrease. All that He says, He's received from above, and it's all true. My job has been to point in His direction. He is God's Son and has received God's Spirit without measure. If you believe in Him, you will have eternal life, but if you ignore Him, you disobey God, and His anger rests on you."

Luke 4:16 - 30 *Little acceptance at home*
One Sabbath, in a Nazareth synagogue, Jesus stood up to read from the passage in Isaiah which said: "The Spirit of the Lord is upon Me, because He has anointed Me to preach the good news to the poor and proclaim the release of the captives and the recovery of sight to the blind. To set the downtrodden free and to proclaim the favorable year of the Lord." He closed the book and sat down. Every eye in the place was on Him, and He said, "Today this passage has been fulfilled in your hearing." As highly as they thought of Him they still couldn't believe He was the Christ because they knew where He lived, and who His parents were. Jesus said, "A prophet receives very little acceptance in his own home town. I tell you this; when Elijah shut up the rain for over three years he was sent only to one widow to help her and when Elisha ministered he only healed one leper: Naaman, the Syrian. These statements of Jesus agitated those listening and they were ready to take Him by force and to stone Him on the outskirts of town, but He slipped through their midst, because His time had not yet come. So Jesus continued to travel and preach.

Luke 5:1 - 11 *Fishers of men*
One day Jesus met His disciples at the shore of Lake Gennesaret. To accommodate the huge crowd, Jesus stood in Peter's boat to teach. When He had finished, He said, "Peter, put your boat out in deep water and let down your nets for a catch." Peter replied, "Master, we worked hard all night and caught nothing, but at Your suggestion we will let down the nets." When the nets were set, they became so full of fish they began to break as the men tried to haul them in. Peter called another boat. But soon the boats were both so full of fish they began to sink. Peter fell at Jesus' feet and said, "You should leave me now Lord for I am a sinful man." He and his business partners, John and James Zebedee, were completely amazed at the haul of fish. Jesus said, "Do not be afraid, from now on you will be fishing for men!" They left the boats and the catch and followed Jesus from then on.

John 4:1 - 43 *Woman at the well*
The Pharisees knew Jesus was attracting more followers than John. Knowing this, Jesus left Judea for Galilee and had to pass through Samaria. He stopped at a popular well that Jacob had given to his son Joseph. Tired from the journey, Jesus was sitting by the well at six o'clock in the evening while His disciples were getting food in town. A woman of Samaria came to draw water. Jesus requested a drink. She said, "Why

would You, a Jew, ask a Samaritan woman for a drink?" (Jews had no dealings with Samaritans.) Jesus answered, "If you knew the gift of God and Who it is that is asking you for a drink you would ask Him for a drink, and He would give you living water." She replied, "Sir, how are You to get this living water out of the well without a bucket? You're not greater than Jacob, who gave us the well and drank from it himself with his sons and cattle!" Jesus answered, "The well water will only satisfy your thirst temporarily. But if you drink the water I give you, you won't thirst again, and it will become a well of water springing up to eternal life." The woman said, Sir, give me some of that water so I won't be thirsty and I won't have to come way out here to drink." He said, "Get your husband and return." The woman said, "I don't have a husband." Jesus said, "That's right, you've had five husbands, and the one you live with now is not your husband, so you have spoken truly." The woman replied, "Sir, I perceive You're a prophet. My relatives worshipped at this mountain, but Your people say we should worship in Jerusalem." Jesus said, "Woman, believe Me, an hour is coming when you won't worship the Father here or in Jerusalem. You're not exactly clear about what you worship. We worship what we know, since salvation is from the Jews. The time is coming and has arrived when true worshippers will worship the Father in spirit and truth; that's the type of worshipers He wants. God is a Spirit and those who worship Him must worship in spirit and truth." The woman said, "I know that The Savior is coming and He will clear everything up." Jesus said, "You're talking to Him."

At this point His disciples arrived. They were flabbergasted that He was talking with a woman, but no one mentioned it. The woman left her pot and went into town. She told the men about the Man who told her all she'd ever done, "Could this be The Savior?" she asked. While she was away the disciples offered food to Jesus. But He said, "I have food to eat that you don't know about." They were all saying, "I didn't see anyone bring Him food." Jesus said, "My food is to do the work I was sent to do by God. A farmer says, 'Yep, four more months and we'll harvest.' I say look around, the fields are ready for harvesting now. It has already begun. Those who are reaping are already gathering fruit for eternal life and the sowers and reapers are rejoicing together. The saying is true, 'Some sow and others reap.' I'm sending you out as reapers in a field you didn't sow; that work has been done by others, but you're part of the team."

The people in that town believed what the woman said. So Jesus agreed to stay with them for two days. More of the town's people believed after hearing Him. They said to the woman, "What you said about Him was true, now we believe because we've heard for ourselves. This Man is the Savior of the world."

Matthew 5 and 7 (add Luke 11:5 - 13 and Luke 18:1 - 8 about prayer) *Sermon on the Mount*

The crowds followed Jesus into the country. Then, Jesus taught the multitudes that came to him on the mountain saying:
"The poor in spirit are blessed because they have the kingdom of heaven. Those that mourn are blessed because they will be comforted. The gentle are blessed because they will inherit the earth. The ones who hunger and thirst for righteousness are blessed because their hunger will be satisfied. The merciful are blessed because they will receive mercy. The pure in heart are blessed because they will see God. Peacemakers are blessed because they will be called the sons of God.

"When you are persecuted because you are trying to do the right thing you are blessed because you will receive the kingdom of heaven. When men insult you and say evil things about you falsely, be happy, you will be rewarded in heaven. The prophets before you had the same things done to them. You are the salt of the earth. If salt loses its saltiness it might as well be used to pave a walkway. You are the light of the world. A light is not lit just to be covered by a basket; it is set on a table to give light to the room. Let your life show people who God is, the way a light shines in a room and provides light.

"I haven't come to abolish the law but to fulfill it. Everything written in the law will be fulfilled. Your righteousness will have to exceed that of the religious leaders if you want to see the kingdom of heaven.

"They say do not murder, but I say if you are angry with someone it's as substantial as murder. If you're on your way to make an offering to God, and you are in a quarrel with a friend, go make peace with your friend and then make the offering.

"You've heard it said, don't commit adultery. Well I'm saying if you look at a woman with lust in your heart, you've committed adultery. If your right eye makes you stumble, cut it out, it is better to lose one eye than your soul. You've heard it said; whoever divorces his wife should give her a certificate of dismissal. I say if you divorce for any other reason than infidelity, and you marry again, you are committing adultery.

"It is said, 'Do not make false vows but complete them before the Lord. But I say don't make any oaths at all. What do you have to make an oath to, the heaven or the earth? God made the heaven and the earth. Let your yes be yes and your no, no.

"It's written, 'an eye for and eye, a tooth for a tooth.' But I say; if someone strikes you on your right cheek, turn your left to him also. If someone forces you to go a mile, go two. If someone takes your coat, give him your shirt as well. You've heard it said, 'Love your neighbor and hate your enemy. I say love your enemy, pray for those who persecute you. God makes rain fall, and the sun rise on both the evil and the good. If you love only those who do good to you, what's so special about that? Even sinners love people who are good to them! You are to be perfect, even as your Father in heaven is perfect."

Be careful to do your good works stealthily. If you are doing good things just to be seen and recognized, that's all you'll get. Do your good works anonymously and let God be the only one who sees them, He will reward you. Same thing when you pray. Oh how the religious leaders love to stand in public and say long prayers. They have received their reward from their many admirers. "

"When you pray, go into your closet privately where no one can see you. God will hear you. Don't repeat the same words in vain repetition like the heathen do. Pray along these lines; 'God in heaven, Your very name is great and I have utmost respect for who You are. May You be the king of my life, like You are the king in heaven. Please provide what I need here on earth. Please forgive me when I do wrong and I will also forgive others when they do wrong to me. Keep me away from things that would draw me away from You. You have the power and all the glory is Yours. Amen.' Forgive others, because you'll most certainly need God to forgive you!"

"Suppose one of you had a friend who came to your door at midnight and asked for three loaves of bread. Your first answer would probably be, 'Hey pal, I'm asleep and the pantry door is locked, I can't get you any bread.' He is your friend, but the bed is warm. However, if he keeps knocking and knocking, sooner or later you haul yourself out of bed and get the guy his bread!" Ask and it shall be given to you, seek and you will find. Knock and the door will be opened to you. If your child asked you for a piece of bread, would you give him a stone, or if he asked for a fish, would you give him a snake? You, who are prone to evil, give good gifts to your children. How much more will the Father who is in heaven give good things to those who ask Him. "

Then Jesus told this parable about continuing to pray and not giving up: "There was a judge who did not fear God nor respect man. A widow in his jurisdiction petitioned him for protection against an opponent. He had no inclination to grant the petition, but he knew that she would persist indefinitely, so he granted her petition just to be done with it. Then he said, 'Certainly God will not delay in delivering the elect who pray to him day and night.' I say He will not delay; but will the Son of Man find faith on the earth when He comes?"

"When you fast don't put on a gloomy face and neglect your appearance so everyone will know what a devout person you are. Get dressed up, have a smile; God knows what you're doing. Don't lay up treasure for yourself on earth. It will rot or perhaps be stolen. Lay up your treasure in heaven, where no thieves or termites exist. Your eye is the lamp of your body. If your eye is clear the whole body is full of light. But if your eye is bad the light in you is darkness."

"No one can serve two masters, he will love one and hate the other. That's the way it is with money. You cannot serve money and God. I am telling you not to worry about your everyday needs: food, drink, and clothing. The birds certainly don't sow and reap and gather into barns, but God takes care of them. Aren't you much more important than they are? Who can add a single day to his life by being concerned about daily needs? Look at the flowers, they don't toil or shop, but Solomon in all his glory was never as finely arrayed as them. If God so clothes the grass in the field, how much more will He care for you? So don't worry about your daily needs. He knows everything that you need. Those with no thought of God can spend their energy worrying about these things. When you seek the kingdom of heaven first, all these necessities will be taken care of. Don't worry about tomorrow; it will have enough trouble of its own."

"Don't judge others, or you will be judged. In fact, the way you judge others is the way you'll be judged. How often you will point out a small speck in your brother's eye, when you have a log in your own eye. Hypocrite! Take the log out of your own eye first, so you can see to help your brother with his speck! Don't give what is holy to dogs or throw your pearls before pigs. They'll just walk all over them.

"Ask, and it will be given to you; seek, and you will find; knock and the door will be open to you. "Treat others in the same way you would like to be treated. This sums up the law in one sentence. The gate that leads to life is narrow and few find it."

Beware of false prophets. They come as innocently as sheep, but they are ravenous wolves that would just as soon eat you alive. You will know them by their fruit. Good trees do not produce bad fruit. Not everyone who says to Me, 'Lord, Lord,' does the will of My Father. Many will say on the last day, 'Lord, didn't we prophecy in Your name, didn't we cast out demons and do miracles?' I'll say to them, I never knew you; depart from Me, you lawless people."

"Those who hear My words and act on them can be compared to those who build their homes upon a rock foundation. Great storms can come upon that structure, and it will not fail. Those who hear my words but don't act on them are like those who build their house on sand. When the storm comes, that house will fall."

Mark 1:21 - 28 *First exorcism*
Everyone that heard Jesus' teaching was amazed by it. He taught as one with authority, not at all what they were used to from their religious leaders. In time, they went to a town named Capernaum. Jesus went into a synagogue to teach. A man with a demon cried out, "Why are You coming to destroy us? I know who You are! You are the Holy One of God!" Jesus said, "Be quiet and come out of him." The demon threw the man down in a convulsion as he came out of him. People discussed among themselves how amazing it was that Jesus had power over demons. They wondered where His power came from. People were hearing about Jesus all over the region.

Luke 4:38 -44 *Healing*
Jesus and His disciples went to have dinner at Simon's house. But when they arrived, Simon's mother-in-law was ill with a fever. Jesus took her hand and healed her. Then she got up and helped serve dinner. All that evening people were bringing the sick to Jesus, and He was healing them. Early in the morning while it was still dark, Jesus slipped away and was praying by Himself. Simon and his companions found Him and told Him everyone was looking for Him. Jesus said, "Let's visit some of the other towns nearby. I was sent to preach there too." So Jesus began preaching, healing and casting out demons all over the region

Mark 1:40 - 45 *First leper healed*
A man with leprosy approached Jesus and said, "You have the power to heal me if You want." Jesus said, "You're right, and I will." The leprosy left the man immediately. Jesus sternly warned the man not to broadcast the healing, but to go to the priest as prescribed by the law. But the man went out and told anyone who would listen about his miracle.

Matthew 8:5 - 13 *Officer's faith*

One day as they traveled towards Capernaum, a Roman military officer sent messengers to Jesus with a request. "Lord, my servant is at home, paralyzed, and in pain. Jesus said, "I will come heal him." The officer answered, "Lord, I'm not worthy to have You come to my home. You can just say the word from where You are, and I know he'll be healed. You see I am also a man with authority; I tell one of my men to do something and he does it." Jesus marveled at the officer's faith, "This man has greater faith than any Israelite I've met. I declare to you that many non-Jews will sit at the table with Abraham and Isaac in the kingdom of heaven, while many Jews for whom the kingdom was prepared will be left outside where there will be crying and teeth grinding." Then He turned to the officer and said, "Go on home, the servant is healed just as you've believed." The Roman's servant was healed that very hour.

Luke 7:11 - 17 *Raising the dead*

Jesus went to a city called Nain. As He arrived, a dead man, who was the only son of a widow, was being carried out of the gate for burial. Just about the whole town was there sharing the widow's grief. Jesus felt compassion for her and said to her, "Don't cry." Then He touched the coffin and the pallbearers stopped. Jesus said, "Young fellow, I say to you, arise." The dead man sat up and started talking. Jesus reunited him with his mother. Fear gripped the people, and they began to glorify God saying, "What a great prophet God has sent among us," and, "God has visited His people." The news about Jesus continued to spread.

Matthew 11:2 - 9 *Jesus speaks about John*

Some of John the Baptist's disciples were sent by John to ask if indeed Jesus was the one they were waiting for. John was in jail at the time. Jesus answered John's disciples, "Tell John what you see; the blind are receiving sight, the lame walk, lepers are cleansed, the deaf hear, the dead are raised, and the poor are having the good news proclaimed to them. The person who trusts in Me is blessed. Tell John not to stumble."

After John's disciples left, Jesus talked about John. "What did you go out to the desert to see, a reed that shakes in the wind or a man in flowing silk robes? If you want to see that, go to a palace somewhere. If you went out to see a prophet, that's what you got. John was the messenger who was spoken of in the prophets, who comes before and prepares the way. There has never been a greater man than John the Baptist, but even the least person in the kingdom is greater than he. John is the final prophet, and they have all been rudely treated until now. If you can handle it, John is Elijah; if you can hear it, hear it.

Mark 2:1 - 12 *Hole in the roof*

Jesus was in Capernaum preaching in a house. It was standing room only. A group of men climbed onto the roof with a paralyzed friend, opened a hole through the tiles and lowered him and his cot down with ropes. Jesus was impressed with their faith. He said to the sick man, "My son, your sins are forgiven!" There were religious leaders in the crowd, and they were thinking, "Who does this Guy think He is, forgiving sins?" Jesus perceived their thoughts and said, "Why are you thinking these things? Which is easier to say to the sick man: your sins are forgiven; or get up and walk? To illustrate My authority to forgive sins, I'll say the latter." So He said to the man, "Pick up your cot and go home." The man did just that! Everyone was amazed!

Luke 7:36 - 50 *Woman washes Jesus' feet*

One of the Pharisees invited Jesus to his home for dinner. As they were reclining at dinner, a sinful woman from town brought a vile of alabaster perfume and began to weep at Jesus' feet. She washed them with her tears and hair, and then applied the perfume. The Pharisee said to himself, "If this man were a prophet, He would know what sort of woman this is." Jesus knew his thoughts and said, "Simon, let Me tell you a story. A moneylender had two debtors; one owed him 50,000 dollars, the other 5,000. Neither of them could pay their debt, and he forgave them both. Which do you think was more thankful? Simon the Pharisee answered, "I'd say the one who owed 50,000." Jesus answered, "That's right. You've been noticing this woman attending to Me. When I came in, you offered no water for My feet, but she has washed My feet with her tears and dried them with her hair. You gave Me no kiss; however she's been kissing My feet since she arrived. You didn't offer oil for My hair, but she has conditioned My feet with perfume. Because of all this I say to you, her many sins are forgiven because of her great love. Those who have been forgiven of little, tend to love little as well." Those who were at the table said to themselves, "Who is this Guy, who even forgives sins?" Jesus said to the woman, "Go in peace, your faith has saved you."

Luke 9:57 - 61 *Potential followers*

One day as Jesus and His disciples were walking along a man came up to them and said; "I will follow You were ever You go." Jesus replied, "Foxes have holes and birds have nests, but the Son of Man has nowhere to lay His head." Jesus said to another, "Follow Me." He replied, "Allow me to go bury my father first." Jesus answered, "Let the dead bury their own dead, but you go and proclaim the kingdom of God." Another man said, "I will follow You Lord, but first let me go say good-bye to my family." Jesus answered, "No one who puts his hand to the plow and then looks back is fit for the kingdom of God."

Luke 19: 2 – 10 *(see Matthew 9: 9 – 13 for the call of Mathew, which is similar)*
One day a man named Zaccheus, who ran a very profitable tax collecting franchise, (Jews hated tax collectors), was trying to get a look at Jesus. He was a short fellow and because of the crowd he wasn't successful. So he ran ahead and climbed a tree by the road so he could see Jesus as He passed. When Jesus came by He called up to Zaccheus in the tree, "Come on down Zaccheus, today I will stay at your house!" Zaccheus hurried down and they went to his home. They had quite a gathering with Jesus and His disciples and all of Zaccheus's friends. Zaccheus believed that day. He pledged to correct any fraudulent transactions he may have committed. Jesus said, "Today salvation has come to this house. The Son of Man has come to seek and save those who are lost." There were a good number of unsavory sinners at Zaccheus's lunch party. The Scribes and Pharisees (religious leaders) asked Jesus' disciples why He associated with sinners. When Jesus heard, He said, "I'm like a doctor. I see people who are sick, not people who are well."

Matthew 9:14 - 17 Luke 7:32 & 33 *New wine*
John the Baptist, his followers and Jews in general fasted regularly. Jesus and His disciples never fasted. When asked about this, Jesus replied, "At a wedding party everybody eats and drinks until the bride and groom are there. When they leave, the party stops. If you try to patch an old pair of jeans with new denim, the patch won't hold; the cloth around the new patch will rip. In the same way, no one pours new wine into used wineskins. The new wine will burst the old skins and spill out."

"The people of this generation are like children in a market place who call out, 'We played a flute, and you didn't dance; we played a dirge, and you didn't mourn.' John came fasting and abstaining from wine; I come eating and drinking with sinners. You haven't been accepting of either. You only accept yourselves."

Mark 2:23 - 28 *Lord of the Sabbath*
One Sabbath day Jesus and His disciples were walking through a field picking heads off the grain and eating them. The Pharisees asked why they were breaking the Jewish law by picking food on the Sabbath. Jesus answered, "Remember when David passed through Nob? He needed food, and Abiathar, the priest, gave him the consecrated bread from the tabernacle. That was against the law too. Or have you read in the law how priests in the temple break the Sabbath, but do not break the law?

God made the Sabbath for man, not man for the Sabbath. The bottom line is that I am the Lord of the Sabbath."

Luke 6:6 - 11 *Withered hand healed on the Sabbath*
Later, Jesus went into a synagogue. A man with a withered hand was there. The Pharisees watched to see if Jesus would break the law again by healing the man on the Sabbath. Jesus knew He was being watched. He said, "What is lawful to do on the Sabbath; good or bad, to save a life or to kill? Which of you, who has a sheep that falls into a pit, does not lift it out on the Sabbath? Isn't a man more valuable than a sheep?" The leaders didn't answer. Then Jesus told the man to stretch out his hand. When he did, it was healed immediately! The Jewish leaders began plotting to destroy Jesus from that point on.

Mark 3:7 - 34 *More healings more questions from religious leaders*
Jesus tried to lay low out in the country for awhile, but crowds of folks from all over found Him   In fact, He had to have a boat kept ready at all times in case He was overwhelmed by the crowds. He healed many people and cast out demons. As they were being cast out, the demons would yell, "You are the Son of God!" Jesus warned them to keep quiet. He formally chose his 12 close disciples. Soon Jesus was so busy He didn't have time to eat. Even His own family thought He'd gone a little crazy and tried to get Him to come home.

A man who was deaf and dumb because of a demon was brought to Jesus, and He healed him so he could hear and speak again. The multitudes were amazed and said, "Could this man be the Son of David, our Messiah? The Jewish leaders from Jerusalem said Jesus was possessed by a demon Himself and that was how He was casting out demons! Jesus answered them, "Why would Satan cast out Satan? If his house is divided, he's doomed anyway! The only way a person can enter a strong man's house and steal, is to capture the strong man first. But if I do these things by the finger of God, then the kingdom of God has come upon you. He who is not with Me is against Me. He who does not gather with Me, scatters. When a demon goes out of a man it wanders through dry places seeking rest. When it finds none, it says, 'I will return to where I was.' When it comes, finding its house swept and in order, it goes and finds seven other more evil demons to return with him, and the state of the man is worse than before. This is true: All sins and blasphemies will be forgiven, but speaking against the Holy Spirit will not be forgiven!" He said this in reply to their comments about His having an unclean spirit.

Jesus' family was still concerned about Him, and tried to get word to Him. When Jesus heard His mother and brothers were trying to contact Him, He said, "Whoever does the will of God is My mother, sister, and brother." At the time, He was teaching down by the sea. So many people were there that Jesus got into a boat, and the people sat listening on the shore.

Matthew 13 Mark 4 Luke 8 *Teaching with stories (parables)*
He taught using parables like: "The farmer sowed his seed. Some fell by the road and the birds came and ate it. Some fell on rocky ground where it sprouted but failed to grow because there was little soil and when the sun came up, it was scorched. Some seeds fell among the thorns, but they choked the plants, so they produced no crop. Some seeds fell in good soil. They grew and produced plentifully!

His disciples asked Him about the lessons. He answered them, "I teach in parables to the people because of what the prophets said: 'The people will see and hear, but they won't understand and be saved.' But I will make everything clear to you, My close disciples. I am so thankful that God has chosen to reveal these things to simple folks like you and not to the educated and intelligent. All things have been handed over to Me from God. In fact, no one knows God except the Son and anyone to whom the Son reveals Him. He added, "Come to Me all you who are under a heavy load. Work for Me; learn from Me. I am humble and gentle and I will give you rest. Working for Me is easy; because I give you light loads!

Jesus said, "As the Psalmists say 'I will open My mouth in parables, I will say things that have been hidden since the foundation of the world.' His disciples asked Him to explain the parable of the weeds growing with the crop. Jesus answered, "The one who sows the seed is the Son of Man. The field is the world; the good seed represents the sons of the kingdom, while the weeds are the sons of the evil one. Satan is the enemy who sowed the weeds, and the harvest is the end of the age when the Son of man will send His angels to remove all the stumbling blocks and evildoers from His Kingdom. They will be cast into the fire, where there will be weeping and gnashing of teeth. Then the righteous will shine forth as the sun in the kingdom of their Father.

"The kingdom of God is also like yeast. A woman will put only a little of it in with her dough, but soon the whole loaf is leavened."

The kingdom of heaven is like a treasure in a field that a man finds and hides again. Then with great joy he sells all he has so he can buy the field. The kingdom is also like a merchant who upon finding a pearl of great value sells all he has so he can purchase it.

Yet again, the kingdom of heaven can be compared to a fishing net loaded with fish. The fishermen haul it in, and then separate the good fish into baskets and the bad ones are thrown away. This is how it will be at the end of the age, the wicked will be separated from the righteous and thrown into the furnace where there will be weeping and gnashing of teeth.

The kingdom of God is like the farmer: He sows his seed, but the crop grows by itself; the farmer doesn't understand how. He does go out and harvest though, as soon as the grain is ready!

The kingdom of God is like a farmer who sows his seed, but while he sleeps, an enemy comes throwing weed and thistle seed in with his crop. He decides not to pull out the weeds because he might destroy the wheat, so he waits and harvests all the plants. Then he separates the weeds from the wheat. The wheat is stored in barns and the weeds are burned."

"The Kingdom of God is also like a mustard seed; it's the smallest seed but produces a large tree that even birds find shade in."

Jesus asked the disciples if they understood all these things and they said they did. Then Jesus said, "Every religious leader who becomes a disciple of the kingdom is like the head of a household who brings out both old and new items from his treasure."

As Jesus continued to teach in the synagogues, everyone was amazed at His teaching and wondered where His authority came from. They would say, "Isn't this just the carpenter's son, and don't we know His mother and His brothers, James, Joseph, Simon, Judas, and his sisters too? We know exactly where He came from. How did He get all this wisdom and power to perform miracles? But Jesus replied, "A prophet does not receive honor in his own home town." Jesus did few miracles in Nazareth.

Luke 8:1 – 3 *Female support*
As Jesus traveled from town to town accompanied by his 12 disciples, He was also accompanied by women who had been healed of sickness and had had evil spirits cast out of them. They included: Mary Magdalene, (who had seven demons cast out),

Joanna, the wife of Chuza, Susanna and many others who were contributing from their private funds to support the ministry.

Mark 4:35 - 41 *Calming the storm*
One night they crossed the sea in a boat when a fierce storm came up that threatened to sink the boat. Jesus was asleep at the time. The disciples woke Him up crying, "Teacher, aren't You concerned that we are close to sinking and dying in this storm?" Jesus said, "You guys aren't getting it are you?" Then He commanded the wind to be still. The wind stopped immediately. The disciples were amazed that even the forces of nature obeyed Jesus!

Matthew 8:28 - 34 *Demon(s) exorcised*
They landed the boat in the region of Gerasenes. Two demon-possessed men who lived in the tombs met them at the shore. They had broken every chain used to bind them and cut themselves with stones. When they saw Jesus they cried out, "What have we to do with You, Jesus Son of the Most High God? Please do no torment us." Jesus cast out multiple demons from the men. Jesus allowed the demons to enter a herd of pigs because they requested not to be sent far away. The pigs threw themselves over a cliff. The herdsman reported the incident to the people of the area. When the town's folk saw the demon possessed men in their right mind and heard about the pigs, they asked Jesus to leave the area. The healed men wanted to go with Jesus but Jesus told them to stay and tell people about the great mercy the Lord had shone them.

Mark 5:21 - 34 *Healing (on the way to a healing)*
Jesus left the area by boat. A crowd was waiting when they landed. An official from the synagogue, named Jairus, begged Jesus, "My daughter is close to death, please come touch her and heal her." As they walked to Jairus's house, Jesus was pressed on all sides by the throng. There was a woman in the crowd who had been sick with a female problem her entire life. She had spent all she had on doctors. Her condition was worsening. She believed if she could just touched Jesus' clothes she would be healed. When she was able to touch his cloak she was immediately healed! Jesus felt the healing power release from Him and He said, "Who touched My clothes?" His disciples answered, "Jesus, You're being mobbed and You want to know who touched You?" Jesus saw the woman and she confessed. Jesus said, "Daughter, your faith has healed you. Go your way in health and peace."

Luke 8:49 - 56 *Jairus' daughter*
Some folks came from Jairus' house and announced that his daughter had passed away. Jesus looked at Jairus and said, "Don't be afraid any longer, and just believe."

When they arrived, Jesus allowed only Peter, James and John to follow Him to see the girl. The people at Jairus's house were deep in their sorrow over the loss of the child. Jesus said, "Why cry? The girl is only sleeping." They scoffed at this. Jesus sent them out of the house. He entered the child's room with her parents and His three disciples. He took the girl by the hand and said, "Time to get up little one." The child was immediately up and fully recovered. Jesus told them to get her something to eat and not to broadcast word of the miracle.

John 5:1 - 47 *Another healing offends religious leaders*

While attending a feast in Jerusalem, Jesus saw a man lying by a pool near the sheep gate. He had been sick for 38 years. He was at the pool because occasionally the waters would stir and the one who entered first would be healed. Jesus said to him, "Do you want to be well?" The man answered, "I have no one to help me into the water. I'm never the first in." Jesus said, "Get up, pick up your things, and walk." The man was healed immediately, picked up his bed, and walked.

The Jews saw the healed man carrying his baggage, against the regulation for the Sabbath, and said, "Hey, you're not supposed to be carrying those things on the Sabbath." He replied, "The man who healed me told me to pick them up." The Jews asked, "Where is He?" The healed man couldn't answer because Jesus had slipped into the crowd. Jesus found the healed man at the temple and said to him, "You're well now, don't sin any more or something worse may happen to you." Then the man went and reported to the Jews that it was Jesus who had healed him. The Jews were angry that Jesus chose to heal on the Sabbath. Jesus answered, "My Father works and I work." This made the Jews want to kill Him because He was calling God His Father, making Himself equal with God.

Jesus answered the Jews: "The Son only does what He sees His father doing. The Father loves the Son and shows Him everything. Even greater works are coming. The dead will be raised. Judgment has also been delegated to the Son, so the Son will receive honor. Those that honor the Son, honor the Father. Those who hear Me and believe in God who sent Me, will have eternal life. They won't be judged but will pass out of death into life. An hour is coming when even the dead will hear His voice and be raised. The Father has life in Himself and He has given the Son life in Himself and authority to judge because He is the Son of Man. Judgment will certainly come."

"I can do nothing on My own. I do what My Father tells Me. That's why what I do is good and My judgment is good, because it comes from God. If I said all this of My own accord it would be meaningless. John the Baptist has testified of Me, and the works I do testify that what I say is true. You all search the scriptures but you miss the point. You're too busy being accepted by one another to worry about your relationship with God. The very scriptures you read will be your judgment because they testify of Me."

Matthew 10:1 - 42 *Disciples sent out*
Jesus continued traveling and teaching from village to village. He sent His twelve special disciples out in six pairs with authority to cast out demons and heal sickness. These are the names of the twelve: Simon, (Jesus called him Peter), Andrew (Peter's brother), James and John Zebedee (another set of brothers), Philip, Bartholomew, Thomas, Matthew (the tax collector), James Alphaeus, Thaddaeus, Simon (the Zealot) and Judas Iscariot, (the one who would betray Him).

He gave them these instructions; "Go to the Jews. Stay out of Samaria. Say, 'The kingdom of heaven is at hand.' Heal the sick, raise the dead, cleanse lepers, and cast out demons. You have received freely so give freely. Don't take money with you, or even any extra clothes, a worker is worthy of his support. When you go to a place, find one worthy house and stay there till you leave. Bless the house, but if you are not welcomed, return the blessing back to yourself. If any city doesn't receive you, shake the dust
from that place off your feet when you leave. It will be more tolerable for Sodom and Gomorrah on the Day of Judgment than for that city.

"I send you out like sheep among wolves, so be as wise as serpents and as innocent as doves. Beware of men, they will deliver you up to the courts and whip you in the synagogues. You will be brought before kings and governors for My sake. Don't worry about what to say, it will be given to you at the time. It won't be you speaking but the Holy Spirit speaking through you. Family and others will reject you because of Me. People will think they're doing God a favor by killing you. If they have called the head of the household a devil, what do you think they'll call you! Don't worry about those who can kill the body but can't hurt the soul. Two sparrows are sold for a penny, you're much more important than them! Any one who confesses Me before men will have Me vouching for them to My Father.

Don't think I've come to bring peace to the world. I came to bring a sword. Families will be divided over Me. If you don't love Me more than your family your not worthy of Me. If you're not willing to give up your life for Me you aren't worthy of Me. He who receives you, receives Me. He who receives you will receive a reward. Whoever gives you a cup of water will be rewarded." After all these instructions they set off.

Matthew 11:20 - 24 Cities *reproached*
Then Jesus began to reproach cities where He had performed many miracles, yet few of the people repented. "Woe to you Choazin, Bethsaida, and Capernaum. If all that occurred in you had happened in Sodom, Tyre or Sidon they would have repented completely. It will be much more tolerable for them in the Day of Judgment than it will be for you."

Luke 13:1 - 9 *Response to some local news*
A news report came to Jesus about how Pilate, the Governor of the region, had killed some people of Galilee and mingled their blood with the blood of their own sacrifices. Jesus replied, "So you think those were killed because they are worse sinners than the others in Galilee? No they weren't. Anyone who doesn't turn away from sin will meet the same fate. Remember the eighteen who were killed while the work was being done on the Siloam Tower, were they any worse than others in Jerusalem? No, and I repeat, unless you repent you will die as well."

Then He told a parable, "A man had a fig tree in his vineyard that did not bear fruit, so he ordered his gardener to cut it down. The gardener replied, 'Let me dig a trench around it and fertilize it. If it doesn't bear fruit next year, then we'll cut it down.'"

Luke 13:10 - 30 Another Sabbath healing, another rebuke from religious leaders
One Sabbath Jesus was teaching in a Synagogue. Jesus saw a woman who had been bent over from a sickness for 18 years. He said, "Woman, you are free from your sickness." As He touched her she began to straighten up and praise God. The leader of the Synagogue was indignant and said to those in attendance, "There are six days to work, so come on those days to be healed, but not on the Sabbath!" Jesus replied, "You hypocrites! Who of you doesn't water his donkey on the Sabbath? Doesn't this daughter of Abraham, who has been ill for 18 years, count more than your donkey? Yet you say she shouldn't be freed only because of what day it is!" The leader was humiliated, but the crowd loved it!

Someone said, "Jesus, are just a few going to be saved?" Jesus answered, "Try to enter by the narrow door. The gate to destruction is wide and many enter it, but the way is narrow that leads to life. Once the door is shut no amount of knocking will get you in.

Many will be outside knocking on that day saying they knew Me and they won't be allowed in." Many who you'd think would be great in the kingdom of heaven will be least and many of those you think would be least will be greatest."

Luke 14:1 – 24 *Jesus seems to like healing on the Sabbath (with religious leaders watching)*

One Sabbath Jesus was invited to eat at the house of a high-ranking religious leader. A swollen and sick fellow was there. Jesus asked the lawyers and Pharisees, "Is it lawful to heal on the Sabbath?" They didn't answer, so Jesus healed the man and sent him away. Then He said, "I know if any of you had an ox fall in a pit on the Sabbath you would pull it out." They didn't say a word.

Jesus noticed how some folks picked out places of honor to sit when they arrived. He advised, "When you get invited to a dinner don't sit in an honored seat. The host might come by with a more important guest have to ask you to move, which by then will probably be to the back of the room. Instead take a back seat, and then when the host sees you he may say, 'Come friend move up here closer to us.' Then you will be honored! In the same way those who humble themselves will be exalted." He also said to the Host, "When you invite folks to a party, don't just invite those who you know will invite you in return. Invite those who won't be able to return the favor. God will remember you at the resurrection.

One of the guests said, "Anyone who eats at the table in the Kingdom of God is blessed!" Jesus told this story, "A man put together a big dinner, with invitations going out to many. When the time came he sent a slave out to announce that the dinner was ready. Everybody who'd been invited started making excuses as to why they couldn't come. So the slave was sent to the street and highways to invite poor, crippled and blind folks into the party. The host said, 'Those that were invited won't taste one bite of this feast!"

Luke 13:31 - 35 Matthew 14:1-13 *Warning*

Some Pharisees came to Jesus and said, "You'd better leave this place because Herod wants You killed." Jesus replied, "Go tell that fox I'll do My work just as I always have. It would not be fitting for a prophet to die anywhere but Jerusalem!

King Herod's concern arose from what he had heard about Jesus and His power. Many were saying Jesus was John the Baptist reincarnate and that was the reason for all the miracles. Others said He was Elijah, others said He was a great prophet like the ones in scripture. Herod felt Jesus was John the Baptist, reincarnated. John and Herod had a history. Herod put him in jail because John had denounced his marriage to Herodias, his brother's wife. Herodias also held a grudge against John. Herod did enjoy talking with John and kept him safe, until Herod's own fateful birthday party. Herod and his guest enjoyed the dancing of Herodias's daughter. Herod was so taken with the performance he offered up to half his kingdom to her. She consulted with her mother and asked that John's head be brought in quickly on a silver platter. Herod was stuck because he had publicly made his offer. So the young woman was given John's head, which she immediately presented to her mother, Herodias. John's disciples collected the body and buried it. They came to Jesus. He tried to get them off by themselves so they could recover, but the crowds wouldn't allow it. They followed them into the wilderness. Jesus felt compassion for all the people because they were like sheep without a shepherd.

John 6 *Jesus feeds 5000 and the repercussions*

Jesus continued to teach the multitude in the wilderness until late afternoon. The disciples recommended the crowds be sent back into the villages to eat. Jesus said, "You feed them." They answered, "It would take thousands of dollars just to have a barbecue for a group this size!" Jesus (with a plan already in mind) said, "How much food do we have?" His disciples disclosed an inventory of five loaves of bread and two fish. Jesus had the people sit in groups of 50 to 100. He prayed over what food they had. His disciples began to distribute food to the over 5000 people who were gathered. Everyone ate till they were full. The disciples collected 12 full baskets of leftovers!

After the meal Jesus sent the disciples ahead, across the sea. He stayed to see the people off and to have a time of solitary prayer. Hours before sunrise, Jesus saw His disciples far out on the sea, struggling against the wind. He walked out onto the sea, meaning to pass them and meet them on the other side. When they saw Him, they were afraid because they thought He was a ghost. Jesus said, "It's Me. Don't be afraid." Peter answered, "If it is You, call me out there with You." Jesus replied, "Come on out." Peter left the boat and was walking out towards Jesus on the water, but with all the wind and commotion he became afraid and began to sink. He cried out, "Lord, save me!" Jesus caught him by the hand and pulled him up. "Peter, you just didn't have enough faith, why did you doubt?" Jesus calmed His disciples and ordered the wind to cease as He and Peter entered the boat. The disciples found themselves immediately across the lake in Capernaum. The disciples in the boat said, "You are certainly God's Son!"

A multitude was waiting for Jesus when He landed. Where ever Jesus went people with ailments gathered on cots waiting to be healed. Many wondered how Jesus had crossed because they knew He hadn't gotten into the boat with the disciples the previous evening. Others arrived in boats from the area where they had been fed. "Teacher, when did You get here?" they asked as they landed. Jesus answered, "You're looking for Me because you ate the meal and were full. Don't work for food that perishes, but seek the eternal food that the Son of Man will give you. God has set His seal on Him." They said, "How can we do the kind of work You're doing?" Jesus answered, "If you believe on the One God sent, you'd be doing the work of God." They said, "OK. Show us a miracle so we can believe. Moses gave our fathers manna in the wilderness, bread right from heaven." Jesus answered, "It wasn't Moses who gave you bread out of heaven, but My Father who gives you true bread from heaven. This is the true heavenly bread that gives life to the world. I am the bread of life. If you come to Me, you will not hunger. If you believe in Me you will not thirst. You all have seen Me, yet you do not believe. Everyone My Father has given to Me will come to Me, and I will not cast them out. I have come from heaven to do God's will, not My own. His will is that I lose none that He has given to Me, and I will raise them up on the last day to receive eternal life."

The Jews were grumbling, "How can He say He came down from heaven when we know His parents?" Jesus answered, "Don't grumble among yourselves. No one can come to Me unless the Father that sent Me draws him. Everyone who has heard and learned from the Father comes to Me. I am the only One who has seen God, if you believe in Me you will have eternal life. I am the bread of life. Your fathers ate manna in the wilderness, and they died. I am the living bread that comes from heaven; anyone who eats of this bread will not die. The bread that I give is my flesh."

The Jews argued, "How can this man give us His flesh to eat?" Jesus answered, "I'm telling the truth; unless you eat My flesh and drink My blood you will not have life in yourselves. He who eats My flesh and drinks My blood will rise on the last day. He abides in Me and will live forever. This isn't manna, this is the real bread from heaven." He said these things in a synagogue in Capernaum.
Many of those who followed Him left because of this teaching. Jesus said, "So this causes you to stumble? If you could see who I really am you would know that the Spirit gives life, the flesh gets you nowhere, yet some of you do not believe." Jesus knew from the beginning who was going to betray Him. "This is why I've told you no one comes to Me unless the Father draws him to Me."

More followers left. Jesus said to the twelve, "Do you want to go too?" Peter answered, "Where would we go? You are the one with the message that leads to eternal life, and we believe You are the Holy One from God." Jesus answered, "Yes, I chose the twelve of you Myself, yet one of you is a devil." He meant Judas, one of the twelve who was going to betray Him.

John 7 and 8 *An active trip to Jerusalem*
Jesus was staying in Galilee because He knew the Jews in Judea wanted Him dead. Jesus' brothers were going to Jerusalem for the Feast of Booths. They wanted Jesus to come and do some miracles, "Come on down with us and show them what You can do. It's no good if You hide it!" Even some of His own brothers didn't believe in Him. Jesus answered, "This isn't the right time for Me. Every time is right for you. The world doesn't hate you. It hates Me because when it sees Me it recognizes its own evil. Go on without Me."

Jesus did go to the feast secretly. There was quite a bit of talk about Jesus. Some said He was a good man. Others said He was leading people astray. No one was saying anything publicly because they feared the religious leaders, who themselves wondered if Jesus would make an appearance.

When the feast was in full swing Jesus went to the temple and taught. The leaders were amazed and wondered how He had gained such knowledge without a formal education. Jesus said, "I teach what I am told by the One who sent Me. If you try to do His will, you will recognize that the teaching is from God. I righteously seek to glorify Him, not Myself. Moses gave you the law, yet none of you follow it. Why do you want to kill Me?" They all said, "Now we know You're crazy! No one wants to kill You!" Jesus answered, "I do a miracle on the Sabbath, and you are offended, yet you circumcise on the Sabbath so the law won't be broken and are offended at Me because I make a man whole on the Sabbath! Don't judge by appearance but judge righteously."

Some in Jerusalem were saying, "Isn't this the one they want dead? Yet here He is in public. Do you suppose they are starting to think He is The Savior? But how could He be? We know where He's from." Jesus answered, "You know Me and where I'm from. It's the One who sent Me that you don't know. I know Him because I am from Him. He sent Me." The leaders wanted Him arrested, but many in the multitude believed in Him. They said, "This man certainly performs miracles like the Savior would!" When the Pharisees heard this they sent officers to seize Him. Jesus said, "I'll only be with you a little longer. You will look for Me but won't find Me. Where I'm gong you can't come." The Jews thought He meant He was leaving the country.

On the day of the feast Jesus stood and cried out, " Anyone who is thirsty come to Me and drink. Living water will spring from your innermost being!" He was speaking about the Spirit whom believers would receive after He was glorified. There were many theories about Jesus, and there was a division in the multitude. Some wanted to seize Him, but no one laid hands on Him.

When the soldiers who had been sent to arrest Him returned empty handed, the Pharisees demanded explanation. "Nobody talks like this man." the soldiers answered. "Have you been led astray as well?" asked the Pharisees, "None of us have believed in Him. The rabble doesn't know the law!" Nicodemus (who was a Pharisee) said, "Our law provides for a proper trial before one is judged." The Jews answered, "What? Are you from Galilee too? Go search the scriptures; no prophet comes from Galilee!"

Jesus spent the evening on the Mount of Olives. Early the next morning, He went back to the temple and a crowd gathered to hear His teaching. The Pharisees brought a woman to Jesus that they had caught in adultery and said, "We caught this woman in the very act of adultery. The Law of Moses says she should be stoned to death. What do You say?" Jesus stooped down and began writing with His finger in the sand, saying nothing. They persisted in asking Him, so He stood up and said, "Let the one who is sinless cast the first stone at her." Then He stooped back down and continued writing in the sand. Slowly all the accusers began to disperse starting with the oldest till finally Jesus was left alone with the woman. Jesus stood up and said, "Where are they? Did no one condemn you?" She replied, "No one Lord." Jesus said, "I don't condemn you either; go now and don't continue to sin"

Later, Jesus spoke to the crowd, "I am the light of the world. If you follow Me, you will not walk in darkness but will have the light of life." The Pharisees replied, "You are testifying for Yourself, and You are not telling the truth." Jesus answered, "Even if I was the only witness, My testimony would be true. I know who I am, where I came from and where I am going. You don't know any of these things. You people judge by appearances. I don't judge anyone, but even if I did, my judgments would be true, because the One who sent Me would be in agreement with Me. Your law says that the testimony of two men is true. I have that; Myself and My Father, who sent Me." They asked, "Who is Your Father?" Jesus answered, "You don't know Him or Me. If you knew Me, you would know My Father also." Jesus was in the temple treasury when He said these things, but He was not arrested because His time had not yet come.

Later Jesus said, "I'm going away, you will look for Me and die in your sin. Where I am going you cannot come. The Jews thought He was planning to kill Himself because He said they could not go where He was going. Jesus said, "You are from below, I am from above. You are of this world I am not of this world. That's why I said you will die in your sins. If you don't believe I am He, you will die in your sins. They asked, "Who are you?" Jesus answered, "What have I been saying from the start? I have many things to speak and judge concerning you. I only say what I have been told by the One who sent Me and what He says is true." The Jews did not understand that He was talking about God. So Jesus said, "When you lift up the Son of Man, then you will know that I am He and I don't speak on My own initiative but only what the Father teaches Me. He is with Me and never leaves Me. I always do what is pleasing to Him."

Many of the Jews were beginning to believe in Him as He said these things. To them He said, "If you abide in My word, then you are truly disciples of Mine and you will know the truth and the truth shall set you free." They asked, "How can we be set free? We are the children of Abraham and we have never been anyone's slaves." Jesus answered, "Everyone who commits sin is a slave to sin. The slave doesn't remain in the house forever, the Son does. So if the Son sets you free, you are free indeed! I know you are the offspring of Abraham, yet you want Me dead, because you haven't accepted My word. I say what God tells Me to, you do what your father tells you." They answered, "Abraham is our Father." Jesus said, "If you are Abraham's children, then act like him. You are seeking to kill Me, a man who has told the truth. This is something Abraham did not do. You are doing the deeds of your real father." They replied, "We were not born out of wedlock! We have one Father: God." Jesus said, "If God were your Father you would love Me because I came from Him. I haven't come on My own, He sent Me. You can't understand Me because you can't hear what I'm saying. Your father is the devil and you do what he desires. He was a murderer from the beginning and he does not stand in the truth. Lying is natural for him. He is the father of liars. So you can't hear the truth. Which of you can convict Me of sin? I speak the truth and you can't hear it. He who is of God does hear, but you can't because you're not of God."

The Jews said, "It's clear you are a foreigner with a demon." Jesus answered, " I don't have a demon. I honor My Father, but you don't honor Me. I don't seek glory for Myself, but there is One who does, and judges also. This is the truth; anyone who keeps My word will not see death." The Jews argued, "Now we know You are demon possessed! Abraham and the prophets died, yet You say if anyone keeps Your word, they won't die! You're not greater than Abraham or the prophets. Just who do You claim to be?" Jesus answered, "I am not glorifying Myself. My Father is glorifying Me. The One you say is your God, but you do not know Him. I know Him. If I said I didn't know Him, I'd be a liar like you. I know Him and keep His word. Your father Abraham rejoiced to see My day, and he did see it and was glad." The Jews said, "You're not fifty years old, yet You say You've seen Abraham!" Jesus said, "Before Abraham was born, I am." At this, the Jews picked up stones to kill Him, but Jesus hid Himself and left the temple.

Luke 10:1 - 24 *Jesus appoints seventy*
Jesus appointed 70 others to go out in pairs, to every place He would be visiting. He gave them the same basic instructions He had given the 12 when they had been sent out. Jesus also pronounced woes upon the cities that did not receive the message. "He who rejects Me rejects the One who sent Me." When the 70 returned they were joyous that even the demons obeyed them when
they used Jesus' name. Jesus said, "I saw Satan fall from heaven like lightning. I have given you authority over the enemy and nothing will injure you. Don't rejoice in this. Rejoice that your names are recorded in heaven!"

Luke 11:37 - 53 *A garden party with religious leaders*
One day Jesus was invited by a Pharisee to have lunch in his home. Jesus and His disciples did not follow all the many and various Jewish customs regarding washing. When they arrived, they went straight to the table for lunch. The Pharisees considered this un-holy behavior and confronted them on it. Jesus answered, "Isaiah was right when he said you all serve God with your words but not with your hearts. You pay more attention to rules than you do to knowing God. You even put silly rules above more important matters. For instance, your rules say once something has been set aside for some specific "Holy" reason, it mustn't be used to help anyone else. Yet you wouldn't use it to help your father and mother, who the law clearly says to honor." Isaiah was right when he said of this generation, "This people honors Me with their lips, but their hearts are far from Me. They worship Me in vain because they follow their own rules."

One of the legal experts who was in attendance said, "You not only offend the Pharisees, but You also offend us with these statements." Jesus answered, "Woe to you lawyers also. You lay heavy burdens on your followers and take none on yourselves. You claim to admire the prophets, yet you would kill them just as your fathers did. From the death of Abel to the killing of Zechariah will be charged against this generation. You chose not to enter a real relationship with God and you hinder those that desire to." The religious leaders became hostile. They questioned Him closely on many subjects, hoping to catch Him in something they could use to accuse Him.

Matthew 15:10 - 20 *What defiles a man*
Jesus spoke again saying, "Things from outside the body, going into the man, cannot defile him. It's the things that come out of a man that make him unholy. Whatever goes into the man goes through his stomach and out. But the things that come out from inside a man's heart like sexual immorality, thefts, murders, adultery, coveting, envy, slander, pride, and foolishness; all these things come from within and that's what defiles a man. His disciples came to Him and said, "Jesus, don't You know You're offending the Pharisees with this kind of rhetoric?" Jesus answered, "Every plant My Father did not plant will be pulled up by the roots. Leave the Pharisees alone; they are blind guides, leading the blind. If a blind man leads another blind man, certainly both will fall into a pit."

Matthew 15:21 - 28 *Helping non-Jewish folks*
The crowds around Jesus were so big they were stepping on one another. Jesus went to Tyre, trying to escape the crowds. He entered a house secretly but was soon found by a non-Jewish woman whose daughter had a demon. Even though she acknowledged Jesus had been sent to the Jews, she knew He could help her daughter. Her faith and persistence earned Jesus' respect, and her daughter was delivered from the demon.

Mark 7:31 - 37 *Healings/accusations*
Jesus left Tyre and went to the region of Decapolis. A demon possessed man, deaf and blind, with unclear speech was brought to Him. Jesus put His fingers in the man's ears then spit on His own finger and touched it to the deaf man's tongue. Jesus said with a deep sigh, "Be opened." The man could hear and speak again. The multitudes were saying, "Could this Jesus be the Son of David?" The Pharisees said, "He cast out demons by Beelzebub, the chief of demons.

Matthew 15:29 - 39 *More fed*
Multitudes were coming to Jesus. They would lay their sick and lame at Jesus' feet, and He healed them. The people were amazed when they saw the dumb speak, the lame walk, and the blind see. They glorified the God of Israel. Another situation arose when Jesus had a hungry multitude around Him. He said, "Let's feed these folks, they've been out here three days. If we send them away hungry, they'll faint on the way." His disciples wondered how they would feed so many with the few fish and

loaves of bread they had. Again, Jesus distributed the small amount they had and it was multiplied to feed over 4000, with seven baskets of leftovers collected after the meal.

Luke 14:25 – 35 *Counting costs*
When Jesus saw all the multitudes that were beginning to follow Him, He said to them, "Any one who isn't willing to leave family and home cannot be My disciple. Whoever isn't willing to go to the death chamber in My name can't be My disciple. Count the cost. Don't be like the man who starts building a house and can't complete it because he's run out of funds. Be like the King who sits down and carefully calculates his ability to beat a larger force. If he knows he can't he can send a delegation to negotiate terms. I'm an all or nothing type of commitment. True disciples are like salt. But if salt loses its flavor its worthless for any use.

Luke 15: 1 - 10 *The returning son*
Many tax collectors and sinners followed Jesus. The Pharisees grumbled, "This man receives sinners and even eats with them!" Jesus said, "Each of you knows how wonderful it is to find something after its lost. If a man finds a lost sheep, or a woman a lost coin, they will be telling all their friends how happy they are that they've found what was lost! This is the same way it is in heaven when a sinner repents."

"Listen to this story; a certain man had two sons. The youngest asked for his share of the inheritance. Just a few days after receiving his riches, he went to a distant place and squandered his estate on loose living. When everything was gone, a famine came on that land. He got a job feeding pigs. He ate the same food that he was feeding the pigs. He finally came to his senses and thought to himself, 'My father's servants have it much better than me. I will return home and confess how foolish and sinful I've been. I will never be accepted as before, but perhaps I can work as a servant for my father.' As he approached his old home, his father saw him coming and ran out to embrace him. The son said, 'I have sinned against you and God. I am no longer worthy to be called your son.' The father called his servants and said, 'Take my son, dress him in fine clothes, and put our family ring on him. Then prepare a banquet and let us celebrate, because my son was dead, but has come back to life. He was lost, but now is found!' So the party began. The older son who had stayed home was in the fields. He noticed the party as he was returning from his labor. He called one of the servants to inquire about the party. When he heard it was for his brother, he was angry and refused to come in. His father went out to talk to him. The older son said, 'I have served you and obeyed all of your commands my entire life, yet you have never put on a party like this for my friends and I. Now my brother returns, after spending your money on whores, and you put on a party!' The father replied, 'Son, you have always been with me and all I have is yours, but we had to celebrate. This brother of yours was dead and now he lives. He was lost, and now he's been found!'"

Luke 18:9 - 14 *Self righteousness*
Jesus told this parable about those who trust their own righteousness and view others with contempt. "Two men went to the temple to pray, a Pharisee and a tax-collector. The Pharisee prayed, 'God, I thank Thee that I am not like others: swindlers, unjust, adulterers, like this tax collector. I fast twice a week and pay tithes.' The tax collector couldn't even lift his eyes to God, he gripped his chest and said, 'God forgive me, I am a sinner.' I tell you the tax collector left the temple justified; the Pharisee did not. Everyone who exalts himself will be humbled. He who humbles himself will be exalted."

Luke 16:1 - 31 Luke 12:13 - 21 Mark 12:41 -44 *Money*
"Here's another story; there was a rich man whose money manager was under performing. The manager was required to come in to give a report of his activities. He knew he was going to be fired. He had no other skills and devised a plan that would net many friends who owed him favors after his dismissal. He called those on his books who owed his boss money. He fixed the books so each of them owed much less. The rich man complimented the manager because he had acted shrewdly. The people of this age are shrewder in relation to their own generation than the sons of light. If you make friends by means of riches, when it fails, you will see how valuable these friendships really are. He who is faithful in little will be faithful in much; he who is unrighteous in little will be unrighteous in much. So if you're unfaithful with money, who will entrust true riches to you? If you can't be faithful with that which belongs to others, how can you be faithful with your own? No one can serve two masters; he will hate one and love the other. You cannot serve God and money."

The Pharisees scoffed at these statements because they loved money. Jesus answered, "You justify yourselves in the sight of man. God knows your thoughts, and what is highly regarded by man is detestable to God. All the works of Moses and the prophets were announced until John, but the Gospel of the kingdom has been preached since then, and everyone is forcing his way into it. It would be easier for heaven and earth to disappear than for any item of the law not to be fulfilled."

Jesus continued, "Listen to this story: There was a rich man who lived extravagantly, and there was a man named Lazarus who was so poor and miserable, dogs licked his sores as he begged for crumbs at the gate. They both died. Lazarus went to Abraham's reward but the rich man went to Hades. The rich man lifted his eyes from his torment and saw Abraham far away with Lazarus reclining with him. He said, 'Abraham, please send Lazarus to give me a sip of water.' Abraham said, 'The tables certainly have turned between you and Lazarus. He can't come over to you. The chasm can't be crossed. The rich man said, 'Then send Lazarus to my family so they can avoid this.' Abraham answered, 'They have Moses and the prophets to tell them.' The man in Hades replied, 'They will believe if someone returns from the dead to tell them.' Abraham concluded, 'If they don't believe Moses and the Prophets, they won't believe if someone rises from the dead."

Someone in the crowd said, "Teacher, tell my brother to divide the family inheritance with me." Jesus answered, "Who appointed Me a mediator for you?" Then He said, "Beware of every form of greed. Even when you are rich, your life does not consist of your possessions. Listen to this story: A man owned a large farm that was very productive. He didn't have enough room to store all his crops so he tore down his barns and built bigger barns. When the work was complete he said, "I have goods stored up for many years to come, I'll take it easy, I'll eat, drink and be merry!" God said, 'You fool, this very night your soul is required of you, who owns your barns now?' So it is with him who lays up treasure for himself but is not rich with God."

One day a rich man came to Jesus wanting to know what he must do to obtain eternal life. After reviewing some "ten commandment" type issues which the man had always observed, Jesus instructed him to sell all he had, give it to the poor, and to come follow Him. With all his wealth the man left down-hearted." Jesus lamented, "It is harder for a camel to go through the eye of a needle, than for a rich man to enter the kingdom." His disciples asked, "How can they be saved then?" Jesus answered, "With God all things are possible!" His disciples remarked, "We have left everything to follow you." Jesus replied, "Those who leave their possessions and family to follow the Gospel will receive rewards on earth and in heaven. They will also be persecuted on earth. Many who are first now will be last and visa versa."

Jesus watched as some of the rich people were putting large amounts of money into the collection box at the temple. When He saw a poor widow make her one-cent contribution He said to His disciples, "That widow has made a larger contribution than all those rich folks who went before her. The rich gave from their surplus, but she gave all she had, money she would use to live on!"

Matthew 12:38 - 42 *Religious leaders ask for a sign*

The Pharisees asked Jesus to show them a sign from heaven as a test. Jesus said, "It's an evil and adulterous generation that seeks a sign. The only sign you'll get is that of Jonah, who was in the belly of the whale for three days. Like him, the Son of Man will be three days in the heart of the earth. The men of Nineveh will stand up in judgment against this generation because they repented at the preaching of Jonah and there is one much greater than Jonah here now! The Queen of Sheba will judge you as well because she marveled at Solomon's wisdom and there is one much greater here now!"

Matthew 16:5 - 12 *No bread?*

After this, Jesus and His disciples were crossing the sea in a boat. The disciples had forgotten to take bread to eat. Jesus said to them, "Beware of the yeast of the Pharisees and of Herod." They thought He was chastising them for not bringing bread to eat. Jesus heard their discussion about this and said, "I can't believe you are talking about not having food! You still don't get it! You hear and see all these things, yet you do not understand it. When I distributed the five loaves to 5000, how many baskets of leftovers were there?" The disciples answered, "Twelve." "When I broke the seven loaves for the 4000 how many baskets of leftovers did you collect?" They answered "Seven." Jesus said, "Hellllooo! Can't you see I'm not worried about bread, but concerned about the evil influence of these religious leaders?"

Luke 12: 2 - 9 *Everything revealed*

"Nothing will be covered up that is not revealed; everything hidden will be known. What you have said in the dark will be heard in the light. What you have whispered in your bedroom will be shouted from the rooftop. Don't be afraid of those who can kill the body, because they can't kill your soul. God has that authority; fear Him! Five sparrows are sold for a dollar, yet God forgets not one of them. Every hair on your head is numbered; you are much more valuable to God than many sparrows. Everyone who confesses me before men, I will confess before the angels of God. But he who denies Me before men shall be denied before the angels of God."

Luke 10:38 - 42 *Most important thing*

During their travels through a certain city, a woman named Martha welcomed Jesus into her home. Her sister Mary sat a Jesus' feet as He spoke. Meanwhile, Martha was busy with the preparations, so she came to Jesus and said, "Aren't You concerned that my sister has left me all the work?" Jesus answered, "Martha, Martha you are worried about so many things, yet Mary has found the most important thing. It won't be taken from her."

John 9:1 - 41 *Healing a man born blind (happened on a Sabbath)*
One day as Jesus and His disciples were traveling they saw a man who had been blind from birth. His disciples asked him, "Teacher, who sinned, this man or his parents that he should be born blind?" Jesus answered, "It wasn't any particular sin. It was so God could do a work in him. We need to do the work of Him who sent Me while it is light. The night is coming on the world when no work can be done. While I am in the world, I am the light of the world." Jesus spat on the ground, made mud, applied it to the man's eyes and told him to go wash the mud off. The man returned seeing! His neighbors, who knew him as a beggar, wondered if it was really him. They thought it must be someone who looked like him. After he assured them, they asked who had healed him. He said, "That Jesus fellow put mud in my eyes, told me to go wash it off, and I was healed." He wasn't able to tell them where Jesus was.

They brought the healed man to the Pharisees. It happened to be a Sabbath when Jesus made the mud and healed the man. When the Pharisees heard how Jesus had accomplished the healing, they said, "We now know this man is not from God because He does not keep the Sabbath." Others were saying, "How could this man do what He does if He were not from God?" They asked the healed man what he thought, he said, "He is a prophet." The Jews then decided the man had not been born blind. They called his parents and questioned them. "So this is your son and he was born blind; how is it that he sees now?" His parents replied, "That's our son, and he was born blind, but we don't know how he got his sight. He's an adult, so ask him." The parents said this because the Jews had already announced that anyone who believed in Jesus would be put out of the synagogue.

So the Pharisees called the healed man before them again and asked how Jesus had performed the miracle. The man said, "We've been over this. Why do you want to hear it again? Do you want to be His disciples too?" This set the Jews off and they said, "Your His disciple. We're disciples of Moses. We know God has spoken through Moses; we don't even know where this man is from!" The healed man said, "Well isn't this amazing; you don't know where He's from, yet He opened my eyes! We know God doesn't hear sinners, but if a man does His will, He hears him. Since the beginning of time has anyone healed a man who was born blind? If this Jesus were not from God, He couldn't do anything." The Jews answered, "You are a sinner yourself and you are teaching us?" They had him removed from their chambers.

Jesus heard that the healed man had been put out, so He found him and said, "Do you believe in the Son of Man?" The man said, "Who is He, so I can believe in Him?" Jesus answered, "The Son of Man is here talking to you." The man said, "I believe," and he worshipped Jesus. Jesus said, "This is why I was sent, so those who do not see may see, and those who think they see become blind." Some Pharisees who were with Him said, "We're not blind are we?" Jesus answered, "If you were blind you wouldn't have sin, but since you think you see, your sin remains."

John 10:1 - 42 *The Good Shepherd*
"Here is the truth: There is one door into the fold of sheep, if you climb in some other way, you're a thief. The one who enters by the door is the shepherd and the sheep recognize his voice. He calls the sheep by name and leads them out. The sheep follow Him because they recognize Him. They don't follow the voice of a stranger." Jesus used this sheep analogy but the Jews didn't understand it.

Jesus said, "I am the door. All who came before Me are thieves and the sheep didn't hear them. I am the door, if anyone enters through Me, they will be saved, come in and out, and find pasture. The thief comes only to steal, kill and destroy. I have come that they can have abundant life! I am the good shepherd. The good shepherd lays his life down for his sheep. A hired shepherd hears a wolf coming and leaves the sheep; they scatter and some are snatched. I am the good shepherd. I know My own and they know Me, even as I know the Father, and He knows Me. I lay My life down for the sheep. I have other sheep that are not from this fold. I must bring them also and they will hear My voice and there will be one flock with one shepherd. The Father loves Me because I lay My life down that I might take it up again. No one has taken it from Me. I lay it down of My own initiative. I have authority to lay it down and the authority to take it up again. This is the commandment I received from My Father."

These words caused a division among the Jews. Some saying He was crazy, but others saying He didn't speak like a crazy person and He possessed the power to heal.

Later at the Feast of Dedication, Jesus was in the temple and the Jews said, "Why are you keeping us in suspense, if You're the Savior, why don't You just tell us?" Jesus answered, "I have told you, and you don't believe Me. The works I do in My Father's name testify to who I am. But you don't believe Me because you are not My sheep. My sheep hear My voice, and I know them and they follow Me. I give them eternal life and no one can snatch them away from Me. My Father has given them to Me. No one is greater than My Father, so no one can snatch them away. The Father and I are One.

The Jews picked up stones to kill Him. Jesus said, "For which of the good works that I've done are you stoning Me?" The Jews replied, "We're not stoning You for any good work; we're stoning You for blasphemy, because you are making Yourself out to be God and You're just a man." Jesus answered, "Your own Law says, `I say you are gods.' and you lift up stones against Me because I say I am the Son of God. Well, the works I do testify that I am the Son of God, so believe in the works if you can't believe in Me. If you look at them, you'll know the Father is in Me, and I am in the Father."

They tried to seize Him, but He eluded them and went out to the wilderness where John had first started baptizing. Many were saying, "Even though John did no miracles, he was surely right about this Jesus. Many came to believe in Him at this time.

John 11:1 - 46 Raising *Lazarus*

Lazarus, the brother of Mary and Martha, (Mary was the woman who anointed Jesus and wiped His feet with her hair), became ill. The two sisters sent a message to Jesus. Jesus said, "This sickness will not end in death, but will bring glory to the Son of God." Jesus loved Lazarus and his two sisters but stayed where He was for two days before He said, "Let's go back to Judea." When His disciples warned Him of the potential danger of being stoned to death in Judea, Jesus said, "There are 12 hours of daylight; the one who walks in the light will not stumble, but the night traveler will stumble because there is no light in him. Our friend Lazarus has fallen asleep. I must go and awaken him." The disciples thought this meant he was getting better. Then Jesus said plainly, "Lazarus is dead. I'm glad I wasn't there for your sakes, so you can believe." Thomas, one of the twelve said, "Let's go to Judea so we can die with Him.

When Jesus arrived in Bethany, where Lazarus had lived, He found that Lazarus had already been dead four days. Bethany was only two miles from Jerusalem, so many prominent Jews were there consoling Mary and Martha. When Martha heard Jesus had arrived in town she went out to meet Him while Mary stayed at home. She said, "Oh Jesus, I wish You had been here so Lazarus would not have died but even now I know God would grant any request You made of Him." Jesus answered, "Your brother will rise again." Martha said, "I know he will rise in the resurrection on the last day." Jesus answered, "I am the resurrection and the life, he who believes in Me shall live even if he dies. All who believe in Me will not die. Do you believe Me?" Martha answered, "Yes I believe that You are the Savior who has come into the world." After she said this, Martha went and secretly told Mary Jesus would arrive soon, so Mary got up and went to Him. When the Jews in the house saw Mary getting up quickly, they followed her thinking she might be going to Lazarus's grave. When she saw Jesus, Mary fell at His feet and said, "If You had been here my brother would still be alive." Jesus wept as He saw how sorrowful everyone was. He asked them to lead Him to the grave. When the Jews saw Jesus crying they said, "This man can heal the blind but did not save His own friend from death."

When they arrived at the grave, Jesus said, "Remove the stone." Martha advised against it, "Jesus, he's been dead four days; by now there will be quite an odor." Jesus said, "Didn't I tell you that if you believed you would see a glorious thing from God?" So the stone was removed. Jesus looked toward the sky and said, "Father, thank You for hearing Me. You always hear Me, but I am saying it so the people around Me can know that You sent Me." Then He shouted, "Lazarus, come forward!" Lazarus, who had been dead, came walking out with his grave clothes still bound. Jesus instructed the people to remove the wrappings. Many of the Jews who had come to Mary believed in Him because of this miracle. But some went back to Jerusalem and reported it to the chief priest.

As they continued to travel and teach in the villages, Jesus asked His disciples, "Who do people say that I am?" They answered, "Some say John the Baptist, others say Elijah, others say You're one of the prophets." Jesus asked, "Who do you say that I am?" Peter answered, "You are the Messiah." Jesus said, "Peter, God has revealed this to you, not flesh and blood. You are a stone and upon this bedrock I will build My church and the very gates of Hell will not prevail against it! I give you the keys to the kingdom of heaven. Whatever you bind or set loose on earth will be handled likewise in heaven." Then He told them not to tell anyone else that He was the Christ.

Matthew 16:21 - 27 *Bad time coming*
Later Jesus began to tell His disciples that He was going to suffer many indignities. He said that the religious leaders would reject Him, and that He would be killed but would come back to life after three days. He was very clear about it. Peter took Him aside and told Him not to talk about it. Jesus reprimanded Peter, "Get behind Me Satan! You are not concerning yourself with what God wants, but only your personal interests." He told all of them, "If you want to follow Me, be prepared to die. If you try to save your life you will lose it, but if you lose your life for My sake you will save it. Why gain the whole world only to lose your soul? The world has nothing to offer that's worth your soul. Don't be ashamed of Me in this evil world, or I will be ashamed of you when God reveals Himself with His holy angels."

Luke 17:11 - 19 *Ten lepers*

Jesus was traveling between Samaria and Galilee when He entered a certain village where ten leprous men stood at a distance to meet Him. They cried, "Jesus, Master, have mercy on us!" Jesus yelled back, "Go show yourselves to the priest." As they were doing this, they were healed of their disease. One of them, who was a Samaritan, returned praising God. He fell at Jesus' feet, thanking Him. Jesus said, "Where are the other nine? Ten were healed and only this foreigner has returned to give glory to God. Get up and go; your faith has made you well."

Matthew 17:24 - 27 *Taxes*

As they arrived in Capernaum, the collectors of temple taxes came to Peter and asked, "doesn't your teacher pay the temple tax?" Peter answered, "Yes." When Peter went into the house where Jesus was, Jesus asked him, "Peter, who do Kings collect taxes from, their family or strangers? Peter answered, "Strangers." Jesus replied, "So the sons are exempt. But just in case we offend these temple tax people, go out and catch a fish, when you open its mouth you'll find a coin sufficient to pay both of our taxes."

Matthew 18:1 - 14 *Like a child*

His disciples approached Jesus wondering how to be great in the kingdom of heaven. Jesus answered, "You have to become like a child to even enter the kingdom. The one who humbles himself like a child is greatest in the kingdom. Whoever receives a child in My name, receives Me but if anyone causes a little one to stumble would be better off with a pair a cement shoes and drowned. Oh it will be bad for those who cause stumbling. Indeed each little one has an angle looking over him. It's like if a man had a hundred sheep. If one is lost he'll search until he finds it. Then he'll rejoice over the one that is found. So you see God doesn't want to see any of these little ones to perish.

Matthew 18:15 – 20 *A sinning brother*

If you know someone who's sinning, go to him alone and talk to him about it. If he continues, go back with a few friends. If he still continues take him to the whole assembly. If he refuses to act correctly after all that, let him go and treat him as if he were an unbeliever. For what you bind here on earth will be bound in heaven. And if two of you agree on earth about a request to God, He'll see it gets done. Whenever two or three of you are gathered in My name, I'll be right there with them.

Matthew 18:21 – 35 *Forgiveness*

Then Peter asked Him, "How many times should I forgive my brother, seven times?" Jesus answered, "Try seventy times seven. The kingdom of heaven could be compared to this story. A king wanted to settle accounts with one of his slaves who owed him millions in silver. Since the slave couldn't pay the king was arranging to have him and his entire family sold. The slave came into the king and begged for payment arrangements. The king had compassion and forgave the entire debt! A few days later the same slave went to someone who owed him a few hundred in silver. His debtor begged for payment arrangements. The slave refused and had him thrown in jail. When the king heard about it he had the unforgiving slave thrown in a torturous prison until his entire debt was paid. So God will treat those who do not forgive their brothers.

Mark 9:2 - 8 *Listen to Him*
Jesus said to His disciples, "Some of you will not taste death until they see the power and coming of the Kingdom of God." Six days later Jesus took Peter, James, and John to a mountain and He was changed before their eyes. His clothing became whiter than any launderer on earth could have bleached them. Elijah appeared with Moses to speak with Jesus. The three disciples were mute with fear. Peter finally suggested that they erect tents for Jesus, Moses and Elijah. A cloud overshadowed them, and a voice came from it, "This is My beloved Son, listen to Him!" Then suddenly it all disappeared and Jesus was left with His three disciples. Jesus told them not to talk about the incident until He was raised from the dead. They had no idea what He meant by "raised from the dead."

Mark 9:9 - 13 *Elijah*
As they continued down the mountain they asked, "Doesn't it say in the prophets that Elijah will come before the Messiah?" Jesus answered, "Yes, it says that, and he has come. They did to him whatever they wished, just as it is written. It's also written that the Son of Man will suffer many things and be treated with contempt."

Luke 9:37 - 43 *Tough demon*
When they got back to the rest of the disciples they found them in a heated discussion with a group of religious leaders. Jesus said, "What's up?" A man in the crowd said, "My son has a demon that causes him to foam at the mouth and throws him on the rocks. Your disciples haven't been able to cast it out. Jesus said, "What an unbelieving generation. Bring the boy to Me." When the lad arrived, he immediately started into convulsions and foaming at the mouth. Jesus determined the boy had been afflicted since birth. The man said, "If you can, would you please help us?" Jesus replied, "If I can? All things are possible to him who believes!" The father said, "Help me with my unbelief!" Jesus saw the crowd was getting large, so He cast the demon

out. The boy looked like a corpse when the demon had left. Jesus took him by the hand and raised him. Later, in private, His disciples asked Him why they couldn't cast it out. Jesus told them it was a tough demon that required prayer and fasting.

Matthew 17:22 & 23 *Foretelling*
They traveled stealthily through Galilee. Jesus began plainly to explain to His disciples about His death. He said, "I will be turned over to the authorities and executed, but I will rise three days later." His disciples didn't understand and they were afraid to ask for an explanation.

Matthew 18:1 - 6 *How to be greatest*
One evening after arriving at their quarters, Jesus asked His disciples what they had been talking about that day as they walked. They didn't want to answer because they had been arguing about which of them was the greatest. Jesus sat them down and said, "If one of you wants to be first, he should be last and serve the rest. He brought a child before them and said, "Whoever receives a child like this in My name not only receives Me but also receives the one who sent me. The truth is, unless you become as humble as children you can't enter the kingdom of heaven. It will be terrible for whoever causes any of these little ones to stumble."

Mark 9:38 - 41 *Who is with us*
John said, "We saw someone casting out demons in Your name. We tried to stop him because he's not one of us." Jesus said, "Don't stop him. Anyone who does a miracle in My name won't be able to say anything bad about Me. He who is not against us, is for us. Whoever gives you a cup of water because you are My follower will not lose his reward. Whoever causes a believer to stumble would be better off with his feet set in concrete and thrown into the sea."

Luke 9:51 - 56 *Sons of Thunder*
One day, men who He had sent ahead to a certain village, returned saying the village would not receive them. When James and John Zebedee heard this they said, "Jesus, should we command fire to come down from heaven and destroy the village?" Jesus replied, "You two can be a bit much! I didn't come to destroy men's lives but to save them." So they went on to another village.

Matthew 19:1 - 12 *Quiz*
Jesus and His disciples traveled to Judea. The Pharisees there tested Him with questions. "Is it lawful for a man to divorce his wife?" Jesus asked, "What does the law say?" They recited, "Moses permitted a man to write a certificate of divorce and send

her away." Jesus answered, "He wrote that because of your hardness of heart. God made man, male and female. When they marry they become one flesh. That was instituted by God and it should not be separated." Later His disciples questioned Him again on the subject. Jesus said, "If you divorce your spouse and take another, you commit adultery." His disciples replied, "It would be better not even to get married!" Jesus answered, "Not everybody can accept this, but some men were born to not be married, some have been made that way by man and others have obtained the ability to live unmarried for the sake of the kingdom of heaven."

Mark 10:13 - 16 *Children*
Many brought their children to Jesus. His disciples thought He was wasting His time and energy on the young. Jesus corrected them, "The kingdom of God belongs to the child-like. If you don't accept the kingdom of God like a child you won't enter it at all."

Matthew 20:17 - 19 *Foretelling*
As they approached Jerusalem, Jesus again warned them about what would happen, "I will be arrested by the religious leaders. They will hand Me over to the Romans, who will mock Me and kill Me. After three days, I will rise again."

Matthew 20:20 - 28 *Serve to be great*
Mrs. Zebedee along with her sons, James and John, drew Jesus aside and asked if they could sit on His right and left side when He obtained His glory. Jesus asked, "You don't understand what you're asking for. Are you able to drink the cup that I drink?" They replied, "We are able." Jesus answered, "You'll drink from the cup, but it's not My call who will sit at My right or left. Those places will be filled by those for whom it has been prepared." The other disciples began to feel indignant with James and John. Jesus called the twelve to Him and said, "Worldly rulers lord over their realms. But with you, whoever wants to be great must be the servant of the rest. Look at Me, I didn't come to be served, but to serve, and give My life as a ransom for many."

Mark 10:46 - 52 *Blind beggar*
A blind beggar named Bartimaeus and a companion were by the side of the road. When they heard Jesus was coming by they began yelling, "Jesus, son of David, have mercy on us." Many tried to quiet them down. Jesus called for Bartimaeus and his friend to be brought to Him. "What do you want?" "We want to regain our sight." Jesus answered, "Your faith has made you well." The men immediately regained their sight and followed Jesus on the road.

Mark 11:11 - 24 Luke 17:7 - 10 *Jesus curses a fig tree*
Jesus took a quick look around the temple and then went back to Bethany for the night. The next day, on the way back into town, Jesus was hungry. He saw a fig tree in leaf and approached it to get some fruit, but the tree didn't have any; it was not fig season. Jesus said to the tree, "May no one ever eat fruit from you again." His disciples heard Him say it. The next day as they passed the same fig tree, the disciples noticed it had withered. They pointed it out to Jesus. He replied, "If you have faith, anything can happen. You could say to a mountain, 'Move,' and it would move if you didn't doubt. I'm telling you; anything you ask for, with belief, will be given to you. If you have the faith of a mustard seed you could say to this mulberry tree: 'Be uprooted and planted in the sea.' and it would obey you.

Remember this however: Which of you who own slaves say to them when they come in from the field, 'Sit and eat immediately'? Rather you say, 'Cook me a meal, get dressed properly to serve it to me, and afterward you can have dinner.' Does the slave deserve any special reward because he's done what he was told? So, when you do all these things that are commanded of you, say, 'We are just slaves doing what we're told.'"

Luke 20:1 - 8 *More testing from religious leaders*
Jesus was teaching each day at the temple. The chief priests and the religious leaders were bent on destroying Him. They couldn't find anything against Him, and the people hung on every word He spoke. The chief priest came to Jesus to test Him, "By what power or authority do You work miracles?" Jesus answered, "Let Me ask you a question, if you answer, so will I. Was John's baptism from heaven or from men?" This put the leaders in a corner, if they answered, 'heaven,' then Jesus would ask why they didn't believe in John. If they answered, 'from man,' then they'd have the crowd to contend with because they believed John was from God. So they answered, "We don't know." Jesus replied, "Neither will I tell you by what authority I do these things."

Mark 12:1 - 12 *The vineyard*
Jesus presented this parable: "A man planted a vineyard. He put a wall around it and built a tower for it. Then he rented it out and went on a journey. At harvest time he sent a slave to collect his portion of the harvest. The renters beat the slave and sent him back with nothing. The owner then sent other slaves; some were wounded, others killed. Finally the owner sent his own son, thinking they would have to pay him. The renters reasoned that if they killed the son they would gain his inheritance, so they killed the owner's son. What will the owner do? He will come and destroy the renters! Have you not seen the scripture: 'The stone the builders rejected has become the chief corner stone,' this came from the Lord and it is marvelous in our eyes!"

Luke 20:20 - 26 Matthew 22:23 - 33 Matthew 22:41 -46 Mark 12:28 - 34 Luke 10:29 - 37 *Testing continues*

This story angered the religious leaders even more because they could tell He was speaking against them. They sought even more fervently to trap Jesus. They sent some legal experts to question Him. "Jesus, we know how wise and true You are. Please tell us, is it lawful to pay tax to Caesar or not?" Jesus answered, "Why are you testing Me? Bring Me a coin to look at." Jesus looked at the coin that was presented to Him and said, "Whose picture is on the coin?" They answered, "Caesar's." Jesus replied, "Pay Caesar what is his and pay God what is His."

Some of the leaders who did not believe in life after death, questioned Him, "We know in the law that if a man dies with out bearing children from his wife, his brother should take her and have children. Let's say a woman is widowed by a man, then, widowed by his brother, and on down the line through seven brothers. Whose wife would she be in the after life?" Jesus answered, "You all don't understand the scriptures or the power of God. In heaven people are not married, they are like angels in that regard. The scripture does teach eternal life. Remember when God appeared to Moses in the burning bush? He said, 'I am the God of Abraham, Isaac and Jacob.' He is the God of the living not of the dead."

One of the leaders saw that Jesus was wise and asked Him an honest question, "What is the most important commandment?" Jesus answered, "Love God with all your heart, mind, soul, and strength. The second is: Love your neighbor like you love yourself. These are the greatest two commandments." The leader agreed, "Yes indeed these two are more important than burnt offerings and sacrifices." Jesus could see that the leader was honest and said, "You are not far from the kingdom of God."

Another leader wishing to justify himself asked, "Who is my neighbor?" Jesus told this story: "A man was traveling from Jerusalem to Jericho when he was robbed, beaten, and left half dead. A priest passed by but instead of stopping he crossed to the other side of the road to avoid becoming involved. A Levite came along and did the same. Finally a Samaritan came by. He put ointment and bandages on the man's wounds, put the man on his own donkey and took him to an Inn. The next day he told the innkeeper, 'Take care of him, I will pay any charges when I return.' Now I ask you who proved to be the man's neighbor? The Pharisee replied, "The one who helped him." Jesus answered, "Correct; now go and do the same."

Matthew 22:41 -46 *The religious leaders decide to stop asking questions*
As Jesus continued to teach, He said, "How is it that your leaders say the Christ is to be the son of David? Didn't David himself call the Christ 'Lord' in the Psalms? How is He a son and a Lord?" The people loved it when Jesus confounded the Pharisees. The Pharisees decided to stop asking questions.

Matthew 23:1 - 37 *Jesus' advice about religious leaders*
Jesus advised His listeners, "Be careful of the religious leaders. They love to be highly respected and get good seats at gatherings. They rob widows in private and say long prayers in public. They will receive a greater condemnation. Their religion is all confused; they make rulings on what's more binding to swear upon; the gold in the temple or the temple itself and other similar distinctions that are incorrect. They tithe down to the smallest mint leaf in their garden, but ignore weightier provisions of the law concerning mercy and justice." "Woe to the religious leaders; they wash the outside of a cup and leave the inside dirty with robbery and self indulgence. They should clean up the inside first. They are like freshly painted tombs: they look great on the outside, but inside are dead men's bones. They build monuments to the prophets and say, 'If we had been alive during their time we would not have shed their blood.' How wrong they are! They will continue to kill prophets even as they have until now, and they will be judged as guilty!"

Matthew 24:1 - 14 *Temple to be demolished (beginning of end times warnings)*
As they were leaving the Temple, one of the disciples said, "Teacher, look at how wonderfully these stones have been laid in this building!" Jesus answered, "Not one of these stones will be left on the other." Peter, James, and John questioned Him privately as they sat on the Mount of Olives, "Tell us when these things will happen. What will be the sign they are coming?" Jesus answered, "Don't let anyone mislead you. Many will come claiming to be Me. There will be wars and rumors of wars, famines and earthquakes will come, do not be afraid, these are like the beginning of birth pangs. The good news about Me will be preached to every nation, and then the end will come.

Mark 13:9 - 13 *Don't worry about what to say*
You will be delivered to the courts and flogged. You will stand before governors and kings for My sake. Don't be worried about what to say. Just say what's given to you at the time because it won't be you speaking but the Holy Spirit. You will be hated by everyone because of My name, but the one who endures to the end will be saved."

The Story Bible for Adults

Matthew 24:15 - 24 Luke 21:25 - 28 Matthew 24:32 - 44 Luke 12:36 - 48 Luke 17:22 - 37 Luke 12:49 - 56 Matthew 25:1 - 13
Luke 19:12 - 27 Matthew 25:31 - 46 *Warnings about the end of the age*

"When the ABOMINATION OF DESOLATION is standing where it should not be, the people in Judea should get out of town! Don't get your stuff; just leave! Hopefully it won't occur in winter. It's not going to be a good time to have a youngster to haul around. It will be a time like never seen before nor will ever come again. The citizens of Jerusalem will fall by the sword and be led captive into many nations and the city will be trampled under foot until the time of the Gentiles is complete. Everyone would be destroyed except God has shortened those days for the Elect's sake."
Jesus continued, "Many false Christs will appear. They'll be so convincing that many will follow them. Remember I've told you this in advance. The sun will be darkened; the moon will not give its light. The stars will fall from the heaven, and the powers in the heaven will be shaken. Then you will see the Son of Man coming in the clouds with great power and glory. He will send out His angels to gather the Elect from the whole earth and heaven.

When a fig tree puts out leaves we know the harvest will come soon. So when these things occur you'll know that the end is knocking on the door. No one knows the exact time. That's why you need always to be ready. Think of it this way: If your boss leaves and doesn't say when he'll return, you definitely want to be working when he comes back! So stay alert!" No one knows the exact hour these things will occur, not even the Son.

"When the master of the house leaves, happy is the servant who is found working when he returns! He should be prepared to run to the door to great Him when he returns. I'll tell you the Master will serve those workers himself, at his own table. Be ready no matter what time it is: nine at night or three in the morning. The servant who is found resting will be thrown out." Peter asked, "Is this parable directed just to us or to everyone?" Jesus answered, "Who is the faithful manager whom the master puts in charge of his servants to see that they are provided for at the proper interval? Blessed is the manager whom the master finds doing so when He returns. That manager will be put in charge of all his Master's possessions. But the manager who says in his heart, 'It will be a long time before the Master returns.' Then he beats the servants and gets drunk. When the Master returns and finds this, that manager will be cast out and punished. The one who knows these things will be held more accountable than the one who is ignorant of them. He who has been given much will have more expected of him.

The coming of the Son of Man will be just like the days of Noah. There were eating and drinking and marriage parties right up to the time the ark door was closed. On that day, there will be two men together in a field; one will be taken the other left. Two women will be working together, one will be taken the other left." His disciples asked, "Where will they go?" Jesus said, "Where the body is, vultures will gather. No one knows when this will happen. It's like the head of the house that didn't know when the thief was coming to steal his property. If he had known, he would have been on alert and would have stopped the thief.

I have come to cast fire upon the earth. How I wish it was already kindled, but I have a baptism to go through and until it is complete, I am distressed. Do you think I've come to bring peace on the earth? No, I have come to bring division! From this time on, a household will be divided, a father against a son, a daughter against mother, a daughter-in-law against her mother-in-law. You can predict the weather by the conditions you see in the sky, but you do not see the signs of the times."

The kingdom of heaven is like ten girls invited to a wedding feast. They all start with oil in their lamps. Five of the girls are wise and take flasks of extra oil because they don't know when the groom will arrive. When he comes, they have oil to light their lamps, but the other's lamps have run out. They will ask the wise girls for oil but there won't be enough to go around, so while the girls without oil for their lamps are off buying oil, the groom comes, the party begins, and the door is shut. The five foolish girls arrive and are not let in. So be on alert. You do not know the day or the hour.

His disciples still thought the kingdom would be coming immediately, so Jesus told them this parable: "The kingdom of heaven is like a nobleman who goes on a journey to receive a new kingdom for himself. Before he leaves he entrust his riches to his servants. He gives one servant 10,000 dollars, another is entrusted with 5,000 and another 2,000, each according to his ability. When he returns from his journey, he settles accounts with his servants. The one who received 10,000 dollars has invested wisely and returns 20,000. The servant given 5000 returns 10,000. The master is happy with both and rewards them with more lucrative positions. Then the one who received 2,000 comes and says, 'I know you're a hard man and often harvest where you have not planted. I didn't want to lose your money so I hid it in the ground. Here it is, the whole amount.' The master says to that servant, 'If you knew I was a hard man, you should have at least put the money in the bank so it returned some interest!

You're fired! Get out of my sight. Your 2,000 will be given to the one who was given 10,000!" So those who have will be given more and those without will be cast out, like worthless employees, in the dark where there is weeping and gnashing of teeth.

"When the Son of Man comes, His angels will separate the righteous on His right, and the un-righteous will be moved to His left. To the righteous on His right He will say, 'Come into My kingdom you good and faithful servants, for you fed Me when I was hungry and gave Me drink when I needed it. You helped Me when I was in prison.' They will say to Me, 'When did we do that?' I will answer, 'Whenever you helped even the least of My brothers you helped Me!' Those on the left will say, 'When did we not help You?' I will answer, 'Every time you denied help to the least of these you denied it to Me.' These will be cast into eternal punishment which has been prepared for the devil and his angels, but the righteous will be given eternal life."

Matthew 23:38 - 39 *Jesus laments for Jerusalem*
"Oh Jerusalem, who kills the messengers God has sent you. How I wanted to gather you under My wings like a hen gathers her chicks, but you rejected Me. When you see Me again you will certainly be happy and say, 'Blessed is He who comes in the name of the Lord.'

John 11:45 - 57 *Formalized plans*
News of Jesus' miracles continued to pour into the office of Caiaphas the high priest. A council was convened. "What are we going to do about this man? He is performing so many signs, everyone believes in Him. If this continues, the Romans will become involved and our nation will be destroyed." Caiaphas said, "Let's be smart about this, it is better for one man to die so our nation and everyone else may live." (He didn't say this of his own initiative, but because he was high priest that year. It was a prophecy that Jesus would die for the Jews and for all His other children scattered through the world.) From that day forward, they formalized their plans to kill Jesus.

Jesus and His disciples left the area discreetly. The Passover feast was approaching and many were wondering if Jesus would attend. The Jews had issued an order that if He was seen, it should be reported so He could be arrested.

John 12:1 - 8 *Mary pours a fortune on Jesus' feet*
Six days before the Passover Jesus went to Bethany, the same town Lazarus lived in. He was having dinner at the home of Simon the leper. Martha was serving, and Lazarus was at the table with Jesus when Mary entered with a very expensive bottle of

perfume. She poured it on Jesus' feet and wiped it with her hair. Some felt the valuable perfume had been wasted. Judas, the one who would betray him, said indignantly, "That perfume was worth what most people make in a year. Why didn't we sell it, to help the poor?" (Judas wasn't concerned for the poor. He handled the moneybox and pilfered from it.) Jesus answered, "She has prepared Me for burial. She can keep the rest and use it for My actual burial. What she has done will always be remembered. The poor will always be here; I will not."

Luke 21:1 -11 John12:-*19 Jesus received on a donkey*
As they approached Jerusalem, Jesus sent two disciples into one of the outer villages to pick up a donkey. He told them where it would be and what to say if questioned. They found everything as He had told them. When villagers questioned them about taking the donkey, they answered, "The Lord has need of it." They were not detained from bringing it.

Jesus entered Jerusalem on the donkey. This was done to fulfill the prophecy that says: "Behold your king is coming to you, gentle and mounted on a donkey." The crowd laid palm branches down in His path crying, "Hosanna! Blessed is He who comes in the name of the Lord! Blessed is the coming kingdom of our father David!" His disciples didn't understand what was going on at first but realized afterwards that these things were happening just as the prophets had predicted. Many in the crowd had been present when Lazarus was raised. Many others came because they'd heard of it. The Pharisees said to one another, "Our warnings to the people about this man are doing no good. The whole world seems to be going after Him." Some of the Pharisees said to Jesus, "This is ridiculous. Tell Your followers to stop the yelling." Jesus answered, "If they become quiet, the stones will cry it out!"

Luke 22:3 - 6 *Judas defects*
Judas arranged a secret meeting with the chief priest. A deal was struck, involving the exchange of money. Judas would deliver Jesus, away from the crowds, because the Jews were concerned about a riot if they seized Him publicly.

John 12:9 - 11 *A plan in flux*
Many Jews came to Bethany when they heard Jesus was there. They didn't come just to see Jesus only, but to see Lazarus, the one who had been raised from the dead. Because of this, the chief priest approved a plan that would have Lazarus killed with Jesus because so many had come to believe through his resurrection.

John 12:20 - 26 *Greeks come asking about Jesus*
Greeks who had come to Jerusalem to worship at the Passover came to Philip and asked him if they could meet Jesus. Philip told Andrew and together they approached Jesus. Jesus answered them, "It time for the Son of Man to be glorified. Unless a seed dies, it bears no fruit. He who loves his life will lose it. He who does not regard his life will keep it forever. Those who want to serve me should follow me. Where I am, my servant will be also and My Father will honor him."

John 12:27 - 36 *Jesus is troubled*
Jesus said, "I am troubled down to My soul. Should I ask God to save Me from the very thing I was sent to do? Father Glorify Your name!" Just as He had said this, a voice from out of heaven said, "I have glorified it and will glorify it again." Some of those standing around said it had thundered. Others said an angel had spoken to Him. Jesus said, "The voice didn't come for My sake but for your sakes. Judgment is upon the world and now the ruler of the world shall be cast out. I will be lifted up, and I will draw all men to Myself." The crowd was asking, "If the Messiah is to remain forever, how can He say, 'The Son of Man is to be lifted up?'" Jesus said, "The light will be with you for a little while longer. Walk in it while you can, so you may become sons of light."

John 12:37 - 50 *"I am the light of the world"*
Jesus did so many signs before the people but most still did not believe and even those that did, hesitated to admit it for fear of their reputation. But Isaiah had prophesied that the eyes of the people would be blinded. Jesus' final statement to the multitude was, "He who believes in Me, believes in the One who sent Me. He who sees Me sees the One who sent Me. I have come as a light to the world. He who believes in me no longer lives in darkness. I did not come to the world to judge it. But those who reject Me will be judged because I never spoke on My own initiative. I only said what I was told to say. The words I've spoken lead to eternal life."

Matthew 26:17 - 19 *Passover plans*
His disciples asked Jesus where He planned to eat the Passover meal. He instructed them to enter the city. There would be a man carrying a pitcher of water, he would have a room for them. The disciples found it exactly as the Lord had told them.

John 13:1 - 35 *The last supper*
As they were at the table for supper, Jesus got up and washed the feet of the disciples. Peter resisted but Jesus compelled him to accept the service. Jesus said, "You all call

Me Teacher and Lord, which is correct. If the Lord and Teacher washes your feet, so you should serve each other with humility as well. I do this as an example for you."

Later as they ate, Jesus announced that one of the twelve would betray Him. They were upset and each of them said, "Surely not me!" Jesus said, "The one who dips his bread in the bowl with Me will betray Me. It would surely be better for this man if he had not been born." After He said this, Judas dipped his bread in the bowl and took his last bite of supper. Jesus said, "Go and be quick." The disciples thought Judas was being sent out on an errand.

As soon as Judas had left, Jesus said, "Now the Son of Man and God are glorified. Soon, as I said to the Jews, I will be going and you won't be coming with Me. It is very important that you love each other. This is how others will know you are My disciples."

John 14:1 - 31 *Jesus speaks with His disciples*
"Don't be worried. Believe in God and Me. There are many rooms in My Father's house. I am going to prepare one for you, so you know I'll certainly be coming back to get you so we can be together again." Thomas asked, "Where are You going, and how do we get there?" Jesus answered, "I am the way there. I am the truth and the light; no one can get to God except through Me. If you know Me, you know God. If you've seen Me, you've seen God." Philip said, "Lord, show us the Father and that will be all we need." Jesus answered, "Philip, We've been together for a long time and you still don't know Me? Don't you believe that I am in the Father and He is in Me? I'm not saying this on My own. The Father who is in Me does the works you've seen. The person who believes in Me will do even greater works, because I am going to My Father. Whatever you ask in My name I will do it so the Father will be glorified in Me. If you love Me you'll follow My orders. I will ask the Father and He will send you another Helper, He will be with you forever. He is the Spirit of Truth, who the world cannot receive, because it doesn't know Him. He will be with you and live in you. I won't leave you alone; I will come to you. In just a little while the world won't see Me any longer, but you'll see Me, because I live, you will live too. Then you will know that I am in My Father and I am in you and you are in Me. He who follows My orders loves Me and he will be loved by My Father and I will love him and disclose Myself to him."

Judas (not the one who betrayed Jesus) said, "What has happened that you'll disclose Yourself to us and not to the world?" Jesus answered, "Anyone who loves Me will do what I've said, My Father will love him and We will come and live with him and in him. He who does not love Me, doesn't do what I've said. The things I've told you come from God, and I've told them to you while I've been here with you. The Helper, the

Holy Spirit, will be sent by My Father, in My name. He will teach you everything. He'll help you remember all the things I've told you. I'm leaving peace for you. My peace isn't like the peace the world gives you. Don't be worried or afraid. If you understood now, you'd be rejoicing that I'm leaving because I'm going to My Father and He is greater than Me. I've told you all this before it happens, so you will be able to believe in Me. We don't have a whole lot more time. The prince of this world is coming, but he has nothing to do with Me. This is all happening so the world will know that I love My Father and I follow His orders."

John 15:1 - 8 *"I am the vine"*
"I am the vine, and My Father is the vineyard keeper. All the branches in Me that do not bear fruit He removes, those that are productive, He prunes, so they will bear more fruit. You are clean because of the message I've given you. Stay connected to Me because a branch cannot bear fruit unless it is connected to the vine. He who stays connected to Me and with whom I stay connected, will bear much fruit. You can't do anything apart from Me. If you don't stay connected to Me, you will wither. Withered branches are cut off and burned. When you stay connected to Me, if you ask anything in My name, it will be done for you. Then you'll bear much fruit because you are My disciples and My Father will be glorified.

John 15:9 - 27 *"I chose you"*
I have loved you, just like My Father has loved Me. Live in My love. If you follow My orders, you will live in My love, just like I live in My Father's love and follow His orders. I say all this so My joy may be fulfilled. This is My order, love one another just as I loved you. There is no greater love than when a man lays down his life for his friends. You prove you are My friends when you follow My orders.

You are truly My friends now because a master wouldn't tell his slaves everything like I am telling you. You didn't choose Me, I chose you. You are to bear lasting fruit. God will help you by providing what you ask in My name. Love one another, that's a command. The world will hate you just as it has hated Me. You are not of the world, I chose you out of the world, that's why it hates you. I am persecuted, and you will be too. This happens because the world does not know the One who sent Me. If I had not come and spoken to them and done works no one else has done, then they would not have sin. But I have come, and now they have no excuse. He who hates Me, hates My Father also. All this is happening to fulfill the prophecies. When the Helper comes, that is the Spirit of truth, who comes from the Father, He will bear witness of Me. You will too, because you have been with Me from the beginning.

John 16:1 - 32 *Final thoughts*
I'm telling you these things so you won't stumble. The time is coming when you'll be expelled from the synagogues. You will be killed by those who think they are doing God a service by doing so. I've waited to be so frank about your fate because I've been with you. Now that you understand I'm leaving, you're sad, but I tell you the truth, it is to your advantage that I go. The Helper will not come until I have left. When He comes, He will convict the world concerning sin, righteousness, and judgment: concerning sin because they do not believe in Me, concerning righteousness because I will be with the Father, not here with you, and judgment because the ruler of this world has been judged. I have many other things to say to you but you can't understand them now. But when He, the Spirit of Truth comes, He will guide you into all truth. He won't speak on His own initiative, but whatever He hears, He will speak. He will also show you what is to come. He will be with all who are mine. Soon I am going away and you won't see Me; then in a little while you will see Me again."

His disciples didn't understand where He was going or how long He'd be gone. Jesus knew they had questions and said, "I know you are confused about where I'm going and how long we will be separated. You will weep and lament. The world will rejoice while you are sad, but your sadness will be turned to joy. It will be like a woman's labor; the turmoil and pain are turned to joy when a new life is begun. After your sorrow, you will see Me again, and no one will be able to take your joy away. You won't be asking Me any questions then. You'll ask the Father for anything, and He will give it to you in My name. I won't be making the request for you. You will ask the Father directly. He loves you because you have loved Me. In that day I won't be speaking figuratively like I've had to here. In that day you will ask anything of the Father in My name, and it will be done for you. I came forth from the Father and am now returning to Him."

The disciples replied, "Now You are speaking clearly, not using figurative speech." Jesus said, "Do you believe now? An hour is coming, in fact it's already here when you will all be scattered, each returning to his own home, leaving Me alone. But I will not be alone, because the Father is with Me. I have told you these things so you can have peace. In the world you will have tribulation, but have courage; I have overcome the world."

Mark 14:22 - 25 *The Sacrament*

While they were eating, Jesus took bread, broke it and said, "This bread is My body, take it and eat it in remembrance of Me." Then He took His cup and passed it around saying, "This is My blood which is poured out for many. Drink it because this is the new agreement between God and man. I won't drink any more wine until I drink it with you in the Kingdom of God."

John 17:1 - 26 *Final prayer*

Then Jesus lifted His eyes towards heaven and prayed, "Father, the time has come to glorify the Son, so the Son may bring glory to You. You have given Me the authority to impart eternal life to those You have given to Me. Eternal life is knowing You, and Jesus Christ whom You have sent. I glorify You here on earth, having accomplished the work You have given Me to do. Now glorify Me together with You, with the glory I had with You before the world existed. I have manifested Your name to the men You gave Me from out of the world. They now understand that I came from You, and they believe that You sent Me. I am leaving the world and they are staying. I pray You would keep them united like You and I are united. The world hates them because they are not of the world. I don't ask that they be taken out of the world but that they be protected from the evil one."

"Keep them in Your word, which is truth. As You have sent Me into the world, so I send them. I do not ask for these alone but also for those who believe through their word. I pray that they be united even as You and I are, so the world will know that You sent Me. I want them to be with Me and see the glory You gave Me before the creation of the world. The world has not known You, but I have, and these men believe You sent Me. I have made You known to them. May the same love that You have for Me be in them and may I be in them.

Matthew 26:31 - 35 *Jesus knows they will all desert Him*

Jesus said, "The scriptures say, "I will strike the shepherd and the sheep will be scattered. You all will desert Me but I will rise and meet you in Galilee. Peter, Satan has demanded permission to sift you like wheat, but I have prayed for you, that your faith would not fail. When you have finished your testing, strengthen your brothers. Peter said, "The rest of these fellows may fall away, but I'll stick by you." Jesus answered, "Peter, before the rooster crows tomorrow you will have denied me three times." Peter insisted that even if he was to be killed, he would not leave his side." All the disciples were saying the same thing.

Luke 22:35 - 38 *Two swords*
Jesus said, "Formally I sent you out without money, just a bag and sandals. Did you lack for anything?" They answered, "No, nothing." Jesus continued, "Well the game is changing, now I say take money along, buy a sword. It is written, 'He will be numbered with the transgressors.' This is about to be fulfilled in Me." The disciples said, "Here, we have two swords." Jesus answered, "That is enough."

Mark 14:32 - 42 *In the garden*
They arrived at the Garden of Gethesemane, and Jesus took Peter and the two Zebedee brothers further into the garden and said, "Wait here while I go pray." He went to a different area in the garden and began to pray. He prayed that if possible His death might be avoided: "Dad, I know all things are possible for You, Isn't there some way we could avoid this? Still I am here to do Your will, not mine." When He returned to His disciples they were asleep. Jesus said, "Simon, you're sleeping. You couldn't stay up with Me for one hour? Keep praying; you're entering a tough period. I know the spirit is willing but the flesh is weak." Then Jesus went to pray again on the same matter as before. An angel appeared to Him and strengthened Him. He was in such distress that He was sweating blood. When He returned they were asleep again. They didn't know what to say to Jesus. Jesus went to pray a third time, and they were snoring away when He returned. Jesus said, "Get up. The time has come. I am now being betrayed into the hands of sinners."

John 18:1 - 9 *Kiss of Judas*
Judas was approaching with a large band of armed men. He met Jesus with a kiss saying, "Teacher." This was a signal to his mob indicating who to arrest. Jesus said, "Whom do you seek?" The leaders of the mob said, "Jesus the Nazarene." Jesus answered, "I am He." At this the mob fell backward on the ground. When they got back up Jesus said, "I am the one you seek, let these others go." So none of the disciples were arrested, just as Jesus had said.

Mark 14:47 - 52 *Jesus arrested*
Peter pulled a sword and cut the ear off a slave of the high priest named Malchus. Jesus stepped in and said, "Enough of this! If I wanted, I could call a legion of angels to our assistance." He touched Malchus's ear and healed it. Then Jesus said, "Why are you here with clubs and swords? I was in the temple teaching every day. This is all just as the scriptures said it would be." All His disciples fled from the scene. One young man was there wearing only a linen sheet. They grabbed him by the sheet, but he escaped running away naked.

The Story Bible for Adults

John 18:12 - 24 *Jesus before Annas*

Jesus was taken to Annas first. Annas was Caiaphas's father-in-law. It was Caiaphas who said it was better for one man to die than for the whole nation to perish. Peter followed at a distance. Annas questioned Jesus about His teachings and His disciples. Jesus said, "I've been teaching publicly, why are you asking Me like I have spoken in secret?" One of the officers struck Jesus saying, "It is not appropriate for You to address the high priest this way." Jesus said, "Why strike Me when I am telling the truth?" Jesus was taken to the temple where the temple guards mocked and beat Him. Jesus was blindfolded and beaten. The guards said, "Prophesy, who is the one that hit You?"

Matthew 26:57 - 68 *Jesus before the Council*

Before the Council, false witnesses were brought in against Jesus. The testimony centered on the statement Jesus made about rebuilding the temple in three days after its destruction. None of the testimony was consistent. Jesus was saying nothing. Finally the high priest said, "Why do You make no comment? Don't You hear what's being said about You?" Still Jesus kept silent. Then the high priest asked, "Are You the Christ, the Son of the Blessed One?" Jesus answered, "I am, and you will see the Son of Man sitting at the right hand of Power, coming with the clouds of heaven." With this comment the high priest tore his
clothes and said, "What more evidence do we need, He is guilty of blasphemy and deserving of death." Jesus was led away. Some spit at Him, others beat Him and slapped Him. They were all mocking Him.

Mark 14:66 - 72 *Peter's denials*

Peter was down in the courtyard when a little girl came by and said, "Didn't I see you with Jesus." Peter denied it saying, "I don't know Him or what you're talking about." He went out to the porch area and another person said, "There is one of them." Peter again denied it. Then more said, "You must certainly be with Him; you're a Galilean too." At this Peter began to curse and swear, "I don't know what you're talking about!" Jesus was being led through at that moment, and He looked at Peter. Then the rooster crowed. Peter remembered what Jesus had said and began to weep bitterly.

Matthew 27:3 - 10 *Judas's remorse*

Meanwhile, Judas returned to the elders and said, "I have betrayed an innocent man." The elders responded, "That's your problem, not ours." Judas threw the silver he had received into the sanctuary. He went away and hanged himself. With the money, the elders bought a field to bury strangers, just as Jeremiah prophesied.

Luke 23:1 - 5 *Pilot defers to Herod*
Jesus was taken to Pilate, the Roman governor of Judea. The Jews did not enter Pilate's court, the Praetorium, because the Sabbath was approaching and they didn't want to defile themselves, so Pilate came out to them. They made numerous accusations against Jesus saying He stirred up the people and referred to Himself as a king. When they mentioned that Jesus had started His ministry in Galilee, Pilate said, "Herod, the Galilean governor, is in town take the Galilean to him.

Luke 23:6 - 12 *Herod's interview*
Herod was very pleased to have an opportunity to interview Jesus. But Jesus provided no entertainment. He didn't answer any of Herod's inquiries. The priests who had accompanied Jesus to the interview were vehemently accusing Him. Herod and his soldiers treated Jesus with contempt. They put a fancy purple robe on Him and sent Him back to Pilate. Herod and Pilate, who had always had an adversarial relationship, became good friends from that day forward.

Luke 23, John 18 and 19, Mark15 *Jesus before Pilot*
Jesus was returned to Pilate. Pilate asked the Jews, "What accusation do you bring against this Man?" The Jewish leaders answered, "We would not have delivered Him to you if He were not an evil doer." Pilate answered, "Deal with Him yourselves, I find no fault in Him." They answered, "We are not permitted to put anyone to death."

Pilate then went back into the Praetorium were Jesus was held and asked Jesus, "Are you the King of the Jews?" Jesus answered, "Are you saying this on your own or did others tell you that about Me?" Pilate replied, "I'm not a Jew, am I? Leaders of Your nation have delivered You to me. What have You done?" Jesus answered, "My kingdom is not of this world. If it were My servants would be fighting to protect Me from this, but My kingdom is not of this realm." Pilate asked, "So You are a king?" Jesus answered, "That is correct, I am a king. For this I was born and came into the world, to bear witness of the truth. Everyone who is of the truth hears My voice." Pilate said to Him, "What is truth?" Then he went back out to the Jews and said, "I find no guilt in Him." Pilate was in a quandary. He perceived Jesus was being delivered because the Jewish leaders were envious of His popularity with the people. Also, his wife had warned him saying, "Have nothing to do with that righteous man because I suffered greatly in a dream because of Him."

It was a custom, that during the feast, Rome would release one prisoner. Pilate suggested Jesus, knowing the priest had delivered Him because of envy for His popularity with the people. But the priests stirred up the crowd to ask for Barabbas instead. Pilate asked, "What am I to do with the one you call: "King of the Jews?" They yelled back, "Crucify him!" Pilate answered back, "I find no fault in Him." But they yelled all the more loudly, crucify Him, crucify Him!" Because the crowd was about to riot, Pilate sent Him away to be whipped.

Jesus received the Roman whipping, called a scourge. Then the Roman soldiers decided to have some sport with Him. They dressed Him in purple and forced a crown of thorns over His head. They beat Him and mockingly bowed before Him, saying, "Hail, King of the Jews." They beat Him on the head with a reed rod and hit Him in the face. Then Pilate came out again and said, "I am bringing Him out to you, so that you know I find no fault in Him." Jesus came out wearing the purple robe and the thorny crown. Pilate said, "Behold the Man!" When the chief priests and officers saw Him they yelled, "Crucify Him, Crucify Him!" Pilate answered, "Crucify Him yourselves, I find no fault in Him." They said, "According to our law He must die, because He said He is the Son of God."

This caused even more concern for Pilate. He went back to Jesus and said, "Where are You from?" Jesus gave no answer. Pilate said, "Don't You understand I have the authority to release You or have You crucified? I would start answering questions if I were You." Jesus answered, "You have no authority over Me that wasn't given to you from above. For this reason, those who delivered Me to you have the greater sin.

Pilate continued his efforts to have Jesus released but was rebuffed at every turn by the Jews who said, "If you release this Man, you are no friend of Caesar. Anyone who makes himself out to be a king is an enemy of Caesar." Finally Jesus was brought out again and Pilate said, "Behold your king!" The Jews yelled back, "We have no king but Caesar. Crucify Him!"

Pilate sat in his judgment seat and washed his hands. Jesus was sent away to be crucified. Jesus carried His own cross part of the way to the place of the crucifixion, then a man who just happened to be passing by was forced to carry the cross. His name was Simon of Cyrene, (He was the father of Alexander and Rufus). There was a multitude following Jesus. The women following along were weeping and lamenting Him. Jesus turned to them and said, "Don't weep for Me, weep for yourselves and your children. The time is coming when barren women will seem lucky. If the world does this while the tree is green, imagine what they will do when it's dry."

Matthew 27:33 - 37 *Jesus nailed to the cross*

They arrived at the crucifixion area, a hill known as the skull. They nailed Jesus on the cross. Two thieves where crucified on either side of Jesus. Jesus was saying, "Father, forgive them. They don't know what they are doing." They offered Him some pain reliever mixed with wine, but Jesus refused it. A sign written in three languages was put on the cross that read: JESUS THE NAZARENE, THE KING OF THE JEWS. Some of the chief priests complained to Pilate saying, "The sign should read: 'He said, I am the King of the Jews.'" Pilate answered, "What I have written stays."

Matthew 27:39 - 43 Jesus *mocked by the crowd*

The crowd mocked Jesus saying, "You, who were going to tear down the temple and rebuild it in three days, save Yourself! If You are the Son of God, come down from the cross." The soldiers who had crucified Him said, "Really, if You are the King of the Jews You should come down from there!" The chief priest said, "He is not the King of the Jews. If He were, He would be coming down. He helped others but He can't even help Himself. If He would come down from the cross, then we would believe in Him."

John 19:23 - 26 *Mary and John at the cross*

Around noon the sky became darkened. It remained dark for about three hours. The soldiers gambled for Jesus' clothes. (His outer tunic was seamless, woven in one piece. They didn't want to rip it up.) This fulfilled prophecy written by David. Jesus' mother, Mary, was standing nearby with her sister and Mary Magdalene. A disciple Jesus loved was also standing there. Jesus said to His mother, "Woman, this is your son." And to the disciple, "This is your mother." Mary lived with that disciple and became a member of his household.

Luke 23:39 - 43 *Thieves hanging with Him*

One of the thieves hanging there with Him said mockingly, "If You are who You claim, save Yourself and us!" The other thief replied, "Don't you fear God? We are receiving a just sentence, this man has done nothing wrong." To Jesus he said, "Jesus, remember me when You come into Your kingdom." Jesus answered, "Today you will be with Me in Paradise.

John 19:28 - 29 *Thirsty*

Jesus said, "I am thirsty." He was offered some sour wine on a sponge.

The Story Bible for Adults

Mark 15:33 - 35 *Forsaken*
As His time on the cross was near an end, He cried out, "My God, My God, Why have You forsaken Me?" At this point some in the crowd thought He was crying out for Elijah.

John 19:30 *Finished*
Jesus said, "Father, into Your hands I commit My spirit." And finally He said, "It is finished." Having said this, He breathed His last.

Matthew 27:51 - 54 *Temple veil ripped*
At that moment, the veil in the temple ripped from the top to the bottom. The earth trembled and the tombs were opened and many dead saints were raised. After Jesus had been raised from the dead, many folks in Jerusalem saw these dead saints. The military officer in charge who saw Jesus die said, "Surely this was the Son of God."

John 19:31 - 37 *Religious leaders worried about the Passover Sabbath*
The Jews were concerned. The next day was the Sabbath and they didn't want dead bodies still hanging on the crosses on that high day. So they requested that the legs be broken to bring death more quickly. The two criminals' legs were broken. When they came to Jesus, they saw He was already dead. One of the soldiers pierced His side with a spear. When he removed the spear, blood and water poured out of the wound. So the scripture was fulfilled: "Not one of His bones was broken," and "They looked on Him that they had pierced."

Luke 23:50 -56 *Burial*
A man named Joseph of Arimathea, a member of the Council who did not approve of what was done to Jesus, gathered his
courage and approached Pilate to request the body of Jesus. After Pilate confirmed through the military officer handling the crucifixion that Jesus was indeed dead, he released the body to Joseph. Mary Magdalene, Mary the mother of James, Joses and Salome assisted in preparing the body as best they could for a quick burial before the Sabbath. Jesus was laid in an un-used tomb that Joseph owned.

Matthew 27:62 - 66 *Guards at the tomb*
The Jews approached Pilate saying, "When that deceiver was still alive, He said, 'After three days I will rise again.' So give orders that the grave should be secured and guarded so His disciples won't be able to steal Him to continue the deception by saying He has risen from the dead." Pilate answered, "Take your own Temple Guard and

make the grave site as secure as you know how to." So the guard was placed. A huge stone was rolled in place to close the tomb, and a seal was set on the stone. Jerusalem was quiet as the Sabbath was observed.

Mark 16:1 - 8 *The women see an angel at the tomb*
Early in the morning, on the first day of the week, Mary, Salome, and Mary went to the grave to complete the burial. On the way, they were concerned as to how the stone could be moved. When they arrived, they found the stone already moved away and they saw an angel who said. "Don't be afraid. I know who you're looking for, but why should you look for the living in a place for the dead? Jesus has risen, just as He said He would. Look inside you will see where He had been laid. Go tell His disciples to go to Galilee as He had instructed them and He will meet them there." The ladies ran from there to tell the disciples.

Mark 16:9 - 11 *Disciples get the news*
The disciples were all hiding behind closed doors. When they got the news from the women, the general consensus was unbelief. Peter and John ran to the tomb. John arrived first and Peter pushed in behind. They found Jesus' burial clothes lying there with the face cloth rolled up by itself. They still did not understand the scriptures about how He must rise again from the dead.

John 20:11 - 18 *Mary sees Jesus*
Later Mary peaked again into the tomb. She saw two angels sitting where His head and feet had been. They asked, "Why are you weeping?" She answered, "Because they have taken away my Lord and I don't know where they have laid Him." When she turned around, Jesus was standing there, but she thought He was the gardener. Jesus said, "Woman, why are you crying? Who are you looking for?" She said, "Sir, if You have moved Him, just tell me where you've put Him and I'll make sure He is taken away." Jesus said, "Mary!" At this she said, "Teacher!" and fell at His feet. Jesus said, "Stop clinging to Me Mary, I have not yet ascended to My Father. Go tell your brothers that you have seen Me and that I have ascended to My Father and theirs." Mary returned to their hiding place to tell the disciples.

Matthew 28:11 - 15 *The payoff*
When the soldiers guarding the grave reported to the elders about the previous evening's events, they received assurances they would not be punished and were paid a large sum of money to say Jesus' disciples stole the body while they slept. This false report is still circulated among the Jews to this day.

Luke 24:13 - 33 *Jesus appears to men on the road*

Later that day, two men who had been following Jesus were walking on a road towards a village called Emmaus, about seven miles from Jerusalem. They were talking about all that had taken place. Jesus, Himself, joined them and asked, "What are you discussing so urgently as you walk along? They didn't recognize Him. One of the men, named Cleopus, answered, "You've got to be the only person visiting Jerusalem who has not heard of the things that have happened!" "What things?" Jesus asked again. "The things about Jesus of Nazareth, a mighty prophet in words and deeds who was delivered to the Romans by our chief priest and crucified. We were hoping He was going to be the deliverer of Israel. It's been three days since these things occurred. Some of our women have been to the tomb. His body was missing and they claim to have seen angels. Some of the men have followed up; Jesus' body was gone, but they didn't see Jesus alive either."

Jesus answered, "You two are surprisingly dim to not understand what the prophets have spoken! Wasn't it necessary for the Christ to suffer these things and to enter His glory?" Then Jesus explained the scriptures about Himself, starting with Moses and moving forward through all the prophets. The men convinced Jesus to stay with them and eat. After they had sat down, as He broke the bread to give them, their eyes were opened. They realized who He was, and He disappeared from their sight. They realized then how their hearts had burned from the moment He began speaking with them. They returned immediately to Jerusalem, to where the disciples were holed up.

Luke 24:34 - 43 *Jesus appears to the disciples*

They found out Peter had seen the Lord, Mary had given her report, and they gave their news. As they were all wondering about it, Jesus Himself appeared to them. He said, "Peace be with you. Why are you troubled and why are doubts entering your hearts. Look at Me, touch Me, I am not a ghost to be afraid of. A ghost would not have flesh and blood that you can touch. As joyful as they were, they were still doubtful, so He asked for some fish to eat, He ate it before them.

John 20:24 – 29 Thomas doubts

Thomas, one of the twelve, had not been present at any time the Lord had appeared. He said, "Until I have seen the scars on His hands and put my hand into his side, I will not believe. Eight days after he said this Jesus appeared to them again. Jesus offered Thomas an opportunity to touch his scars. Thomas said, "My Lord and my God." Jesus said, "You believe because you've seen Me. The ones that believe with out actually seeing are blessed!"

Matthew 28:16 - 20 Mark 16:14 - 19 *The Great Commission*
Jesus said, "All authority has been given to Me on earth and in heaven. As My Father sent Me, now I am sending you. Go to the whole world and make disciples from every nation. Baptize them in the name of the Father, the Son, and the Holy Spirit. He who believes and is baptized will be saved. He who does not believe will be condemned. If you forgive the sins of any, they will be forgiven, if you retain the sins of any, they will be retained. Signs will follow you: demons will be cast out, healings will be accomplished, new tongues will be spoken, and you will be protected from poison and snakes. Teach the new believers to observe

all that I commanded you. I am sending the promise from My Father upon you. Stay in town until you have received power from heaven. I will be with you until the end of the age."

John 20:1 - 25 *Jesus appear to the disciples on a fishing trip*
For the most part, the disciples remained in Jerusalem praising God in the temple. Jesus did appear again at the Sea of Tiberias. In the dark of morning a group of disciples, including Peter, John, James, Thomas, Nathanael and two others were finishing up a rather unproductive night of fishing. The boat was no more than 100 yards from shore. Jesus, whom they did not recognize, stood at the shore and called out, "Boys, no fish yet?" They answered, "No fish." Jesus instructed, "Throw the net to the right side of the boat and you will find a catch." Soon the net was so full they were having trouble handling all the fish. John Zebedee looked up and said to Peter, "It is the Lord!" Peter, who had been stripped for work, threw on his outer clothing and jumped into the sea. The others continued to bring the boat in. They had 153 fish and not a tear in the net!

When they got to shore they found a fire crackling, with fish and bread already cooking. Jesus said, "Bring some of the fish you've caught." No one was questioning who this stranger was now. They all knew it was Jesus. After breakfast Jesus said to Simon Peter, "Simon, do you love Me more than these?" Peter answered, "Lord, you know I love you!" Jesus said, "Tend My lambs." Jesus asked him again, "Simon do you love Me?" Peter answered as before. Jesus said, "Shepherd My sheep. After a third exchange Jesus said, "Tend My sheep." Then Jesus said to Peter, "When you were young you were free to go where you pleased. When you are old, you will not be free, and you will be forced to go where you do not want. Always follow Me." Jesus said this to prepare Peter for how he would die. Peter saw John following and asked, "What about him?" Jesus answered, "If I want him to remain until I come, what is that to you? You follow Me." Now this has caused a saying that John would remain until the

Lord's return. Jesus never said that. He told Peter, "If I want him to remain until I come, what is that to you?"

So these are some of the things that Jesus did. There were many other things, but if they were all written down, I suppose the world could not contain the books.

The Acts of the Apostles

Acts 1:1-11 *Jesus' final instructions and departure*

For 40 days after His resurrection, Jesus presented Himself on many occasions. He provided many convincing proofs and spoke to His disciples concerning the kingdom of God. Finally, He gathered them together on the Mount of Olives and commanded them to wait in Jerusalem until the promise of the Holy Spirit was delivered to them. He reminded them, "John baptized with water, but soon you will be baptized with the Holy Spirit."

The disciples asked, "Will You now restore the kingdom to Israel?" Jesus answered, "It is not for you to know the times or epochs which the Father has established by His own authority. But you shall receive power, when the Holy Spirit has come upon you. You will be My witnesses in Jerusalem, in all of Israel, and even to the remotest parts of the world."

After He said this, Jesus was lifted up into the clouds out of their sight. As they were gazing intently into the sky, two men in white clothes stood beside them. They said, "Why are you Galileans looking into the sky? Jesus, who has been taken up into heaven, will return in the same way you've watched Him go."

Acts 1:12-26 *Judas replaced*

The disciples: Peter, John, James, Andrew, Philip, Thomas, Bartholomew, Matthew, Simon the Zealot, the other James, and Judas (not the betrayer), returned to the upstairs room they were sharing in Jerusalem. They were united in one mind and prayed continually with the women, Mary, Jesus' mother, and His brothers.

At a gathering of one hundred twenty believers, Peter stood and addressed the group. "The prophecies said one who was among us would betray the Lord. He's ended up dead and a burial field has been bought with the price he received for his betrayal. It says in the Psalms that we should find another to take his place. Now this replacement should be one who has been with us from the beginning, and he will be a witness with us of the Lord's resurrection." Two men were put forward for the position, Joseph and Matthias. They prayed, "Lord, You know which of these You want." Then they drew lots and the choice fell on Mathias, so he was numbered with the eleven apostles.

Acts 2:1-47 *Holy Spirit arrives, fellowship grows*

On the Day of Pentecost, the believers were all together. Suddenly a noise came from heaven like a violent rushing wind, and it filled the whole house where they were gathered. It looked as if tongues of fire came to rest on each of them. They became filled with the Holy Spirit, and they began to speak in different languages. Many Jews were in Jerusalem for the feast of Pentecost, along with many proselytes from all over the world: Parthians, Medes, Elamites, Mesopotamians, and many other places. When the visitors heard the sound they came to check it out and were amazed that this group of Galileans were all praising God in the native languages of all the folks visiting for the holiday. It created quite a stir. Some thought the Galileans were drunk because of the way they were carrying on. The visitors and local Jews were all wondering what kind of event they were witnessing.

Peter stood up with the eleven and addressed the crowd. "Listen to my words. These men are not drunk as you suppose, it's just nine o'clock in the morning! This is happening in fulfillment of a prophecy spoken by Joel, 'In the last days I will pour out My Spirit on mankind. There will be dreams and visions, your sons and daughters will prophesy, before the great and glorious day of the Lord comes.'"

"Men of Israel, Jesus the Nazarene, who was here in Jerusalem working miracles and wonders, that you saw yourselves, was delivered up to the Romans according to a pre-ordained plan of God. Godless men killed him, but God raised Him up again, putting an end to the agony of death, because it was impossible for death to hold Him. David spoke in the Psalms saying that death wouldn't be able to hold Him, that He would not see decay. But David died, we know where his tomb is. However, God promised him that one of his descendants would sit on an eternal throne. We're here to tell you that Jesus, whom you crucified, is that promised Lord and Savior."

When those listening heard these words, they were pierced to the heart and asked what they must do. Peter replied, "Turn from your sins and be baptized in the name of Jesus Christ. Your sins will be forgiven, and you will receive the Holy Spirit!" About three thousand new believers were added to the fellowship that day. Everyone devoted themselves to the teaching of the apostles, and they ate and prayed together.

There was a sense of awe among the new believers. Many signs and wonders were taking place through the apostles. Property was held in common. Many were selling all they had and sharing the proceeds with anyone who had need. They all went from house to house, taking meals together and being joyful and glad. They were constantly praising God and gained favor with the people. Their number was growing each day.

Acts 3 *Lame beggar healed, Peter finds a Preacher's grove*
One afternoon Peter and John went to the temple at the normal prayer hour. A man sat begging at the gate called Beautiful, as he did every day. He had been crippled from his mother's womb. He asked Peter and John for spare coins as they went by. Peter said, "Look at us." The crippled man looked up expecting to receive a contribution and Peter said, "I don't have any money, but what I do have, I give to you: In the name of Jesus Christ of Nazareth...walk!" Peter took the lame man's right hand and pulled him up. His feet and ankles were immediately strengthened, and he stood up with a leap! He stood there correctly and began to walk and leap with them into the temple.

Everyone in the temple was drawn to the commotion caused by the leaping, praising, and healed beggar. They recognized the man as the crippled beggar who sat each day at "Beautiful" gate. A sense of amazement permeated the crowd. Peter, seizing the opportunity, spoke: "Why do you look at us with such amazement as if we had healed this man through our own power or piety? The God of our fathers: Abraham, Isaac and Jacob, has glorified His servant, Jesus, the one whom you delivered to the Romans and disowned when Pilate tried to have Him released. You asked for a murderer instead of the Holy One of God. But God has raised the Prince of Life. We are witnesses to the fact. It is on the basis of faith in His name that this man has been given perfect health as you can all plainly see."

"Now brothers, we know you and your leaders acted in ignorance in regard to Jesus, but all this was announced long ago by the prophets. So repent and return, your sins will be wiped away, and you will gain refreshment in the presence of the Lord! Jesus has been sent for you. Remember what Moses said, "God will raise up a prophet like me, and you will give heed to Him. To ignore Him would certainly bring condemnation! Even God's promise to Abraham clearly states that 'All the earth will be blessed by Abraham's seed.' God has raised Him up to turn you from your wicked ways!"

Acts 4 *Peter and John arrested*

When the priests, temple guards, and other Jewish leaders came and heard them talking about Jesus and His resurrection, they were not pleased. They put Peter and John in jail. Many who had already heard Peter's words were converted. The new believers that day pushed the number of men in their fellowship above five thousand.

The next day Peter and John were brought before the elders. Annas, Caiaphas, John and Alexander, all of high priestly descent, were in attendance. They asked, "By what power or by what name have you done this?" Peter, filled with the Holy Spirit, stood up and said, "Gentlemen, if we are on trial for healing this man, let it be known to you and all Israel that it was accomplished in the name of Jesus Christ the Nazarene, whom you had crucified and whom God raised from the dead. It is by His name that this man stands before you in good health. Jesus is the One spoken of in the prophets, 'The stone rejected by the builders has become
the chief cornerstone.' There is salvation by no other means under heaven."

Peter and John's confidence was clearly apparent to the council. They remembered seeing them constantly with Jesus. The high priests made no answer but went out of the meeting area to talk the situation over. "We can't hide the fact that a noteworthy miracle has been accomplished through these un-educated fellows, that lame man is walking for everyone to see. But we must warn them not to speak in this name any longer."

So they went back in, gave Peter and John stern warnings and sent them home. Peter offered no guarantees that they would stop sharing what they had seen themselves, but they were released that morning. They went home and told the believers everything that happened. They remembered a Psalm that predicted that the leaders of the earth would stand against the Lord's Anointed One, so the opposition did not surprise them. They realized more clearly how Jesus had given Himself up according to God's plan. They prayed for strength and courage to share the good news about Jesus. They all became filled again with the Holy Spirit and spoke openly about the good news with boldness.

There was an abundant grace upon the new church. There were no needy people among them, because those who had property were selling it and sharing the proceeds with whoever needed it. Sometimes those who sold their property would give the Apostles the proceeds so they could oversee the distribution. A fellow the apostles called Barnabus (son of encouragement) owned a tract of land. When he sold it he gave the proceeds to the apostles.

Acts 5:1-12 *Ananias and Sapphira*
A married couple, named Ananias and Sapphira, sold a piece of property. But they held some of the money back for themselves and presented the rest to the apostles as if it were the total amount of the sale. When Ananias made the presentation, Peter said, "Ananias this was your land to do with what you wanted and the money you received was also all yours. Why have you chosen to lie to the Holy Spirit this way? You haven't lied to men but to God!" When Ananias heard these words, he died right on the spot. He was taken out and buried. Later his wife Sapphira came in. Peter asked, "Is it true Sapphira, that you sold this property for such and such a price?" She answered, "Yes, that was the amount we received." Peter said, "Why is it that you and your husband have agreed to put the Holy Spirit to the test? Behold those who buried your husband are now at the door for you." She died immediately and was buried with her husband. A great fear swept the church when these things were reported.

Acts 5:13-42 *Multiple arrests*
The fellowship continued to grow even though many were afraid to be associated with them for fear of the Jews. The apostles performed many miracles that couldn't be denied. Many sick people would line up in Peter's path, hoping to be healed by his shadow passing over them.

The high priests and religious leaders rose up in jealousy and placed the apostles in jail. An angel appeared at the jail that evening. He opened the doors and instructed the apostles to go to the temple and preach the whole message of this Life. They got to the temple at daybreak and started teaching. That same morning, the high priests called a meeting of the entire Council and the Senate of the sons of Israel. A captain and his men were sent to the jail to bring the prisoners before the Council. They returned reporting that the locks and guards were in place, but when the prison was opened, there were no apostles inside.

As the Council and the captain were wondering what would come of this situation, a messenger informed them that the apostles, who had been in prison, were now in the temple teaching the people. The captain and his men were sent to retrieve the apostles from the temple. They were able to bring them in without trouble. They had been afraid the people might stone them.

Back before the Council, the apostles were rebuked. "We gave you strict orders not to teach in this name, yet you've filled the city with the teaching and intend to bring the man's blood on us!" Peter and the apostles answered, "We follow God's orders, not man's. God has raised Jesus up and it was you who sent him to the cross. Jesus has been raised to the right hand of God Himself and is the Savior to grant Israel repentance and forgiveness of sins. We are witnesses to this along with the Holy Spirit, whom God gives to those who believe."

The Council was cut to the quick. They fully intended to have them slain, but Gamaliel, a respected teacher of the Law, ordered the apostles out of the room and gave this address to the Council. "Gentlemen, be careful what you do to these men. A few years ago a fellow named Theudas came along claiming to be somebody and hundreds followed him, but when he was slain, his followers dispersed and nothing came of all his talk. Then Judas of Galilee rose up around the time of the last census, when he perished all his people split up. I advise you to leave this group alone. If they are following a plan devised by men it will soon pass as these others did. If their actions are from God, there's nothing you can do to stop it and you will find yourselves fighting against God."

The Council took his advice. They had the apostles flogged, they warned them to discontinue teaching in the name of Jesus and released them. The apostles went away feeling greatly privileged to be able to suffer shame for Jesus' name. Everyday they continued preaching about Jesus in the temple and from house to house.

Acts 6 and 7 *Stephen martyred*
As the numbers of believers in the fellowship increased, an argument arose between Jewish believers from out of the area and local Jewish believers. The out-of-towners felt their widows were being overlooked in the daily serving of food. The apostles summoned the congregation and said, "This shouldn't be our problem, and we should be concentrating on the teaching of the word, not serving tables. Select seven good men who are filled with the Spirit and put them in charge of food distribution. Everyone agreed. They selected Stephen, a man full of faith and the Holy Spirit, Philip, Prochorus, Nicanor, Timon, Parmenas, and Niolas, who was from Antioch. The apostles laid their hands on these men, and they took over the food service end of the ministry.

The fellowship continued to grow in Jerusalem. Many Jewish priests were becoming believers. Stephen, full of grace and power, was performing great wonders and signs in public. An influential synagogue sent representatives to argue with Stephen, but they weren't able to cope with the Spirit and wisdom he showed. They retained false witnesses, stirred up a mob and hauled Stephen before the Council. They accused him of incessantly speaking against the temple and the law, and claiming Jesus would return to destroy Jerusalem and change the customs handed down by Moses. When his accusers looked at Stephen, his face appeared to them like an angel's. The high priest said, "Are these accusations true?"

Stephen answered, "Our father Abraham was instructed by God to leave the land he was living in and go to a new place. He ended up right here in Israel. Abraham received great promises about blessings on and through his offspring. But he was warned they would be aliens in a foreign land for four hundred years. Abraham also received the seal of his contract with God, which is called circumcision. Abraham's son was Isaac; Isaac's son was Jacob and Jacob's sons were the twelve patriarchs. The patriarchs became jealous of Joseph and sold him to Egypt. But God was with Joseph, and he rose to the position of Governor of Egypt. A famine came upon the whole world. Our fathers learned the only bread was in Egypt and on their second visit to Egypt to buy bread; Joseph made himself known to them. The entire clan of 75 people moved to Egypt and multiplied into a nation."

"Moses was born at a time when the Pharaohs had long forgotten Joseph. Our fathers were slaves and Hebrew males were being killed at birth. Moses was miraculously taken in by Pharaoh's daughter who raised him as a son with all the knowledge of Egypt. When he reached age 40 he visited his Hebrew brothers and killed an Egyptian who was mistreating one of them. Instead of viewing Moses as a potential deliverer, the Hebrews made Pharaoh aware of Moses's deed against the Egyptian. Moses was forced to flee far away to Midian. Forty more years passed and Moses had two sons. An angel of the Lord appeared to him in a burning thorn bush. God spoke to Moses and informed him that Israel would be delivered from Egyptian slavery. Which Moses did by performing many wonders and signs. Moses told the people, 'God will raise up another prophet like me.' Israel rejected Moses. They asked Aaron to make them gods to follow because Moses had been up on the mountain a few weeks and no one knew if he was ever coming back. God turned away from the Israelites and they served the hosts of heaven. For 40 years in the wilderness, our fathers were mostly disobedient."

"God provided a design for the tabernacle in the wilderness and Joshua brought it with him as he drove out the inhabitants of the land promised to our fathers. Then David came and found favor in God's sight. David's son, Solomon, built God a house, but we all know God doesn't dwell in houses. The heavens themselves are His throne; He has made all things."

"You people are a stiff-necked people. Which one of the prophets did you not persecute and kill? They all announced the coming of the Righteous One, and you have rejected Him as well. You receive the law as ordained by angels, yet you do not keep it."

These words of Stephen cut them to the quick and they gnashed their teeth at him. Stephen, full of the Holy Spirit, looked up to heaven and said, "Behold I see heaven opened and Jesus standing at the right hand of God!" The crowd covered their ears and fell upon Stephen with one impulse. They drove him out of the city and began stoning him. A young man named Saul watched
the coats of the mob that was stoning Stephen. As Stephen fell to his knees, he cried out, "Lord, don't count this sin against them!" Having said this, he died.

Acts 8 *Phillip spreads the Word*
Saul was in full agreement with this act.

Stephen's martyrdom was followed by a full-scale persecution of the church in Jerusalem, and the believers were all scattered, except for the apostles. Saul led the purge against the church, going house to house, hauling as many believers as he could into jail. Those who were scattered preached the good news wherever they went. Philip went to a city in Samaria and proclaimed Christ. Everybody was listening because of the signs he was performing; paralyzed and lame were healed, unclean spirits were cast out and the whole city was rejoicing.

There was a man from the city named Simon. He was a very successful magician and made great claims about himself. He was said to have "The Great Power of God." All the people believed the message of Philip and were being baptized. Simon himself believed. After he was baptized, he continued with Philip and was continually amazed at the miracles that were taking place.

When the apostles in Jerusalem heard that converts were being won in Samaria, they sent Peter and John to pray for them so they might receive the Holy Spirit. When Simon saw them doing this, he offered them money saying, "Give me this authority too, so when I lay my hands on people they will receive the Holy Spirit." Peter replied, "Your heart and thoughts are darkness, thinking you could buy this gift with money. You'll have no portion of this. You need to pray that your evil will be forgiven you! I see you are in the bondage of iniquity." Simon replied, "Please pray for me yourselves, that nothing you've said will fall on me!" When Peter and John had finished solemnly testifying, they started back to Jerusalem and taught in some of the cities along the way.

An angel of the Lord appeared to Philip and said, "Go follow the old desert road out of Jerusalem that heads towards Gaza." On the road he met an Ethiopian who was in charge of all the treasure of Candace, the queen of Ethiopia. He had come up to Jerusalem to worship. As he was returning home on the old road, he was reading from the prophet Isaiah. The Spirit prompted Philip to catch up with the chariot. He heard the Ethiopian reading these words from Isaiah: "He was led as a sheep to the slaughter. As a lamb is silent before its shearers, so he did not open his mouth." Philip asked if the Ethiopian understood what he was reading. The man replied, "I don't know if the prophet is speaking of himself or someone else. How can I understand unless someone will teach me?" So Philip started from that place and used many other scriptures to show that Jesus was the Christ.

As they passed some water, the Ethiopian said, "There's water! What is stopping me from being baptized right now?" Philip answered, "If you believe with your whole heart that Jesus is the Lord you can be baptized!" "I believe!" replied the Ethiopian. So they went into the water, and Philip baptized him. As they came up from the water, Philip was snatched away by the Spirit. The Ethiopian continued on his way rejoicing. Philip found himself at Azotus. He kept preaching in all the cities he passed through on his way to Caesarea.

The Letter from James

James, Jesus' brother in the flesh, was reputed as one of the pillars of the church along with Peter and John. He wrote a letter to the Jewish Christians that were spreading all over Israel, Samaria, and Galilee during this time because of the ministries of Philip and others like him. James encouraged the believers to show their faith with action and by separating themselves from the evil influences of the world. He informed them that the troubles they were having shouldn't surprise them. He noted the prophets as examples of those who had suffered trouble before them. The trials that Christians face would actually work out for their good ultimately, by making them more patient and reliant on God.

James wrote that believers needed to be very careful about what they said with their mouths. He advised them to be quick to hear and slow to speak. He noted that a man who was in control of what he said, was in control of his whole being. He taught that temptation to do wrong didn't come from God but from our own sinful thoughts, which sometimes would turn to actions and could lead to death.

James said that all Christians were equal in God's sight and commanded them not to criticize or condemn each other. The rich were no better than the poor. He instructed the churches to have an attitude of impartiality. He concluded his letter with the admonition that members of the church should be honest with one another, that they should confess their sins to each other, and should help each other stay on the right path.

<>

Acts 9:1-31 *Saul*

Saul meanwhile continued breathing threats and murder against the church. He had secured letters from the high priest, allowing him to journey to Damascus to collect believers and bind them for a rough trip back to Jerusalem. As he approached Damascus, a bright light from heaven suddenly flashed around him. He fell to the ground and heard a voice saying, "Saul, Saul, why are you persecuting me?" Saul asked, "Who are You Lord?" The voice said, "I am Jesus, whom you are persecuting. Get up and enter the city, you will be told what to do." The men who where traveling with him heard the voice but saw no one. When Saul got up, he was blind. They led him into Damascus where he remained blind. He fasted for three days.

There was a disciple in Damascus named Ananias. The Lord appeared to Ananias in a dream and said, "Ananias go to Straight Street, to the house of Judas and ask for a man named Saul of Tarsus. He is praying there and is seeing a vision of a man named Ananias coming to lay his hands on him so he can see again." Ananias answered, "Lord, I've heard of this Saul fellow. He has done much harm to the believers in Jerusalem and is on a mission now to arrest believers here in Damascus and return them to Jerusalem." The Lord answered, "Go to him, he is an instrument of mine, to carry the good news to the Gentiles, to kings, and to Israel. He will learn how much he will have to suffer for My name's sake."

Ananias did as he was instructed. As he laid his hands on Saul it seemed scales fell from Saul's eyes, and he regained his sight. Saul had some food and drink. He spent several days with the disciples in Damascus. Saul was very effective in proving from scripture that Jesus was indeed the Christ. Many were still afraid of him because of his reputation. After many days of effective preaching by Saul in Damascus, the Jews were so provoked by his persuasive abilities that they conspired to murder him. The plot reached the disciples so Saul was slipped out of town in a large basket that was let down over the city wall.

When Saul arrived in Jerusalem, many there were not convinced of his conversion and remained afraid of him. But Barnabas took Saul to the apostles and convinced them of how effective Saul was in Damascus, boldly proclaiming the name of Jesus. Saul was stirring up enough trouble in Jerusalem with the out-of-town Jews that another plot was advanced to have him killed. At this point the disciples got him out of town and into Caesarea, and then finally back to his hometown of Tarsus.

Acts 9:31- 10:48 *Peter travels Gentiles receive the Holy Spirit*
The church throughout Judea, Samaria, and Galilee continued to grow in numbers and in the comfort of the Holy Spirit. Peter was traveling through all these areas. While in Lydda, he came upon a man named Aeneas who had been paralyzed in bed for eight years. Peter said to him, "Aeneas, Jesus Christ heals you, stand up and walk." Immediately he arose. Many from Lydda and Sharon saw the healed man and believed in the Lord.

In a town not far away, named Joppa, there was a disciple named Tabitha. She had a reputation for good deeds. She fell ill and died. They washed her body and laid it in an upper room. When they heard Peter was just over in Lydda, they sent word asking that he come immediately. When Peter arrived, he went up to where the body lay. Many widows were in the room showing Peter all the lovely garments and tunics Tabitha had made while she was alive. Peter sent the women out and knelt by the bed. He said "Tabitha, arise." She sat up. Peter took her by the hand and led her back to her friends. Peter stayed many days in Joppa at the house of a tanner named Simon.

In Caesarea there was a military officer named Cornelius. He was in command of the Italian cohort. He was a devout man who gave generously to the Jewish people. One afternoon an angel appeared to him and said, "Cornelius, all your good works ascend to God like a memorial. Send some men to Joppa to bring a man named Peter back here. He's staying at the house of a tanner named Simon, near the sea." So Cornelius sent two servants and a soldier to Joppa.

The next day as Cornelius's men were finding their way to Simon's house, Peter was up on the roof, rather hungry before lunch. As the food was being prepared, Peter fell into a trance. In a vision, the sky opened and an object like a sheet came down. On the sheet were all kinds of animals: birds, four-footed animals, and even crawling creatures. A voice said, "Get up Peter, kill and eat." Peter answered, "No way Lord. Some of these animals are unclean. I wouldn't eat them!" The voice returned, "What God has cleansed is no longer unholy." This happened three times. Finally the sheet was taken up into the sky.

While Peter was pondering all this, Cornelius's men had found the gate to Simon's house. The Spirit told Peter to go with the men because they had been sent to get him by the Spirit Himself. Peter went downstairs and heard the men's story about the angel and Cornelius. The next day Cornelius's men, Peter, and some of the believers from Joppa traveled to Caesarea.

Cornelius was waiting for them with his family and some of his close friends. When Peter arrived, Cornelius bowed and worshipped him. Peter said, "Stand up. I'm just a man like you." When Peter entered and saw all the people who were assembled he said, "Normally it would be unlawful for me, a Jew, to be in here with all you Gentiles. But God has shown me that I shouldn't think of any man as unholy or unclean. That's why I've raised no objection as to why you asked me here, uh, but why did you ask me here?" Then Cornelius related the story of the angel's appearance and instructions and said, "So we're here to listen to what you have to say to us."

Peter said, "It's clear to me now that God is not concerned about what nationality a person is, only that he hears and obeys the truth. You all have heard about the things that have gone on in Israel, beginning after the baptism proclaimed by John. You have heard about Jesus of Nazareth and all the miracles and signs He performed in Jerusalem and all over Israel. You've also heard about how He was put to death on a cross. Well, I can tell you that God has raised Him up. He appeared to many of us and ate with us. He is the Savior that has been promised to us through the prophets. God has appointed Him as Judge of both the living and the dead. Through Him you can receive forgiveness of your sins." While Peter was speaking, the Holy Spirit fell on them and the Gentiles were speaking in tongues and praising God along with the Jews. The Jews were amazed that Gentiles were receiving the Holy Spirit. Peter said, "If these folks can be baptized by the Holy Spirit, they can certainly be baptized in water as well!" So they were baptized, and Peter stayed with them for a few days.

Acts 11:1-19 *Non-Jews may be saved!*
News of the Gentiles receiving the word of God reached Jerusalem before Peter did. Apostles and brethren who were circumcised took issue with Peter because he had eaten with non-Jewish people. Peter explained in orderly sequence what transpired

from the angel's visit with Cornelius, to his own vision, to the Holy Spirit falling on the Gentiles. He concluded by saying, "Who was I, that I could stand in God's way?" With this explanation they quieted down quickly and said, "Well then, Gentiles can also receive repentance that leads to life."

Acts 11:20-30 *Antioch*

The believers that were forced from Jerusalem during the time of Stephen's martyrdom continued to spread the word outside Jerusalem. A group of Jewish believers in Antioch began sharing the good news with Greeks and other non-Jewish people. Many of them turned to the Lord. The church in Jerusalem soon heard about them, and they sent Barnabas off to Antioch. When Barnabus saw what was happening, he rejoiced and offered encouragement from a resolute heart to remain true to the Lord. Barnabus was full of the Holy Spirit and had great faith. Many more were brought to the Lord through his preaching. Barnabus left Antioch for Tarsus, to find Saul. He brought him back, and they spent a full year teaching considerable numbers of new believers. Disciples were first called Christians in Antioch.

Some prophets from Jerusalem came to Antioch. One of them named Agabus stood up and indicated by the Spirit that a worldwide famine was coming. All the believers in Antioch gave an offering, as they were able, to help the church in Jerusalem. They sent the collection to the elders in the hands of Barnabus and Saul.

Acts 12:1-23 *Herod and Peter*

During this period Herod arrested some of the Christians and mistreated them. He put James Zebedee, John's brother, to death. When Herod saw that this pleased the Jewish leaders he had Peter arrested as well. This was during the feast of unleavened bread. Peter was held under heavy security. Herod planned to bring him before the people after the Passover. Many believers were praying about Peter's situation.

The night before Herod planned to bring him to trial, Peter was sleeping, chained between two soldiers, with two more in front of his cell door. An angel appeared in the cell with a great light. He struck Peter in the side to wake him up. The angel said, "Get up quickly." As he did his chains fell off. The angel continued, "Get dressed and let's get out of here. As this was occurring, Peter didn't know if it was real or a vision. They went out to the final gate leading to the city, which opened for them by itself.

When Peter was out on the street, the angel disappeared. At this point Peter realized it wasn't a vision because he was out in the street.

He went to a house owned by Mark's mother. They were having a prayer meeting for Peter inside. Peter knocked on the door and a servant girl named Rhoda came to answer. When she recognized Peter's voice, she ran into tell the others without opening the door! The people at the meeting thought Rhoda was crazy. Meanwhile Peter was still outside pounding on the door. They were truly amazed when they realized it was him. He signaled them to keep quite and told them about his escape. He instructed them to tell the other apostles, and he went on to another place. There was quite a commotion at the prison when the warden learned Peter was gone. Some of the guards involved were executed.

Herod left Judea and went to Caesarea. A few days later, Herod was arbitrating a problem between two of his cities. He was dressed in his official robes and the people proclaimed they were hearing the words of God, not a man. Herod was struck by an angel and died a miserable death because he did not give God the glory.

Acts 12:24-13:3 *Saul's first missionary mission begins*
The word of the Lord continued to spread. Barnabus and Saul completed their delivery mission in Jerusalem so they returned to Antioch, taking John, who was also called Mark, with them.

The church in Antioch was fully functional. It had teachers and prophets. During a period when they where together ministering to the Lord, the Holy Spirit said, "Set apart Barnabus and Saul for the work I have called them to do. Additional prayer and fasting was offered. Then they laid hands on them and sent them away on a missionary journey. They took John Mark with them as a helper.

Acts 13:4-52 *Great success and resistance*
Their first stop was in Salamis. They began to proclaim the word of God in the Jewish synagogues. They aroused the interest of the proconsul of the Island named Sergius Paulos. He wanted to hear the word of God. The proconsul had a man attached to him named Elymus, who was a Jewish false prophet and magician. He sought to hamper the word as it was delivered to the proconsul. Saul would have nothing to do with the interference. He said to Elymus, "You are an enemy of the truth and are full of deceit and fraud. You're going to be blind for a time." A dark mist covered Elymus sight and he needed someone to lead him around. This sign had a clear impact on the proconsul, who believed, and was amazed at the teaching of the word of God.

Saul (also known as Paul) and his companions left the island by boat and arrived in Pamphylia. John Mark left the team and returned to Jerusalem. They continued to Antioch in Pisidia and on the Sabbath they went to the Jewish synagogue and sat down. They were invited to speak after the reading of the prophets.

Paul stood and motioning with his hand, he said, "God chose Israel and made them great in number, way back in Egypt. Then with an up-lifted hand He led them out of Egypt and put up with their whining for 40 years in the wilderness. Then God delivered the land to them by causing them to defeat the seven nations living there. They had judges to deliver them from their enemies for a time but finally they asked for a king. God gave them Saul from the tribe of Benjamin for 40 years. After he was removed, God raised up David to be their king. Now God Himself called David, 'A man after My own heart.' God Promised Israel a Savior from David's offspring, that is Jesus.

"John the Baptist came with a Baptism of repentance and said, 'Someone is coming after me whose shoelaces I am unworthy to untie.' The one he spoke of, the Savior, the promised descendant of David, the One we are sent to tell you about, is Jesus Christ of Nazareth. The leaders in Jerusalem, even though they read these prophets every Sabbath, failed to recognize Him. Though they found no guilt in Him, He was delivered to Pilate to be crucified. He suffered and died just as the prophets predicted. Then they pulled Him down off the cross and laid Him in a tomb."

"But God raised Him from the dead! He appeared to those who had been following Him throughout His ministry, which started in Galilee. They have become His witnesses and now we have been sent all the way out here to proclaim the good news to you: That God has fulfilled His promise. In the second Psalm it is written, 'You are My Son; today you have been born from Me.' This is the same Son of whom another Psalmist said, 'You will not allow Your Holy One to see decay.' Because He rose, Jesus did not undergo decay! Let it be known brothers, that through Jesus, forgiveness of sin has been proclaimed to you. Through Him, everyone who believes is freed from all things. The law of Moses was unable to free you from these things. Pay special attention because you don't want to fall into the category spoken of by the prophets. 'Behold you scoffers, I am accomplishing a work in your days that some of you will not believe even though it is carefully described to you.'"

This sermon was very popularly received! The people begged Paul and Barnabus to return the next Sabbath to speak again. Many Jews and God-fearing Jewish converts followed Paul and Barnabus, who encouraged them to continue in the grace of God.

The next Sabbath nearly the whole city came out to hear the word of God! When the Jews saw the crowds they began to make contradictions and even to blaspheme because of their own jealousy. Paul and Barnabus spoke boldly to the Jews saying, "It was appropriate for us to first proclaim the word to you. But you repudiate it and judge yourselves unworthy of eternal life. So we're taking the message out of the synagogue and delivering it to the Gentiles, as it says in scripture, 'I have placed You as a light to the Gentiles, that You should bring salvation to the ends of the earth.'"

This made the Gentiles rejoice and many were converted. The Jews meanwhile pooled all their resources to drive Paul and Barnabus from the region. Paul and Barnabus shook the dust from their feet in protest and continued on to Iconium. The disciples they left were continually filled with joy from the Holy Spirit.

Acts 14 *Iconoum*
When they arrived in Iconium they entered the synagogue and preached in such a way that many believed, both Jew and Gentile. The unbelieving Jews stirred up the minds of some of the Gentiles and made them embittered towards the brethren. They spent a long time there preaching boldly. God was also certifying their words with signs and miracles. But the city remained divided. A plot hatched by both Jew and Gentile leaders to have them killed became known to Paul and Barnabus, so they fled the area and made stops in the cities of Lyconia, Lystra, Derby, and all the surrounding regions preaching the good news.

In Lystra, Paul was speaking publicly. There was a man in attendance who was lame from birth. When Paul's eyes met his, Paul perceived he had the faith to be healed so he ordered him up on his feet. When the crowd witnessed the miracle they proclaimed in the Lyconian language, "The gods have become like men and are among us!" They called Barnabus: Zeus, and Paul: Hermes, because Paul was their chief speaker. The priests of Zeus, whose temple was just outside the city, came in with oxen and garlands to offer sacrifice to them. When Paul and Barnabus heard this they tore their clothes and cried out, "No! We are men like you! We're preaching the good news to you so you will turn from these vain beliefs, to the living God, who created the earth and the sea and all that is in them. He has permitted you to go your own way, but now has made a way for all men to enjoy his goodness!" Even with these words they had difficulty restraining the crowd from offering sacrifice to them.

Jews from Antioch and Iconium came to Lystra and won a multitude to go against Paul. They stoned him and dragged him outside the city thinking he was dead. The disciples, thinking Paul was dead, were surprised when he got up and went back into the city! The next day Paul and Barnabus went to Derby.

After they preached the good news in Derby and made disciples there, they began their journey home. They stopped in each city they had preached. In each city they encouraged the believers, appointed leaders, and laid hands on them. They finally returned to Antioch where they had begun and reported all the things God had accomplished on the mission. They remained in Antioch for a long time with the church.

Acts 15:1 *Judaizers*
Men from Judea came to Antioch preaching that Gentiles needed circumcision to be saved. Paul and Barnabus had great dissension and debate with them. Some of these "Judaizers" also drifted into the region of Galatia where Paul and Barnabus had just established churches. Paul wrote "The Letter to the Galatians" in response to this situation.

The Letter to the Galatians
Paul started all his letters by identifying himself as an apostle who was specially called to his work by God Himself, not some worldly institution. He immediately addressed the Judaizers' claim that Christians must be circumcised and follow Jewish customs to complete their salvation. He repudiated it completely, saying that if Christians could have a right relationship with God through following a law, then Jesus wouldn't have had to die on the cross. Paul proclaimed a curse on anyone who would add any requirement other than faith in Jesus Christ to the salvation message.

Paul recounted his own conversion and activities as they related to his receiving the message of salvation. He spent several years in Arabia after his conversion and then many more in Tarsus receiving the message before he began to actively minister. He claimed that the message was revealed to him directly by the Lord, not from other men's teaching. His trips to Jerusalem had only been to confirm his beliefs, not to be instructed. He added some rebukes against Peter and others who fellowshipped with Gentiles when the Jews were not present and avoided contact with Gentiles when the Jews were watching.

Paul made points from the Old Testament about how Abraham was justified by faith, before the Law was delivered, and before he had received the seal of circumcision. He explained how Christ fulfilled all the requirements of the Law for Christians, so there wasn't any distinction now between Jew and Gentile; they were both saved by Christ's sacrifice on the cross. Paul encouraged the people in Galatia to live their lives in a manner appropriate to their position with Christ, to serve and love one another and not to concentrate on evil desires.

<>

Acts 15:2-35 Church meeting
After much debate with the Judaizers who had come to Antioch, it was agreed that Paul, Barnabus and certain others from the Antioch church would go to Jerusalem and discuss the issue directly with the elders of the church there. On their trip they encouraged all the churches on the way. When they arrived in Jerusalem they were received by the elders and made a full report of all that had gone on with them. Certain Pharisees, who were now believers, stood up and said, "It is necessary to circumcise the Gentiles and direct them to observe the Law of Moses."

So the apostles and the elders came together to look into this matter. After much debate Peter stood up and said, "You all remember in the early days how God sent me to preach to the Gentiles. He made no distinction between them and us. He cleansed their hearts and gave them the Holy Spirit. So why do you now want to place a yoke on them that we ourselves have been unable to carry? We believe Jews are saved by the grace of the Lord Jesus. It is the same for the Gentiles."

They continued to listen to testimony from Paul and Barnabus concerning all the wonders and signs God had accomplished among the Gentiles on their missionary trip. When they finished, James stood up and addressed the meeting. "Peter has related how God first began taking from the Gentiles a people for His name. And the scriptures are full of references as to how the Gentiles will be blessed and be called by His name. It is my judgment that we do not trouble those who are turning to God from among the Gentiles. We should write them a letter advising them to abstain from things contaminated by idols, from fornication, from things that are strangled, and from blood. They can hear the Law of Moses, it is taught in synagogues worldwide on every Sabbath."

So they sent a letter that summarized the elders' position, that Gentiles did not require circumcision to be saved, back to Antioch with Paul and Barnabus and two brothers from Judea, Judas and Silas. When they arrived in Antioch they delivered the letter and there was much rejoicing at the encouragement it brought. Judas and Silas also delivered lengthy messages. After they had spent some time there, Judas returned to Jerusalem, but it seemed good to Silas to stay in Antioch.

Acts 15:36-16:10 *Paul meets Timothy*
After some days Paul proposed a return missionary mission to all the cities where they had preached on the first trip. Barnabus wanted to take John Mark along. Paul insisted he should not go because he had deserted them in Pamphylia and not finished the first trip. The disagreement was so sharp that Paul and Barnabus parted ways. Barnabus and John Mark sailed to Cyprus. Paul chose Silas, and they departed with the blessing of the church to strengthen all the churches in Syria and Cilicia.

When Paul arrived in the region of Derby and Lystra, he met a man named Timothy who was spoken well of by the disciples in the area. Paul wanted Timothy to join them. Timothy was circumcised because all the Jews in the vicinity knew his mother was Jewish and his father was a Greek. They were delivering the message that had been agreed to by the council of elders in Jerusalem. So the churches continued to grow in number. Paul and Silas moved on, passing through some regions when the Holy Spirit forbade them from speaking the word there. They came to a city named Troas, where Paul had a vision of a man asking that they come into Macedonia.

Acts 16:11 *In Philippi*
They traveled by ship to a city named Neapolis and from there to Philippi, which was a leading city in the region of Macedonia and a Roman colony. They stayed there for many days. On the Sabbath they went to a place by a river they supposed was a place of prayer. There was a gathering of women there so Paul began to share the word with them. A lady named Lydia,
a merchant from a city named Thyatira, who specialized in purple fabrics, received Paul's message and her whole household was baptized. She asked Paul and his team to stay with them.

One day as they were going to a prayer meeting, a woman with the spirit of divination, who was gaining substantial profit for her masters, followed after them saying, "These are the bond servants of the Most High God who are proclaiming the way of salvation." She continued this day after day. Paul became annoyed by it. He turned to her and said to the divination spirit within her, "I command you by the name of Jesus Christ to come out of her!" The spirit left immediately.

When her masters realized her gift (and their mode of profit) had gone, they seized Paul and dragged him before the authorities. When they were before the chief magistrates they said, "These men are throwing our city into confusion, being Jews. They are proclaiming customs that are not lawful for Romans to accept." The crowd rose up together against Paul and his team and the magistrates ordered their robes torn off and had them beaten with rods. After they inflicted many blows upon them they threw them in jail and ordered tight security. With this order, they were thrown in the inner prison and their feet were bound in the stocks.

Around midnight Paul and Silas were praying and singing hymns, with all the other prisoners listening. Suddenly there was a great earthquake that shook the foundations of the prison. All the doors came open and everyone's chains were unfastened. The jailer, who was roused out of sleep, saw all the doors open, and he drew his sword to kill himself because he thought everyone had escaped. Paul called loudly, "Don't harm yourself, we're all still here." The jailer ordered the lights. He came trembling before Paul and Silas and said, "Sirs, what must I do to be saved?" They answered, "When you believe in the Lord Jesus, you and your whole household will be saved." The jailer washed their wounds and took them to his home that night. He and his entire household were baptized.

The next day the chief magistrates sent word to the jail to have Paul and his team released. When the jailer passed the news, Paul replied, "They beat us, who are Roman citizens, in public, without a trial and now they want to cover it up. Tell them to come themselves and release us." When the magistrates heard that Paul and some of his companions were Roman citizens, they were afraid. They appealed to them and brought them out. Paul and his team left the prison and went to Lydia's house where they encouraged the brethren and then left the city.

Acts 17: *Thessalonica, Berea, Athens*
After passing through some other cities, they came to Thessalonica. There was a synagogue there and according to his custom, Paul went there first and reasoned with the Jews from the scriptures for three Sabbaths, providing evidence that the Messiah had to suffer and be raised from the dead. He proclaimed Jesus as the Christ. Some were persuaded and joined them along with some of the leading women of the city. The leaders of the synagogue became jealous. They recruited wicked men from the market place to form a mob and set the city in an uproar. The mob went to Jason's house looking for Paul and his team. When they didn't find them, they dragged Jason and some of the brethren before the city officials saying, "The men who have upset the

world with their message are now here! Jason has welcomed them, and they all serve a king named Jesus, not Caesar." Jason was able to post bond and gain his and the brethren's release.

Paul and Silas were sent away that night to Berea. When they arrived there they went to the synagogue and began again to present Jesus as the promised Messiah. The people of Berea were more noble minded than those in Thessalonica. They received the message and searched the scriptures daily to confirm the message. Many believed, Jew and Greek, men and women. When the Jews in Thessalonica heard Paul and Silas were in Berea they went there to stir up a crowd against them. The believers sent Paul towards Athens by sea. Silas and Timothy remained in Macedonia. When Paul's group arrived in Athens, he sent his escorts back with instructions to send Timothy and Silas as soon as possible.

Being stuck in Athens, a city full of idols, was not pleasant for Paul. He reasoned with the Jews in the synagogue, with God-fearing Gentiles at their gatherings, and in the market place to whoever would listen. Some of the Epicurean and Stoic philosophers conversed with him. Some thought he was an idle babbler, others thought he was a proclaimer of strange deities, because he was preaching Jesus and His resurrection. Paul did generate enough interest to be taken to the Areopagus to make a presentation. (Athenians and visitors to the city loved to hear and talk about new things.)

Paul stood up in the Areopagus and said, "Men of Athens, I can see that you are very religious in all respects. You even have an altar with the inscription: TO AN UNKNOWN GOD. You don't know this God, but I can tell you about Him. He made the world and everything in it. He doesn't live in temples made by men, nor does He need any service from men, since He Himself gave life to men. He made every nation on earth and appointed their times and boundaries. He is not far from any of us. His divine nature can't be accurately represented in gold, silver, or stone. He has overlooked the times of ignorance and is now declaring that men everywhere can turn towards Him. He has fixed a day in time when the world will be judged, according to the righteousness of one Man, whom He has appointed and certified by raising Him from the dead."

When Paul started the resurrection message many began to sneer at him but some said they wanted to hear from him again. Paul left the Areopagus and some men followed him believing. One, named Dionysius, was an official in the Areopagus.

Acts 18:1-5 *Corinth*

Paul left Athens and went to Corinth where he met a Jew, named Aquilla and his wife Pricilla. They had come to Corinth because Claudius had ordered all Jews to leave Rome. Paul worked with them in their tent-making business, (Paul was trained in this trade), and he spent every Sabbath at the synagogue trying to persuade Jews and Greeks. When Silas and Timothy arrived from Macedonia, Paul devoted himself full time to the word and his ministry.

The Two Letters to the Thessalonians

Timothy brought news about the church in Thessalonica. They were doing generally well but there were some questions because false teachings and teachers were already creeping in. Paul, along with Silas and Timothy wrote two letters to the church in Thessalonica during his stay in Corinth. Paul expressed his thankfulness to God at how the Thessalonians were enduring in their faith even though it was causing some hardship for them. Paul differentiated his teaching and methods from false teachers. He reminded them of how he set an example of hard work and asked for nothing in return from them. No one could accuse Paul of bad motives in his approach to ministry. He wasn't in it for the money.

Paul assured them that he wanted to come visit them again himself but indicated Satan had prevented him so far. This is why he sent Timothy in his place. Paul encouraged the church folks to live exemplary lives, so others would be drawn to the faith and God would be glorified.

Paul also spoke of the day that Christ would return. He indicated it would come unexpectedly. He spoke of a time when dead believers would be raised and Christians alive on the earth would be caught up with them in the air on that day. He had to clarify some of these statements in his second letter to them. Many seemed to think he was saying the day was just around the corner. Some false teachers even claimed it had already occurred. Paul taught that there would be a great rebellion against the truth before the day of the Lord. The Anti-Christ, who was already secretly at work, would raise himself up and position himself in the temple of God to be worshipped. A great deception would be coming that would lead many astray.

Acts 18:6-17 *Corinth*

The Jews in Corinth ultimately rejected Paul's message. He shook the dust from his garments and said, "I've done all I can do to convince you; your eternal fate is in your own hands. Now I will take the message to the Gentiles." Paul had meetings in a house owned by Titus Justice that was located next to the synagogue. Crispus, one of the leaders of the synagogue, came to believe in Jesus. His conversion influenced others towards the faith. Jesus appeared to Paul in a vision one night and said, "Don't hold back any longer, speak freely, do not be silent. I am with you and I will protect you because I have many people in this city." Paul stayed another year and a half preaching and teaching in Corinth.

While Gallio was proconsul of the area, the Jews rose up with one accord against Paul and took him before the judgment seat. They said, "This man persuades men to worship God contrary to the law." As Paul was about to defend himself, Gallio said to the Jews, "If these accusations had anything to do with a violent crime I might listen to you, as it is you're bothering me with questions about names and words in your own law. Look after this yourselves, I will not be a judge for you on these matters." Gallio sent them away from the judgment seat. The Jews then took hold of one of the leaders of the synagogue, named Sosthenes, and beat him in the sight of Gallio, who took no concern in the matter.

Acts 18:18-19:20 *Ephesus*

After staying in the area for many more days, Paul boarded a boat for Syria with Pricilla and Aquilla. He made one stop in Cenchrea where he had his hair cut for the purpose of beginning a vow. They came to Ephesus and Paul entered the synagogue to reason with the Jews. They asked him to stay longer but he said, "I will see you again if it is the Lord's will." He left Pricilla and Aquilla in Ephesus. Paul continued on through Caesarea and finally arrived back in Antioch. After spending some time there he left again and traveled through the Galatian region strengthening the brethren there.

Back in Ephesus a very eloquent man named Apollos began to make an impression with his powerful presentation of the scriptures. He was persuasive and accurate in his presentation about Jesus, but he was acquainted only with the baptism of John. Pricilla and Aquilla were able to take him aside and start bringing him up to date. He took his message to the Achaia region with the blessing of the brethren and was very effective in his public demonstrations of scripture.

Later Paul came back through Ephesus, while Apollos was traveling in Achaia, and found twelve new believers, who like Apollos previously, knew only about the baptism of John. Paul preached to them about the baptism of Jesus and the Holy Spirit. They were re-baptized and received the Holy Spirit.

After about three months in Ephesus, some men in the synagogue became hardened, disobedient and spoke evil about the "Way". Paul separated from them and began conducting his discussions at the school of Tyrannus. He was there for two years and many signs and wonders accompanied his ministry. Handkerchiefs or aprons were even taken from Paul, laid on sick people, and they were being healed!

Some Jewish exorcists attempted to cast out demons saying, "Come out in the name of Jesus, who Paul preaches about." The demon answered one of them, "I know Jesus, and I know Paul, but who are you?" At this the man who was demon possessed overpowered the Jewish exorcist, sending him running, beaten, and naked.

Those who practiced magic were coming to believe in Jesus. They publicly repented by burning their books on magic. When they added up the price of the books it was worth more than all of them would make in a year. The word of the Lord was spreading all over the area!

The First Letter to the Corinthians

A group from Corinth came to Ephesus with news and some questions for Paul that had come up as a result of a previous letter he had written. His first concern were divisions in the Corinthian church. Factions were developing around individual teachers. Paul answered this problem by emphasizing that the message of Christ is not divided and is not delivered by a teacher but by the Holy Spirit Himself. It isn't a message that can be broken down through worldly wisdom. Different teachers had different jobs. Paul used Apollos and himself as examples, but it was God who gave power and certified the message. Paul recounted how he kept his messages simple.

Paul delivers severe judgment against the church for allowing a man to maintain sexual relations with his father's wife. Paul instructs the church to cast the man from the fellowship. He instructs the Corinthians that sin has the power to enslave a person, sexual sin in particular. He assures them of their freedom but warns them not to become slaves to anything but God. Christians' bodies are actually the temples of the Holy Spirit so they should keep them holy.

Paul answered specific questions from the Corinthians on marriage and eating habits. He also explained his habit of not receiving payment from those he ministered to. He offered instruction on orderly worship and the use of spiritual gifts. He explains that although gifts like teaching, healing, and speaking in unknown languages were helpful and good, only one spiritual gift was the greatest: the gift of love. All the other gifts lose their use in heaven, but love endures forever.

Paul finishes the letter by defending the validity of the resurrection of the dead. He explains that if Christ didn't rise from the dead, then Christianity was false and he would be foolish to stay with it.

Acts 19:21- 20:1 *Ephesus*

Paul became convinced that he needed to go to Jerusalem. He also felt compelled, at some point, to go to Rome. His plan included visiting Macedonia again and visiting the churches on his way to Jerusalem, so he sent Timothy and Erastus ahead while he stayed in Asia for a while.

A man in Ephesus named Demetrius, who made a living making silver products memorializing Artemis, the goddess of Ephesus, stirred up quite a ruckus against Paul and the Way. He called a meeting of other craftsmen who benefited from the Artemis concession and announced, "Gentlemen you know our prosperity depends on the people's devotion to Artemis. This Paul fellow is preaching that handmade gods aren't gods at all! Not only is this bad for business but our own goddess Artemis could be dethroned from her magnificence!" These words enraged the gathered craftsmen and they all yelled, "Great is Artemis of the Ephesians! A huge, disorganized crowd grew and headed to the city theater. They weren't sure of what they wanted to accomplish, other than yell their true devotion to "Artimis of the Ephesians!" Which they did for about two hours. Finally the town clerk was able to quiet the mob by assuring them that the image of Artemis had indeed fallen from heaven and the Ephesians were still the guardians of her temple. All these facts were established and undeniable. However, if any charges were to be brought by Demitrius and his union against Paul and the Way, it would have to be done lawfully. These words quieted the crowd and everyone went home.

After the uproar had finished, Paul gathered the disciples, gave them exhortations and left on his journey to Macedonia. He ministered his way through Macedonia and while on this leg of his trip was joined by Titus, who brought more news and questions from the church in Corinth.

The Second Letter to the Corinthians

This letter to the Corinthians is very personal in nature. Paul had indicated he would try to come to them on his way to Macedonia. He explained that he went north through Asia and across to Philippi because he didn't want to come in the spirit of discipline. He expressed his satisfaction that the Corinthians had received his last rather harsh letter with a positive result. Paul encouraged them to restore the man who had been banished from the church.

Paul spent a good deal of the letter talking about how tough it has been spreading the Gospel. He reports being beaten, jailed, and shipwrecked. Many false teachers seem to be saying that Paul is not a true apostle. Paul defends his apostleship by the fruits of his ministry. He is certainly an apostle to the Corinthians because he was the first to bring the message of Christ to them.

The letter is full of hope of what is to come for the Christians. Things can get very bad in this evil world but when Christ comes to establish his kingdom, Christians will receive new bodies. This has been guaranteed and sealed by the fact that Christians are given the Holy Spirit.

Paul reminds them that he is taking a collection from all the churches for the church in Jerusalem. He encourages the Corinthians to be generous in their giving for this cause and to begin collecting it so it would be ready when Paul comes through.

<>

Paul left Macedonia and traveled down into Greece to visit the Corinthians. While he was there he wrote a letter to the budding church in Rome.

The Letter to the Romans

Paul's letter to the Romans is his most complete presentation of the message he was preaching wherever he went. His first point is the fact that all men are sinful by nature and are separated from God as a result. Everyone, everywhere, falls into this unfortunate category. Paul explains how God gave the Law through the Jews to highlight and clearly define man's sinfulness. No one is able to live up to the requirements of the law. Because of this, the Law is not able to make anyone right with God. The human race is under a sentence of death and separation from God because of personal sin in each of its members.

Paul explains that God has created a solution for the problem by sending His own unique Son. Christ came to pay the price for sin. His death on the cross is the paid ransom. It is because of faith in Christ that believers are saved from their sins, not because of any good thing they might be able to do.

Paul continues to discuss the life of believers who have accepted Christ. They are still plagued by a sinful nature that comes from the flesh, but by trusting in the Spirit that God gives them, they can become more and more the type of people God wants them to be. Everything that they go through as Christians is designed by God to bring them into closer conformity with what he wants them to become.

Paul also explains that God's promises to the Jews are still in effect. He has used them in many ways, and Jesus Himself came from the Jews, but now their eyes are blinded and God is allowing everyone into a right relationship with Him through His Son.

Paul encourages Christians to live in a manner worthy of their new relationship with God. When Christians serve God, it enables them to show love and sensitivity to others.

<>

Acts 20:2-21:16 *Pushing towards a certain fate in Jerusalem*
After three months visiting the Corinthians and ministering in Greece, the Jews hatched a plot, and Paul left the area. He traveled again through Macedonia. Timothy and a group of others accompanied him on this leg. They stopped in Troas in Asia for about a week.

On the last night of their stay, Paul was teaching late into the night, in a well-lit third-floor room. As Paul continued his long message, a young man, named Eutychus, who was sitting in a windowsill fell asleep and tumbled three floors to the ground. Paul hurried down and covered the young man with his own body. He embraced the young man and assured every one he would be fine, then he went back up and continued the service. He spoke until dawn. Every one was encouraged because the boy was alive.

Paul was in a hurry to get to Jerusalem so they took a seagoing route past Ephesus. When he put in at Miletus he called for the elders in Ephesus. When they arrived,

Paul delivered this message to them: "You all know I have done my best to proclaim Jesus as Savior to you from the time I arrived in Asia. I did so even as problems and trials came upon me because of plots from the Jews. I continued to build upon the foundation I laid, never holding anything back that might be of help to you. Now I am compelled to go to Jerusalem. The Holy Spirit has told me clearly and often that problems and imprisonment are waiting for me. But finishing the course of ministry set out for me by Jesus Christ is my only concern. I doubt you will see me face to face again. Now it is your job to guard the flock that God has assigned you to oversee. Be on your guard, savage wolves will come in to try to rob the flock. Some of you will even turn to speaking false messages and draw disciples away for yourselves. So be alert and remember how I was a servant among you. I wasn't after money; I took care of my own needs and those who were with me. Jesus said, 'It is better to give than to receive.'" There was crying and grieving as they all prayed together. They all went together as Paul and his team boarded the ship.

After a few stops and ship changes, Paul and his team stopped at Tyre. They stayed seven days with some believers they found there. The brethren in Tyre warned Paul again, through the Spirit, that harm awaited him in Jerusalem. When it came time to leave, the disciples, along with their wives and children, escorted Paul's group out of the city and onto the ship.

Their next stop was in Caesarea where they lodged with Philip the evangelist. Again Paul received prophetic warnings that he would face imprisonment in Jerusalem but he said, "I'm ready to die in Jerusalem." Everyone began to understand Paul's resolution on the matter and stopped trying to dissuade him. Some additional disciples from Caesarea joined Paul's group as it headed towards Jerusalem.

Acts 21:17-22:29 *Paul before the mob*
James and the other elders in Jerusalem received them gladly. Paul gave a complete report about all that had been accomplished among the Gentiles and there was much rejoicing. Then the elders said to him, "Paul, as you know thousands of Jews are believers, and they are zealous about following the Law of Moses. They have heard that your teaching encourages believers to forsake the law, not to circumcise their children, and not to walk according to customs. We are in a quandary because they will certainly hear you are in town. Here is our plan. We have four men who are just finishing up a vow. Take them to the temple and pay the expenses for their purification, along with your own, (Paul was completing a vow as well). They will see that you follow the law yourself and there is nothing to what they have heard about you. We have already written a letter to the Gentiles instructing them that they

should abstain from meat sacrificed to idols, from blood, from what is strangled, and fornication." So Paul did as he was advised.

When the seven days of purification were close to completion, Jews from Asia saw Paul in the temple and began stirring up the crowd saying, "Men of Israel, there is the man who preaches all over the world against the law and this temple. He even has defiled the place by bringing Gentiles into the temple." They said this because they had seen Paul in town with one of the Gentile Ephesians who had accompanied them on the trip to Jerusalem. They assumed Paul had brought him into the temple. The false accusations worked. The crowd abducted Paul, beating him as they dragged him out of the temple. Word made it to a Roman army unit nearby that there was a major disturbance at the temple. They rushed to the scene and grabbed Paul away from the mob who were close to beating him to death, and shackled him with chains as they moved him towards the barracks.

The Romans weren't able to determine why the mob was so moved against Paul. Too many Jews were yelling too many things. They carried Paul as they approached the barrack's stairs because of how violently the crowd was after him.

As they were taking Paul into the barracks he addressed the captain in Greek, "May I say something to you?" The captain replied, "If you know Greek, you must not be that Egyptian who stirred up a revolt recently." Paul answered, "No, I am a Jew from Tarsus which is a big city. Please allow me to address the people." The captain did allow it. Paul turned and motioned with his hand. There was a great hush that became even more pronounced when he began his defense in the Hebrew dialect:

"I am a Jew from Tarsus, but I was raised in Jerusalem. I received my education in the law from Gamaliel, so my background is firmly based in following the law and being zealous for God. At the beginning I was in opposition to the Way, tracking down converts and throwing them in jail. These facts can be verified through the Council of elders. I was on a trip to Damascus to arrest new disciples in "The Way" when a bright light flashed from heaven." Paul continued to recount the story of his conversion on the road to Damascus and his return to Jerusalem. "When I returned to Jerusalem, I was in prayer in the temple when I fell into a trance. Jesus appeared and said, 'Get out of Jerusalem quickly because they won't accept what you say about Me.' I said, 'They certainly know I was zealous for the law. I had believers imprisoned and beaten. I stood by holding the cloaks of those who killed your servant Steven.' Jesus answered,

'Go! I will send you far away to the Gentiles.'"

The crowd listened until he made this statement, then they all threw off their cloaks, threw dust in the air and cried out as one, "Away with him, he should not be allowed to live!" The Roman captain had him brought into the barracks and had him stretched out to be tortured, so they could get him to admit why the Jews were shouting so vehemently against him. Paul asked him, "Is it lawful for you to whip a Roman citizen before he has been convicted of any crime?" "You're a Roman citizen?" the captain asked, "I had to buy my citizenship for a large price. How did you acquire yours?" Paul answered, "I was born into mine." Paul was immediately released, and the regional commander was concerned that Paul had even been bound.

Acts 22:30-23:11 *Paul before the Council and bound for Rome*
The next day the Jewish council was ordered to convene and the Romans brought Paul before them. Paul looked intently at the group and said, "I have lived my life with a clean conscience before God to this day." Ananias commanded the man standing next to Paul to strike him in the mouth. Paul said to Ananias, "God will strike you, you whitewashed wall. You sit there trying me in accordance to the law and have me struck in violation of the law!" One of the bystanders said, "You are reviling the high priest!" Paul replied, "I was not aware; I know it is not lawful to speak against a ruler of the people."

Paul saw that there were Sadducees and Pharisees on the council, two groups with a long-standing dispute concerning life after death and the existence of angels, the Pharisees believing in both, and the Sadducees believing in neither. So Paul stood and cried, "I am a Pharisee, the son of Pharisees. I am on trial for my hope in the resurrection of the dead!" A dissension was raised in the council that intensified to an uproar with some of the Pharisees saying; "We find no fault with this man. Perhaps an angel or a spirit has spoken to him. As the arguments continued to intensify, the Romans ordered troops to get Paul out of there
because they were afraid he might be torn to pieces! So he was returned to the barracks.

That night Jesus appeared to Paul by his bed saying, "Take courage, just as you have been My witness in Jerusalem, so you must also testify about Me in Rome."

Acts 23:12-24:27 *Paul in the legal system*
The next day a group of more than 40 of Paul's enemies was organized among the Jews. They bound themselves under an oath that no one of them would eat or drink

until Paul was killed. So word from the council was sent to the Romans to bring Paul before them again for more investigation. They planned to kill Paul as he was being transferred. Paul's nephew heard about the plan and sent a secret messenger to the Romans informing them of the plot. So the Romans moved Paul to Caesarea with a guard of 200 soldiers, and 70 horsemen. Paul rode on a horse as well. He was being taken to Felix, the Governor of the area. This is the letter that was sent by the regional commander to be given to Felix:

> "From: Claudius Lysias
> To: The most excellent governor Felix
>
> Greetings,
> The Jews arrested this man, and they were about to slay him. Having learned he was a Roman citizen, I came upon them with troops and rescued him. Hoping to ascertain a charge, I brought him before their council. He was accused over questions about their Law, but no accusation deserved death or imprisonment. When I found there was a plot against him, I sent him at once to you and informed his accusers to bring their charges against this man before you."

So Paul was taken to Felix. When governor Felix had read the letter he asked Paul were he was from. When he found Paul was from Tarsus he said, "I will have you lodged in Herod's official residence. Your accusers have been ordered to come here to bring their charges."

Five days later Ananias arrived with his attorney, Tertullus, and some of the other elders. Tertullus began his opening statement, "Most excellent Felix, we have attained much peace as a result of your reforms that have been carried out. We acknowledge your part in all this. We don't want to weary you any further, so with your approval we present these charges. We have found this man to be a real pest. He is a fellow who stirs up dissension among Jews throughout the world, and he is a ringleader in the sect of the Nazarenes. He was attempting to desecrate the temple when we arrested him. We wanted to judge him according to our own law, but then Lysias, the regional commander came along and violently took him from us. Now we have been ordered to come here and make our charges. If you examine him yourself, you will be able to ascertain that these charges are accurate." The Jews joined in the attack, asserting that these were the facts.

When the governor nodded for Paul to speak, he responded, "Knowing that you have been a judge to this nation for many years, I cheerfully make my defense. I arrived in Jerusalem only twelve days ago. I did not have public discussions with anyone, in the temple, in any synagogue, or in the city. I certainly didn't incite any riots! They can't prove any of the charges they have brought you. But I must admit, according to the Way, which they call a sect, I serve the God of our fathers and hold true everything that is written in the Law and the Prophets. I have a hope in the same God these men cherish, that there will be a resurrection of both the righteous and the wicked. In view of this I try to maintain a clean conscience before God and men."

"When I arrived in Jerusalem I was in the temple finishing a purification ceremony with others who were completing an oath according to our law. There was no uproar, until a group of Jews from Asia, who should be here if they have an accusation against me, started one. I can't imagine what uproar I caused, except when I made a statement about the resurrection when I was on trial before them."

Felix had some knowledge about The Way and delayed decision saying, "When Lysias comes, I will decide this case. Paul was returned to Herod's mansion, where he was allowed some freedom and his friends were free to provide for him and to visit. A few days later Felix brought his wife to speak with Paul, and Paul shared freely about faith in Jesus Christ. When they were discussing righteousness, self control, and the coming judgment, Felix got uncomfortable and said, "That's enough for now, I'll talk to you again." Felix hoped at some point Paul might offer him money for his release, so occasionally he would spend time talking with Paul. Two years passed. Felix was succeeded by Festus and as a favor to the Jews; Felix left Paul under house arrest.

Acts 25-26 *Paul before Festus and Agrippa*
Festus, the new governor, spent his first couple of weeks in the province visiting Jerusalem. The Jewish leaders brought charges against Paul there, urging that he be brought to Jerusalem for trial. They planned to set up an ambush to kill him on the way. Festus replied that he was going to Caesarea soon; they should come with him and he would hear the case there. Festus spent another week and a half before he left for Caesarea.

The Jews came to Caesarea the day after Festus's arrival. Festus took his seat on the tribunal and ordered Paul to be brought in. The Jews made a number of serious charges they couldn't prove. Paul said in his own defense, "I have broken no laws, Jewish or Roman!" Festus still seemed to want to do the Jews a favor and said, "Well, will you go to Jerusalem to prove your position in a proper trial. Paul answered, "I am standing before a Roman tribunal. I know I have broken no Jewish laws. If I had, I would be willing to die, but none of these charges are true, so no one can turn me over to them. I appeal to Caesar." After consulting with his council, Festus said, "You have appealed to Caesar, to Caesar you shall go."

Several days later King Agrippa and Bernice arrived in Caesarea to welcome Festus to his new job. During their stay Festsus reviewed Paul's case with Agrippa and concluded his review saying, "I'm in a bit of a quandary. I've had him held in order to send him to Rome, but the case is only about some disagreements over their law and about a dead man named Jesus who Paul says is alive." Agrippa said, "You have an interesting case here. I would like to hear from Paul myself."

So the next day Agrippa and Bernice entered the auditorium amid great pomp, accompanied by Roman generals and the prominent men of the city. When they were all properly seated, Paul was brought in. Festus addressed them first. "Before you is a man whom the Jews vehemently say should not be allowed to live any longer. He has appealed to Caesar and I have agreed to send him, but I am in a quandary as to how to make my report that will accompany him. So I have brought him before you, especially you, King Agrippa, so that after your investigation you might have some in-put as to how I should prepare my letter to Caesar."

Agrippa said to Paul, "You are permitted to speak for yourself." Paul stretched out his hand and began making his defense. "I feel fortunate for this opportunity to make a defense before you, King Agrippa, because you are familiar with Jewish law and customs. You are aware of the hope the Jewish people have. My belief in the fulfillment of that hope is why I am on trial here today."

Paul continued to recount his early zeal for Judaism and his persecution of the early believers, his trip to Damascus and his conversion. He recounted Jesus' words to him regarding his ministry to the Gentiles. "The Lord said, as I lay next to the Damascus road, 'Get up, I have appeared to you, to appoint you a minister and a witness, not only of that which you have seen but also those things I will reveal to you. Delivering you from the Jews and from the Gentiles. You will preach a message to the Gentiles to open their eyes, so they will turn from darkness and the dominion of Satan, to God, to receive forgiveness of sins, and an inheritance among the others who are sanctified by faith in Me.'"

"I was not disobedient to this heavenly vision, King Agrippa. Starting there in Damascus and now all over the world, I have preached the message of repentance and living in a manner appropriate to that repentance. This is the reason some of the Jews seized me in the temple. My message proclaims that the promises of the Prophets and Moses have taken place. That the Christ was to both suffer and to rise again from the grave and to be the light of both Jew and Gentile."

While Paul was talking, Festus interrupted in a loud voice, "Paul, you're out of you're mind. All you learning is driving you mad!" Paul answered, "I'm not out of my mind, most excellent Festus, I am speaking in sober truth. King Agrippa knows about these things. I am sure none of these things has escaped his notice, because they have not been done in a corner. King Agrippa, do you believe in the Prophets? I know that you do!" Agrippa replied, "Paul, in a short time you'll have me turned into a Christian!" Paul answered, "Short time or long, I want all to be in the same position as I am, except of course, these chains I am in." The king, Bernice, the governor, and all those who were seated with them, arose and moved aside for a conference. All agreed, that if he hadn't appealed to Caesar, Paul could have been set free. As it stood, Paul was to be sent to Rome.

Acts 27 *Sailing to Rome*
Paul, with some companions and other prisoners were placed on a ship for Rome. Julius, the centurion in charge, treated Paul with courtesy. At stops along the way, Paul was allowed to disembark and rest with friends. Paul and his companions were transferred to an Alexandrian ship in Lycia. From there the trip moved slowly because of the wind. They sailed south of the Island of Crete, stopping at a place called Fair Havens. They were way behind schedule, and the remainder of the trip promised to be dangerous. Paul provided warning that continuing would prove disastrous, but the captain and the centurion decided to at least try for Phoenix on the island of Crete. They hoped to winter there.

When a moderate south wind came up, they weighed anchor. Before long a strong northeaster came upon the ship, and they had to give way to it. The storm became fierce and survival was uncertain. The second day they threw cargo overboard, the third day the ships rigging was jettisoned. After many days in the storm, Paul stood and encouraged everyone saying, "Don't be afraid, tonight an angel appeared to me and assured me that I would stand before Caesar in Rome and all aboard would survive." One night, after two full weeks of weather, the crew took soundings that seemed to indicate they might run aground. The ship's crew made an attempt to escape on the ship's boat, on the pretense that they were making some repair. Paul alerted the

Roman centurion, who stopped them and cut the ship's boat loose. Later that night Paul said, "It's been fourteen days that we've been battling the sea, and no one has hardly eaten a thing. Everyone should take nourishment and be assured; not a single one of us will be lost!" There were two hundred and seventy six people on the ship. Having said this, Paul took bread, gave thanks to God
in the presence of them all, and they became encouraged as they ate.

In the morning they could see a shoreline and a beach. They resolved to drive the ship into it but they struck a reef on the way in. The ship began to break up in the waves. The soldiers were preparing to kill the prisoners so they wouldn't escape when the centurion stopped them. He wanted Paul to get to Rome. So every one abandoned ship. They all made it to shore, either swimming or grabbing anything that would float.

Acts 28:1-15 *Malta*
The natives of the Island of Malta were very friendly. They provided shelter for everyone. Paul gathered a pile of sticks to throw onto a fire when a viper snake jumped up because of the heat and attached itself to Paul's hand. When the natives saw this, they concluded Paul was a guilty murderer. Paul shook the snake into the fire. After a long wait, the natives concluded he was a god, because he hadn't even become ill! After three days on the island Paul learned that the father of Publius, the leading man of the island, was ill with fever and dysentery. Paul prayed and laid hands on him, and he was healed. After that the rest of the people on the island, who had diseases, came to Paul and were cured.

After three months on the island, Paul and his companions were placed on an Alexandrian ship that had wintered on Malta. The cruise to Italy was uneventful. Paul was met south of Rome by some believers and was much encouraged by them. They escorted him into Rome where Paul was allowed to live by himself with a guard.

Acts 28:16-31 *Two years in Rome*
After three days he met with the leading Jews in Rome saying, "Brethren though I have done nothing against our people or our customs, I was delivered as a prisoner to the Romans. When they examined me, they found no crime, but the Jews objected and I was forced to appeal to Caesar. I want to explain myself to you because this imprisonment is for the sake of the hope of Israel." They replied, "We haven't heard anything from Jerusalem about you, good or bad. But we have only heard negative

comments about this new sect, so we would like to hear what you have to say." So a date was set for Paul to make a presentation to the Jewish leaders in Rome.

When the day arrived, a large number came to Paul's lodging, to hear his presentation. Paul spent the entire day trying to persuade them about Jesus from the Law and the Prophets. Some were being convinced, others did not believe so that a dispute arose between them. As they were leaving, Paul quoted the prophet Isaiah: "Go to this people and say: 'You will hear but not understand; you will see but not perceive.' The heart of this people is dull; they have closed their eyes." Paul concluded, "I will also present this message to the Gentiles, and they will listen." They Jews left with their dispute continuing.

Paul stayed for two more years in Rome, living in rented quarters. He welcomed all who came to him and continued to preach and teach concerning Jesus Christ without being hindered.

While he was under house arrest in Rome, Paul wrote four letters that appear in the New Testament. Three of the letters: Ephesians, Colossians, and Philemon were written together and sent from Rome at the same time with two of Paul's helpers, Tychicus and Onesimus.

The Letter to the Ephesians

The letter begins with an explanation of how God has always had a plan to bring a family of saved and forgiven people together. The entire plan revolves around the fact that the sins of man are paid for by the sacrifice of Christ on the cross. Christ is at the center of the plan and the universe. He always has been and always will be the focal point of creation.

The church is the body of Christ here on earth. Christ is the cornerstone spoken of in the prophets, and His church is the temple built from Jews and Gentiles together. Because Christians are part of God's family, they have quick access to Him and are assured of His welcome.

Because Christians are all part of this family of God, they have a responsibility to act like children of God. Specific examples of how Christians are to act in marriage, in a family and in the work place are offered. Paul ends the letter by noting that Christians are engaged in a spiritual battle. God provides the equipment His children need to fight in this warfare.

◇

The Letter to the Colossians

Paul carefully explains that Jesus Christ is the unique Son and revealer of God to mankind. He has all the same characteristics as God. He was in charge of creation and holds creation together. By His work on the cross, He has allowed all things to be brought back to God. Christians gain their acceptance by God entirely through Him. Believers have a new unbreakable connection with Him in His death and resurrection.

Paul warns again about false teachers that want to require additional efforts on the part of believers to secure their right relationship with God. He then gives recommendations about appropriate conduct for those that believe.

◇

The Letter to Philemon

This is a personal letter from Paul to his friend Philemon. One of Philemon's slaves, named Onesimus, had separated himself from his master and become involved with Paul. Paul requests that Philemon now accept his slave back, not only as a valuable servant but also as a fellow believer and brother. Paul looks forward to a visit with Philemon when he is free.

◇

The last of Paul's letters written during his first imprisonment in Rome was sent to the Philippians. Paul had some back and forth messaging with them, and they had recently sent a gift to support Paul in his incarceration.

The Letter to the Philippians

Paul openly expresses his special love for the Philippians. They had always shared and participated in Paul's work. Paul is careful to tell them that the work is continuing even though he is imprisoned. Many are becoming bolder as a result of his lockup. Even though Paul would be satisfied to die in jail, he is confident he will be returning to see them.

Paul encourages them to follow the example of humility Jesus gave when He chose to leave the glory He had in heaven to come to earth to save mankind. Because of this Jesus will ultimately receive worship from every person.

Paul warns against false teachers who would cause the Philippians to trust in their own efforts as a way to gain a right relationship with God. Paul points out that if any man could trust in his own efforts it would be him, but everything he has accomplished is worthless except for what Christ has done in him. Paul points out that he is in no way perfect but he always forgets his past mistakes and presses forward towards the good calling he has received in Christ.

Paul assures them that God will provide all of their requirements and thanks them for their gift. He notifies them that Timothy will be coming to them soon and provides a hearty endorsement for his helper.

<>

Paul was released from imprisonment in Rome and continued to travel. He wrote his first letter to Timothy and a similar letter to Titus during these travels.

The First Letter to Timothy

Paul's letter to Timothy provides instruction about protecting the message he had been called to spread. He is to accomplish this by teaching the sound doctrine he has learned and by living in a fashion that will not raise any question about his devotion and that will provide an example to others.

Guidelines were provided for behavior in worship. Paul delineated specific qualifications for those that Timothy would select for leadership in the church. Paul warns Timothy that false teachers will come and many would follow them. Timothy was not to waste time arguing meaningless points, but to clearly guide his congregations into the essentials of the faith. Timothy was instructed to keep himself in spiritual shape for his task by continuing in his regular study of the scriptures and prayer.

<>

The Letter to Titus

Paul gives Titus many of the same instructions he gave to Timothy. He was instructed to encourage a standard of conduct in the church that would be exemplary. Old men were to be self-controlled and worthy of respect. Young men were to live wisely and seek to do good deeds. Slaves were to obey their masters. Older women were to train the younger women to respect their husbands. All these activities were reasonable because of the great mercy Christ had already shone.

<>

It would seem by the tone of his second letter to Timothy that Paul had landed in jail again and was nearing the end of his "race."

The Second Letter to Timothy

Paul truly loved his young assistant. The love was certified by their shared love and zeal for the Lord who had called them both. Paul wants to see Timothy as soon as possible.

Timothy is encouraged not to be ashamed of the gospel even though Paul is in jail because of it. Paul encourages him to continue in the faith just as Paul has. They are soldiers in a war. They need to stay true to their training and to their commander. Paul warns Timothy that times won't get easier; they'll get tougher. Timothy must continue in living good Christian life in good times and bad times.

Paul is satisfied that he has fought the good fight, that he has run the race hard all the way. He is looking forward to the prize at the finish.

There are seven additional letters that made their way into the New Testament. Hebrews, I and II Peter, and Jude were all written within 10 years of Paul's last letter to Timothy. The last three, I, II, III John where written over twenty years after Paul's last letter to Timothy.

The Letter to the Hebrews

The anonymous writer of Hebrews begins his letter confirming the Lordship of Christ. He is presented as being greater than any angel and greater than Moses or Abraham. He is the complete revelation of God. He has fulfilled the entire law. He is not only the Christian's Savior but also his high priest. Christ is an everlasting high priest who has been tempted like all men but is perfect in every way. He is the only way to God.

Christ's sacrifice on the cross is the perfect sacrifice, so it replaces the old sacrificial system. Jesus only needed to be offered once, not again and again like the sacrifices in the old covenant. The believer's sins are forgiven because of Christ's sacrifice.

As forgiven children of God, believers should push forward towards a holy life. The faith Christians have in their new relationship with God will help them live appropriately. As they endure through troubles, their character will become stronger.

<>

Peter's two letters

Peter was probably in a Roman jail when he wrote these two letters. The general consensus was that things were going to start getting pretty rough for those who acknowledged Jesus Christ as King. Peter's letters were primarily written to encourage. He states that since Christians have their position as God's people because Jesus paid the ransom required for sin, they should strive to live accordingly; holy, with much love for others and constantly trying to grow more in these characteristics.

Because the world is watching, believers should do good things, be good citizens and behave lovingly, especially with their families. Christians should also strive for unity with each other and know that final victory is coming. Jesus will judge the universe. The leaders are to be motivated by service to God, not financial gain.

In his second letter, Peter begins identifying the traits Christians are to strive for: faith, high morals, knowledge of the truth, self-control, perseverance, kindness, and love. He states that if believers work towards these characteristics, it will be difficult for them to stumble. Peter assures them also about his being a witness to all the things they've heard about.

He warns about all the false teachers that will arise. They are an unsavory lot. Most started in the right way, and then left it. Their primary problem is that they have become entangled with worldly pleasures again. Their teaching simply allows them to continue in whatever earthly pleasure they happen to be captive to. They will be judged. Peter concludes with the sureness of Christ return and the final judgment. The entire universe will be consumed by fire and a new heaven and earth will be established. Because these things are surely coming, Christians should remain steadfast to the true faith.

<>

Jude's Letter

Jude had intended to write about the basics of salvation, however he felt compelled to encourage his readers to contend for the true faith against false teachers that were infiltrating in the church. False teachers are in the same league with all of God's enemies through time. They are constantly trying to gain position through flattery or fault finding. The appearance of false teachers hasn't been a surprise. Jude concludes with encouragement to resist these elements and hold true to the faith. Jesus will help them in this effort.

<>

The last of the letters are from the apostle John, written late in his life.

The First Letter of John

John was a firsthand witness to the life of Jesus: a life that created the opportunity for Christians to obtain eternal life. The message he writes about he learned directly from Jesus who is God and is represented by light. Christians are to walk in that light not in the darkness. Believers aren't perfect; they'll fall short and sin, but when they do Jesus is always willing to forgive. Christians are to follow the commandments of

Jesus, which John boils down to two things: to believe in Jesus and to love one another. The love Christians have is the true measure of their faith.

John admonishes his readers not to be connected to the evil in the world: lust, pride, and materialism because the world will pass away. There are anti-Christs in the world that are liars, who add or subtract from the true message. Some were denying that Christ had actually lived as a man.

God's love for the world is illustrated in the fact that Jesus came as a man to this world and gave himself as a sacrifice for sin. Because He first showed this kind of love, He becomes the motivator for Christians to love in the same way, and to avoid sin.

<>

The Second Letter of John

John's second letter is a personal letter to a lady of some prominence. He is joyful that she is keeping the faith and that some of her children are also believers. He warns her about false teachers. He looks forward to seeing her in person.

<>

The Third Letter of John

This letter is written to John's good friend, Gaius. John is joyful at how well he is doing in his faith. Gaius has been very helpful with traveling teachers. Another man, Diotrephes, has not only been unhelpful, he has rejected John's authority; and encouraged others to do the same as it pertains to supporting the traveling teachers. Demitrius, another fellow, has been helpful.

John hopes to make a visit soon.

<>

Late in the Apostle John's life, he was exiled to a prison Island named Patmos. It was there that he received the Revelation that is recorded in the final book of the Bible.

The Revelation of Jesus Christ to John

Revelation 1-3 *Jesus' letters to the churches*
Revelation begins with letters from Jesus to churches in the Asian provinces. The letters both commend and warn each of the churches. God's views are positive towards assurance, faith, and service. He views lawlessness, immorality, lifeless faith, and compromise negatively.

Revelation 4-6 *Seven seals*
John is then taken into heaven in a vision. He sees heavenly worship and the unfolding of the judgment that is to come upon the earth. Jesus opens seven seals. The first seal reveals a great leader who wins many battles. The second one opens a time without peace, full of war and killing. The third seal speaks of a time of famine, while fourth shows a season of death by war, famine, and disease. The fifth reveals the questioning of those who have been martyred for their faith in Christ as to how much longer God will with hold His judgment against evil. The sixth sparks a massive earthquake and great upheaval in heaven. Every one on the earth, great and small, is aware judgment from God has come and they hide in caves.

Revelation 7 *144,000 witnesses*
A massive scene in heaven follows. 144,000 are chosen as witnesses from the 12 tribes of Israel. After this a multitude of people dressed in white are seen before the throne of God. It is revealed to John that these are the ones delivered out of the great tribulation on earth. God covers them and wipes away all their tears.

Revelation 8-9 *Seven trumpets*
The final seal is broken and it reveals seven angels with trumpets. The first trumpet delivers fire that burns a third of the vegetation on earth. The second affects the sea and a third of it is polluted. The third trumpet pollutes a third of the fresh water on earth. The fourth trumpet darkens a third of the sun, stars and moon. The fifth trumpet opens the abyss, and demons are allowed to attack those who do not have the seal of God upon them. No one is killed, but for five months the tormented ones wish they could die. The sixth trumpet unleashes an army of 200,000,000 from the east who wreak havoc on the people of earth. Even after all this, the ones left alive refuse to turn from their evil ways.

Revelation 10-11 *Two witnesses*

Before the seventh trumpet, John sees a mighty angel come to earth. Seven thunders answer his great shout which sounds like a lion's roar. What was said by the thunder remains unknown because John was instructed not to write it down. John eats the small scroll held by the angel then he measures the temple and learns of two witnesses that will come to the earth. No one can hurt them. They have incredible power. The beast that comes out of the bottomless pit makes war against them and defeats them. All the people of earth rejoice and give gifts at their passing. But after three and a half days of lying dead in Jerusalem's main street, the two witnesses are given new life and called into heaven. A mighty earthquake shakes Jerusalem and 7000 people are killed. The seventh trumpet announces that judgment is surely coming.

Revelation 12 *The Dragon and the Woman*

John sees some significant events in heaven. A woman clothed with the sun is giving birth to a child. A dragon with seven heads, ten thorns, and wearing seven crowns is waiting to devour the child as it is born. God protects the woman and the child, who is to rule all nations. John sees a war in heaven with Michael and his angels fighting the dragon and his angels. The dragon was cast to earth. There was rejoicing in heaven, and the dragon again tries unsuccessfully to attack the woman where she is being protected for a time in the wilderness.

Revelation 13 *Beasts earth and sea*

Then John sees a beast come from the sea. One of the beast's heads is mortally wounded but is healed. The people of earth worship the dragon for giving this healed beast such power. The beast speaks against God, wages war against God's people and rules the entire earth. This is a great opportunity for true believers to endure to the end. Another beast comes and makes the world worship the first beast. He works such wonders that everyone who belongs to the world believes in him. He makes a statue of the first beast that begins to speak, and the people worship it. A system is put in place where all the people take a mark on their hand or forehead in order to buy or sell anything. The mark is the number 666, which represents a man.

Revelation 14 *Winepress*

Then John sees the Lamb standing on Mount Zion with the 144,000 witnesses. Then he sees an angel flying through the heavens proclaiming the time to fear and glorify God had certainly arrived. Another angel came proclaiming the fall of Babylon. A third angel announced that those who had taken the mark on their hand or forehead would be judged. Jesus is then seen harvesting the world for His people and an angel harvesting grapes for the wrath of God's wine press.

Revelation 15-16 *Wrath poured out*
Another significant event is seen in heaven; seven angels prepare to pour out the final plagues that will bring God's wrath to completion. John also sees the believers who had been victorious over the beast and his statue standing on a crystal sea praising God. The gates of the temple in heaven were open, but nobody could enter until the last seven plagues were poured out. These last plagues were much like the trumpets. The sixth angel poured his bowl on the Euphrates River, which caused it to dry up. This allowed the kings of the east a dry march westward toward the valley of Armageddon where the kings of the earth had been led for a final battle. Finally the seventh angel emptied his bowl and a cry went out, "It is finished!" The earth was ravaged with a mighty earthquake and hailstones weighing up to 70 pounds!

Revelation 17 *Great prostitute*
Then one of the angels who had poured out the plagues on the earth spoke to John. He said, "Come with me and I'll show you the judgment that's coming upon the great prostitute. John was taken to the wilderness where he saw a woman sitting on a beast with seven heads and ten horns. She was drunk and her cup was filled with obscenities and immoralities. She represented the great city that rules over all the kings of earth. She sat on waters that represented the masses of people from every nation. The angel told John that the heads and horns of the beast represented kings who will give their authority to the beast. They war against the Lord, and they hate the woman (the prostitute). God will put a plan in their minds that will carry out His purpose.

Revelation 18 *Babylon judged*
Then another angel with great authority came out of heaven with a mighty shout, "Babylon is fallen, that great city has fallen. It has become a hideout for demons and buzzards, the rulers of earth have committed adultery with her and grown rich because of her luxurious living!" Another voice warned all God's people to keep away from her. She will be judged double for all her sins. All the rulers and merchants of the world are amazed at how Babylon could fall so quickly. All the products and fine things they traded are gone in one hour!

Revelation 19 *Wedding feast*

Next John heard the sound of a vast crowd praising God in heaven. They were excited because the time for the wedding feast of the Lamb had come. The bride was prepared and wore the finest white linen, (which represents the good deeds done by believers). Then heaven opened up and a white horse was standing there. The One sitting on it was called Faithful and True. He had many crowns and was dressed in pure white; on his robe and thighs were written, "King of kings, Lord of lords." Down on earth the kings were gathering to fight against Him and His army. The battle that ensued was quick and decisive. The beast was captured and the armies of the world destroyed.

Revelation 20 *One thousand years*

Satan is then bound and thrown into the bottomless pit for a thousand years. Then all those who had not taken the mark or who had been killed for their trust in Jesus reigned with Him for a thousand years. At the end of this period, Satan will be let out and will deceive the nations again; but he will be finally and forever destroyed and cast into the lake of fire along with all those whose names were not written in the Book of Life.

Revelation 20-21 *The curse is lifted*

Then John saw a new heaven and earth. The New Jerusalem came out of heaven sparkling like a bride prepared for her husband. This new city was in the shape of a cube with 1400-mile long sides made of gems and pure gold. There was no need for sun because God and the Lamb are its light. The curse is lifted. The tree of life is planted by a river that flows from the throne of God. Jesus Himself says, "See, I am coming soon, and My reward is with Me. I am the A and the Z, the first and the last, the beginning and the end." The Spirit and the bride say, "Come, let us drink from the water of life without charge." Finally John says, "Amen, come Lord Jesus!"

CPSIA information can be obtained at www.ICGtesting.com
Printed in the USA
LVOW10s1347230216

476359LV00027B/844/P